ORGANIZATION PLANNING
Cases and Concepts

THE IRWIN SERIES IN MANAGEMENT
AND
THE BEHAVIORAL SCIENCES

L. L. CUMMINGS and E. KIRBY WARREN
CONSULTING EDITORS

JOHN F. MEE   ADVISORY EDITOR

Organization Planning.
Cases and Concepts

Edited by.

JAY W. LORSCH, S.M., D.B.A.
Professor of Organizational Behavior

PAUL R. LAWRENCE, M.B.A., D.C.S.
Wallace Brett Donham Professor of
Organizational Behavior

Both of the
Graduate School of Business Administration
Harvard University

1972 **RICHARD D. IRWIN, INC.**
and
THE DORSEY PRESS Homewood, Illinois 60430

Irwin-Dorsey Limited, Georgetown, Ontario L7G 4B3

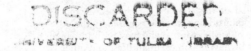

Case material of the Harvard Graduate School of
Business Administration is made possible by the
cooperation of business firms who may wish to remain
anonymous by having names, quantities, and other
identifying details disguised while basic relationships
are maintained. Cases are prepared as the basis for
class discussion rather than to illustrate either effective
or ineffective handling of administrative situations.

ISBN 0–256–00456–0
Library of Congress Catalog Card No. 72–79316
Printed in the United States of America

To the Original Teachers of
Administrative Practices

Professors Learned
Roethlisberger
Hower
Lombard
and
Glover

Acknowledgments

THE MATERIAL in this volume is the result of several years' effort in developing a course at the Harvard Business School on behavioral science approaches to designing organizations. As a result, we are indebted to the various research assistants and doctoral candidates who have contributed to both the cases and conceptual papers that are included. In the earliest stages of this development, John J. Gabarro, now an assistant professor at the Harvard Business School, was a major force in the development of the teaching cases and the ideas contained in the conceptual summaries. John J. Morse, now assistant professor at the University of California at Los Angeles, was responsible for the Rockford Container cases; and Stephen A. Allen III, now assistant professor at Harvard Business School, and Stevan Trooboff worked on several of the conceptual notes. Miss Jeanne Deschamps assisted in much of the work and took a major role in the writing of the Samantha case. In subsequent years, case material and conceptual material was added by Martin Charns, now assistant professor at Carnegie Mellon, and Martin Knestrick.

In addition to all of these contributors from the Harvard Business School, we are indebted to Professor Jay Galbraith of the Sloan School of Management at Massachusetts Institute of Technology for permission to use his paper.

We are also appreciative of the help of several dedicated secretaries who contributed to this work in numerous ways: Mrs. Ann Walter, Miss Mary Lou Ryder, and Mrs. Susan Christiansen.

All material in this volume with the exception of the Galbraith paper was originally copyrighted by the President and Fellows of Harvard College, and we are grateful for their permission to include it. None of the material included is to be reproduced without written permission.

Boston, Massachusetts   J.W.L.
September 1972   P.R.L.

Contents

READINGS ON ORGANIZATIONAL THEORY

Introduction

THIS BOOK is intended to help advanced students of organizational behavior and management develop their skills in thinking about and acting on issues of organizational design. By organizational design we mean *the systematic planning and creation of organization structure, measurement and reward schemes, and personnel development programs, to divide up the organization's work while still achieving unified effort toward the organization's goals.* To accomplish these purposes, both readings and cases have been included. The readings provide summaries of several of the more widely known conceptual models of organizational structures and processes. In the space available, it has not been possible to treat any of these models exhaustively. Rather, an attempt has been made to provide sufficient understanding so that as the student reads about them and applies them to the cases, he can make judgments about the strengths and weaknesses of these approaches. The cases which have been included were selected not only because of their utility in learning to use the conceptual models but also because they deal with the wide range of organizational design issues faced by today's managers, for example, designing and managing matrix organizations, building cohesive organizations from newly acquired units, designing organizations to operate computer controlled processes, and forming organizations to undertake new kinds of businesses, etc.

One major question which may be on the reader's mind even after this brief introductory paragraph is why it is important to be able to apply conceptual frameworks for understanding organizational issues. Why isn't one's common sense or intuition sufficient?

1

Like the problem solver in other fields, the manager concerned with organizational issues needs analytic tools which will provide him with ways of thinking about the problems he faces and the solutions available. We often fail to recognize that we use these tools in thinking about human problems, but as William Foote Whyte has pointed out:

> When we set out to build an organization, we have in mind a theoretical model of an organization. When we set out to change an organization, we have in mind a theoretical model of what the reorganized structure should resemble. A man of action may deny that he is guided by any theoretical model. That is only to say that his assumptions about organizations remain implicit and are thus not available for conscious analysis and evaluation. . . .[1]

Whyte continues by making the important point that we can be more effective action takers if we are explicit about the models we choose to use. If we are explicit about these models, we will be less apt to become confused as to what is the map we are using to describe the territory (the organization) and what the territory itself is. Similarly, by being explicit about them we can hold our assumptions about the organizations up to the light so we and others involved can evaluate them and determine their validity.

The Problem of Selecting Organization Models

Even if we are explicit about the organizational models we use, we still have difficult problems because the existing and more thoroughly developed organizational models which administrators use often seem to contradict each other. This is true both in terms of their underlying theoretical premises and in terms of their action implications. Looking first at the theoretical premises of various models which seem to contradict each other, Alvin Gouldner has observed that one confusion in organizational models stems from the fact that some are "rational models" while others are "natural system models." Gouldner defines these two types of models as follows:[2]

The Rational Model of Organizational Analysis

In the rational model, the organization is conceived as an "instrument"—that is, as a rationally conceived means to the realization of expressly announced group goals. Its structures are understood as tools deliberately estab-

[1]William F. Whyte, "Models for Building and Changing Organizations," *Human Organization*, Spring–Summer 1967.

[2]Alvin Gouldner, "Organizational Analysis," *Sociology Today*, eds. Robert K. Merton, Leonard Broom, Leonard S. Cottrell, Jr. (New York: Basic Books, Inc., 1959), pp. 404–6.

lished for the efficient realization of these group purposes. Organizational behavior is thus viewed as consciously and rationally administered, and changes
in organizational patterns are viewed as planned devices to improve the level
of efficiency. The rational model assumes that decisions are made on the basis
of a rational survey of the situation, utilizing certified knowledge, with a deliberate orientation to an expressly codified legal apparatus. The focus is,
therefore, on the legally prescribed structures—i.e., the formally "blue-
printed" patterns—since these are more largely subject to deliberate inspection and rational manipulation.

This model takes account of departures from rationality but often tends to
assume that these departures derive from random mistakes due to ignorance
or error in calculation. Fundamentally, the rational model implies a "mechanical" model, in that it views the organization as a structure of manipulable
parts, each of which is separately modifiable with a view to enhancing the
efficiency of the whole. Individual organizational elements are seen as subject
to successful and planned modification, enactable by deliberate decision. The
long-range development of the organization as a whole is also regarded as
subject to planned control and as capable of being brought into increasing
conformity with explicitly held plans and goals.

THE NATURAL-SYSTEM MODEL OF ORGANIZATIONAL ANALYSIS

The natural-system model regards the organization as a "natural whole," or
system. The realization of the goals of the system as a whole is but one of several important needs to which the organization is oriented. Its component
structures are seen as emergent institutions, which can be understood only in
relation to the diverse needs of the total system. The organization, according
to this model, strives to survive and to maintain its equilibrium, and this striving may persist even after its explicitly held goals have been successfully
attained. This strain toward survival may even on occasion lead to the neglect
or distortion of the organization's goals. Whatever the plans of their creators,
organizations, say the natural-system theorists, become ends in themselves and
possess their own distinctive needs which have to be satisfied. Once established, organizations tend to generate new ends which constrain subsequent decisions and limit the manner in which the nominal group goals can be
pursued.

Organizational structures are viewed as spontaneously and homeostatically
maintained. Changes in organizational patterns are considered the results of
cumulative, unplanned, adaptive responses to threats to the equilibrium of the
system as a whole. Responses to problems are thought of as taking the form
of crescively developed defense mechanisms and as being importantly shaped
by shared values which are deeply internalized in the members. The empirical focus is thus directed to the spontaneously emergent and normatively sanc-
tioned structures in the organization.

The focus is not on deviations from rationality but, rather, on disruptions
of organizational equilibrium, and particularly on the mechanisms by which
equilibrium is homeostatically maintained. When deviations from planned
purposes are considered, they are viewed not so much as due to ignorance or

error but as arising from constraints imposed by the existent social structure. In given situations, the ignorance of certain participants may not be considered injurious but functional to the maintenance of the system's equilibrium.

The natural-system model is typically based upon an underlying "organismic" model which stresses the interdependence of the component parts. Planned changes are therefore expected to have ramifying consequences for the whole organizational system. When, as frequently happens, these consequences are unanticipated, they are usually seen as divergent from, and not as supportive of, the planner's intentions. Natural-system theorists tend to regard the organization as a whole as organically "growing," with a "natural history" of its own which is planfully modifiable only at great peril, if at all. Long-range organizational development is thus regarded as an evolution, conforming to the "natural laws" rather than to the planner's designs.

More recently Walter Buckley has made a similar point indicating that many of the inconsistencies in current organizational models stem from the fact that some have been developed through the use of an analogy with a mechanical system which is in equilibrium, while others are developed on the premise that organizations resemble a biological system which has homeostatic properties.[3] More importantly, perhaps, Buckley offers an alternative—modern system theory—which he feels is more consistent with the observed functioning of organizational systems. He points out that organizations or "sociocultural systems," as he terms them, are different from biological and mechanical systems in one important respect. Sociocultural systems are morphogenic; that is, they have the capacity to change or elaborate their form, structure, or state. This is a characteristic of biological systems in only the longest term sense, that is, biological evolution, and is rarely, if ever, a characteristic of mechanical systems. He goes on to suggest that this morphogenic process in organizational systems takes place as members change their expectations as to what is acceptable behavior through the processes of interaction and information flow. He suggests that modern system theory offers a way of understanding this process directly without arguing from analogy. In using the readings and cases in this book, the reader will have an opportunity to test out the premise in Buckley's approach; but now we can see, at least, that one source of contradiction in the widely used organizational models has been their tendency to view organizations as either mechanical-rational phenomena or as natural-biological phenomena instead of as social-psychological phenomena.

For the reader concerned with how to use these tools, all of this may seem highly abstract. But it has significance in the action ramifications facing the administrator, because the authors who have developed theories from these different analogies have reached quite different conclu-

---

[3]Walter Buckley, *Sociology and Modern Systems Theory* (Englewood Cliffs, N.J.: Prentice-Hall, Inc., 1967).

sions. If we select a mechanical-rational model, for example, we may place great emphasis on clarifying responsibility and authority and on developing clearly defined reporting relationships from top to bottom of the organizational hierarchy. On the other hand, if we are attracted to models with a natural system or biological base, we may be more concerned with developing an organization where trust and openness are the norms, and where there is the fullest possible involvement of all members in decision making.

Similarly, if we use a mechanical-rational model, we may be very optimistic about changing the organization. Determine what the new structure should be rationally and communicate it to the responsible managers and the change will be accepted. According to this view the equilibrium can be easily and predictably altered, much as we could alter the functioning of mechanical systems by changing the gear ratio. Reliance on a natural system model can lead us in the opposite direction—organizational change is a natural growth process and difficult to plan. At the extreme, this latter model can lead to the pessimistic view that organizations are practically impossible to change. To many students either of these models may seem extreme and inappropriate. Yet, many, if not most, managers implicitly or explicitly rely on one (particularly the rational model), and sometimes on an eclectic mixture of both, as they think about organizational design issues.

To understand why these two classes of models are so widely used, it is helpful to develop at least a general understanding of the kinds of tools (or models) which have generally been available to administrators prior to the later 1960s. This is accomplished by the first two readings. The first on "Two Universal Models," which describes the "classical" and "participative" models, has a clear connection to Gouldner's rational and natural systems dichotomy. The second reading, "Sociotechnical and Cognitive Model," describes two other widely recognized models which have captured more of the complexity of organizational phenomena. From these readings, one should get not only a better understanding of the current state of organizational theory but also some understanding of what makes a useful model for attacking organizational problems.

These four models, obviously, are not an exhaustive list of the models developed by organizational theorists and utilized by practitioners. They have been selected for discussion for several reasons: First, and most obviously, to draw on a larger number of models would be even more confusing and is impractical, given the time available. Second, these four models are probably the most widely used today by both practitioners and students of organizational phenomena. Many of the other models in the literature are permutations of these, or, at the least, have close historical antecedents to these models. Third, these models provide dramatic examples of some of the apparent contradictions in organization theory. Finally, by examining these four models, we can gain a good understanding of the factors which seem important in selecting a useful conceptual model. By using them as examples, we can lift up for examination some of the practical issues confronting organization designers as they attempt to apply any model.

As the reader becomes involved in this task, a word of warning may be appropriate. We are not attempting to build a case which supports one or two models and indicts the others. Rather, we want to explore the strengths and weaknesses of all of these models and to compare them to see where they diverge and where they converge. The following list of general questions may help as a catalyst for thinking:

1. What are the assumptions about man and his motivation which underlie each model? Do they seem valid?
2. What are the major propositions in each model about organizational and interpersonal phenomena, for example, differentiation, integration, conflict resolution, influence, communication, etc.
3. What was the model builder up to? Where did he get the data for his propositions or assumptions? Did he intend that the model be used in the way you need to use it? Was he developing a descriptive model or a more action-oriented prescriptive model?
4. How can reasonably intelligent authors and researchers arrive at such different models?
5. What are the strengths and weaknesses of the model? Is the model useful? Can it be applied across the range of problems with which you want to deal? Can you obtain the kind of data which is required to use the model as an analytic tool?

The emphasis in these questions on understanding what makes a useful model is especially important as one moves on to the other readings, all of which describe the developing contingency approach to organization theory.[4] The first of these readings describes the work of James Thompson and Joan Woodward. The paper by Lorsch and Lawrence relates their empirical work to the theoretical work of Thompson. Finally, the paper by Jay Galbraith ties all this work, plus that of others, into a view of an organization as an information processing system.

Finally, it should be stressed that the greatest understanding of these models and their usefulness can come only from trying them in the crucible of real issues. The cases which have been included represent our best attempt to capture the complexity of live organizational problems in black and white. While it is our belief that the contingency approach is the most useful conceptual scheme so far developed, we believe that others can only become convinced of this through trying these and the other models described here on the case situations.

---

[4]Paul R. Lawrence and Jay W. Lorsch, *Organization and Environment: Managing Differentiation and Integration* (Boston: Division of Research, Harvard Business School, 1967).

Two Universal Models

JAY W. LORSCH
STEVAN TROOBOFF

THE CLASSICAL and participative models of organization closely parallel Gouldner's rational and natural system models mentioned in the Introduction. Gouldner's rational model which views the organization as composed of manipulative parts clearly coincides with the classic model's authors' view of organizational structure. The natural system model is akin to the participative model in that both are cognizant of accounting for the individual's needs within the structure of the organization. However, while Gouldner stresses the interdependence of the organization's component parts and the organization's tendency to maintain its equilibrium as characteristic of the natural system model, the participative model of organization does not mention explicitly these strivings for organizational balance.

In studying the classical and participative models, you might find it helpful to bear in mind the passages from Gouldner quoted above in the Introduction. By better understanding the theoretical contradictions between rational and natural system models, you should be able to develop a better understanding of the classical and participative models.

THE CLASSICAL MODEL OF ORGANIZATION

Despite the fact that the classical model of organization might seem old-fashioned or outdated when compared with some of the behavioral science ideas, it is extremely important, historically and in terms of current practice. Historically, the classical model is deeply entrenched in our culture. Max Weber's writings on the structure of the bureaucracy have a strong parallel to the classical model in terms of the mechanical approach to the problems of organizational design.[1] And the work of

---

[1] A. M. Henderson and Talcott Parsons, eds., *The Theory of Social and Economic Organization* (Glencoe, Ill.: Free Press and Falcon's Wing Press, 1947).

7

Frederick Taylor in subdividing tasks through time and motion studies gave strong impetus to and is based on the "sound principles" of the classical model.[2] Even today many businessmen adhere to the principles of the classical model in thinking about organizational issues.

The classical model focuses primarily on the relationship between two groups—management and the (production) workers. In discussing these two groups, the classical authors make many assumptions and value judgments about the individuals. For instance, workers are viewed as instruments, solely motivated by economic motives, existing to carry out organizational objectives. Managers, on the other hand, are characterized as rational, omniscient, and possessing outstanding personal qualities such as kindness and fairness. However, despite these qualities, the manager's role defines him as having to be firm with workers.

Because of the model's view of the workers as "economic man," rewards and punishments to the workers should be economic in nature. An astute classical manager would give detailed instructions to his subordinates. Then, according to the model, he must measure or assess exactly what has been done by the workers and if the employee should be rewarded or punished for his performance in executing the task.

The classical authors recognized that the task assigned to the worker would often create an inherent conflict for the employee between his personal goals and those of the organization. Under the model's assumptions, however, the workers are expected to accept the superordinate goals of the organization. The resolution of this conflict and the ensuing acceptance by the worker of the corporate position were to be resolved by fitting the "right" man into the "right" job. This fit was to be defined by personal characteristics such as physical strength, manual dexterity, or specific craft skill. Further, in addition to this fit of the individual and the job skills required for a specific task, heavy formalization of procedures was to minimize the potential conflict by clearly defining what was expected of organization members. This emphasis on formal organization, formal communications, and formal job and task descriptions would keep the worker oriented toward the organization's goals rather than his personal objectives.

Organizational Patterns

The classical organization resembles the pyramid shape displayed in Exhibit 1. At the top point of the structure is the omnipotent manager and the workers. Within this structure, both the chain of command and the channels of communication are vertical. The vertical chain of com-

---

[2]Frederick Winslow Taylor, *Principles of Scientific Management* (New York: Harper & Row, 1947).

mand stipulates that each person in the organization is to have only one superior or boss, for according to the classicist it is impossible for an organization to adapt itself to the complexities of dual command. Similarly, each member is to have authority delegated to him which is equal to his responsibility. In the channels of communication, information is expected to flow downward in accordance with the authority structure and upward only in relation to the results of task performance.

EXHIBIT 1

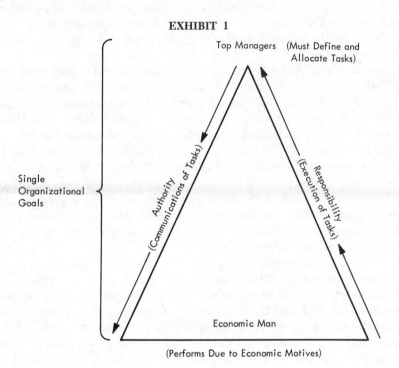

(Performs Due to Economic Motives)

Organizational States and Processes

Specialization. Within this pyramid structure, specialization is a major tenet of how tasks are to be assigned. The principal goal the classical authors were concerned with, apropos of specialization, was to divide the tasks of the organization so that each individual would have the narrowest task; while, at the same time, the total activities of all individuals would add up to the organization's superordinate goals and objectives. This is so because it was assumed that men differ in capacity and skill and can better their individual performance through specialization, that a man can't learn everything in a lifetime, and that no individual can perform more than one task at a time. Men were therefore assigned specialized tasks of a finite nature within their departments. In turn, the men were expected to become highly skilled at performing that particular task.

Most of the classical modelists discussed this specialization in terms of assigning the specific tasks to functional departments. Luther Gulick, however, in discussing this departmentalization, felt that in addition to organizing subunits along functional lines according to the process being used (i.e., production, accounting, engineering, etc.), subunits could be organized by the major goal of the unit (purpose being served, e.g., product), by the clientele dealt with by the unit, or by the place where the service is rendered.[3]

Coordination. As highly specialized as this pyramid structure and the individuals within it appear to be, the classical authors' emphasis that the sum of the individual tasks would equal the overall organizational goal indicates their recognition of the need for coordination or integration. Primarily, the integration of the highly specialized efforts towards the singular and centrally determined corporate goal was expected to be achieved because subgoals would add up to the superordinate goal. Any flaws in this approach would be dealt with through the management hierarchy. In other words, individuals in the organization's hierarchy with appropriate authority are expected to delegate tasks in a manner which will turn out to be an integrated effort. If this doesn't work, they are expected to coordinate subordinate efforts.

While the classicists primarily relied on this hierarchical pattern for achieving integration, Gulick again was one notable exception.[4] He identified several other factors which might affect the integration process. Specifically, he felt that the problems of coordination would vary according to the size of the company, the simplicity or complexity of the organization and its operations, and the company's static or dynamic qualities. Fayol also saw size as a factor influencing the hierarchy's capacity to achieve organizational integration.[5] He believed that a staff would be required by a larger organization to improve coordination by facilitating the dissemination of information.

Conflict Resolution. For the most part, the classical authors ignored the topic of conflict resolution. They believed that the structure they had designed alleviated the possibility of conflict within the organization. The few classical authors who did recognize the need for tools to resolve intraorganizational conflict, relied on the philosophy that conflicting ideas or actions should be "pushed up the hierarchical pyramid for a de-

---

[3]Luther Gulick and L. Urwick, eds., *Papers on the Science of Administration* (New York: Institute of Public Administration, 1937).
[4]Ibid.
[5]Henri Fayol, "The Administrative Theory in This State," in Gulick and Urwick, *Papers on the Science of Administration.*

cision." It was the manager's responsibility to arbitrate disputes between hostile subordinates.

Sources of the Classical Model

The classical model is descriptive of the early organizational structures with which we are all familiar—the church, the military, and the railroads. We can easily picture the military organization as a pyramid with the commander in chief at the top and the structure spreading out below down through the majors, lieutenants, noncommissioned officers, and finally privates. Each individual reports to one other individual on his execution of a specifically designed task. And, the cumulative total of these tasks should add up to the mission of the entire military organization.

Descriptions of the classical model can be found in the works of Fayol (1916), Koontz and O'Donnell (1950s), Newman (1963), Gulick and Urwick (1937), and Mooney.[6] While there are a number of variations in their thinking about the model, depending on their own experience and the time during which they were writing, the views expressed in this short note were mostly universal as concern all organizations. That is, while there might be minor variations from these principles, they were to be rigorously adhered to in all organizations regardless of task, location, and, to a large extent, size. In essence, applying these principles to the design of organizations facing any and all conditions would lead to effective permanence of the organization.

THE PARTICIPATIVE MODEL

Whereas the classical model of organization is largely derived from an analysis of the early experience of practitioners, the participative model is derived from the work of behavioral scientists. The participative model is one which many students tend to think of as McGregor's "Theory Y".[7] While the model's assumptions about individuals are closely akin to McGregor's thinking about people, the model has assumptions and implications which are more far-reaching than Theory Y.

Consequently, in studying the model, you should be careful not to fall into the trap of saying "That's Theory Y and I know that" but rather delve

---

[6]Ibid.; Harold Koontz and Cyril O'Donnell, *Principles of Management* (New York: McGraw-Hill Book Co., Inc., 1968); William Henry Newman, *Administrative Action* (Englewood Cliffs, N.J.: Prentice-Hall, Inc., 1963); Gulick and Urwick, *Papers on the Science of Administration* (Columbia University, 1937); James D. Mooney, *The Principles of Organization.*

[7]Douglas M. McGregor, *The Human Side of Enterprise* (New York: McGraw-Hill Book Co., Inc., 1960).

into the participative model more carefully in an attempt to compare and contrast it with the classical model. This comparison should not only be in terms of the assumptions about the individuals imbedded in a participative model but in terms of the various organizational states and processes and how they vary from the classical set of assumptions.

The Individual

According to the participative authors, the individual in the organization is engaged in a multidimensional process of development. Within this dynamic developmental process, the individual is seen as moving through the process of maturity. As he matures, this individual's needs, goals, and desires tend to move in a specific direction. The individual seeks to be in a position of relative independence in which he has some level of self-determination about his future. He begins to seek deeper, more constant, and increasingly complex interests with which to be challenged. And, he also seeks a greater depth to his behavioral interaction within the organization.

At the same time the individual is experiencing these personal changes, his process of thinking about the organization and his position within the organization begin to change. His time perspective begins to become more long range in thinking about his goals and growth in the organization. In the future, he is concerned about having an equal or superordinate position with respect to his peers.

In other words, the maturity process described above is one in which the individual is seeking self-actualization. The individual wants control over himself. He is developing a sense of integrity and feeling of self-worth.

Organizational States and Processes

According to the participative theorists, the overall objective of the organization is to achieve a satisfactory integration between the needs and desires of the members of the organization and the persons functionally related to it such as consumers, shareholders, and suppliers.

It is assumed that management can make full use of the potential capacities of its human resources only when each person in the organization is a member of one or more effectively functioning work groups, thus participating in the overall organizational effort. Further, it is required that these groups have a high degree of group loyalty, effective skills, and high performance goals.

These groups are to be linked together into an overall organization by means of people who hold overlapping group membership. Exhibit 2 depicts what this overlapping organization looks like. The individual who is represented by an "X" in the exhibit is referred to as the "linking pin."[8]

Under the participative modelists' assumptions, the linking pin is a key figure in the organization. He provides a means of transmitting information and influence throughout the organization to achieve integration. Formalized groups such as ad hoc committees and staff groups or meetings across two levels of the organization are designed to augment interaction and the flow of communication and information throughout the organization.

EXHIBIT 2

An Introduction to Organizational Models
(the linking-pin organization)

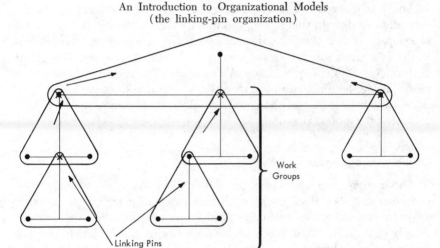

Interaction within the System

The participative organization modelists make a number of assumptions about interaction within the system both at the level of the individual and in light of the entire organizational system.

At the individual level, integration of the individual into the entire organizational system is described by the principle of supportive relationships. This principle states that organizational interaction should be conducted so that individuals will view their interactions as supportive. That is, that in all interactions and in all relationships within the organization, the individual in light of his background, values, and expectations will

---

[8]A term coined by R. Likert, *New Patterns of Management* (New York: McGraw-Hill Book Co., Inc., 1961).

feel these interactions build and maintain his sense of personal worth and importance.

The participative modelists believe that high managerial goals are a precondition to high subordinate goals. And that in order for the subordinates to accept these goals without resentment, the supportive relationships described above should exist. Further, they believe the maximum participation in decision-making and supportive behavior, defined by the model, help establish these high goals and produce a high level of commitment to the goals' achievement.

Supportive behavior and group decision making, according to the participative model, contribute to good communications and coordination within the framework of overlapping groups. The best-performing organizations, according to this model, are those which motivate the individual to cooperate, not compete. In achieving this cooperation, the group leader is accountable and must accept final responsibility for the group performance. However, in spite of the leader's responsibility for group performance, he must consider accepting group decisions with which he does not concur if he feels he could adversely affect group loyalty by not following the group's decisions.

Organizational Change

The participative model of organization views change as a total system codification rather than an atomistic alteration. That is, if a manager wishes to create a change in the participative organization, he can not merely change one small piece of the organization but he has to prepare the entire organization, since under the model's linking pin design the entire organization would be affected.

Consequently, according to the participative designers, change should start by altering the most influential causal variables affecting what you want to change. Then, there should be systematic plans prepared to modify all other affected parts of the organization in carefully coordinated steps.

Conflict Management

The change method described above would involve each individual in the change process, securing each person's commitment to the proposed change, and therefore minimizing the potential for any conflict. In fact, under the model's assumptions, all conflict is managed by the participation of the individuals in joint decision-making processes such as the change process. During the decision-making period, ideas may be challenged. But once this group makes a decision, be it a meeting of four or five or the collective "group" of an entire organization, the participative theorists see everyone as committed to the decision since they helped reach that determination. And if conflict does arise, the participative modelists believe that individuals who trust each other and are seeking to cooperate with one another will be able to resolve this conflict.

Sources of Data

While the participative model is closely linked to the thinking of later researchers like McGregor and Argyris, and to a greater extent on the work of Rensis Likert and his colleagues at the University of Michigan, the deepest roots of the participative model are in the work of Kurt Lewin.[9] While there are some differences in the various researchers'

EXHIBIT 3

An Introduction to Organizational Models

If a manager has:

Well-organized plan of operation
High performance goals
High technical competence
(managers or staff assistants)

And if the manager manages via:

Causal Variables	Direct hierarchical pressure for results including the usual contexts and other practices of the traditional systems	Principle of supportive relationships, group methods of supervision, and other principles of systems

His organization will display:

Intervening Variables	Less group loyalty Lower performance goals Greater conflict and less cooperation Less technical assistance to peers Greater feeling of unreasonable pressure Less favorable attitudes toward manager Lower motivation to produce	Greater group loyalty Higher performance goals Greater cooperation More technical assistance to peers Less feeling of unreasonable pressure More favorable attitudes toward manager Higher motivation to produce

And his organization will attain:

End-Result Variables	Lower sales volume Higher sales cost Lower quality of business sold Lower earnings by salesmen	Higher sales volume Lower sales cost Higher quality of business sold Higher earnings by salesmen

N.B. The same principle applies to other than sales organizations.

Taken from Rensis Likert, *The Human Organization* (New York: McGraw-Hill Book Co., Inc., 1967), p. 76.

---

[9]McGregor, *Human Side of Enterprise;* Chris Argyris, *Personality and Organization* (New York: Harper & Row, 1957); Kurt Lewin, *Resolving Social Conflicts* (New York: Harper & Row, 1948).

points of view, they all find common ground in their universal application of the model. That is, irrespective of time, size, location, or nature of business, they all feel that the participative model is the way in which an organization should and can be most effectively designed.

The conclusion is based on the researchers' studies of organizations which have shown that in the highest performing organization, many of the kinds of behavior defined and described by the participative modelists are present.

Although it is impossible to review all the research on the participative model, Exhibit 3 is a flowchart of the general pattern of research findings.

The Sociotechnical and Cognitive Models

STEPHEN A. ALLEN III

JOHN J. GABARRO

THE SOCIOTECHNICAL and cognitive models contrast strikingly with
the universal models of the classical and participative theorists. The
major difference is that they do not offer a simple, universally applicable
prescription for organizational design and behavior. Both of these models
are intended to help understand the context of the organization's specific
situation and the factors bearing on the organization in that situation. As
such, the two models recognize that behavior in organizations is conditioned by such factors as environment, individual motives, values, differences in goals, etc. They differ in the extent to which they deal with these
relationships explicitly and the extent to which they offer prescriptions.

The sociotechnical and cognitive models have been chosen for study
because they are two conceptual schemes that are well accepted by behavioral sciences and provide a more complex view of the organization
than the universal models do. These two models have also served as the
conceptual antecedents for recent "contingent" approaches to organizational design. (By contingent we mean behavioral science approaches
which systematically take into account the differences between organizations because of differences in their tasks and members' needs.) The
sociotechnical and cognitive models have influenced the work of Woodward, Thompson, and Lawrence and Lorsch.[1]

SOCIOTECHNICAL MODEL

The sociotechnical model views the organization as a system interacting with its environment—a system in which behavior is influenced by

[1]Joan Woodward, *Industrial Organization: Theory and Practice* (London: Oxford
University Press, 1965); James D. Thompson, *Organizations in Action* (New York:
McGraw-Hill Book Co., Inc., 1967); Paul R. Lawrence and Jay W. Lorsch, *Organization and Environment* (Boston: Division of Research, Harvard Business School,
1967).

`17`

human, technological, social, and organizational inputs. All of these variables are interdependent so that a change in one influences the others.

Several theories of organizational behavior can be included under the sociotechnical mantle, but they all have several themes in common: multiple causation of behavior, the concept of the organization as a system, and the realization that the informal social system is not generally the same as the formal social system. There are two traditions—the Tavistock school and Homans' social system theory of group behavior—which travel under the sociotechnical label; and they will be the focus of this paper.

From Homans' study of organizations as social systems we get such notions as the "formal" and "informal" organization and such concepts as sentiments, activities, interactions, norms, values, and their interrelationships.[2] Homans' interest was in behavior in the human group and how it affected and was affected by the organization structure, rather than in the organization structure itself. His work was heavily influenced by Roethlisberger and Mayo and their classic Hawthorne studies and was built on much of their pioneering research.[3]

The second tradition is the sociotechnical system approach or "Tavistock school" of organizational theory, so named because of the work done by Rice, Trist, and Miller at the Tavistock Institute in England.[4] Unlike Homans, the Tavistock theorists emphasize the organizational structure rather than the face-to-face group. Their focus is on how the organizational structure affects and is affected by its members.

The Organization as a System

Implicit in both traditions is the notion of system. Homans saw "the relationship between group and [its] environment as essentially a relationship of action and reaction." He also identified the systematic nature of the relationship between activities, sentiments, interactions, and the resulting behavior in the organization.

While Rice and Miller[5] deal with the system concept differently from Homans, the notion of a system is also central to their work. In the Tavistock model, the organization is seen as an open system exchanging resources with its environment in the form of an input-conversion-output

---

[2]George Homans, *The Human Group* (New York: Harcourt, Brace & World, 1950), chaps. 1, 4, 5, and 6.

[3]F. Roethlisberger and William Dickson, *Management and the Worker* (Boston: Harvard University Press, 1943).

[4]Albert Kenneth Rice, *Productivity and Social Organization* (London: Tavistock Publications, 1958); Eric Trist, *Organizational Choice* (London: Tavistock Publications, 1963).

[5]E. J. Miller and A. K. Rice, *Systems of Organization* (London: Tavistock Publications and Trinity Press, 1967), p. 9.

process. Figure 1 shows an organization as such a process. The enterprise takes in raw materials, energy, and manpower, and exports products, wages, etc. The ability of an organization to satisfy and adapt to its environment determines its success or failure. Similarly, each constituent activity in the organization, such as product divisions, or marketing, production, and research functions, is viewed as an open system.

FIGURE 1

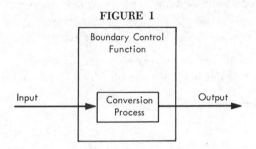

Organizational States and Processes

In the Tavistock model, the input-conversion-output process is carried on to accomplish the organization's "primary task," that is, the task which it performs to survive. Normally, each organization has one primary task, although some organizations such as a teaching hospital have more (i.e., therapy, teaching, research). The organization is built around its primary task. Likewise, each unit in the organization is built around its own discrete subtask. The Tavistock assumption is that the organization's effectiveness and satisfaction of its members are both affected by how well the organization is structured to perform its primary task, and thereby satisfy the demands of its environment.

The model prescribes that differentiation should be based on the nature of the primary task, and around its "prevalent cleavages." Miller suggests that these cleavages naturally occur along one of the following three dimensions:[6]

1. Technology—the material, means, techniques, or skills required for a task.
2. Territory—that geography of the task performance.
3. Time—the task parameters in terms of time, i.e., shifts, turns, tours, etc.

Further subdifferentiation should also be done around these cleavages so each group is performing a whole task. No differentiation should violate task needs.

---

[6]Eric J. Miller, "Technology, Territory and Time—The Internal Differentiation of Complex Production Systems," *Human Relations*, Vol. 12, No. 3, pp. 243–72.

Unlike the classical theorists, the Tavistock authors clearly see that differentiation creates a need for integration. In the Tavistock model's view, differentiation creates the need for a managing system to reintegrate functions so that "constituent tasks add up to the whole task." A management performs this function by defining and reviewing the primary task and by having appropriate regulatory measures at the boundaries of the differentiated operating systems. The Tavistock assumption is that carefully differentiated tasks will reduce integration problems. Rice gives the student or practitioner the following guidelines:[7]

1. Integration is easier with autonomous territorial separation.
2. When each sub-unit has a whole task which is measurable, integration is easier.
3. Controls must follow lines of differentiation.

Little is said about the process of conflict resolution other than the implication that conflict will be minimized if the organization is properly structured around primary tasks:[8]

In general, we can say that without adequate boundary definition for activity, systems' and groups' organizational boundaries are difficult to define and frontier skirmishing is inevitable.

Homans' treatment of conflict rests on the belief that organizational units with different tasks, people, and formal organizations are expected to have different behavioral characteristics. Thus, the process of conflict resolution will be influenced by these differences. Homans does not, however, deal explicitly with how conflict between different organizational units can be resolved.

Homans also identifies as a second type of conflict the differences between social norms of members and the requirements of the organization. Again, he does not deal with this explicitly, other than to imply that both types of conflict, as well as interdepartmental integration, are handled by the organization's leaders in their roles as managers.[9]

Assumptions about Human Behavior

Briefly, Homans sees man as a complex system of perceptions, values, and motives, Homans' elements of behavior are activities, sentiments, and interactions with others. According to this approach, these three elements are in a constant state of interdependence with each other, the individual's personality, and the "external system."

---

[7]A. K. Rice, *The Enterprise and Its Environment* (London: Tavistock Publications and Fletcher & Sons, 1963), chap. 24.

[8]Miller and Rice, *Systems of Organizations*, p. 42.

[9]Homans, *Human Group*, pp. 406–14.

Rice and Miller and the Tavistock school have similar assumptions but express them differently:[10]

An individual experiences satisfaction or deprivation from his work because of:

1. the interpersonal and group relationships he has in the activity system;
2. the harmonies or disharmonies of these relationships with his memberships in other groups [such as family, profession, etc.];
3. the satisfaction or deprivation he experiences in the activities themselves [i.e., the work itself].

Expanding on this latter point, they also assert that individual satisfaction will be maximized when the primary task is differentiated in a meaningful way and based on the real requirements of the task. They also recognize, however, that human needs should influence structure:[11]

Human needs may be treated as constraints on the performance of the primary task—the work must be meaningful and the task must be acceptable to individuals.

Implicit in this last statement is the assumption, also acknowledged by Homans, that the motives of individuals are not necessarily those of the organization.

Formal and Informal Aspects of the Organization

For this reason, Homans and the Tavistock group view the organization as consisting of a "formal organization" as well as an "informal organization." (The "formal organization" is called the "task group" by Rice and the "external system" by Homans. The "informal organization" is called the "sentient group" by Rice and the "internal system" by Homans.) Both Homans and Rice point out that the formal and informal organizations influence each other, although, as one would expect, Homans places greatest emphasis on the informal organization and Tavistock on the formal.

Where the Homans approach and the Tavistock model disagree, however, is in the degree to which formal and informal organizations should be congruent. Homans suggests that wherever practical, the formal organization should coincide with the informal.[12] But Miller and Rice take a different view:[13]

---

[10]Miller and Rice, *Systems of Organizations*, p. 30.
[11]Rice, *Enterprise and Its Environment*, p. 252, also pp. 186–89.
[12]Homans, *Human Group*, chap. 14.
[13]Miller and Rice, *Systems of Organization*, pp. 253 and 260.

. . . We have made the hypothesis that forms of organization in which the task and sentient groups coincide may have relatively short term effectiveness; in the longer term such groups can inhibit change and hence lead eventually to deterioration of performance.

The Tavistock model does not prescribe congruence between task and sentient groups. Rather, it suggests the creation of "sentience" (values and norms) based on commitment to change.

Usefulness of the Sociotechnical Approach

As can be seen from the above discussion, the major strengths of both Tavistock and Homans' sociotechnical models lie in their systematic treatment of the complex realities of organization life, thereby allowing us to identify the diverse causes of behavior in organizations. Unlike the classical and participative models, the sociotechnical model lends visibility without becoming a simplistic, and oftentimes misleading map. Its limitation is that although the model is very useful in analyses, the complexity of the reality which it captures makes it difficult to use as a design tool without practice and formal training.

Taken separately, the Tavistock model is very useful for thinking about division of work and organizational "fit" to primary tasks (although it provides little specific criteria to the practitioner for identifying the primary task). Homans' social system theory by itself is a conditional model which can be applied realistically to a variety of situations in understanding and predicting behavior.

THE COGNITIVE OR DECISION-MAKING MODEL OF ORGANIZATIONS

When we speak of the cognitive or decision-making model of organizations, we are referring to the analytical approach and set of concepts developed by Herbert Simon, James March, and their colleagues at the Carnegie Institute of Technology.[14] This approach to the analysis of complex organizations was developed by the authors mainly to aid them in building quantitative models of decision processes. Because their work is aimed mainly at an academic audience, proceeds at a fairly high level of abstraction, and employs many variables, it usually proves to be fairly rough going for the student who has had no previous exposure to it and who has only limited time to master the concepts. The purpose of this paper is to summarize the major concepts and the general thrust of the cognitive model. It is not intended as a definitive statement of the cognitive model, but rather seeks to provide an overview.

---

[14]James G. March and Herbert A. Simon, *Organizations* (New York: John Wiley & Sons, Inc., 1958).

Basic Elements of the Model

These authors employ three basic elements to explain and predict the functioning of large, complex organizations. These elements are:

1. Cognition—the perceptual and information processing mechanisms of individuals and organizational units.
2. The decision or problem-solving process—the sequence of tests and operations that individuals and organizational units go through to structure and solve a problem.
3. The administrative or organizational setting—the way in which tasks have been subdivided and the mechanisms through which these subtasks are coordinated.

These three elements can be studied in a concrete, operational manner by identifying the goals which are held by individuals and subunits within the organization, and by determining the nature of the communications which flow among these individuals or subunits (e.g., the channels through which information flows, the frequency of communications, the quality of information, etc.).

March and Simon state that both the classical organization theory and the economic theory of the firm are severely limited in their ability to explain organizational behavior because they ignore major portions of the three elements described in the preceding paragraph. The classical model focuses mainly on the problems of subdividing and assigning tasks; and while this is an important element of organization, it is only a starting point. For instance, March and Simon (1958) note:

> One peculiar characteristic of the assignment problem and of all the formalizations of the departmentalization problem in classical organization theory is that, if taken literally, problems of coordination are eliminated. Since the whole set of activities to be performed is specified in advance, once these are allocated to organization units and individuals the organization problem posed by these formal theories is solved. . . . We need a framework that recognizes that the set of activities to be performed is not given in advance, except in the most general way—that one of the very important processes in organizations is the elaboration of this set of activities, and the determination of which precise activities are to be performed at which precise times and places (pp. 25–26).

The authors' argument with the economic theory of the firm focuses on the economists' simplifying assumptions that price and output decisions are made by an individual entrepreneur who has perfect information (e.g., about the marginal revenues and costs associated with units of output). In reality these decisions are made by a group of managers whose goals are often in conflict with each other and who possess very imperfect information. Thus, organizations tend to "satisfice" rather than optimize profit by the very nature of their decision processes.

Major Organizational Processes

Now let us consider the March and Simon view of the organizational decision process. Stated simply, an organizational decision is the execution of a choice made in terms of objectives from among a set of alternatives on the basis of available information. The authors overlay this simple notion of decision making with a complex set of assumptions concerning the cognitive limitations of human beings and the behavioral effects of specialization. In essence, the individual is viewed as "a choosing, decision-making, problem-solving organism that can do only one or a few things at a time, and that can attend to only a small part of the information recorded in its memory and presented by the environment" (p. 11). This is why we have organizations; they are institutional mechanisms for factoring a complex set of problems into subproblems which are simple enough to be handled by the human mind. These same limitations of human cognition also lie at the heart of the problem of achieving coordination. Perhaps the best way to elaborate this last point is to consider how March and Simon view the processes of differentiation, integration, and conflict resolution.

ASSUMPTIONS REGARDING DIFFERENTIATION, INTEGRATION, AND CONFLICT RESOLUTION

Specialization

Whether an organization divides work on the basis of purpose (major ends to be achieved) or process (major activities to be performed) and the manner in which these bases of specialization are interspersed in an organization are a function of a number of factors, for example, the size of the organization, the complexity and interdependence of the activities to be performed, and the degree to which activities can be routinized or programmed. Specialization per se is not as important to the March and Simon schema as the behavioral effects which it produces.

Specialization leads individuals and groups to identify with subgoals of the organization. In other words,

When tasks have been allocated to an organizational unit in terms of a subgoal, other subgoals and other aspects of the goals of the larger organization tend to be ignored in the decisions of the subunit. In part, this bias in decision-making can be attributed to shifts in the focus of attention. The definition of the situation is simplified by omitting some criteria and paying particular attention to others (p. 152).

At the same time, specialization leads to a particular channeling of information to and from the specialized unit. Thus, marketing and manufacturing executives in the same organization will have very different goals and communication patterns. They will focus on different aspects of the world and tend to perceive similar events somewhat differently.

Notions such as identification with subgoals and channelizations of communications lead to the view of the total organization as a coalition of units and/or individuals whose goals are imperfectly rationalized with one another and who differ both in the information they possess and their perceptions of the organizational world.

Coordination

"The problem of arranging the signaling system for interdependent conditional activities is the coordination problem" (p. 28). Different bases of specialization require different *degrees* of coordination. Specialization by purpose entails greater self-containment and thus lower coordinative costs than process specialization.

Organizations use different *types* of coordination depending on the degree to which the situation can be standardized. Coordination by plan, or preestablished schedule, is used where the situation is more stable and predictable. Coordination by feedback, which entails the transmission of new information, is relied upon more heavily where conditions are more variable and unpredictable.

Factors Affecting Interunit Conflict

The relationships which March and Simon see between differentiation and integration can best be summarized by examining their model of interunit conflict. Exhibit 1 details the major factors affecting the level of conflict, which may be viewed as lack of integration. The authors discuss this diagram as follows:

> The existence of a positive *felt need for joint decision-making* and of either a *difference in goals* or a *difference in perceptions* of reality or both among the participants in the organization are necessary conditions for intergroup conflict (p. 121).

We have already considered some of the ways in which specialization leads to differences in goals and perceptions. Two other factors which affect differences in goals are also noted in Exhibit 1. If overall organization goals are operational and tied to reward systems, differences in subunit goals will tend to be reduced. Similarly, the less the mutual dependence on limited resources, the greater the difference in goals which can be tolerated. This condition has been termed "organizational slack" by

March and Simon. "Slack" is defined as the differences between the resources available to the organization and the total requirements of the members of the organizational coalition. Where "slack" is positive, there is lower conflict (1) because there is less felt need for joint decision making and (2) a greater difference in subunit goals can be tolerated.

EXHIBIT 1

Factors Affecting Intergroup Conflict within an Organization*

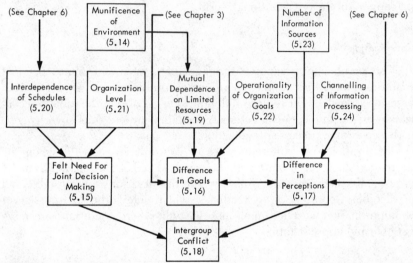

*James G. March and Herbert A. Simon, *Organizations* (New York: John Wiley & Sons, Inc., 1958), p. 128.

Two additional factors are seen as affecting the felt need for joint decision making: One is the degree to which subunit tasks are interdependent. The second factor is organizational level—the higher the level, the greater the felt need for joint decision making.

Quasi-Resolution of Conflict

We have considered several factors which contribute to interunit conflicts. How do organizations manage these conflicts? Cyert and March argue:

. . . that most organizations most of the time exist and thrive with considerable latent conflict of goals. Except at the level of non-operational objectives, there is no internal consensus. The procedures for "resolving" such conflict do not reduce all goals to a common dimension or even make them obviously internally consistent. . . . We assume that conflict is resolved by using local rationality, acceptable-level decision rules, and sequential attention to goals (p. 117).

Essentially the assumption here is that organizations seldom confront conflicts directly. Conflict is managed by (1) delegating responsibility for subgoals to individual departments (local rationality); (2) by employing decision rules that are either consistent with a number of goals or at a low enough aspiration level to produce "slack" (acceptable-level decision rules); and (3) by attending to different goals at different times (sequential attention to goals).

CONTRIBUTIONS AND USEFULNESS OF THE MODEL

Although the cognitive model may seem overly complex and at times unnecessarily "jargonesque," it provides a number of useful insights into the functioning of complex organizations. As an analytical approach, it leads us to view organization as a *process* which evolves from the interaction of structure, human cognitive mechanisms, and the nature of the decisions which must be made. In this sense, it is a *dynamic* model which emphasizes the development and adaptation of organizational systems under varying conditions. As a set of concepts this model is also insightful. It points both to the behavioral effects of specialization and to the coordinative problems posed by specialization.

From a theoretical standpoint the cognitive model has at least three limitations: First of all, it gives only limited explicit recognition to the effects an organization's environment may have on processes of specialization and coordination. Second of all, it emphasizes individual and group cognition but ignores the social processes through which power and status positions evolve in organizations. Finally, its treatment of conflict resolution borders on the tautological. The authors essentially state that conflict is resolved by avoidance. While organizational slack, sequential attention to goals, etc., are undoubtedly important elements in conflict situations, leadership and intergroup bargaining would also seem to be important factors.

Practitioners and students frequently question the practical utility of the cognitive model because it contains much analysis and no prescriptions. Further its hypotheses have not been systematically tested with empirical data. The authors, for their part, unabashedly disavow any interest in prescription. The more useful question for the student is, "Do the analytical approaches and concepts employed by this model allow me to better understand the functioning of complex organizational systems?" If the answer is yes, then it becomes the student's task to apply his insights to the design and development of more effective organizations.

The Theories of Joan Woodward and James Thompson

MARTIN P. CHARNS

JOAN WOODWARD and James Thompson are organizational theorists who have attempted to find and describe patterns of similarities among—and differences between—different types of organizations. Both authors have chosen variables in technology of organizations as key elements in their classifications. Woodward in *Industrial Organization: Theory and Practice*[1] describes the findings of her study of the organizational structure of 100 manufacturing firms located in the south of England. Thompson, on the other hand, has drawn primarily upon other literature in organizational behavior and related fields in developing his conceptualizations of organizations.[2]

JOAN WOODWARD[3]

Joan Woodward, believing that the concept of the firm as a sociotechnical system had been accepted but had remained largely an abstraction at operator and management levels, began a study to determine conditions under which behavior inside organizations became standardized and predictable. She desired to link technical variables in the manufacturing situation to elements of organization and the management process. In her South Essex study of 100 manufacturing firms, Woodward found that organizational characteristics did not appear related to either size of the firm or business efficiency. Woodward then classified firms in terms

---

[1]Joan Woodward, *Industrial Organization: Theory and Practice* (London: Oxford University Press, 1965).

[2]James D. Thompson, *Organizations in Action* (New York: McGraw-Hill Book Co., 1967).

[3]The basis for the majority of the material in this section comes from Joan Woodward, "Automation and Technical Change—The Implications for the Management Process," presented by J. J. Rackham and reproduced with permission in Harvard Business School Case HP 670.

of the technology characterizing their production processes into the three main groupings of (1) firms that produced units or small batches generally to customers' individual orders; (2) large-batch and mass-production firms; and (3) firms producing on a continuous-process basis. (The firms were subsequently classified into 11 subgroups, which will not be discussed here.) Woodward believed this classification produced what was in effect a crude scale of technology in terms of three related variables of (1) the stages in the historical development of production processes; (2) the interrelation between the items of equipment used for these processes; and (3) the extent to which the operations performed in the processes were repetitive or comparable from one production cycle or sequence to the next. In moving along the scale from small batch to continuous flow, the technology was better known and understood and lent itself to increasing exercise of control over manufacturing operations. Targets could be set and reached more effectively in continuous-flow production than they could in the most up-to-date and efficient batch-production firms. In continuous-flow production, factors likely to limit performance could be allowed for, whereas no matter how well-developed production control procedures might be in batch production, there would be a degree of uncertainty in the prediction of results. In unit production —especially in prototype manufacture—the difficulties of exercising effective control were greatest.

Organizational Differences

Among the three different categories of organizations, Woodward found differences in terms of organization and management practices. In her sample, she found that the small-batch and unit-production firms had a median number of levels of authority of 3, with a range of 2 to 4. Among the large-batch firms, the median was 4 and the range from 3 to 8, and among process-technology firms the median was 6 and the range from 2 to 17. Woodward's description of this finding is shown in Figure 1.[4] Similarly, in span of control of first-line supervisors and in the ratio of managers and supervisors to other personnel, Woodward found significant differences among the three groups of firms, and these differences did not appear related to the size of the firm (Figure 1A). Woodward's findings are summarized in Table 1.

Woodward believed that the location of responsibility for production was related to the structural differences which she found. In process production an error could cause a considerable loss to the process if it continued unchecked or unnoticed. One result of this fact was the con-

---

[4]Figures 1 and 1A are Exhibits 2 and 3 from Joan Woodward, *Management and Technology* (London: Her Majesty's Stationery Office, 1958).

FIGURE 1

The Number of Levels of Authority in Management Hierarchy

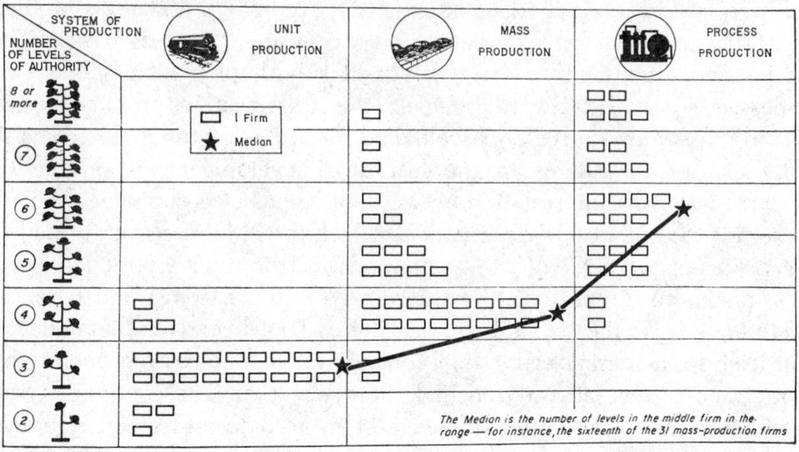

centration of that portion of the control function which is not a part of the process itself into the hands of managers and supervisors.

Woodward also found that on certain of the characteristics, firms at the extremes of the technical scale resembled each other, a finding which was also true for less easily measured characteristics. There was a tendency for organic management systems to predominate in jobbing and continuous-flow production, while mechanistic systems predominated in the middle ranges. Clear-cut definition of duties and responsibilities were characteristic of firms in the middle ranges, while flexible organization

FIGURE 1A

Span of Control of First-Line Supervision

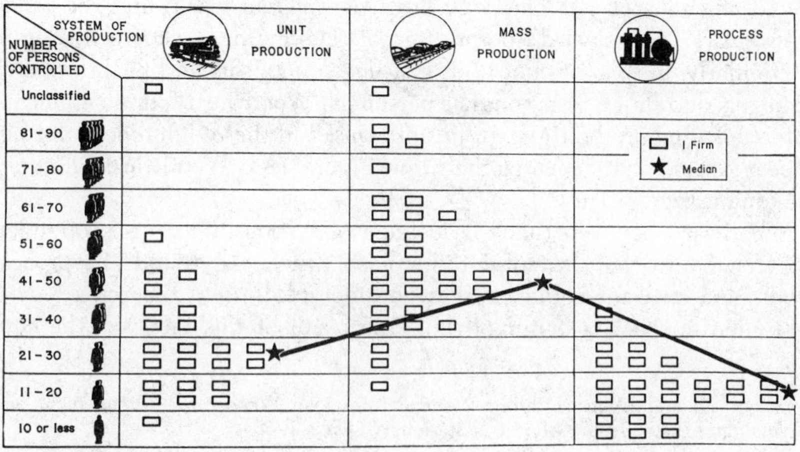

TABLE 1

Organizational Characteristics as Related to Technology

	Type of Technology		
Organizational Characteristic	Unit and Small Batch	Large Batch	Process
Number of firms in study............	24	31	25
Levels of management authority:			
median	3	4	6
range.........................	2–4	3–8	2–17
Median span of control	23	48	15
Range of ratio of managers and supervisory personnel to other personnel	1:24 to 1:49	1:14 to 1:18	1:7 to 1:8

with a high degree of delegation of authority and responsibility for decision making and with permissive and participative management was characteristic of firms at the extremes.

In both process and unit production, stress was laid on the importance of managers being technically competent. In process production, the technical competence was intellectual, based upon qualifications and knowledge, whereas in unit production it was intuitive, based on long experience and know-how.

The two groups of firms at the extremes of the scale also had in common the characteristic of homogeneous organizational and behavior patterns. The physical work flow and the nature of the manufacturing process appeared to place considerable restrictions on organizational choice. In batch production the physical work flow did not impose such rigid restrictions, with the result that technology did not as much determine organization as define the limits within which it could be determined. In batch production the management process was not as much a function of the technology as of the control system, which in turn depended upon both technology and social and economic factors.

Structure and Success

When firms were grouped on a basis of their production systems, the outstandingly successful ones had at least one feature in common. Many of their organizational characteristics approximated to the median of their production group. For example, in successful unit-production firms the span of control of the first-line supervisor ranged from 22 to 28, the median for the group as a whole being 23; in successful mass-production firms it ranged from 45 to 50, the median for the group being 49; and in

The mediating technology involves the linking of clients or customers who are or wish to be interdependent.[7] Examples are the commercial bank, which links depositors and borrowers; the insurance firm, which links those who pool common risks; and the telephone utility. Complexity in the mediating technology comes not from the necessity of having each activity geared to the requirements of the next but rather from the fact that the mediating technology requires operating in standardized ways, and extensively, for example, with multiple clients or customers distributed in time and space.

In the intensive technology a variety of techniques is drawn upon in order to achieve a change in some specific object; but the selection, combination, and order of application are determined by feedback from the object itself.[8] It is a custom technology whose successful employment rests upon the availability of all capacities potentially needed and upon the appropriate custom combination required by the individual case. A good example of an intensive technology is a general hospital. The combination of dietary, x-ray, laboratory, and housekeeping services together with the various medical specialties, pharmaceutical services, occupational therapies, social work services, and religious services can be determined only from evidence about the state of the patient.

Technology and Structure

Thompson assumes that structure is a fundamental vehicle by which organizations achieve bounded rationality. By delimiting responsibilities, control over resources and other matters, organizations provide their participating members with boundaries within which efficiency may be a reasonable expectation. The resulting spheres of bounded rationality are interdependent, and structure must also facilitate their coordinated action. Thompson characterizes interdependence as (1) *pooled,* (2) *sequential,* or (3) *reciprocal.*

In a situation characterized by pooled interdependence it is not necessary that parts of the organization are dependent upon each other in any direct way. Yet they may be interdependent in the sense that unless each performs adequately, the total organization is jeopardized; failure of any one part can threaten the whole and thus the other parts. A multidivisional company in which the divisions operate in different markets and have different technologies but where they draw upon a common pool of resources (such as financial resources) is an example of a situation having pooled interdependence.

Where direct interdependence in a serial form can be pinpointed, we have sequential interdependence. Here one organization unit is directly

---

[7]Ibid.
[8]Ibid., p. 17.

dependent upon another (e.g., when the output of one division is the input for another). In situations characterized by sequential interdependence, it is always possible to specify the order of interdependence. Sequential interdependence implies that there is also an aspect of pooled interdependence; sequentially interdependent units both make contributions to and are sustained by the whole organization.

Reciprocal interdependence refers to the situation where outputs of each unit become inputs for the others. Each unit involved is penetrated by the other. An illustration of reciprocal interdependence is an airline which contains both operations and maintenance units. The maintenance unit produces a serviceable aircraft, which is an input to the operations unit; the product (or by-product) of operations is an aircraft needing service, which is an input to the maintenance unit. In situations having reciprocal interdependence there are aspects of pooled and sequential interdependence, but the distinguishing aspect is the reciprocity of the interdependence, with each unit posing contingency for the other.

The three types of interdependence contain increasing degrees of contingency, moving from pooled to sequential to reciprocal. The increasing degrees of contingency make the three types of interdependence increasingly difficult to coordinate and thus, Thompson postulates, more costly to coordinate.[9]

The type of coordinating mechanism which is used by an organization in a specific situation is directly dependent upon the type of interdependence characterizing the situation.

Coordination by *standardization* is appropriate with pooled interdependence. Standardization involves the establishment of routines or rules which constrain action of each unit or position into paths consistent with those taken by others in the interdependent relationship. The set of rules must be internally consistent, and this requires that the situations to which they apply be relatively stable, repetitive, and few enough to permit matching of situations with appropriate rules.

Coordination by *plan,* which involves the establishment of schedules for the interdependent units, is appropriate for the situations having sequential interdependence. Here, there is not the same high degree of stability and routinization that are required for coordination by standardization. Coordination by plan is more appropriate for more dynamic situations, especially when a changing task environment impinges on the organization.

Coordination by *mutual adjustment,* which involves the transmission of new information during the process of action, is appropriate for more variable and unpredictable situations and is called for by situations of reciprocal interdependence.

The three types of coordination, in the order introduced, place increas-

---

[9]Ibid., p. 55.

ingly heavy burdens on communication and decision, and thus present increasing costs to the organization. Thompson proposes that organizations group positions to minimize these coordination costs.[10] Thus, given that organizations can group positions on one of several different bases, such as upon (1) common purpose or contribution to the larger organization, (2) common processes, (3) particular clientele, or (4) geographical considerations,[11] and that organizations are not unidimensional, the question becomes one of setting the priorities in applying the criteria for grouping. This Thompson suggests is determined by the nature and location of interdependency, which is a function of both technology and task environment.[12]

To reduce costs of coordination, an organization will give first priority to grouping so as to minimize the more costly forms of coordination. Organizations seek to place reciprocally interdependent positions tangent to one another in local groups which are autonomous from the rest of the organization within the constraints set by plans and standardization. Once an organization has handled reciprocal interdependence, priorities on grouping of positions are placed on meeting sequential interdependence by placing these positions tangent to each other. Third priority is placed upon grouping positions homogeneously to facilitate coordination by standardization.

First-order groupings, however, may not be able to deal satisfactorily with all reciprocal interdependence, and even if the basic groups do satisfactorily deal with reciprocal interdependence, sequential and pooled interdependence may still have to be handled. Thus, when reciprocal interdependence cannot be confined to intragroup activities, organizations seek to link the groups involved into a second-order group. Thompson views this clustering, or combination of interdependent groups, as the first step in a *hierarchy*. After grouping units to minimize coordination by mutual adjustment, organizations seek to place sequentially interdependent groups tangent to each other in a cluster, or second-order grouping. After units are clustered to solve problems of reciprocal and sequential interdependence, organizations seek to cluster groups into homogeneous units to facilitate coordination by standardization. In more complicated organizations the criteria of reciprocal and sequential interdependence tend to exhaust the clustering possibilities before this third criterion can be exercised. Then organizations seek to blanket homogeneous positions under rules which cut across group boundaries, and to blanket similar groups under rules which cross divisional lines. Organiza-

---

[10]Ibid., p. 57.

[11]These four bases were suggested by Luther Gulick in Luther Gulick and L. Urwick, eds., *Papers on the Science of Administration* (New York: Institute of Public Administration, 1937).

[12]Thompson, *Organizations in Action*, p. 57.

tions employing such rules which cut across multiple groupings develop liaison positions linking the several groups and the rule-making agency. For example, staff specialists such as controllers at intermediate levels in the organization are often intended to serve a liaison function.

The liaison positions are appropriate for situations having pooled interdependence, and requiring formulation, interpretation, and application of rules for standardization. Organizations employ other devices to deal with other types of interdependence that is not contained by the formal structure. They rely on committees to accomplish coordination not handled by the formal structure in situations of sequential interdependence and upon task-force or project groupings in situations of reciprocal interdependence.

Environmental Factors and Organizational Integration

JAY W. LORSCH
PAUL R. LAWRENCE

Introduction

IN THE PAST few years, the study of ecology of organizations has been given an important impetus by the work of Perrow, Thompson, Udy, Woodward, and others.[1] Each of these studies had conceived of the demands external to the organization in slightly different terms. For example, Woodward reports that the structure of industrial organizations is related to the type of manufacturing technology with which the firm is dealing (job shop, batch, in process); Thompson relates the internal structure of the organization to the nature of its environment in a homogeneous-heterogeneous continuum and a stable-shifting continuum. Yet all of them, including our own recent study, seem to point to the fact that an important environmental characteristic which is related to the internal structure of the organization is the position of the environment on a certainty-uncertainty continuum.[2]

In our own study, for example, we have found that organizations operating in uncertain and diverse environments tend to have units which are more highly differentiated in terms of the internal structure of units and the members' goal, time, and interpersonal orientation. Organizations in this type of environment tend to have more elaborate mechanisms for achieving integration among functional units and have relatively evenly distributed influence patterns over decision on critical issues. In contrast,

---

[1] Charles Perrow, "A Framework for the Comparative Analysis of Organizations," *American Sociological Review*, Vol. 32, No. 2 (April 1967); James D. Thompson, *Organizations in Action* (New York: McGraw-Hill Book Co., Inc., 1967); Stanley Udy, *Organization of Work* (New Haven, Conn.: HRAF Press, 1959); Joan Woodward, *Industrial Organization: Theory and Practice* (London: Oxford University Press, 1965).

[2] Paul R. Lawrence, and Jay W. Lorsch, *Organization and Environment: Managing Differentiation and Integration* (Boston: Division of Research, Harvard Business School, 1967).

organization in more stable and less diverse environments have less differentiated units and tend to rely on the hierarchy as the major means for achieving integration and have a more pointed distribution of influence on critical decisions.

While there is this area of seeming agreement between these studies, the timing of the completion of all of them is such that it has been impossible for us or any of the other authors to build systematically on the work of each other. In this paper we would, therefore, like to take a small step in this direction by attempting to relate our work to one important aspect of Thompson's set of propositions. In doing this, we are going to assume that there is the rough correspondence suggested above between our own concepts of environmental certainty and diversity and Thompson's continuums of homogeneity-heterogeneity and stable shifting. Rather than focusing on this point of convergence between Thompson's theory and our own findings, we want to concentrate on another aspect of the environment (*the nature of the required interdependence*) where Thompson's formulations are more refined than our own and tend to illuminate our own findings further.

Environmental Characteristics à la Lawrence and Lorsch

Before doing this, it is useful to restate more fully the constructs we have utilized to describe environmental variables. As suggested above, one of the major variables with which we have been concerned is the *certainty* or *uncertainty* of the environment and its *diversity* or *homogeneity*. Rather than being concerned with the certainty of the environment as a unitary entity, we have recognized that complex organizations—those with more than one unit—actually have segmented their environments into parts. Consequently, we have identified the relative certainty of each of these parts of the environment. For example, each of the 10 industrial organizations in our study was dealing with a market subenvironment (the task of the sales unit), a technoeconomic subenvironment (the task of the production units), and the scientific subenvironment (the task of the research or design unit). Each of these subenvironments had a different rate of change of information, differing time spans of feedback, and different certainty of information at any given point in time. Since these are the important dimensions of certainty which we were able to identify, we can say that each of these subenvironments had a different degree of certainty. How similar or different these parts of the environment were on the certainty-uncertainty continuum determined whether the total environment was diverse or homogeneous. For example, in one of the environments studied, the container industry, all parts of the environment were relatively certain and the total environment was characterized as homogeneous. On the other hand, in a second environment, the plastics industry, the parts of the environment ranged from a highly certain technoeconomic subenvironment to a very uncertain scientific sector; and the total environment was characterized as diverse. As we have suggested above, the diversity of the environment was related to the state of differentiation of structure and managerial orientation within the organization.

A second characteristic of the environment with which we have been concerned is *the dominant competitive issue* in the environment. In the plastics environment this was the issue of innovating new products and processes; for the container industry the dominant issue was the scheduling and allocation of production facilities to meet market demands. The dominant competitive issue was also related to the final environmental characteristic which has been of interest to us—*the pattern and degree of interdependence required between units*.

In all three environments studied (plastics, consumer foods, and containers), the tightness of interdependence required was found to be identical. However, there was an important difference in the pattern of units around which this interdependence was occurring. As shown in Figure 1, in plastics and in foods (where the dominant competitive issue was also innovation), the tight interdependence was between research, sales, and production. In the container industry, with the dominant issue of scheduling and allocating manufacturing facilities, the tight interdependence was required only between production and sales.

FIGURE 1

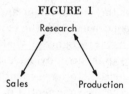

Thompson's Typology of Interdependence

To this point, Thompson's theoretical formulations do not seem at all inconsistent with the environmental characterisitics on which we have focused. However, as mentioned above, his scheme suggests another characteristic which we did not consider—*the type of interdependence required*. He has identified three types of interdependence:[3]

Pooled—where each part renders a discrete contribution to the whole and each is supported by the whole, but no direct interaction is required between the units of the organization.

---

[3]Thompson, *Organizations in Action*, pp. 54–55.

Sequential—when "direct interdependence can be pinpointed between them (the units) and the order of the interdependence can be specified." This interdependence is "not symmetrical."

Reciprocal—when "the outputs of each (unit) become the inputs for the others" . . . "under conditions of reciprocal interdependence each unit involved is penetrated by the others."

While Thompson uses these constructs primarily in dealing with the relationship between technology and structure, he points out that they also have relevance to understanding the relationship between environment and structure. It is in this later context that we wish to build on Thompson's formulations. Not only can this typology of interdependence be utilized to understand the required and actual coordination within the technological core of the organization but it also seems to have utility in understanding the entire pattern of differentiation and integration between units.

Thompson also argues that these types of interdependence "form a Guttman type scale," ranging from pooled toward reciprocal interdependence.[4] The simplest organizations have only pooled interdependence, while moderately complicated ones have pooled and sequential, and the most complicated organizations have all three types present. As we shall illustrate below, data from our study tend to support both the validity of the typology itself and the idea that it represents this sort of continuum. However, the three environments in our study required that organizations deal, to some extent, with all three types of interdependence. Nevertheless, this typology has proved useful because, as Thompson suggests, in each of the environments we have found that one or two types of interdependence had priority, depending on the major competitive issue.[5]

Types of Interdependence in Three Environments

As we suggested earlier, our attempts to review our own data in the light of this typology were post hoc and based on our clinical impressions. We have not been able to systematically measure the presence of each type of interdependence. In spite of this we are relatively confident, based on our intensive study of the three industrial environments, that in the plastics and food environment the dominant type of interdependence between functional units was reciprocal in nature, while in the container environment it was a combination of the pooled and sequential types.

Since the dominant issue in the plastics and food environment was product and process innovation, the members of the research and produc-

---

[4]Ibid., p. 55.
[5]Ibid., p. 57.

tion units and the sales and research units had mutually to reach joint decisions about numerous complex issues, such as product characteristics, customers' requirements, process methods, etc. Clearly, this required a reciprocal interdependence between these units. In the container environment, the critical demand for interdependence was around the major issue of production scheduling to meet market requirements. Sequential interdependence was called for with the sales unit aware of market requirements initiating on the production function. But this critical interdependence was also of a pooled type because to meet a sellers' market, allocation decisions had to be made in regard to scarce production capacity. The nature of the primary interdependencies in the environments is illustrated in the diagrams in Figure 2. It should be empha-

FIGURE 2

Primary Types of Interdependence in Three Environments

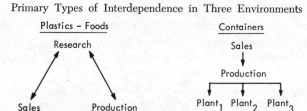

sized that we have only pointed to the critical type(s) of interdependence required. The other types were also present. For example, in the plastics and food environment sequential interdependence was required between sales and production to schedule production orders. Similarly, in the container industry reciprocal interdependence was required between production and research to solve short-term technical and quality problems. In all three environments pooled interdependence was also required to allocate financial and human resources. The reason, however, for pointing to the dominant type of interdependence required is that this appears to have had an important impact on the internal structure of the organizations in each environment.

Interdependence and Internal Structures

That this connection between the type of interdependence required and structure might exist has been suggested by March and Simon and by Thompson.[6] Thompson, following March and Simon, predicts that the coordination required by pooled interdependence would be achieved

---

[6]James G. March and Herbert A. Simon, *Organizations* (New York: John Wiley & Sons, Inc., 1958).

through reliance on *standardization*—that is, establishing standard decision rules and procedures. He argues that in cases where sequential interdependence is required, coordination will be achieved by *plan*. This involves the formulation of schedules for the units concerned which will
govern their action. Reciprocal interdependence, according to Thompson's predictions, will mean that coordination is achieved through
mutual adjustment. In these situations, coordination will be achieved by
interaction and feedback between representatives of the units involved.
As Thompson points out, this may or may not represent superior-subordinate relations through the hierarchy, but may also represent peer interaction across unit boundaries.

Thompson goes on to make another point, which is highly relevant
to this discussion. The three types of interdependence from pooled to
reciprocal place an increasing load on the communication and decision-
making mechanisms in the organization. Pooled and sequential interdependence which can be managed by rules and/or plans require less
face-to-face communication and decision making than the reciprocal
type, which requires members to engage in direct contact to achieve
coordination.

Thompson's (and March and Simon's) formulations were largely in the
form of untested propositions. The data from our 10-organization study
provide an opportunity, at least crudely, to test empirically these ideas
and to add another important set of variables to our empirically derived
conceptual model. To do this, we will briefly compare the environmental
elements in the three environments studied and the internal characteristic of the economically effective organization(s) in each environment.[7]
Before discussing this data, two points should be made: First, our use of
the concept of "integration" is similar, if not identical, to the meaning of
Thompson's concept, *coordination*. Second, all of the data presented with
the exception of the type of interdependence required and the proportion
of special integrating personnel have been reported in detail elsewhere.[8]
For this reason, the data are presented in a summarized form only.

Looking first at the plastics organization and its environment, as we
suggested above, the parts of this environment have quite diverse degrees
of uncertainty, ranging from a very uncertain scientific part of the environment to a relatively certain technoeconomic portion. This diversity
led to the high degree of differentiation between the functional units.

---

[7]In the food and container environments we studied one effective organization and
one less effective organization by common economic criteria. In the plastics industry,
we studied two highly effective organizations, two moderately effective organizations,
and two which were operating at a relatively low level of economic performance. For
the purpose of this discussion, we will treat only one of the high performing plastics
organizations, since they both had directly similar internal characteristics.

[8]Lawrence and Lorsch, *Organization and Environment*.

Our initial conclusions were that this differentiation and the tight inter-dependence required *between* units necessitated the proliferation of integrating devices beside the hierarchy (i.e., teams, units, and roles) which we found in the two effective plastics organizations. However, the Thompson typology of interdependence provides a further explanation of why these particular types of integrative mechanisms were developed rather than reliance on plans and procedures. In this environment, the reciprocal interdependence required seemed to be closely connected to the relative uncertainty in the research and market parts of the environment. This uncertainty was so high that managers and scientists had to constantly provide feedback to each other and make joint decisions. Thus, integrating roles, departments, and teams provided mechanisms for specialists to manage this type of interdependency, through direct contact with each other and with persons in special integrating roles. Procedures and plans would not have met the needs of this type of interdependence.

That this was in fact the case is supported by other evidence in Figure 3. The primary interaction pattern to achieve integration in the effective plastics organization was in groups or teams. Groups of managers, engineers, and scientists were in constant sessions, exchanging information and solving mutual problems. Similarly, the wide distribution of influence throughout the several levels of the organization's hierarchy is important evidence that mutual feedback and conflict resolution were taking place at many levels of management. Finally, the fact that the integrating unit had higher influence than any of the functional units is consistent with the reciprocal nature of interdependence between the basic units. This group of integrating personnel was in a position to facilitate the search for conflict resolution, so that the members of the basic units would seek a mutual solution to their problems.

We should emphasize that by pointing to the consistency between this type of interdependence and these integrative mechanisms, we are not departing from our earlier conclusions that the degree of differentiation had an important impact on the integrating devices which are required for an organization to perform effectively. The fact that the degree of differentiation does have an important impact on internal structure can be seen from comparing the effective plastics and food organization. Both were operating in environments, according to our evidence, which required mutual interdependence. Yet the plastics organization had more complicated integrative devices (teams and departments as well as roles). It also had a higher proportion of special integrating personnel than did the food organizations. The best explanation of these variations between the structure of these two highly effective organizations seems to lie in the fact that the functional units within the food organization were less differentiated from each other than were the units in the effective

FIGURE 3

Environmental Factors and Organizational Integration

Industry	Environment Diversity	Dominant Type of Interdependence	Actual Differentiation	Integration Devices	Special Integrating Personnel as Percent of Total Management	Interaction Pattern	Hierarchical Influence	Unit Having High Influence
Plastics	High	Reciprocal	High	Teams, roles, departments, hierarchy, plans, and procedures	22*	Team	Evenly distributed	Integrating unit
Foods	Moderate	Reciprocal	Moderate	Roles, plans, hierarchy, procedures	17*	1 to 1 peers	Evenly distributed	Sales and research
Container	Low	Pooled-sequential	Low	Hierarchy, plans, and procedures	0	1 to 1 superior-subordinate	Top high Bottom low	Sales

*This proportion was constant for the high and low performer within these industries.

plastics organization. The differences between the integrating mechanisms in these two organizations was more one of type than of degree. Thus the integrative mechanisms in both organizations were designed to achieve reciprocal interdependence, but because of its greater differentiation the plastic organization had developed more elaborate mechanisms (teams and an entire integrating department), while the food organization relied on individual coordinating roles. Similarly, the plastics organization had almost 25 percent of its professional and management personnel acting in special integrating positions, while this proportion was only 17 percent in the food organization.

Yet, in spite of these differences, the food organization seemed to have developed integrating mechanisms suited to reciprocal interdependence. The individual coordinators usually met on a one-to-one basis with one specialist peer and then another until they could help reach a mutual solution to problems. Teams were only used to deal with especially problematic issues. Like the plastics organization, the influence was distributed among all levels of the management hierarchy. Since there was no integrating department, the highest influence among the functional units was shared by the sales and research units. This was consistent with the environmental demands since much of the reciprocal interdependence had to be achieved between these two units, which were centrally involved in process and product innovation.

While the food and plastics organizations were facing somewhat similar environments and thus had developed somewhat parallel integrating mechanisms, the effective organization in the container industry provided a clear contrast with both of them. This organization's environment was less diverse than either food or plastics and thus required less internal differentiation among units. The required interdependence was a combination of sequential and pooled. Given the degree of differentiation and the requirement for these types of interdependence, it is not surprising to find that most of the integration was carried out through the hierarchy and by plan with superior-subordinate pairs involved and with most of the decision-making influence at the upper levels of the hierarchy. With less complex types of interdependence and smaller differences between units, the hierarchy along with standard schedules was able to provide the communication and conflict resolution necessary, and no special integrating roles were necessary. As the high influence of the sales unit suggests, the information about market requirements was gathered in this unit and passed up the hierarchy to the top sales manager. This manager, along with the chief executive officer, managed the sequential and pooled interdependence by deciding how the production resources of the several plants were to be allocated. The production schedule was developed by them weekly and then passed on to the production unit and its several plants.

Based on this description, we feel that our data generally support Thompson's ideas about the types of interdependence and the kinds of integrating devices which are necessary to deal with each type. They may not confirm all of his propositions precisely, but they clearly point in the same general direction. We should stress, however, that our findings in several ways go beyond Thompson's formulations. First, we have established that it is not just the type of interdependence which influences the structure of integration devices, but also the degree of differentiation present. Second, we have found that while these differences in type of integrating devices existed between organizations, especially effective organizations, in these different environments, the key factors which distinguished effective and less effective organizations in any one of these environments were the behaviors used typically to resolve conflicts and reach decisions.

For example, in the plastics environment all six organizations had developed essentially the same sorts of integrating devices (departments, teams, and roles). In fact, all of these organizations had approximately the same proportion of total management and professional personnel in integrating positions (22 percent). This was also true in the food environment where the proportion of integrating personnel was 17 percent in both the high performing and the less effective organization. Perhaps the factors which did make the most important difference between the effective and less effective organizations in each of the three environments was the extent to which the organization had a pattern of influence, both interunit and hierarchical, which met the demands of the environment and the extent to which conflict was confronted and problems solved. As we suggested above, the pattern of influence in the effective firms was consistent with the type of interdependence required. While the specific influence patterns did vary depending on environmental demands, we found that in the effective organization in all three environments there was a higher reliance on confrontation to resolve conflict than in the less effective organization. Similarly, there was less reliance on smoothing over conflict or on forcing a resolution.

Thus, we conclude that Thompson's typology of interdependence provides us with additional insight into the meaning of our field data. But our data clearly indicate that we must consider more than just the formally prescribed integrating mechanism to determine whether an organization's internal state and processes are consistent with its external demands.

Summary

Obviously, the conclusions drawn here must be considered somewhat tentative. Nevertheless, we feel that combining these constructs of

Thompson's with our own model provides further insights into the relationship between organizational form and environmental demands. This typology of interdependence enables us to understand more clearly why certain formal mechanisms for achieving integration are relevant in different environmental situations.

Beyond this, however, our analysis points to the importance of interpersonal skills for achieving integration in organizations operating in dynamic and diverse environments. In these industries the large number of managerial personnel performing integrative roles were, in effect, using their own personal problem-solving skills to resolve the new interdependency issues that were constantly arising. As any specific issue repeatedly arose, it was, of course, subject to programming and future resolution by plan or standardization. But a viable solution had to be found through face-to-face discussions before this programming process could begin. The data suggest that more elaborate integrative mechanisms were necessary in these settings but were not sufficient to achieve integration. Personal skills of confrontation were also needed.

Organization Design: An Information Processing View

JAY R. GALBRAITH

THE DESIGN of large organizations has passed through a number of stages of inquiry. The first stage consisted of the theorizing of Taylor, Fayol, and others around concepts such as functional foremanship and line-staff. Partly as a reaction to the amount of formalization in the first stage, the second stage can be characterized as emphasizing informal organization. Since it grew out of the Hawthorne Studies, the second stage had a predominantly empirical flavor. This empirical tradition has carried over to the third and current stage, but the focus has shifted back to formal structure variables such as spans of control. The third stage is also distinguished by the conclusion that there is no one best way to organize. There is also a corollary that any way of organizing is not equally effective. The best way depends on the situation. It now appears that current research is leading to a convergence of thought on ways to define situations that distinguish when alternate organization forms are most or least effective.

The purpose of this paper is to develop the convergence and elaborate upon it. First, some of the representative empirical studies will be reviewed. Second, what appear to be the primary conditioning variables are defined and related to information processing. Third, an information processing model of the organization design problem is presented which attempts to explain variations in organization structures. Finally, some empirical studies are related to support the model.

Review of Empirical Studies

In the 1960s some empirical studies began to appear which concentrated on organizations as aggregate units. This was a change from the emphasis on attitudes, job satisfaction, and small groups. It is from these aggregate studies that the convergence has appeared.

One of the first macro studies was reported by Burns and Stalker (Burns and Stalker, 1961). They reported about 20 case studies on British

49

and Scottish manufacturing firms. On the basis of personal observation, they distinguished between two types of organization. One was labeled as mechanistic. This organization had well-defined responsibilities, a well-defined hierarchy of authority, and many rules and procedures. Most of the work was planned in advance, and the communication was primarily vertical through the chain of command. The second type of organization was called organic. By contrast, this organization had undefined responsibilities and authorities, few rules, and communication was in all directions.

The principal finding of the study by Burns and Stalker was that each form of organization was appropriate to a particular market environment. The mechanistic form was effective in markets which were stable and had little change in technology. For markets characterized by rapid changes in products and technologies, the organic form seemed to be more effective. Thus the rate of change of the market and the technology was a variable which distinguished the appropriateness of alternative organization forms.

A second study concerning 100 English manufacturing firms reported comparable findings (Woodward, 1965). In this study the conditioning variable was the type of production process operated by the firm. The organizations were ranked on a scale of increasing technological complexity. On the low end were job shops producing small batches to customer order. The middle range was made up of large batch, assembly processes. The high end of the scale consisted of process industries such as oil refineries. The low to high also characterized the predictability and controllability of the process.

The principal finding of the research was that the organization form varied with the type of production process. Also it was discovered that those organizations which did not have the appropriate form were judged as ineffective. Some examples of findings were that the number of levels in the hierarchy and the span of control of the chief executive varied directly with the complexity of the production process. The spans of control of the management hierarchy decreased with increases in production complexity. The study supports the argument that there is no one best way to organize. According to these results, the best way depends on the production technology.

The third and most recent study has combined the results of the first two (Harvey, 1968). The argument put forth by Harvey was that the scale of technical complexity used by Woodward really measured the amount of change in the firm's products. The job shop was a custom designer producing to customer order while processing industries produced standard products for a finished goods inventory. By measuring the number of new products produced, Harvey reproduced some of

Woodward's findings using his scale. Therefore, the appropriate way to organize depended on the number of new products introduced.

A fourth study has introduced an interesting variation (Hall, 1962). The first three studies accounted for variations in structure between organizations, based on the market served and technology operated. Hall's proposition is that the predictability of the task should account for structure variation within an organization as well as between organizations. The proposition was tested in 10 organizations with the result that departments with predictable tasks had a well-defined hierarchy of authority, greater division of labor, and made greater use of procedures. Departments with less predictable tasks exhibited these characteristics to a lesser degree. This study adds to the generality of the previous findings.

The last study to be described is one which has combined the approaches of the previously mentioned studies (Lawrence and Lorsch, 1967). Their proposition was that there are two dimensions to the organization design problem. The first problem is to organize each subtask in a manner which facilitates the effective performance of that subtask. To the extent that subtasks vary in their predictability, then different structures should be applied. This phenomenon was called *differentiation*. In addition, the organization had to provide for the *integration* of the subtasks into the successful completion of the whole task. The appropriate way to integrate depended upon the number of new products or predictability of the organization's task. This approach would account for task predictability differences which existed between and within organizations.

The results of the study, carried out with 10 organizations in three industries, strongly supported the propositions. That is, the successful organizations had differentiated internal structures when the subtasks varied in predictability. They also adopted integrating mechanisms in proportion to the amount of differentiation and the amount of new product introduction. The study confirms again the proposition that the predictability of the task is a basic conditioning variable in the choice of organizational forms.

The empirical studies that have just been reviewed were chosen partly because they had one feature in common. That is, the independent variable was directly related to the predictability or certainty of the task. In addition there are some other studies with similar findings but the relation between the independent variable and predictability is less direct (Meyer, 1968; Blau, Heydebrand, and Stauffer, 1966; Blau, 1968; Bell, 1967; Stinchcombe, 1959). However the independent variable is quite consistent with task predictability. Thus the certainty or predictability of the task is emerging as one of the primary determinants of organizational forms. What remains is to explain *why* this is so. This is the task of the remainder of the paper.

Task Predictability and Information Processing

The relationship between task predictability and organization form is probably like many social science relations in that there are multiple and interacting influences. One explanation was put forth and tested by Lawrence and Lorsch. Their concept of differentiation implies that as tasks vary in predictability, the attitudes of the task performers vary in systematic ways. For example, the predictable task requires personalities with low tolerance for ambiguity while unpredictable tasks require high tolerances. In addition, there is another reason which is more highly related to the overall configuration of the organization. This reason is also suggested by Lawrence and Lorsch.

The basic proposition is that the greater the uncertainty of the task, the greater the amount of information that has to be processed during the execution of the task. If the task is well understood prior to performing it, much of the activity can be preplanned. If it is not understood, then during the actual task execution more knowledge is learned which leads to changes in resource allocations, schedules, and priorities. All these changes require information processing during task performance. Therefore the greater the *task uncertainty,* the greater the *amount of information* that must be processed in order to insure effective performance. From this proposition it follows that variations in organizational forms are variations in the ability to process varying amounts of information.

The relation must be stated more explicitly and developed further if it is to be useful in further theory development. What has been hypothesized so far can be stated in functional form

$$I = f(u) \tag{1}$$

where

I = the amount of information that must be processed to insure effective performance.

u = degree of uncertainty concerning the task requirements such as resources needed, time to complete, etc.

Another factor influencing the amount of information to be processed is the size of the organization. The greater the size, the greater the amount of information. But there are other factors which are related to size. For a given size firm, more information must be processed if there are many occupations represented than if there are few. Similarly for a given size firm, the greater the number of products the more information must be processed. Thus it is the *number of elements relevant for decision making* that influences the amount of information to be processed. The functional form now becomes

$$I = f(u, N) \tag{2}$$

where

N = number of elements relevant for decision making such as number of departments, number of occupational specialties, clients, products, etc.

As it stands, equation (2) is still incomplete. The reason is that uncertainty is a necessary but not a sufficient condition to guarantee the need for communication during task execution. The other necessary condition is some degree of *interrelatedness or interdependence* among the elements. That is, the behavior in one department must directly affect the goal accomplishment of another. Then as one unit learns more about its task it cannot unilaterally change schedules and priorities. It must communicate with other units that would be affected by a schedule change and resolve the decision in the best interest of the collective.

There is considerable variation in the amount of interdependence in organizations. The kinds of variation can be illustrated by considering a large research and development laboratory employing some 500 scientists and engineers. Further assume that there are 250 projects all of which are pursuing the state-of-the-art. Thus we have a large number of elements and high task uncertainty. However, there is little need for communication. All the projects are small and not directly connected to other projects. Therefore a schedule delay or a design change does not directly affect other design groups. The only source of interdependence is that the design groups share the same pool of resources—men, facilities, ideas, and money. But once the initial resource allocations are made, the only necessary communication between design groups is to pass on new ideas (Allen, 1969). This type of interdependence has been termed as *pooled* (Thompson, 1966, pp. 54–55).

If the nature of the projects is changed from 250 small independent projects to two large projects, a different pattern of interdependence arises. The large projects will require sequential designs. That is, a device is first designed to determine how much power it will require. After it is complete, then the design of the power source can take place. Under these conditions, a problem encountered in the design of the device will directly affect the group working on the design of the power source. The greater the number of problems the greater the amount of communication that must take place to jointly resolve problems.

The second example describes a situation which is more complex and requires greater amounts of information processing. The second example has all the problems that were described in the first example. There must be budget and facilities allocations made under conditions of uncertainty. There must be a flow of new ideas among the technical specialties. But in addition, the second example requires information processing and decision making to regulate the schedule of sequential activities. This is because there is greater interdependence in the second example.

The interdependence or interrelatedness of the design groups can be increased above what is described in the second example by the degree to which "design optimization" is pursued. Optimization means that a highly efficient device is desired and any change in the design of one of the components requires redesign of some others.

This can be illustrated by an automobile engine and body. The handling qualities of a car depend on the weight of the engine. The engine compartment can hold only a certain size of engine with its accessories. The drive shaft and differential can handle only a limited amount of torque. Changes in the weight, size, or output of the engine may necessitate changes in the body of the automobile. These interrelations and many others must be taken into account in the design of an automobile.

Actually, in the case of the passenger automobile there is a good deal of flexibility with regard to the body-engine match. The engine compartment is usually large, the parts of the suspension are easily changed, and the drive shaft probably has plenty of excess torque-carrying capability. Engines of a variety of shapes and sizes are frequently placed in the same body. But this need not be the case. In high performance automobiles, the size of the engine compartment is frequently sharply constrained by aerodynamics considerations. There may be efforts to lighten the whole automobile by making the parts of the drive system and body as light as possible, given the required strengths. In such a situation, the flexibility in the size, shape, and performance of the engine placed in the body is sharply reduced or eliminated (Glennan, 1967).

Thus the high performance auto is a highly interrelated system while the passenger car is a flexible, loosely coupled system. The same is true of the organizational subunits which must design these systems. Any change in engine design for the high performance car must be communicated to the group designing the body so that an optimal fit is still achieved after the change. This is less true for the passenger car. Therefore the organization designing the high performance car must be capable of handling the information flows described in examples one and two for budgets, ideas, and schedules and also those for all the design-redesign decisions deriving from the interrelated design. The amount of information that must be processed increases as the amount of interdependence increases.

The functional equation now becomes

$$I = f(U, N, C) \qquad (3)$$

where

C = amount of connectedness or interdependence among the elements that are necessary for decision making.

While it is too early to completely specify equation (3), some hypotheses can be made concerning its general form. First, it is probable that the amount of information is a monotonically increasing function of the independent variables (e.g., $\delta I/\delta U \geqq 0$). Second, at some point the function increases at a decreasing rate (e.g., $\delta^2 I/\delta U^2 \leqq 0$). Both functions in Figure 1 are consistent with this hypothesis.

FIGURE 1

Information Processing as a Function of Task Uncertainty
Holding Connectedness and Size Constant

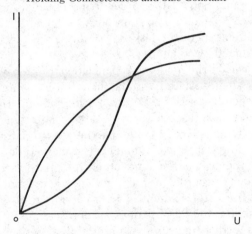

The most significant property of equation (3) is that in analysis of variance terms, the interactive effect dominates the independent effects. This was illustrated with the first example of the research and development laboratory that was characterized by many small projects, a high degree of uncertainty, and large size. There was little need for communication because the subunits were not interdependent. Similarly, the automobile assembly line is characterized by large size and a high degree of interdependence. However there is little need for communication since the predictability of the task allows most of the activity to be specified in advance of task execution. Therefore it is hypothesized that it is the interaction between the three variables which will account for the amount of information to be processed. It follows that the interaction effect will primarily account for variations in organizational forms. The most complex form occurs for tasks that are highly uncertain, highly interdependent, and large in size. The aerospace programs are good examples of such complex tasks. At the other extreme, the simplest form of large organization is one with a predictable and loosely coupled task. The distinguishing feature between the simple and complex structure is the capability to process large amounts of information. The remainder of the paper presents a model which describes the mechanisms that simple organizations adopt to increase their information processing capacities.

AN INFORMATION PROCESSING MODEL OF ORGANIZATION

In this section an organization design model is developed. The model attempts to explain how simple organizations increase their information processing capacities to become complex organizations. The model is based on the assumption that in order to be effective, the information processing capacity of an organization must be equal to the information processing requirements of the task. The information processing requirements are determined by equation (3).

In order to develop the model of organizational forms with various information processing capacities, assume there is a large organization with a highly interdependent set of activities. Further assume the subtasks are differentiated and make use of a functional specialization. The problem now facing the organization is to obtain an integrated pattern of behavior across all of the interdependent subunits. The magnitude of the integration problem depends on the amount of information that has to be processed in order to coordinate the interdependent subunits. In the situation just described, the amount of information varies with the uncertainty of the task. For the purpose of exposition, assume first that the task is predictable and then increases in uncertainty. As the uncertainty increases, the amount of information will increase. As the amount of information increases, the example organization will adopt integrating mechanisms which are hypothesized to increase its information processing capabilities. Let us begin with a predictable task and the simplest forms of integration mechanisms. Figure 2 will serve as the representation of the formal authority structure of the example organization.

1. Rules and Programs

The simplest method of coordinating interdependent departments is to specify the behaviors in advance of their execution (March and Simon, 1958, chap. 6). The organization's employees are taught the job-related situations with which they will be faced and the behaviors appropriate to those situations. Then as situations arise daily, the employees act out behaviors appropriate to the situations. If everyone adopts the appro-

FIGURE 2

Representation of Formal Authority Structure

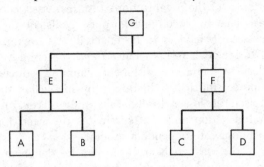

priate behavior, the resultant aggregate response is integrated or coordinated.

The primary virtue of rules is that they eliminate the need for further communication among the subunits. If an organization has hundreds of employees, they cannot all communicate with each other in order to guarantee coordinated action. To the extent that the job-related situations can be anticipated in advance and rules derived for them, then integrated activity is guaranteed without communication. However, rules have a limited range of usefulness. To the extent that rules are limited, the organization must rely on additional integration mechanisms.

2. Hierarchy of Authority

The use of rules is limited in the amount of complexity that can be handled. For tasks with multiple job-related situations, the number of rules necessary to coordinate interdependent behavior becomes too large to learn. At this point the formal hierarchy of authority is employed on an exception basis. That is, the recurring job situations are programmed with rules while the infrequent situations are referred to higher levels in the hierarchy. If all the interdependencies are to be considered, the exception should rise in the hierarchy to the first position where a shared superior exists for all affected subunits. For example, if department A (see Figure 2) encounters an exceptional situation which also affects department D, the situation should rise to G for resolution. The combination of rules for repetitive situations and upward referral in the hierarchy for exceptional situations guarantees an integrated or coordinated organizational response to the situations faced by the organization. The combination is effective as long as the number of exceptional situations remains within the capacity of the hierarchy to process them. As the task uncertainty increases, the hierarchy gets overloaded and additional mechanisms are needed.

3. Planning

As the uncertainty of the organization's task increases, coordination increasingly takes place by specifying outputs, goals, or targets. Instead of specifying specific behaviors to be enacted, the organization undertakes processes to set goals to be achieved and the employees select behaviors which lead to goal accomplishment. Planning reduces the amount of information processing in the hierarchy by increasing the amount of discretion exercised at lower levels. Like the use of rules, planning achieves integrated action and also eliminates the need for continuous communication among interdependent subunits.

An example of the way goals are used can be demonstrated by considering the design group responsible for an aircraft wing structure. The group's interdependence with other design groups is handled by technical specifications elaborating the points of attachment, forces transmitted at these points, centers of gravity, etc. The group also have a set of targets (not to be exceeded) for weight, design man-hours to be used, and a completion date. They are given minimum stress specifications below which they cannot design. The group then design the structures and assemblies which combine to form the wing. They need not communicate with any other design group on work-related matters if they and the interdependent groups are able to operate within the planned targets.

The ability of design groups to operate within the planned targets depends on two factors: The first is the degree to which the task is understood and predictable. This is necessary in order to determine the nature of the interdependence and elaborate meaningful subgoals. The other factor is the complexity of the pattern of interdependence. If there are multiple linkages between numerous subunits, then a complicated model is needed in order to compute the magnitude of the subgoals. For example, job shop scheduling is a difficult problem not because the task is uncertain but because the model needed for subgoal elaboration is computationally infeasible. The result caused by both uncertainty and complexity is the same. In the process of task execution the subunit must violate some of the planned targets unless additional decisions are made. In the case of uncertainty, targets are missed because they were based on incomplete knowledge. For complexity, targets are missed because known factors had to be ignored when determining the goals.

The violation of planned targets usually requires additional decision making and hence additional information processing. The additional information processing takes place through the hierarchy in the same manner as rule exceptions were handled. Problems are handled on an exception basis. They are raised into higher levels of the hierarchy for resolution. The problem rises to the first level where a shared superior exists for all affected subunits. A decision is made, and the new targets are communicated to the subunits. In this manner the behavior of the interdependent subunits remains integrated.

In summary, the organization adopts integrating mechanisms which keep the amount of information processing within its capacity to process information. These mechanisms are adopted *in addition to* not *instead of* the previous mechanisms. Therefore, if an organization is using planning processes then it is also using the hierarchy and rules. The examples used so far have exaggerated the mechanistic behavior of the organization in order to highlight the information processing aspects of organization behavior. The mechanistic model which has been described so far uses only vertical information flows. It is doubtful that any real organization operates this way. But the mechanistic model serves as a base from which alternative organization designs can evolve.

The ability of an organization to successfully utilize coordination by planning, hierarchy, and rules depends on the combination of the frequency of exceptions and the capacity of the hierarchy to handle them. As the task uncertainty increases, the number of exceptions increases until the hierarchy is overloaded again. Therefore the organization must again take organization design action. It can proceed in two ways: First, it can take action to eliminate the need for processing information and therefore reduce the number of exceptions referred up the hierarchy. Second, the organization can take action to increase its capacity to handle more information. The two methods for reducing the need for information and the two methods for increasing processing capacity are shown schematically in Figure 3. In the next sections each of these

FIGURE 3

Alternative Organization Responses to Increased Task Uncertainty

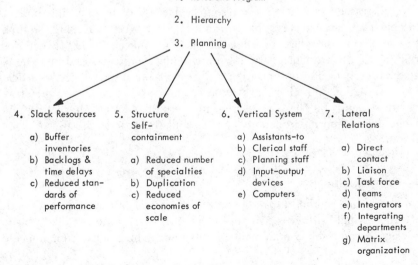

1. Rules and Program

2. Hierarchy

3. Planning

4. Slack Resources	5. Structure Self-containment	6. Vertical System	7. Lateral Relations
a) Buffer inventories		a) Assistants-to	
b) Backlogs & time delays	a) Reduced number of specialties	b) Clerical staff	a) Direct contact
c) Reduced standards of performance	b) Duplication	c) Planning staff	b) Liaison
	c) Reduced economies of scale	d) Input-output devices	c) Task force
		e) Computers	d) Teams
			e) Integrators
			f) Integrating departments
			g) Matrix organization

methods and the costs and benefits will be discussed individually. In reality, the organization will balance the use of each of these methods. It is the choice of balance that determines the organizational form.

4. Slack Resources

As the number of exceptions begin to overload the hierarchy, one response is to increase the target levels so that fewer exceptions occur. For the example of the wing design group, an increase in the completion date of several weeks will significantly reduce the likelihood that an exception will occur. Therefore completion dates can be extended until the number of exceptions that occur are within the existing information processing capacity of the organization. This has been the practice in solving job shop scheduling problems (Pounds, 1963). Job shops quote delivery times that are long enough to keep the scheduling problem within the computational and information processing limits of the organization.

Similarly the budget targets or the technical specifications can be relaxed. The degree of design optimization can be reduced thereby creating a flexible design. For manufacturing operations, buffer inventories can be added between sequential operations. All of these examples have a similar effect. They represent the use of slack resources to reduce the amount of interdependence between subunits (March and Simon, 1958; Cyert and March, 1963). With reference to equation (3) the amount of information that has to be processed is reduced by reducing interdependence. This keeps the required amount of information within the capacity of the organization to process it. It follows that the greater the uncertainty, the greater the additional inventory or schedule delay necessary to maintain the balance between information required and capacity to process it.

The strategy of using slack resources has its costs. Relaxing budget targets has the obvious cost of requiring more budget. Increasing the time to completion date has the effect of delaying the customer. Inventories require the investment of capital funds which could be used elsewhere. Reduction of design optimization reduces the performance of the article being designed. Whether slack resources are used to reduce information or not depends on the cost relative to the cost of other alternatives. As technologies and environments vary so will the cost of the use of slack resources.

5. Authority Structure

The second method for reducing the amount of information is to modify the formal authority structure. The direction of the modification is toward greater self-containment of the units which must communicate (i.e., those which are most interdependent) (March and Simon, 1958, pp. 158–61; Thompson, 1967, chap. 5). The effect of such a change is to break up one large problem into several smaller independent subproblems. The total amount of information processing and decision making needed to coordinate the smaller independent subunits is less than that needed to coordinate the large integrated unit. An example will help illustrate why this is so.

It was assumed earlier that the example organization had a high degree of interdependence because it was functionally specialized. Figure 4 (a) shows a functionally specialized manufacturing firm. In this form, joint problems involving mechanical-fabrication, or assembly-sales, etc., must rise to the general manager for a decision. If there are many new products being introduced, these joint problems arise frequently and overload the general manager. One response is to change the authority structure to one of three identical product groups which are functionally specialized. This form is represented in Figure 4 (b).

The form in Figure 4 (b) self-contains the interdependent units. It reduces the amount of information processing by reducing the number of levels through which joint decision problems must pass. The information processing is reduced by bringing the decision-making power down to where the information exists. In addition, the product group form multiplies the number of people making trade-off decisions concerning engineering, manufacturing, and marketing. If the rate of change of market activities is great enough, the three product group executives will be overloaded. In this case the self-containment can be carried lower in the organization as illustrated by Figure 4 (c). This brings decision making lower in the organization and multiplies the number of the decision makers considering the interdependent activities.

Thus, the greater the task uncertainty, the lower the level in the hierarchy at which self-containment will occur. This means the organization's response to increased task uncertainty is to decentralize or to increase the decision-making influence of the lower levels. The integration is maintained in spite of the fact that decisions are made with only local knowledge. The local knowledge is sufficient to encompass all interactions due to the self-containment of the authority structure.

Like the use of slack resources, changes to the authority structure will create costs for the organization. The first kind is a loss of economies of scale of manufacturing equipment. In Figure 4 (a) the organization needs only one large machine, in (b) it needs three smaller machines, and finally in (c) it needs nine machines. In each case the cost of the machines for the same processing capacity is greater. The other cost is associated with either a loss of expertise or duplication depending on the organization's response. In a functional engineering organization there can be two electrical engineers—one electromechanical and one elec-

FIGURE 4

Formal Authority Structure Representing High Interdependence
(*a*) to High Independence or Self-Containment (*c*)

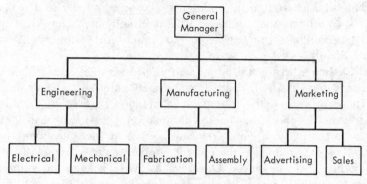

a) Functional Specialization

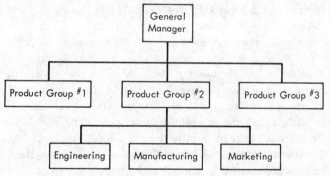

b) Product Groups with Functional Specialization

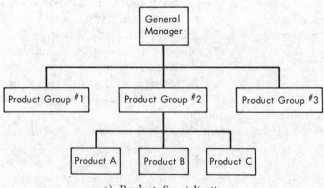

c) Product Specialization

tronics. If the structure is changed to two product groups, two electrical engineers are still needed but will be required to generalize across electromechanical and electronics applications. (This assumes that more knowledge is required to generalize across disciplines than across products.) If a high level of expertise is necessary, the organization can maintain one electromechanical and one electronics engineer for each product group. But now there is duplication involved. Four engineers are required instead of two.

Despite these costs, the organization may reduce specialization because it is believed to be less costly than customer delay or inventory carrying costs. Likewise manpower duplication in capital intensive operations may be an insignificant cost. Also for very large operations self-containment may not reduce specialization to the point where it is costly.

6. Vertical Information Systems

The first pure strategy of increasing the capacity of an organization to process information is to operate directly on the vertical, formal information system. The purpose of the action is to reduce the number of exceptions flowing up the hierarchy. This can be accomplished by reducing the plan-replan cycle. Thus by making up schedules more often, the number of missed due dates can be decreased (Carroll, 1966; Galbraith, 1968).

The reason a reduction in the plan-replan cycle reduces exceptions is that every plan begins to decay in usefulness immediately after it is conceived. The longer one operates with a plan the less useful it is. The greater the task uncertainty, the greater the rate of decay. Thus to maintain a given level of plan usefulness, the decision frequency must be greater, the greater the task uncertainty. A highly predictable plant can be scheduled once a month. Therefore about every four weeks the status of all jobs in all departments is updated and a new schedule is generated. This serves to guide operations for the next four weeks. In another shop where there are frequent engineering changes, absenteeism, and machine breakdowns, the same schedule effectiveness is maintained by weekly updates and rescheduling. In this case there is four times the amount of information processing and decision making at planning times. But it does keep the number of exceptions to a minimum between schedule changes. This is a more efficient way to operate since it is more economical in terms of managerial time, delays resulting from exception handling, and time devoted to information collection. That is, if one large planning effort is made every week, less decision-making resources are consumed than if 10 exceptions resulted in 10 small planning changes.

The additional information processing and decision making is achieved at the cost of adding assistants-to, by adding scheduling staffs, and by adding clerical personnel. Also with an advantage of approximately

100,000 to 1, computers are used in place of manual processing of quantitative information. Computers are combined with various forms of input-output devices to provide access to data. All of these devices increase the capacity to process more information. The costs of these devices is to be balanced against loss of economies of scale, customer delay costs, and inventory carrying costs. The experience with computers in job shops has shown that their application has reduced slack resources by reducing the average time to complete an order (Buffa, 1968, chap. 12).

7. Lateral Relationships

The second way to increase the capacity of the organization to process greater amounts of information is to establish lateral relations and undertake joint decisions (Landsberger, 1961; Strauss, 1962; Dutton, Walton, and Fitch, 1966; Simpson, 1959). These lateral relations can take many forms. It is hypothesized that the form and extent of the relations is directly related to the predictability of the task. In order to develop the different forms let us move from certain to highly uncertain tasks. It is also hypothesized that the lateral forms are cumulative. That is, each form is adopted and added to the previous forms. They are not a substitute for other lateral forms.

a) Direct Contact. The simplest and least costly form of lateral relationship is direct contact between managers affected by a problem. For example, refer to Figure 2. If department A is about to overrun its schedule on an item which goes next to department D, the manager of A could refer the problem upward to G for resolution. G would decide who would work overtime or suggest some other solution. Alternatively, A could contact D directly and they could reach a mutually agreeable joint decision. To the extent that problems can be resolved in this manner, then the number of exceptions flowing up and down the hierarchy is reduced. The top managers are left free for only those decisions that cannot be solved by direct contact between managers.

The problem that arises when direct contact is used is that an entirely new set of behaviors is required from the managers. They must now be able to behave cooperatively and to be able to reach joint decisions with peers without an authority relationship. This requires a reward system designed to facilitate the kinds of behaviors necessary to meet the information processing requirements of the task (Zander and Wolf, 1964). It also requires skills and techniques for conflict resolution (Lawrence and Lorsch, 1967, chaps. 3 and 5).

b) Liaison Roles. When the volume of contacts between any two departments grows, it becomes economical to set up a specialized role to handle this communication. Liaison men are typical examples of specialized roles designed to facilitate communication between two interdependent departments and to bypass the long lines of communication involved in upward referral. Liaison roles arise at lower and middle levels of management.

c) Task Forces. Direct contact and liaison roles, like the integration mechanisms before them, have a limited range of usefulness. They work when two managers or functions are involved. When problems arise involving seven or eight departments, the decision-making capacity of direct contacts is exceeded. Then these problems must be referred upward. For uncertain, interdependent tasks such situations arise frequently. Task forces are a form of horizontal contact which is designed for problems of multiple departments.

The task force is made up of representatives from each of the affected departments. Some are full-time members; others may be part-time. The task force is a temporary group. It exists only as long as the problem remains. When a solution is reached, each participant returns to his normal tasks.

To the extent that they are successful, task forces remove problems from higher levels of the hierarchy. The decisions are made at lower levels in the organization. In order to guarantee integration, a group problem-solving approach is taken. Each affected subunit contributes a member and therefore provides the information necessary to judge the impact on all units. Task forces also require the same cooperative forms of behavior mentioned for direct contact (Likert, 1967, chap. 10).

d) Teams. As tasks become less predictable, more problems arise during the act of execution. At some point, the combined use of rules, plans, direct contact, task forces, and upward referral are no longer adequate to the task of maintaining integration. The delays in decisions become long, lines of communication become extended, and top managers are forced to spend more time on day-to-day operations. The next response is to use group problem solving on a more permanent basis. Thus teams are formed around frequently occurring problems. These teams meet daily or weekly to discuss problems affecting the group. They solve all the problems which require commitments that they are capable of making. Larger problems are referred upward.

Teams can be formed at various levels. Actually an entire hierarchy of teams could be designed. The designs of team structures present the same kind of departmentalization problems that are involved in the design of the formal hierarchy of authority. They could be formed around common customers, clients, geographic regions, functions, processes, products, or projects, whichever is appropriate. If the hierarchy of authority is based on common functions such as engineering, production, and marketing, the teams could be formed around products with representatives from each function. Thus the teams involve design decisions concerning the basis of the team, the composition of membership, the levels at which they are to operate, the extent of their discretion, and the frequency of their meetings. The pattern interdependence and basis for the authority structure will determine the basis and composition of membership. It is also hypothesized that the greater the task uncertainty the greater the number of levels at which teams will operate, the more frequent will be their meetings, and the greater will be their discretion.

An interesting example of teams can be illustrated by an aerospace firm's manufacturing operations. The formal authority structure is based on common functions and is illustrated in Figure 5. Teams were formed around the major sections of the aircraft that were being produced. In addition, the groups were physically located around common aircraft sections. All groups working on the wing are located in the same area of the plant. Thus the basis of physical location facilitates the lateral communication process and team structure. The design is an attempt to achieve the benefits of both a functional form and a task or project form.

FIGURE 5

Wing Team Overlaid on a Functional Structure

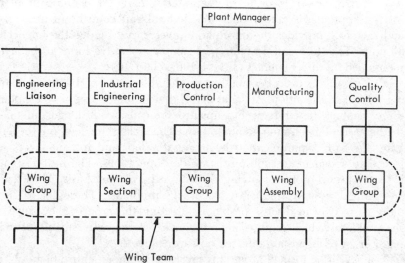

e) Integrating Personnel. As the task uncertainty increases, the proportion of total decisions made at lower levels increases. In addition the amount of discretion increases. At this point the organization becomes concerned about the quality of decisions made at lower levels through group processes. It is desired that these joint decisions be made from the perspective of the general manager. However, the general manager cannot personally check or participate in all decisions. A compromise is to create a number of roles which represent the general manager's perspective. These are called integrating roles (Lawrence and Lorsch, 1967, chap. 3). They carry labels such as product managers, project managers, brand managers, and materials managers. These managers do not supervise any of the actual work but are responsible for integration of the interdependent subunits which are not directly integrated with an authority relationship. The integrators generally acquire power through a direct reporting relationship to the general manager.

It is the function of the integrators to bring the general manager perspective to bear on joint decision problems arising at lower levels in the organization. They will do this by acting as chairmen of task forces and teams considering joint problems. They act as secretaries for the groups and perform many of the group maintenance functions.

In one sense the integrator's role emerges due to the volume of joint decisions reached at lower levels. The volume is related to the predictability of the task. In another sense the integrator's role emerges due to *differences* in the predictability of the subtasks performed by managers who must collaborate in joint decisions. This is the concept of differentiation suggested by Lawrence and Lorsch. Differentiation arises because subunit managers acquire attitudes and modes of operation which are related to predictability of the subtask. However, the attitudes which are necessary for effective subtask performance make collaboration on joint decisions more difficult. The greater the differences in subtask predictability, the greater the differentiation and the greater the difficulty in achieving successful collaboration. Thus for a given volume of joint decision making, the greater the differentiation the greater the need for integrators and the general manager perspective. The integrators represent a device which achieves integration between subunits without sacrificing the differences needed for effective subtask performance.

f) Integrating Departments. As the uncertainty of the organization's task increases further, larger numbers of decisions of consequence are reached at low levels. As the differences between the predictability of subunits tasks increase, the greater the difficulty in reaching joint decisions on these problems. Therefore in order to make the role of the integrator more effective, the organization increases the power of the integrator. The power is increased in several ways. First, the integrator receives subordinates to aid him in carrying out the function. Collectively they form an integrating department.

A second and major change is the reporting of information around the integrator's duties. The usual reporting system for a functional organization shown in Figure 4 (a) is to report actual data versus budget for each function. If the integrators are product managers, then the information system reports product costs and profits in addition to functional information. In this way the teams and integrators have information for decision making and an ability to get feedback to see how well they have done.

The third change is to give the integrator a voice in the budgeting process. Therefore any change in engineering's budget on product No. 1 will require the approval of the product manager on product No. 1. The product manager may not approve a request for overtime funds for engineering because it would be cheaper to wait and have manufacturing work overtime to get the new product back on schedule. This is what is meant by the general manager's perspective.

g) *Matrix Organization.* The final step in the utilization of lateral relationships is the establishment of a matrix organization. The matrix represents another increase in the amount of influence that the integrating department has on the decision-making process. More power or influence is required when a greater amount of decision making is carried on at lower levels in the hierarchy. The increased decision making is a response to increased task uncertainty. That is, in order to handle the required increase in information processing and decision making, more decisions are made at lower levels. This maintains a balance between the information processing requirements of the task and capacity of the organization to process information. The increased power of the integrator is to enable him to maintain the quality of low-level joint decisions.

The matrix organization represents a complete commitment to joint problem solving and shared responsibility. The other lateral relations all utilize joint decision making and shared responsibility but not to the degree that a pure matrix organization does. In this paper a pure matrix organization differs from the previous lateral forms in two ways: First, at some level in the organization, a *dual authority* relationship exists. In Figure 6, an organization chart illustrates the formal authority relationships in a typical aerospace firm. In this case one man is both the technical specialty department manager and the subproject manager. While there are other variations, the main feature is the dual reporting relationship. This feature distinguishes the matrix from the use of integrating departments. The matrix uses integrating departments but with a dual authority relationship in addition.

The other feature of the matrix is a reasonable *balance of power* between the two bases of organizing the work. With respect to Figure 6 this means that reasonable power balances are desired between the technical specialty managers and the project managers. While equal power is an unattainable razor's edge, the power differences are much smaller than the differences in the previous lateral forms. The power balance is obtained and maintained in several ways. The addition of the dual authority relation helps establish the power balance. Also the project manager gets the budget for the project and buys service from the technical specialties. The technical specialties also get funds for work which is not for any specific project. The formal authority structure and the funds allocation process are used to control the power balance.

FIGURE 6

Formal Authority Structure of Matrix Organization

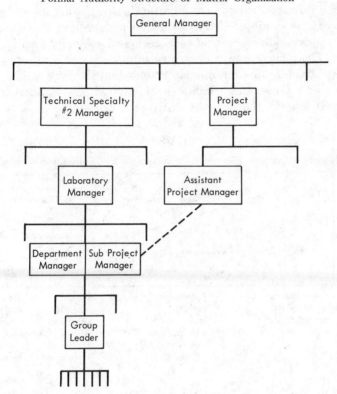

The reason a power balance is desired is that the decisions and preferred solutions to problems cannot be predicted in advance. Rather than
have solutions biased toward the stronger of the technical specialty or
project manager, a balance is maintained. This means the realities of the
problem at hand will determine the preferred solution if the joint decision making is effective. Of course this does not mean that power differences do not arise. Personality factors alone would introduce differences.
In addition environmental changes will affect the power balance. In the
aerospace industry the technical specialties had more power in the early
1960s due to the missile gap crisis and a lag in the space race. Then a
balance occurred with the addition of incentive contracts and PERT-Cost
techniques. Now in the context of the Proxmire Senate hearings and cost
problems on the C-5A aircraft, the project managers have more influence
on decisions. These power shifts have occurred without any change to the
formal reporting relationships. The matrix is thus a very flexible design.

If the volume of consequential decisions made from the project manager's perspective increases still further, the matrix would be abandoned and the authority structure changed to a project form. However, the functional managers would now perform the integrating roles. Therefore no new categories are needed. As a matter of fact there is continuum of relative power differences between technical specialty managers and projects. The relative power or influence on decisions is affected by the authority structure, the information system, and the flow of budget dollars. Figure 7 shows this continuum of *relative* power differences and how it is affected by the authority structure.

FIGURE 7

Relative Decision Power as a Function of the Authority Structure

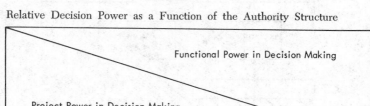

Relative
Power

Functional Power in Decision Making

Project Power in Decision Making

| Functional authority structure with project teams | Functional authority structure with project integrators | Matrix | Project authority structure with functional integrator | Project authority structure with functional teams |

Thus the use of lateral relations represents a method of decentralizing or making decisions at low levels in the hierarchy. Like self-containment, the greater the task uncertainty, the lower the level of decision making. However in order to prevent the making of decisions which affect global goals with only local information, group problem solving is used. In this way all departments pool their local information thereby providing sufficient information to reach a decision affecting global goals. This puts a premium on cooperative behavior, conflict resolution, and joint problem solving.

The work of Lawrence and Lorsch is highly consistent with the assertions concerning lateral relations (Lawrence and Lorsch, 1967; Lorsch and Lawrence, 1968). This is illustrated in Table 1. The plastics firm has the greatest rate of new product introduction (uncertainty) and greatest amount of differentiation. Likewise the plastics industry makes the most extensive use of lateral relations. Figure 8 shows the pattern of influence for the plastics and container firms. Thus the greater the uncertainty the lower the level of decision making, and the integration is maintained by lateral relations.

TABLE 1

	Plastics	Food	Containers
Percent new products in last 10 years	20	10	0
Differentiation	10.7	8.0	5.7
Integrating devices ...	Rules	Rules	Rules
	Hierarchy	Hierarchy	Hierarchy
	Planning	Planning	Planning
	Direct contact	Direct contact	Direct contact
	Teams at 3 levels	Task forces	
	Integrating department	Integrators	
Percent integrators/ managers	22	17	0

Adapted from Paul R. Lawrence and Jay W. Lorsch, *Organization and Environment* (Boston, Mass.: Division of Research, Harvard Business School, 1967), pp. 86–138; and Jay W. Lorsch and Paul R. Lawrence, "Environmental Factors and Organization Integration," paper read at the Annual Meeting of the American Sociological Association, August 27, 1968, Boston, Mass.

FIGURE 8

Influence Graph Showing Influence in Decisions by Level

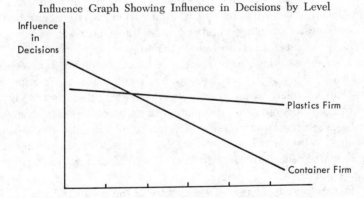

Table 1 points out the cost of using lateral relations. The plastics firm has 22 percent of its managers in integrating roles. Thus the greater the use of lateral relations the greater the managerial intensity. This cost must be balanced against the cost of slack resources, structure variation and information systems.

SUMMARY

Several explanatory statements are needed before summarizing. First, a word of caution is required. All of the above statements are hypotheses. They require testing. The text of the paper makes assertions only for the convenience of eliminating the frequent use of the phrase "it is hypothesized that. . . ." Second, almost all of the propositions have appeared before in various forms. What this paper has tried to do is to put them into a logically consistent framework based on concepts suggested from empirical research.

This paper was based on the premise that certainty of the task is a primary independent variable which distinguishes between the appropriateness of alternative organization forms. The premise was derived from the empirical research performed in the last few years. What is missing in this empirical research is an explanation of why uncertainty should affect organization forms. The model presented here gives a partial explanation of why this is so. The basic explanation was that task uncertainty required information processing during the execution of the task. The effect of uncertainty was hypothesized to be moderated by the interdependence between subtasks and the number of elements (such as number of employees, number of specialties, etc.) relevant for decision making. The result is summarized by equation 3.

The other premise of the paper is that in order to be effective, an organization must design a structure which is capable of processing the amount of information required by the task. The organization can take action either to reduce the amount of information required or to increase the capacity of the structure to process more information. It was hypothesized that the organization can reduce the amount of information by adding slack resources which in turn reduces interdependence between subtasks. This strategy maintains a centralized decision-making process as long as slack is added as uncertainty increases. The other way the organization reduces the amount of information to be processed is to change the authority structure to a more self-contained form. This also reduces interdependence between subtasks. However, it brings the decision-making power down to where the information exists. Therefore the response is decentralization.

The first strategy to increase the capacity of the organization to process more information is reduce the time between successive planning sessions. This requires more information flowing to update the status of files. The change occurs in the formal, sometimes mechanical, information system. It brings information up to the decision makers and results in centralization of decisions. The other response is to use lateral relations between interdependent subunits. It brings decision making lower in the organization and therefore results in decentralization. In order to use decentralized decision making in the presence of interdependence, joint decision making is used.

In reality various combinations of these strategies will be used depending on the relative costs involved. In another paper, the author describes a case study in which an organization is faced with these design choices (Galbraith, 1970).

The implication of this paper for future research is that the research designs must be more complex. The need is for greater control of the interacting variables which affect the information processing characteristics of an organization.

BIBLIOGRAPHY

ALLEN, THOMAS. "Information Flows in Research and Development Laboratories," *Administrative Science Quarterly,* March 1969, pp. 12–20.

BELL, GERALD. "Determinants of Span of Control," *American Journal of Sociology,* July 1967, pp. 100–109.

BLAU, PETER. "The Hierarchy of Authority in Organizations," *American Journal of Sociology,* January 1968, pp. 453–67.

————; HEYDEBRAND, WOLF V.; AND STAUFFER, ROBERT. "The Structure of Small Bureaucracies," *American Sociology Review,* April 1966, pp. 179–91.

BUFFA, ELWOOD. *Production-Inventory Systems.* Homewood, Ill.: Richard D. Irwin, Inc., 1968.

BURNS, THOMAS, AND STALKER, G. M. *The Management of Innovation.* London: Tavistock Publications, 1961.

CARROLL, DONALD. "On the Structure of Operational Control Systems" in *Operations Research and the Design of Management Information Systems* (ed. John Pierce), pp. 391–415. New York: Technical Association of the Pulp and Paper Industry, 1967.

CYERT, RICHARD, AND MARCH, JAMES. *The Behavioral Theory of the Firm.* Englewood Cliffs, N.J.: Prentice-Hall, Inc., 1963.

DUTTON, J.; WALTON, RICHARD; AND FITCH, H. "A Study of Conflict in the Process, Structure and Attitudes of Lateral Relationships" in *Some Theories of Organization.* Eds. Albert H. Rubenstein and Chadwick J. Haberstroh. Rev. ed. Homewood, Ill.: Richard D. Irwin, Inc., 1966.

GALBRAITH, JAY. "Achieving Integration through Information Systems," *Proceedings of the Academy of Management,* December 1968.

————. "Environmental and Technological Determinants of Organization Design: A Case Study" in *Studies In Organization Design.* Eds. Jay W. Lorsch and Paul R. Lawrence. Homewood, Ill.: Richard D. Irwin, Inc., 1970.

GLENNAN, THOMAS. "Issues in the Choice of Development Policies" in Marschak, Glennan, and Summers, *Strategy for R&D,* pp. 13–48. New York: Springer-Verlag Inc., 1967.

HALL, RICHARD. "Intra-Organizational Structure Variation," *Administrative Science Quarterly*, December 1962, pp. 295–308.

HARVEY, EDWARD. "Technology and Structure of Organizations," *American Sociological Review*, April 1968, pp. 247–59.

LANDSBERGER, H. A. "The Horizontal Dimension in a Bureaucracy," *Administrative Science Quarterly*, 1961, pp 298–332.

LAWRENCE, PAUL R., AND LORSCH, JAY W. *Organization and Environment.* Boston, Mass.: Division of Research, Harvard Business School, 1967.

LIKERT, RENSIS. *The Human Organization.* New York: McGraw-Hill Book Co., Inc., 1967.

LORSCH, JAY W., AND LAWRENCE, PAUL R. "Environmental Factors and Organization Integration." Paper read at the Annual Meeting of the American Sociological Association, August 27, 1968, Boston, Mass.

MARCH, JAMES, AND SIMON, HERBERT. *Organizations.* New York: John Wiley & Sons, Inc., 1958.

MEYER, MARSHALL. "Expertness and the Span of Control," *American Sociological Review*, 1969, pp. 944–51.

POUNDS, WILLIAM. "The Scheduling Environment" in *Industrial Scheduling.* Eds. Muth and Thompson. Englewood Cliffs, N.J.: Prentice-Hall, Inc., 1963.

SIMPSON, R. L. "Vertical and Horizontal Communication in Organization," *Administrative Science Quarterly*, 1959, pp. 188–96.

STINCHCOMBE, ARTHUR. "Bureaucratic and Craft Administration of Production," *Administration Science Quarterly*, 1959, pp. 168–87.

STRAUSS, GEORGE. "Tactics of Lateral Relationship," *Administrative Science Quarterly*, 1962, pp. 161–86.

THOMPSON, JAMES. *Organizations in Action.* New York: McGraw-Hill Book Co., Inc., 1967.

WOODWARD, JOAN. *Industrial Organization: Theory and Practice.* London: Oxford University Press, 1965.

ZANDER, ALVIN, AND WOLFE, DONALD. "Administrative Rewards and Coordination among Committee Members," *Administrative Science Quarterly*, June 1964, pp. 50–69.

CASES ON
ORGANIZATIONAL
DESIGN

Complan
Interactive Systems

In 1969 and early 1970 the computer time-sharing industry, then only four years old, was experiencing a shake-out. At a time when the stock market had shown a year of nearly steady decline and the computer software and services industries had fallen in disfavor with investors, many time-sharing companies were merging and others were falling to the wayside or being acquired at fire-sale prices.

The Time-Sharing Industry

The development and growth of the time-sharing industry was described in volume 12 of *Innovation* magazine: "Time-sharing is a special kind of service industry based on the remote manipulation of data via certain combinations of technology—computers, communications, software. This becomes a viable business largely because the technology gets attractively inexpensive to use when its essential costs are shared. . . .

"The customers use keyboard [e.g., teletypes] or graphic terminals linked to a central computer by telephone lines. In effect, each customer believes that the computer operates exclusively in his behalf, for certain supervisory programs within the machine analyze the demands made by various customers and interleave them . . ." so that the response to demands by individual users optimally is given with no noticeable delay resulting from other customers' uses of the machine.

The article described the entry of some companies into the young time-sharing industry, " . . . after suitable juggling had been accomplished among potential customers, a computer supplier, and the phone company, you hired some smart programmers and whipped them like galley slaves to have the software ready on time to meld the whole affair together in an operating system. . . .

"Technically creative people impelled most time-sharing companies. Many of them were started by programmers who were attracted by the idea of capitalizing on what they knew how to do with software—squeeze the most out of computer hardware."

The time-sharing companies soon found that operations were more complex than they had anticipated. One of the main advantages of time sharing—the immediate availability of the computer to several users simultaneously—began to haunt the time-sharing entrepreneurs. Customers could call at any time of the day or night, which was fine until too many customers called at the same time. Then the operating system—a sophisticated design of hardware and software—could answer each individual's requests only after much longer response times than were desirable. If this situation occurred too frequently, customers complained and eventually discontinued using the service. On the other hand, the time-sharing company saw its machine being underutilized for portions of each day. The incremental cost of putting on new customers appeared very low, as the hardware was already there and each additional customer had only a small effect on the system's performance. The *Innovation* article described the outcome of this type of analysis: "If enough companies put enough computer time on the market based on such an incremental pricing strategy, it doesn't take long before the cost competition has all of them selling at below real operating costs unless their computers do run at capacity which . . . degrades service and drives customers away. Then, when people find their services aren't selling, they cut prices. This iteration becomes disastrous when there is no distinction between time-sharing services except price."

As time-sharing technology was commercially developed, many technical problems appeared. Since the technology for time sharing was much more advanced than for traditional batch-mode service and had not been completely debugged, many hardware and software problems were found only after customers began using the systems. Some problems occurred only when special circumstances, such as a unique sequence and timing of customer demands, hit upon a systems design flaw. These errors were especially difficult to fix, for first the error situation had to be discovered and recreated and often little information remained after the error occurred to help discover what had actually happened. Since customers had direct access to the system, it was more vulnerable than batch operations, in which the computer was in a protected environment and was accessed only by the operator. Furthermore, the fact that several customers were using the system at any one time increased the potential damage that a systems error could cause; many users could find that midway through their session with the system it would "crash" and possibly all of the work they had done to that point would be lost and unrecoverable.

Many of the time-sharing companies' customers were not technically oriented, and the companies offered their customers little help in using the service. *Innovation* described this situation:

Few of the companies had made any real investment in a marketing force. Many of them acquired a good peddler, knighted him with a title of vice president for marketing, paid him $25,000 per year plus stock options, and expected him to scare up customers for the computer waiting in the back room. . . . Early in 1968 a salesman who knew little about programming could still go into a scientific research or engineering establishment and offer raw computer time on a central machine via teletype link: the client could then do as he pleased with the system. But it became more difficult to sell this way because there were lots of other customers who examined an offer of a computer and asked: But what do we do with it.

There followed a great rush through 1968 and 1969 to produce libraries of computer application programs. . . . After two years the great flurry of programming activity hadn't produced much of a distinction between time-sharing services after all. Almost every service, large or small, offered the same computer languages and somewhat the same kinds of programs. This similarity of services continued to depress the time-sharing market.

The programming activity had absorbed many of the resources of the companies that had gone heavily on this marketing strategy. Often, however, it became clear only after a program had been developed that it did not have as wide an application as was expected. Often the market for a program was severely limited by the fact that the program itself was technically a fine development but too sophisticated for use and too difficult to understand for more than a small number of customers.

The Time-Sharing Industry in 1970

In 1970, time-sharing companies were retrenching. Few were profitable. As a result of the several mergers in the industry, some time-sharing companies had operations in more than one city (some all across the nation). The central computer facilities in these situations could either be one large computer with multiplexors and leased telephone lines feeding to this computer or separate computer facilities with similar programs in different cities. The choice between these two alternatives was usually made on economic determinations based upon analysis of the capital investments and operating costs, or it was de facto as a result of a merger situation.

Complan Interactive Systems

In mid-1970, Complan Interactive Systems, Inc. was formed as a new time-sharing service. The company's founders believed that if they followed the right strategy and organized properly they could profitably offer time-sharing services. Basing their strategy upon experience they had gained from observing other time-sharing companies, CIS's founders decided to differentiate themselves from the rest of the industry by offering a specialized package of programs and services to initially one specialized market. CIS's potential clients had little knowledge of computer technology but had several applications in which the use of time sharing could make a major positive impact. The company offered its clients a package which included the use of a terminal, access to the company's programs (which were designed to be both flexible in their application and easy to use), initial instruction in the use of the system and applications programs, detailed instruction manuals, and on-going support services. CIS priced its services significantly higher than the time-sharing industry average pricing structure. The company considered its marketing area to be the United States and Canada, and it based its operations on one central computer facility.

Major Tasks

CIS believed that to be successful, it had to offer:

1. a dependable time-sharing system, which meant:
   a) enhancing and modifying the system provided by the computer hardware manufacturer,
   b) providing dependable operations and maintenance of the hardware and software

at 2. a reasonable (but higher than average) price,

with 3. specialized applications programs that:
   a) met specific customer needs,
   b) were easy to use while still being effective,
   c) were modified and augmented as required,

and with 4. extensive customer service and training that would:
   a) assist the customer in effectively using the service, often answering questions that were relatively simple technically;
   b) answer occasional highly technical customer questions;
   c) provide feedback on the customers' views of the system's performance;

d) provide information on additional applications and market potentials.

CIS's president felt that together with support staff, it would be necessary to assemble an organization of about 100 people. He was trying to determine what organizational arrangements would best meet his company's objectives.

Wheeler/Johnson Group Travel

DURING 1969 the Sternin Bank and Trust Company entered the travel business largely through the purchase of Johnson Group Journeys, a Los Angeles based travel agency, and Wheeler's Travel Center, a San Francisco based agency. Sternin had achieved rapid growth and pursued a strategy based upon providing excellent service to its clients. It had considerable management talent and had acted quickly to establish its credit card business. Sternin believed its service orientation and credit card operations gave it a natural inroad into the group travel market.

By the end of 1969 Sternin had decided to consolidate its two travel acquisitions into Wheeler/Johnson, based in San Francisco and having 27 franchised agencies and 8 company-owned agencies. The company considered its prime market to be the group tour market, and it offered 22 different tours having varying degrees of profitability and risk. In addition to the primary task of arranging and selling group tours, the company considered the selling and servicing of franchises to be its secondary task. Sternin management prided itself in the fact that it had used its marketing and management skills to turn many losing acquisitions into profitable operations, and it wondered what organizational arrangements would be most appropriate for its new Wheeler/Johnson travel operations.

Group Tours

The 22-group tour programs offered regularly by Wheeler/Johnson were of one of three types: ITC, affinity, or GIT. All group tours were governed by the rules of the International Air Transport Association (IATA), and the Civil Aeronautics Board (CAB), which among other things set the limits on air rate reductions for any particular group.

The maximum reduced rates were given to affinity groups, which consisted of one homogeneous group of people—that is, people from the same organization. Inclusive tour charters (ITC) were tours that could be sold to the general public. There was no group membership requirement nor were there any eligibility stipulations. A group inclusive tour (GIT) was a program in which regularly scheduled airline seats were purchased at a discount.

These were not the only types of tours; there were numerous variations of the above three, and all were governed by different rules and stipulations which affected the ultimate cost of a tour and its selling price to the public.

Examples of High- and Low-Risk Tours

In the Hawaiian "Aloha Bound" program a 250-passenger airplane had been chartered once a week for 52 weeks. If the seats were completely filled, a profit would be made. If, however, only 200 seats were filled, a loss would be realized because of the high cost of the airplane. In addition to this high plane cost, brochures, advertising, and sales force expenses were other direct costs that had to be realized by Wheeler/Johnson. It was because of these high fixed costs and potential penalty cancellation costs that the Aloha Bound program could be categorized as being a risky profit opportunity for Wheeler/Johnson.

On the other hand, the "China Sails" program could be characterized as a low-risk program since it was being done as a cooperative effort with a major airline. The result of this cooperative effort was that not only had an additional selling arm been added, since the airline reservation desks and airline agency representatives were recommending this tour program, but also the fixed costs had been diminished and diluted since only the seats used were charged and because all advertising and brochure costs were jointly shared.

The Basic Task

The basic task of Wheeler/Johnson Travel Agency was to prepare marketable trips and sell these trips profitably in the form of group tours through company retail and franchise travel agencies as well as through company salesmen. One staff member described the task:

... You don't need a Ph.D. to put together and market a travel program; once you've lived through one program, the next one requires no new talent. You decide where you want to go, what hotel and airline to use, pick a local travel agency at the destination to handle any sightseeing or other options, competitively price the program and that's it.

After you have put together the program, you must design the brochures, distribute them to the agencies and company salesmen, advertise, and then keep track of the reservations as they come in.

It's the same procedure for every program whether it is in the Orient or it is in Europe.

The ideal trip was a destination that had tourist attraction and was not a destination of any other group travel agency. The marketability of these trips was in fact that one was able to travel to these geographical places in a group at less cost than if he traveled alone. However, with the advent of more and more travel agencies entering the group travel market, these virgin destinations had become more difficult to find. Consequently, the marketability of a group tour was not only geographical destination and price but also the caliber of accommodations and quality of service.

Therefore, to put together a marketable trip, Wheeler/Johnson had to:

1. Negotiate advantageous hotel and airline contracts.
2. Be knowledgeable of each destination's accommodations and facilities, that is, know which were the deluxe and which were the adequate hotels; which were on the beach, in the city, or in the country; and know what was the quality of the hotels, bars, nightclubs, and dining rooms as well as the management of each hotel.
3. Be knowledgeable about the historical and cultural attractions of each destination and make sightseeing tours to these attractions available to group members. Likewise, entertainment highlights at each destination, that is, places to dine, to swing, theater, ballet, musical performances, bullfights, cliff diving, etc., had to be known by Wheeler/Johnson and made available to group members.
4. Be able to grease the way for the traveler, that is, in baggage handling, airline checking, customs, transportation to hotels, hotel check-ins, etc., so that traveling in groups became easier than traveling individually.

Selling Group Tours

The task of the company salesmen was to locate civic, fraternal, religious, business, and professional groups, schools, colleges, and unions, and sell affinity group tours from the company product line, or find out what an organization's desires were and make up new trips and itineraries to meet these desires.

The critical elements in making a sale were:

1. Establishing a need and/or creating a desire to sponsor a Wheeler/Johnson group tour. There were various reasons why an organization would be interested in group travel. For example, business and professional groups might purchase a tour for sales meetings, conventions, or incentive bonuses; while civic, fraternal, or religious organizations might desire to sponsor a trip because of the bargain price, camaraderie, or security of traveling with people who had common interests and cares, etc.

2. Creating an impression of reliability and quality: once a desire for group travel had been fostered, the salesmen had to immediately become the organization's experts on travel. To select a destination from the existing product line or to effectively propose a new destination, the salesmen had to be completely knowledgeable about the destination, that is, its accommodations, facilities, options, and competitive advantage over other group travel tours offering the same destination. If a salesman's knowledge was in question, the reliability and quality of the whole program was in question, and either the organization dropped the whole idea or sought another agency to conduct the trip.

Agency Functions and Requirements

Agencies were an extension of the sales force as far as affinity group tours were concerned, but they also served an additional purpose of selling Wheeler/Johnson inclusive tour charters (as described earlier, group. charters made up of individuals rather than members of the same organization). Agencies, however, sold not only Wheeler/Johnson group tours but also competitors' tours. The task was to get the agency to recommend a Wheeler/Johnson tour. Agencies pushed those tours that offered the highest commission, that were easiest for them to sell, and that had the most reliable service. Commission rate was definitely one of the most important aspects to encourage an agency to push a tour, but it was only a starting point. Agency personnel had not traveled to all if any of the destinations they sold, but like the company salesman, they were expected to be expert travel advisors for every destination. These agency personnel depended on the brochures, airline representatives, and group tour representatives to educate them. The more knowledgeable agencies were about a program, the easier it was for them to sell a potential customer, and consequently they tended to push those programs they knew most about. Equally important was the reliability of service, that is, was everything that was promised actually given? For if a customer was not happy with his trip, not only would he not travel a Wheeler/Johnson group tour again but most likely would not return to the independent travel agency recommending the tour.

Competition in Group Tours

Since 1966 when there were practically no group travel operators, five major operators started business (these were Trade Winds, Simmons/Rogal, American International Travel Service, Interludes, and Pathfinders). The increased competition had the effect of making the major competitive issues of destinations and low price just a starting point and making the operational issues of maintaining quality and reliability of service, accommodations, and schedules the dominant competitive issues. As one salesman explained:

There was a time when I could go to an agency or company, show them our product line of destinations, and they would not believe that the price could be so low. But now we have competition which have comparatively priced programs to the same destination. These same agencies and companies now take price for granted and are more interested in the quality and reliability of the service and options offered. They want to know to the last detail what they are getting for their money so they can compare it to our competition's programs.

Prerequisites for Profitability

1.   Critical to making charter trips successful was filling the seats consistently. Because of the very low margin realized from each trip, if a destination with weekly charter departures deadheaded in some cases just twice, all the contribution to overhead from the trip for the entire year might have been lost. This fact emphasized the importance of not only producing new individual and group business but also of insuring repeat business.

2.   There came a time in every charter program when a decision had to be made to cancel the flight and incur the penalty charge of the airline, or to go ahead with the program. Wheeler/Johnson had to know the status of each trip far enough in advance to effectively direct its sales efforts and to give enough lead time for advertising to work. Similarly, there came a time when a destination began to "dry up," either because of increased competition or because of more desirable destinations. Status reports showed when planes should be made smaller or larger, when to add or drop rooms from the hotels, and/or when to drop a destination altogether.

3.   To efficiently make use of its airline contracts, it was necessary weekly to schedule and reschedule departure cities, as well as to group tours together to fill planes, while canceling others. Also, because of the diversity of airline and hotel contracts, all with different provisions, it was necessary to constantly audit contracts with actual results to insure that what was contracted from the airlines and hotels actually came to pass in terms of dollars per mile or dollars per bed.

4.   Because of this diversity of hotel-airline contracts and advertising schedules, each trip had a different break-even point. Consequently, to be able to efficiently make go-no-go decisions or rescheduling and grouping changes, categorizing of cost by trip and by general administrative overhead costs had to be accomplished so that the break-even point of each trip could be established.

Secondary Task

A secondary task of Wheeler/Johnson was the selling and servicing of franchises. For an investment of about $25,000 and a percentage of future gross revenue, Wheeler would sell to an individual a Wheeler franchise. This $25,000 and percent of future revenues obligated Wheeler to train franchise personnel in writing tickets, accounting procedures, selling techniques, and to include them in the around-the-world contacts that Wheeler through the years had generated. Because new franchise owners had very often never been in business for themselves before, they had in the past required constant monitoring and training.

Recreation Products, Inc.

Introduction

By EARLY 1969 Leroy Harden and James Nicklus were indeed satisfied with the rapid growth in Recreation Products, Inc. They were aware, however, that this very growth could produce organizational strains; they were concerned that any such tendencies not be overlooked but be dealt with. They realized that the rapid growth in RPI had moved them further from operational control and might lead to problems in coordination among the functional units. They were also determined that one key current organizational relationship, selling several product groups through a single force, continue to operate as they continued to pursue their strategies of acquisition and rapid growth.

History

In 1964 Nicklus and Harden left McKinsey to look for a company to purchase and manage. After a five-month search, they purchased Gorman Manufacturing Company, an established but unimaginative maker of lawn sprinklers. Gorman had what Nicklus and Harden were looking for: a consumer product with an established reputation for quality but a feeble marketing effort. The two men felt that their MBA education and consulting experience plus an infusion of younger, more aggressive management talent could markedly improve Gorman's profitability and growth.

Recreation Products, Inc. (RPI) developed as the founders expanded their original ambitions into the larger concept of a leisure time recreation company. In early 1969 the firm was an agglomeration of eight youth, recreation, lawn, and sports equipment companies, all acquired in a carefully developed strategy which would eventually take RPI into most areas normally defined as "leisure time" or "recreation." Between 1965 and 1967, RPI grew at about 15 percent. RPI acquired four firms

86

and grew from sales of $1,291,000 to $9,631,000, and its net income after taxes rose from $81,000 to $536,000. Exhibits 1A and 1B present key financial data for the period 1965–68.

The first acquisition was Rich Spray Gun Company, picked up in 1965 and merged into Gorman. Since the two product lines were similar, this marriage was relatively easy to effect organizationally. Next came Tom Carver, Inc., the world's largest manufacturer of archery equipment. Nicklus and Harden were attracted to this company because of potential for savings in operating costs and the possibility of increasing sales by streamlining the organization and providing increased marketing punch.

They felt certain they could accomplish this by substituting RPI management procedures for those of the founder, Tom Carver, a professional archer. Leroy Harden described the situation as it developed:

> Tom Carver is still on the payroll. Only now he is doing what he likes to do best. This includes promoting Carver products by traveling the United States staging archery tournaments and attracting attention to his entourage, a stuffed animal caravan. Tom Carver is to Carver's product line what Colonel Sanders is to Kentucky Fried Chicken.

In 1967 RPI acquired Nile Sled Company, makers of Snowbird sleds since 1889. Once again the pattern was consistent with the general strategy: a branded consumer product with accepted quality but moribund marketing ideas. James Nicklus commented on the marketing inputs RPI had to inject to rebuild Snowbird sales:

> This Snowbird situation really took an effort. This company virtually dominated the sled market during the 1920s. By 1967, they were lucky to have

EXHIBIT 1A

Key Financial Data for Period of 1965–68

	1968		1967		1966		1965	
Sales	$17,662,000		$9,631,000		$7,324,000		$1,291,000	
Gross margin	5,839,000	33%	3,584,000	41%	2,296,000	31%	506,000	39%
Income before taxes ...	1,922,000	11%	1,004,000	10.4%	432,000	6%	138,000	10.4%
Net income	962,000		536,000		235,000		81,000	
Earnings per share	$1.08		$0.76		$0.40		$0.23	
Working capital ..	5,673,000		2,547,000		2,176,000		141,000	
Net plant and equipment	7,095,000		2,686,000		2,360,000		671,000	
Shareholders' equity	8,177,000		1,380,000		676,000		121,000	
Number of plants	7		4		3		2	
Number of employees	1,700		700		530		120	

EXHIBIT 1B

Stock Price Movement
(bid-asked prices)

Insured 4/68	5/1/68	6/1/68	7/1/68	8/1/68	9/1/68	10/1/68
13	33–35	41–44	43–45	45–48	48–51	58–62
Insured 11/1/68	12/1/68	1/1/69	2/1/69	3/1/69	4/1/69	
61–65	68–72	63–67	68–72	55–59	59–63	

Capitalization, 1,039,000 shares
20 percent held by top officers

Sources: Annual reports.

15 percent, and I'll bet part of that was a gift. This company probably survived because nostalgic fathers insisted their children have the same sled they once used. The products were generally overpriced and unwanted by dealers. We had to redesign the sleds to make them competitive, cut prices to chain stores, and really promote them at retail. We also had to win back dealers with special promotional offers as well as the lowered prices.

In 1968, RPI accelerated acquisition growth by absorbing four more companies. First came Brockman Sprinkler. This purchase was designed to widen the product line in lawn and garden equipment. In March 1968, RPI picked up Green Thumb Company, manufacturers and marketers of indoor plant care products. In June the group moved into still another new field by acquiring Quality Arms Company. Quality Arms manufactured quality lines of firearms, both handguns and shoulder guns. This "top of the line" product group included Tournament Caliber firearms for competition accuracy as well as a complete array of hunting rifles and shotguns. Finally, in October 1968, RPI added to its line of winter products by acquiring Alpine Industries, a Canadian maker of toboggans and other winter sporting equipment. Alpine was also intended to provide an entrée into Canadian markets. Thus, by February 1969, Recrea-

EXHIBIT 2

Product Groups and Products

Archery	Firearms	Lawn and Garden Equipment	Winter Products	Commercial and Industrial Products
Tom Carver	Quality arms	Gorman Manufacturing Company	Snowbird	Farm equipment
		Rich Spray Gun Company	Alpine Industries	Private brands
		Green Thumb Company		Government sales

tion Products, Inc. consisted of the broad product groups shown in Exhibit 2.

Strategy

The key elements of RPI strategy were formulated explicitly by Harden and Nicklus during 1966, as a reaction to factors in the environment. They saw two significant trends which strongly affected the growth possibilities of the companies managed at that time. One trend was the rapid *growth* in demand for leisure time products and services. The factors contributing to this demand are generally known: (1) gradual shortening of workweeks, from today's 38–39 hours to estimates of 20 hours by the year 2000; (2) changing population mix, such that the number of young families, ages 25–34, will increase by 46 percent in the next decade alone; (3) rising disposable income per capita, projected to increase by 45 percent by 1975; and (4) increased education and better communication which serve to "socialize" Americans to use their free time actively.

The second trend, equally important in RPI's competitive environment, was the changing nature of distribution methods for leisure products: the emergence of the high-volume mass merchandiser. This evolution brings significant changes in the way goods are moved: self-service, point-of-sale displays, increased importance of packaging, and more sophisticated promotion techniques. It also brings centralized buying of chains and cooperative groups of independents.

The resultant of these two trends is the cornerstone of RPI strategy: to market various leisure time products through a single sales force. Mr. Nicklus commented to the case writer:

This choice is more significant than might seem to be the case at first glance. The most obvious result is, of course, the economies of the selling effort spread over several products. Because the products are not highly technical, one salesman can handle the various lines. Equally significant, however, is an ability to provide the buyers at larger distributors with facts and data quickly and concisely. What we are working toward is a two-tiered sales force: (1) a small number of expert salesmen who can provide these buyers the benefits of our centralized information on several product groups; and (2) a larger number of "retail detail" men who stock shelves, handle promotional material, etc., at the various retail outlets. The result is that we are able to overpower most of our competitors in dealing with buyers; these competitors are still organized as though they were selling to a network of small retailers. In fact, over 50 percent of the sales of products such as ours are sold through mass merchandisers.

Mr. Harden, commenting on questions of strategy, added:

In terms of where we hope to take RPI, we are really still in Phase I. Our present lines can easily be handled by one sales force. The questions I grapple with are what happens when sales of our present groups (and acquisitions to be made in these existing lines) reach $100 million or more and we move into fields such as travel, education, or entertainment. We might have to leave Recreation Products, Inc. at that time as a separate organization and start almost from scratch with the added services. You know, we can go a long way under the umbrella "leisure time" and "recreation."

To provide even more direction to these strategic goals, RPI has translated them into specific financial objectives. The first page of the 1968 RPI annual report sets forth these objectives and invites stock-holders to evaluate the efforts of the management team in its pursuit of their accomplishment.

Since formation of the company in November 1964, our objective has been to build a major business enterprise engaged in the manufacture and market-ing of leisure time products. At that time we established financial and operat-ing goals as follows: (1) 15 percent annual sales increase through internal growth; (2) 50 percent annual sales increase through acquisition; (3) net income equal to 6 percent of sales and a minimum annual increase in earnings per share of 25 percent.

Organizational Structure

In 1969, Recreation Products, Inc. was organized functionally into three major units: marketing, operations (production), and product de-velopment. A fourth unit, the controller, provided centralized accounting, finance, and customer relation activities for the group at the corporate level. While no formal organization chart existed, Exhibit 3 portrays the case writer's impressions of how it might have looked. Approximate ages are presented in this exhibit, and those men with MBA degrees are noted.

Marketing

The marketing unit performed essentially two types of functions: sales management and product management. Since marketing was critical at RPI, product managers occupied key roles in the operations of the firm. Mr. Nicklus indicated the scope of their responsibilities:

I'm sure the concept of the product manager is a familiar one. Most of the large consumer products companies, General Foods, Procter & Gamble, Kellogg, etc., are built on product managers. Around here, though, the term connotes a much broader span of responsibilities than I think exists in most firms. Our PMs are responsible for product strategies, market evaluation, mer-chandising and advertising tools, just as are their counterparts at General Foods. However, a more appropriate term at Recreation Products, Inc. would

EXHIBIT 3

Organization Chart

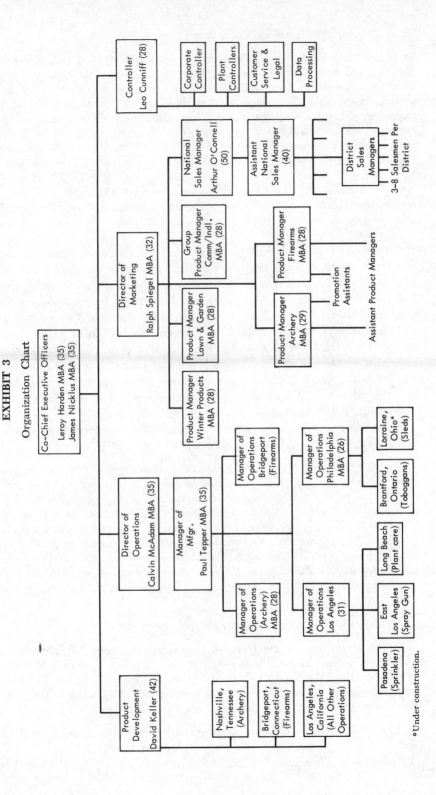

be product *general* manager. We hold these guys responsible for the product planning *and* for monitoring the ongoing situation to see that plans are fulfilled [in reference to the rough organization charts constructed by the case writer]. We don't really believe in these lines and boxes. If problems at a plant are holding back a product's sales, we expect the product manager to be on the phone immediately talking to the plant manager to iron out the problems. You know if I see a forecast not being met, I'll expect that PM to know why this exists, and what he plans to do about it. Similarly, if a PM expects to be under or over forecast in any particular quarter, it is his job to work with the plant manager to adjust production to avoid stocking out or excessive inventories. This information doesn't move up to Ralph Spiegel [director of marketing] and then down. It moves by the shortest route.

Product managers were each responsible for a particular product line: archery, winter products, lawn and garden equipment, firearms. In some instances, a line included more than one type of product; for instance, the PM for lawn and garden equipment handled sprinklers (acquired with Gorman Manufacturing Company), spray guns (once made by Rich), and the indoor plant care products of Green Thumb. The various products in a line might be manufactured at different plants, as is in fact the case in the above example. Thus, the product manager had to maintain contact with various plant people—the manager of operations and men at each specific plant—as well as the sales force and the director of marketing, to do his job.

Bob Vroom, product manager for lawn and garden equipment, described the facets of his job to the case writer:

I'll tell you the one thing I could use most around here, a 30-hour day! But we really relish the work and the responsibility that goes with being a product manager. I spend a good portion of my time at daily "firefighting" chores like attending to a problem raised by a customer or something popping up at the plant. And over the course of a month I am usually engaged in a few specific projects, such as planning a new product or altering packaging on an existing one. Of course, I spend quite a bit of time preparing the budgets and forecasts for next fiscal year. And I guess the remainder of my time is spent in monitoring the current performance of my product line and keeping everyone aware of its status.

Jacob Sanford, product manager for archery, added:

I have to do most of my planning around and between "firefighting" on daily operations. You'll usually find the lights on around here until 9:00, often much later. But I think most PMs do it because of their stake in RPI and their large measure of responsibility for their product line. This stake in the company motivates me to go across functional areas when necessary.

The sales force was divided geographically, with each man responsible for sales of all product lines within his geographic area. In 1969 the national sales area was divided into seven districts, each headed by a district manager. The district managers reported to Arthur O'Connell, the national sales manager. As of 1969 these district managers (DSMs) were dividing their time between selling and administrative duties. The DSM usually handled the larger accounts: centralized buying offices of chain stores and the larger independents. He would sometimes be accompanied by various product managers in calls to these large chains, usually at the beginning of the selling season for a particular product. The purpose of this joint effort would be to provide the intensive information and data mentioned earlier as a critical element of the marketing strategy.

The field salesmen usually called on smaller accounts and handled shelving, promotional material, and similar needs at individual outlets of the chain retailer. Mr. O'Connell commented on the current situation in the sales force.

RPI is really in a state of transition, a state of rapid growth. We began in 1968 with 15 salesmen; by December we had 50. What we are doing is moving toward our eventual target of a two-tiered sales organization. But if you're looking for an established formal organization, I doubt if you'll find it. As the force expands we must be constantly thinking of the future personnel demands. We have men in the field selling who will some day be district or area managers. Some of the men are obviously more talented than others; some possess far greater potential to grow with us. So at the present, our fieldmen have varying assignments. Some perform primarily the "detailing" functions at specific retail outlets. Others do the selling to larger buyers, or at least participate in this effort.

This marketing unit was headed by Ralph Spiegel, a 32-year-old MBA. Mr. Spiegel, a former product manager, had been made director of marketing in early 1969. Since the previous director had left RPI in June 1968, the position had remained unfilled while Messrs. Harden and Nicklus waited for a replacement to develop. In the interim Mr. Nicklus became more deeply involved with coordinating the efforts of the marketing organization.

Operations

Calvin McAdam, 35-year-old MBA, headed the operations organization. Reporting to Mr. McAdam were four managers of operations, each responsible for plants producing a particular product line. In early 1969, Paul Tepper, also an MBA, joined the group as the manager of manufacturing under Mr. McAdam and assumed responsibility for monitoring the day-to-day operations of the various plants. This new position was intended to reduce the extraordinary work load carried by Mr. McAdam.

I'm really glad to have Paul around here. Shifting part of my responsibility to him should permit me to spend some time on areas which I just haven't been able to get around to yet. We really haven't yet fully defined his job, as he has been here only a month. Right now I expect him to be on top of all current operations; that is, assuring the plants are meeting their production plans, meeting their cost reduction goals, and watching inventories.

As you know, I'm usually involved in our acquisitions in the early stages, because we usually have to make a number of significant changes in the production system of these firms. We are committed to our stockholders and the financial markets for making our profit estimates, and that often means getting these acquisitions turned around pronto! I also hope to devote more time now to specific projects, for instance, developing proposals for new plants or additions and developing a uniform labor policy for all plants.

The managers of operations were given full responsibility for the plant or plants under their supervision. They were responsible for translating marketing forecasts into production quotas and for monitoring ongoing operations to assure it met these goals. Allan Temple commented to the case writer on what this responsibility meant:

You know, we're shrewd enough to realize that even though we spend a great effort planning around here, we have to retain the flexibility to react to the inevitable changes. That obviously makes the smooth operation of a product line highly dependent on the personal relationship between guys like me and their product manager. I'm on the phone to Bob Vroom (product manager for lawn and garden products) several times a week. When he sees a likely deviation from the marketing plan, he'll alert me to watch the inventory. If this confirms his thoughts, we will discuss the changes necessary in my production plan. Of course he'll have to justify these changes to Ralph Spiegel [director of marketing], but it will be his decision. I don't see how we'd effectively handle the situation without this continuous personal contact.

Product Development

Most product development activities were centralized in Los Angeles, with only the groups at Nashville, Tennessee (archery), and Bridgeport, Connecticut (firearms), remaining at those particular plants.

David Keller, director of product development, commented to the case writer:

Like the rest of RPI, the product development unit is constantly in a state of transition. We are working toward centralizing everything here at Los Angeles. At the present, the plants at Nashville and Bridgeport are still in need of work on production processes, so there are engineers at these plants.

The typical sequence of a particular project usually began with a suggestion from a product manager for a new or modified product, from a manager of operations for a process change, or from a designer or engineer in the product development group. A preliminary feasibility analysis was done, with time and dollar commitments estimated. Mr. Keller discussed the more frequent contacts he maintained during a project.

During the early phases of a project, I'm in pretty close contact with the particular PM or manager of operations who suggested the project. We gradually develop a cost-benefit analysis to see if the project warrants further work. Gradually, the director of marketing will be brought in, and sometimes the director of operations. And, of course, a "go-no-go" decision on all but very small projects will usually involve the top guys, James Nicklus and Leroy Harden.

Controller

In early 1969 the controller's office had recently been expanded as more and more functions were centralized under the responsibility of Mr. Leo Cunniff, the controller. Typical corporate accounting functions were directed to L.A. even before the group had data processing facilities. Because the A/R and A/P data were there, it was a logical step to establish a central office for handling customer service: orders, complaints, and reports requested by customers. The data processing unit provided data for use by both marketing and operations managers. Mr. Cunniff talked about the current problem areas with the case writer:

At present we have two chief areas of concern. Our present crisis stems from the fact that we are now doing our own data processing in-house, rather than having it done by a service bureau. We're still in the "debugging" stage, so our output isn't getting to product managers or operations people as fast as it should. But this is temporary I'm sure, and we'll get it working.

Secondly, we're now thrashing around the idea of having plant controllers report to their respective plant managers, rather than to me. The intent would be to provide these MOs with more responsive information on their respective operations. The change is now being considered both by myself and by people in operations, particularly Paul Tepper [manager of manufacturing].

The Annual Planning Process

Board Chairman Leroy Harden explained why there was an emphasis on planning at Recreation Products, Inc.:

Given our backgrounds, it's not hard to understand why we are so thorough in our planning efforts around here. James and I were consultants, exposed to a broad range of situations where we could observe a number of different planning systems. Most of our marketing organization comes from companies like General Foods, Procter & Gamble, and Xerox—so we have the benefit of knowing how these rather sophisticated firms went about it. And most of us are MBAs, so I'm sure we're all still recovering from the pounding of "planning is a way of life."

He continued:

Detailed emphasis on planning fits integrally with the style of James and myself here at RPI. We both believe it is possible to make certain types of decisions once, and then disseminate procedures for how these recurring problems should be handled. We have seen so many examples of rather simple decisions being made over and over, each time with a new analysis. In this vein, we are convinced that a strong emphasis on planning forces our people to think in strategic terms. With well-thought plans, the everyday events can be interpreted in the context of the larger plan. Planning also contributes to setting goals and specific action routes to accomplishing these goals.

Because RPI was essentially a marketing organization, planning began with the individual product managers. In late spring product managers began their planning effort for the following fiscal year (beginning November 1). These men were responsible for the preparation of five formal documents, covering in general the industry and market and potential new products, and specifically sales forecasts and budgets for various marketing expenses. The "bottom line" figure for product managers was one which measured sales dollars minus all marketing expenses controllable by PMs, such as advertising and promotion. As mentioned earlier, PMs were held entirely responsible for the performance of their product line. Thus, their completed product plans also specified the efforts they expected to make to increase market share or sales dollars: efforts such as special promotions, new product introductions, intensive advertising campaigns, etc.

As these product plans were the basis for forecasting efforts by other units, substantial pressure existed for these men to produce accurate plans. Ralph Spiegel, director of marketing, explained this to the case writer:

I'm sure it is obvious we use our planning system as a mechanism to coordinate efforts of the various units of the company. As such, it is imperative that we get accurate plans from our product managers. While it is sometimes difficult to do, I try to be just as upset when a PM has underforecast as when he falls short of his goals. Of course, each PM has to project at least a 15 percent annual gain in sales; as a matter of corporate strategy, these are our overall goals. But I want these guys to formulate a marketing strategy they think will be effective, and then give me forecasts based on what they really expect to happen, not just tack 15 percent onto last year's sales figures. We're a long way from being perfect at it, but we are getting closer. And since these PMs have total responsibility for a product line, I believe there is strong motivation to give me good data, rather than leave themselves a "cushion" in their forecasts.

Based on the individual plans of the product managers, the sales organization made its annual forecasts and established targets. The sum of all PM forecasts was reviewed by the national sales manager (NSM) and the director of marketing to determine whether the total load could be handled by the sales force. The figures were broken down by the NSM to specific sales quotas for each district by product line and by quarter. District managers then further divided the district among the various salesmen, again by product line by quarter. Once these quotas had been established, the sales managers have them as a basis for evaluation, unless they receive a formal correction by a PM of his forecast.

On the operations side, the planning effort once again began at the bottom and moved upward. A PM's forecast for his line was given to the manager of operations (MO) responsible for plants producing those products. As the sales forecasts were estimated by quarter, the MOs would then translate this data into volumes by quarter. From this information, production rates, standard cost data, and inventory levels were established; these then became the standards against which these MOs were evaluated.

These MOs were also responsible for initiating requests for capital expenditures. As a part of the annual budgets, managers of operations were expected to submit capital expenditure proposals which met RPI's corporate criteria for ROI and payback period. The director of operations, Mr. McAdam, would review these requests and consult Messrs. Harden and Nicklus if it were necessary to place priorities because of limited available funds.

Once the MOs had established operating forecasts and submitted them to Mr. McAdam, these figures then became the basis for measuring performance. Weekly and monthly reports showing key ratios, operating costs, and inventory were reviewed by Mr. McAdam. MOs were also responsible for initiating a cost reduction program as a part of each annual forecast. They were then measured on meeting these cost reduction targets.

Functional Interfaces

Many of the managers were concerned, in some way or other, with the interfaces between functional areas. While often not stated in precise terms, these men were aware of the potential for problems at these boundaries. The case writer posed this possibility to various managers; the comments below reflect their concern. The problems of multiple products–single sales force will be discussed later and are not specifically mentioned below. Chairman Leroy Harden commented:

I can think of a few ways in which we have tried to "manage these interfaces" as you put it. Clearly the most general fact is our informal communication and the access everyone has to everyone else. Being MBAs James and I expect these men to have an orientation broad enough to fit their job into the more general picture. We also expect them to be problem oriented: to go where they have to and speak to whomever they need, to solve their particular problem.

Secondly, our detailed emphasis on planning and review allows each unit to operate without being totally dependent on other functional units. Once our annual plans are established, the PMs and MOs practically live with each other, going across the functional boundaries. And since PMs have responsibility for meeting sales forecasts, they have what I believe to be a very strong incentive to keep in touch with everyone necessary to do so, everyone being other managers in RPI, the sales force, customers, suppliers.

Last, James and I have mentioned our belief that a lot of decisions in any firm can be procedurized. We hope to have made the process easier for our people by disseminating procedures and criteria. This provides a framework within which our managers can work.

Mr. Temple, manager of operations for lawn and garden equipment, added:

The procedures around here are what I call "methodology procedures," that is, general guidelines. I used to be with a large, rather prosaic metals organization, and there I considered the procedures stifling. Here, they are really the formalized thoughts of Leroy and James. These men really serve as the ultimate resource around here. Whenever there are arguments which can't be resolved they enter the discussion. Leroy usually handles operations and control, while James oversees the marketing side. And believe me, when it gets kicked upstairs, it gets solved.

Calvin McAdam, director of operations, added his thoughts on the topic:

I believe the most critical mechanism for operating across the functions is keeping communications channels open. We have a couple of ways of keeping these channels forced open. First, the mass of written data which flows at RPI serves to provide communication. We get weekly reports and monthly reports on plants; equally precise data is provided on how products are being moved by salesmen. Second, I believe there is a pressure downward to keep information flowing upward. For example, there are plenty of instances where one of my MOs will have indications that some costs are rising, etc., but this would not appear in a report for two or three weeks. I have made it clear that I want such information as soon as they get these first indications. Obviously, this cuts down our reaction time to such contingencies. When I get information on inventories or quality control, for example, the product manager and I can go over it and discuss a possible course of action immediately.

There are, however, a couple of things I'm concerned about as we grow as an organization. I see first signs that we're nearing the size where informal mechanisms become more rigid. I know this has happened personally in at least one instance. In the past, I would react to a PM's first thought that he was over or under forecast by reworking the production plans for the plant involved. Recently, though, I find myself less willing to accept his first indications. There have been times when my quick reaction meant changing a production flow, only to have to reestablish the old volume as the product line got back on forecast. As a result, I generally won't have MOs rework their operating forecasts until the product manager is certain enough of the change to formally commit himself by changing his forecasts in writing.

More significantly, the interface I am most concerned about is that between operations and product development. As I see it no one in PD is responsible for coordinating the efforts of product development people and the operations people on a particular project. I don't believe David Keller [director of production development] can do this; he has to manage so many different projects. As a result, my MOs are really assuming this responsibility by default. This is tough on them, since they already have plenty to do. The solution which comes to my mind is to have one of the product development engineers assume formal leadership of the project group. Then when the project is ready for production it would be handled by the MO.

Walter Grace, manager of operations for winter products, also commented on handling the interdependencies:

I really believe we have just overwhelmed the potential problems by the type of people we have at RPI. We have MBAs with experience in well-run companies or consulting organizations—a collection of good, honest, greedy, capable people. Everyone has that problem-solving orientation imbedded at the business school. When (Ralph) Spiegel was the product manager for archery, they couldn't keep him out of the Nashville plant; he was always snooping around, figuring a way to do something better.

I am not convinced, however, that this alone will permit us to function effectively as we grow. There are a few things I believe we have to try to do. The relationship between PMs and MOs during the planning cycle has to be maintained. I have sensed the tendency for PMs to make their forecasts assuming the best of all possible worlds. Once I even saw a PM complete his unit forecast unaware that his plant would not possibly crank out the predicted volume. I think we have to try and keep a slight bit of manufacturing orientation a part of the PM's perspective.

It also seems likely to me we might end up decentralizing the product development units. Two of them operate out of particular plants already, in Bridgeport and Nashville. And the operations people are already integrally involved in the process. I think the centralized PD group may lose their flexibility across product lines. Perhaps the solution would be "decentralized" product (and process) development at the plants with a headquarters staff providing specific expertise in packaging, materials, design, etc.

Multiple Product—Single Sales Force

Another topic of general concern was that of the single sales force. Mr. Nicklus commented:

We are always thinking about the implications of selling a group of products through a single sales force. While this concept seems to work well for some very large marketing firms, we want to make certain that as we grow in size, we make any modifications necessary to keep this system working here at RPI.

Mr. Nicklus continued his comments in this regard:

What we have really done is encourage a "tunnel vision" perspective on the part of the product managers by giving them full responsibility and rewarding them for performance of their time. To compensate for this, I look to the director of marketing and national sales manager to resolve any frictions which arise. And, of course, I am usually pretty involved in things, especially if a conflict can't be settled.

The national sales manager and director of marketing did have several mechanisms to translate the product managers' forecasts into salesmen's quotas and to monitor their efforts in meeting these quotas. The primary tools have been mentioned previously: the planning process itself and the review to assure that the sales force could handle the total job as determined by the various PMs. In addition, most of the product lines were seasonal in nature, so it was possible to schedule intensive sales efforts for the various products so that they did not occur simultaneously. Thus, the salesmen's yearly routine normally included a sequence of peak efforts plus a continuing selling job of much less intensive nature.

Arthur O'Connell, national sales manager, commented further:

I feel we have good data with which to insure that the salesmen concentrate where it will be most effective. District managers get weekly reports showing sales calls, orders booked, and dollar volume for each man, for each product line. There is also a "super" bonus for the salesman who achieves this target sales goal in *each* product group.

District Sales Manager Jim Grabowski also spoke on this topic:

Our salesman routes himself through his territory, subject to the review of myself and Mr. O'Connell. The frequency with which each customer is called upon is also determined by the individual men, based on our expectation of the importance of the account. Again, his choices are subject to review. By watching the reports for call frequencies and sales by product line, I can usually spot a situation where quotas might not be met. This might be symptomatic of a man feeling low, since he is so distant from us and his home, or it could be just a poor salesman. The super bonus at RPI also depends on every man in the district meeting his overall dollar quotas. Obviously, I'm very interested in finding out about potential trouble spots quickly, for the sake of my bonus as well as those of my men.

There are a couple of other areas I think we have to work harder on. First, we aren't yet getting good communication between the salesmen and product managers. These men in the field can supply valuable information on the market and competitors; we haven't yet brought the two groups together. I think it would also be valuable for the salesmen to provide estimates on potential sales of various lines by customer. This might help the PMs in their forecasts. Secondly, we are still establishing individual quotas from the top down. I've read many places that since we are paying these guys based on their accomplishing these quotas they ought to bear some responsibility for establishing them.

Incorporating Acquisitions

Leroy Harden described the acquisition process:

We've had enough experience at making acquisitions to have distilled a few generalizations. The process can be visualized in four stages.

First, James and I evaluate the opportunity in the context of our established strategy. Does this situation fit? Can it take us where we want to go? Next we enter a period of negotiating with the present owners as to the value of the firm. Being human, these owners generally want more than a firm is worth; sometimes they seem to expect us to pay them for value we intend to introduce by making changes.

The third stage is probably the most critical: that is to arrange for integrating an acquisition into Recreation Products, Inc. We take a *task force* into the new firm; usually someone from marketing, operations, and control. Each of these men analyzes the situation he finds and is responsible for developing an "action plan." This plan should tell us, in specific language, what has to be done to turn this company into a contributor to the company. We spend quite a bit of time as a task unit, preparing changes we believe necessary.

The action plans indicated what types of inputs RPI expected to inject into an acquisition, both in the immediate future and over the longer term. In most cases to date the immediate emphasis was on reducing general overhead expenses and instituting cost control measures in the plants. More significant were the sophisticated marketing ideas and techniques which RPI brought to bear; products were added and others discontinued to strengthen the line; some products were altered and improved to be more attuned to changes in the markets, and more emphasis was placed on providing retail outlets with data helpful in making their decisions as to product mix and space allocations.

Potential acquisitions could reach Messrs. Harden and Nicklus through a variety of sources. Product managers might suggest a firm for its addition of products to the existing line. Salesmen could pass back information on possible candidates. Outside sources, such as business brokers, etc., might supply leads. And Mr. Harden and Mr. Nicklus spent much of their time keeping up on possible acquisition sources.

Walter Grace contributed some thoughts on possible dysfunctions in the acquisition process:

I think we might be failing to gear up for longer term development of an acquisition. There is tremendous pressure to turn a problem situation around as quickly as possible because we can't afford the losses which could be incurred. We are committed to earnings growth, and we can't have our existing operations support a losing situation for long. As a result, we tend to cut it apart if necessary to accomplish our transition quickly.

While a change in ownership and operating procedures was bound to have an impact on existing personnel, the severity of the changes varied and could be considerably less disruptive than is implied above. In a typical company before acquisitions, much of the administrative work was usually handled by the owner and one or two assistants. On several occasions these people, who were often involved in negotiating the role, had elected not to remain with the company. Plant personnel were usually retained, although the force might have been reduced by some amount. Engineers and most plant supervisors remained with the firm. In most cases, the original companies relied on manufacturers' representatives for their sales effort. Therefore, no large sales force had to be disbanded.

RPI had not yet faced the difficulties of acquiring a larger company with a highly technical product line. They had not yet faced the situation of having to rely on existing managers for detailed market information, or on engineers for highly technical product and process characteristics. Mr. Grace commented on this subject:

As we grow and take larger firms, we will probably face the possibility of having to keep existing management. As we get further from where we are, we might in fact need them for their expertise to compensate for our not knowing the specifics of the business.

Implications of Growth

Many of the managers realized that a continuation of the rapid growth at RPI could mean changes in its structure or procedures. Thus, many had comments relevant to a discussion of the implications of this potential growth. Mr. Harden commented:

I devote quite a bit of time thinking about this. "Growth" for RPI means something distinct from what it has for most other firms, and even conglomerates. In addition to extrapolation of trends in existing products or markets, growth often means to us completely new markets. This usually means subsuming an existing firm, with its own ways of doing things, into our present organization. Whereas conglomerates normally operate new acquisitions as semiautonomous units, we incorporate them into our present structure. As we move further from our existing lines into leisure services, for instance, we will have to learn new tasks, develop new expertise. I think you'll agree, it's exciting and certainly very challenging.

I see growth forcing us to gradually replace our informal access to one another with more formal mechanisms. Not that we want to but I think size and distance will force us to. James and I will always want as much personal involvement as possible, but I believe size, and in time diversity, will force us to spend more of our time working with acquisitions and less working with the existing lines. In fact, hiring Paul Tepper is a step in the direction of providing for someone to monitor our established operations. Calvin McAdam will now spend more time working on acquisitions and special projects.

Our growth potential poses a unique pressure on James and myself, that is, providing the opportunities for our existing management team to develop and grow. We have been able to attract such talent by giving them responsibility and challenging tasks today, but also by promising them opportunities for more of both tomorrow. I personally feel a greater pressure to provide these opportunities than I do to perform for the "auction judges" of the financial markets.

The potential growth of the sales force at RPI was well planned, and in rather specific detail. The broad intention was for the size of territory covered by each man to gradually contract as he (1) penetrated more of the potential customers in his area, (2) carried more products and possible new product lines, and (3) convinced each customer to take more products from the lines offered. Indices had been developed to anticipate when new men were needed and where each new man would go. This planning for the force's expansion extended five years into the future and was closely watched for accuracy and relevance to the next time interval. Plans were also developed to add to the administrative capabilities of the sales force by adding additional levels of zones, regions, etc. Ralph Spiegel, director of marketing, made additional comments on the subject:

The potential always exists here for competition among the product managers for the resources of RPI, in several aspects. Already, I can see the competition for the efforts of the sales force. Arthur and I try to control this by translating the individual forecasts into a total forecast and insuring it can be met. The plans for expansion of the sales force are also designed to reduce this potential bottleneck.

A second potential bottleneck could develop, I feel, in competition among PMs for product development or capital expenditure dollars. Right now product development effort is allocated on a "first-come-first-served" basis. If a PM wants a new product, process change, etc., he will request a product from David Keller. David will accept projects which meet our established ROI criteria until his budget is exhausted. Thus, the only way we can determine priorities among products is to bring in James Nicklus. And yet we might want a disproportionate share of product development going into a product with greater growth potential, for example.

A final possibility is that the nature of our selling task will change as we grow, and as our sales force matures. Right now the effort is primarily on building the sales of a narrow line to a customer who bought it from the firm which we took over. A secondary emphasis is on developing new customers. As we mature, I think greater emphasis will be placed on getting a particular customer to carry all our lines. We will also find a way to get better information back from the field. And I think we might gradually increase our efforts in providing customer service. While we are prepared to provide such service now, many of our customers don't know yet how much help we can provide.

Another existing mechanism for providing for growth in the sales force was the unit bonus system for rewarding districts. Jim Grabowski, a district sales manager, discussed this:

We know that one thing which can seriously damage a salesman's morale is to have part of his territory taken away after he has cultivated it. We have tried to cope with this by placing a heavy reliance on the total effort of a *district* as the basis for determining bonuses. Then, as we contract these territories, we hope the transition will be smoother. This team effort feeling also helps keep my men from feeling they are alone in the field. I think it brings them one step closer to RPI.

Walter Grace, manager of operations for winter products, also commented on the ramifications of growth at RPI:

I don't think we are really geared up to provide for product introduction in the long run. I think this is because of our strategy of acquiring new lines by acquisition. However, we must continue to innovate with new products to remain competitive. Many of these innovations must come from within the present organization rather than by acquisition.

Calvin McAdam, director of operations, added his thoughts on the implications of growth:

I think we have to do two things with our people as we expand. First, James and Leroy will of necessity be less involved in ongoing operations. We have to compensate for their not being the final arbiter around here. More importantly, we still must attract capable people into the organization. This, I think will be more difficult than it has been in the past. We'll have less to offer in terms of growing with the firm, as most of us are the benefactors of getting in on the ground floor. Someday we'll have to attract people on the same criteria as does General Foods.

Torrence Industries (A)

IN JULY 1965, Robert Duncan, operations manager of Torrence Industries, Automotive Division, was considering whether he should extend the use of "manufacturing teams" throughout the division's Euclid Works (one of its three manufacturing plants). The idea for these teams had evolved from the creation of one team in September 1964 to deal with serious manufacturing problems in the compressor department of the Euclid Works (when this new product was manufactured for the first time). Bob Duncan felt that the team in the compressor department had enabled the general foreman of the area, quality control, production control, and the engineers (plant, factory, industrial, and product) to get together and solve major preproduction problems related to this new product. As he put it, "This approach has resulted in improving the operation of the pump department significantly."

He wondered, however, whether these teams would work as well in other areas of the Euclid Works and whether several teams could operate as well as this one had. He also wondered to what extent the "crisis atmosphere" surrounding the compressor team had contributed to the success of the participants in reaching joint decisions and taking action.

He was also concerned about how to proceed if he decided to form teams in other parts of the works. Should these teams be organized by product (as was the case in the compressor department) or by manufacturing process? At what level of management should he form these teams? Which of the functions in the works should be represented in the teams? Should he attempt to measure the effectiveness of these teams as control centers or in some other way? Finally, he wondered whether he should plunge into these teams throughout the works at once or on a more gradual basis—perhaps one team at a time? If the teams were successful in the Euclid Works, he could then extend them to the division's other two plants.

The Automotive Division

Torrence Industries, with headquarters in Pittsburgh, Pennsylvania, was a highly diversified company with annual sales volume in 1965 of approximately $900 million. Its products ranged from chemicals and plastics to electronic components to automotive and aircraft parts. The Automotive Division, which was headquartered in Cleveland, Ohio, at the Euclid Works, manufactured automotive parts. The three major products of the Euclid Works were rear axle assemblies, power drive assemblies, and automobile air-conditioning compressors. These parts went into automobiles, trucks, and off-road equipment. About 70 percent of these products were sold to original equipment manufacturers (OEMs), while the balance was sold as replacement parts. The replacement parts business was particularly important as it enabled the division to stabilize its manpower requirements in spite of the seasonal and cyclical swings of orders from original equipment manufacturers. Bob Duncan explained this:

The 30 percent of our gross in the aftermarket gives us flexibility in scheduling, which enables us to stabilize our manpower. We try to balance out the automotive cycle by using the down periods to build replacement parts for inventory. Only two men have been laid off in the past three years.

John Einhorn, the Euclid Works manager, indicated that the division was a product innovator in its field. Division product engineers developed new products, on which Torrence Industries held the patents. Torrence then sold the OEMs on using the products in their vehicles. Einhorn put it this way:

Most of our products are developed by our engineers. We figure how we have to manufacture the product competitively and make a profit. For example, the compressor was developed here, then sold to our customer. We like to think of ourselves as innovators in the industry.

Also important along with this innovative ability was the division's manufacturing flexibility. Bob Duncan stated: "One of our strengths is our ability to handle many variations of our product line at different volumes."

The organization of the Automotive Division is shown in Exhibit 1 and that of the Euclid Works in Exhibit 2. The functions of most of the departments in the exhibits are evident from their titles. However, some clarification is required apropos of the several engineering departments. The engineering department at the division level (Exhibit 1) was involved with product and development engineering for all plants of the division. The other engineering departments, as shown in Exhibit 2 (plant, factory, and industrial), were responsible for Euclid only. The factory engineering department was responsible for process development, process estimating, tool engineering, project engineering service, supply stores, tool building and tool maintenance. This department had an organized project engineering section under one supervisor covering the plant

EXHIBIT 1

Automotive Division Organization Chart*

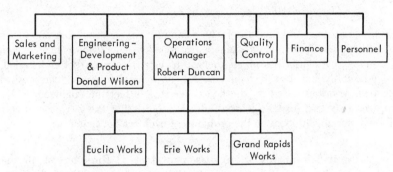

* Names appear only for persons mentioned in the case.

EXHIBIT 2

Euclid Works Organization Chart*

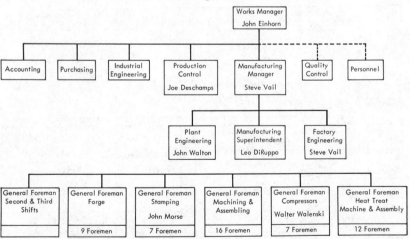

*The only change in the organization chart between 1965 and 1967 was that in 1967 one man was acting as both manufacturing and factory engineering manager. In 1965 he was only factory engineering manager. Dotted lines indicate division units which are operationally responsible to the works manager. Names are given for only those persons mentioned in the case.

based on their expertise by process, such as forging, stamping, machining, etc. The organization of this section had been altered to this arrangement during early 1965, so that there was now a factory engineer responsible for working in each area to which there was a general foreman assigned (see Exhibit 3): forge; stamping; machining and assembling power drive; compressors; heat treat, machining, and assembling axles. Steve Vail, manager of factory engineering, explained the thinking behind this change:

We just recently changed the factory engineering concept from one of division by expertise to matching engineers to areas of general foremen. I feel that the conflicts over priorities about the use of experts can be better handled if they (the individual factory engineer and the general foreman) can work out their own priorities based on the floors' needs. We feel the engineers will develop the necessary technical capability. We hope that this way the engineer will be better able to focus on the problems of each control center.

As Exhibit 2 indicates, there was a total of 51 foremen on all three shifts. Typically, each foreman supervised about 15 production workers. There were 1,250 management, engineering, and production personnel at the Euclid Works, the largest of the division's three plants.

EXHIBIT 3

Automotive Division

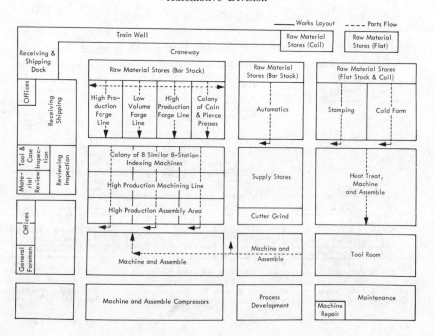

Leo DiRuppo, manufacturing superintendent, described how production workers were recruited and promoted:

Most of our skilled people (e.g., toolmakers) are production workers who worked themselves up to skilled. Our (Union) contract calls for letting production workers bid on the jobs in the toolroom. These guys go to school nights to learn the trades and then apply for the jobs in the toolroom. About 80 percent of the men in the toolroom started out as production workers. Ninety percent of the grinding department started in the shop.

Leo also explained that most of the production supervisors were high school graduates, many of whom had taken management courses at Western Reserve University. He concluded, "being a supervisor here is a tough job."

Manufacturing Technology

Euclid Works was located in a modern building with manufacturing space of approximately 300,000 square feet. Division engineering and other offices were located in another wing of the building. As Exhibit 3 indicates, the production flow for power drive assemblies, axle assemblies, and compressors was established through a planned layout program.

Jim Reasor, industrial engineering manager, discussed this as it related to the three major commodities of the works:

Our engineered layout combines some of the advantages of line production with some of the flexibility of a colony arrangement for machines.

The objective of the layout program is to have families of machines in one area which allow manufacturing expertise on common equipment [colony] and yet get the line approach for high production and low cost.

The general flow of material is from the vendors through receiving, receiving inspection into the craneway as raw bar steel, coil, and flat stock. The craneway runs the length of the west side of the plant and feeds the start operations, which transform the raw metal by hot forging–semihot metal forming, metal removal from bar stock, stamping in presses, or cold forming by use of coldheading machines. The material from the start operations is then stored, which permits optimum production scheduling of start operations and machining operations independently. Material is then released to the machining lines where little in-process inventory is carried until machining is complete. All components are brought together at assembly points which are related to the machining line. The total assembly is transported to shipping, which uses the same loading docks as receiving.

The planning of a colony-line layout along with the intermittent in-process storage areas for (a) start operations of forging, automatics, stampings, and cold formed parts; (b) machined parts through machining lines; and (c) sub-assembly and total assemblies allows maximum flexibility of using machines for high-production OEM runs and short runs for service requirements.

All planning and scheduling of production is based on EOQs (economic order quantities) for purchasing of material and EMQs (economic manufacturing quantities) for internal manufacturing.

The compressor production line was located in the southeast corner of the plant and was set up as a high-volume production line. This commodity was of limited part variation which permitted the machining and assembly operations to be joined together by automatic handling devices. The operators received the parts at close proximity to their work station, and the parts were automatically disposed of and transported by conveyors or chutes to the next operation.

In general, the plant has two commodities arranged in line-colony layouts which are highly flexible in tools, machines, and handling of parts to facilitate the many product and volume variations.

The third commodity, the compressor, is a relatively fixed designed product of high volume which permits a single-purpose high-volume line to be used for manufacturing.

The size of production runs for axle and power drive assemblies varied, depending upon whether the product was for OEM or the replacement market. Products for OEMs, generally, were manufactured in runs of 40,000 to 50,000 and could be scheduled through the plant on almost a production-line basis as they moved across the line-colony arrangements. Lots for the replacement market were usually much smaller, frequently in the range of 50 to 500 pieces, and these were handled more on a job shop basis.

In total, for all three commodities, 700 product variations were produced annually. This required, including replacement parts for past years, 5,000 different parts to be manufactured annually and an inventory of 6,000 parts. (Parts had to be inventoried for 7–10 years after their original introduction.)

Because of this number of parts, the addition of new service parts, and the annual model changes of the automotive manufacturers, about 25 percent of the jobs had to be retooled or modified at the Euclid Works each year. (This compared, for example, with only 3 percent at the Erie Works of the division.) This retooling in most cases involved a major floor change of the machine and the tools, and required the work of one of the factory engineers as well as the setup man. In addition, as regular job changes were made based on manufacturing schedules, setup men or setup and operators had to change the "setup" of the machinery to run current production requirements. This was especially complex in a number of areas where the processes were automatically controlled; for example, certain stamping machines.

Orders for products from OEMs were received on a monthly basis. As a result, some machines might have 40 setup changes a month. On other machines, there might be only four setups. According to Leo DiRuppo, manufacturing superintendent, efficient scheduling was crucial: "The secret of this business is getting full utilization of the machines on a five-day basis—keeping them running at all times, so we schedule them as tight as we can to reduce downtime for maintenance and repair. We don't want idle machines."

In addition to these setups, the manufacturing superintendent pointed out the importance on long runs of pulling drills and similar tools regularly, "say every 500 pieces to touch them up." According to DiRuppo this could be the difference between obtaining 1,000 or 10,000 pieces per drill.

Another important factor in the manufacturing process, according to works department managers, was quality. Close tolerances had to be maintained on most operations; often to 1/10,000 of an inch. Leo Di-Ruppo discussed this fact: "Quality requirements have really tightened in the auto industry in the past few years because of the safety program we are on. We have continuous surveillance inspection by the motor companies."

In addition to these factors, the case writer observed that managers were concerned about direct labor hours used, indirect labor hours used, tool costs, equipment maintenance costs, supply costs, etc. Charts reflecting these statistics were posted in the offices of the general foreman, plant superintendent, and manufacturing manager.

The Compressor Crisis

In the spring of 1964 the Automotive Division, in general, and the Euclid Works, in particular, were presented with a major challenge when a large-automotive customer, on short notice, placed a sizable order for a new air-conditioning compressor which had been developed and designed by Automotive Division engineers. While the division marketing group had been working on obtaining this order for several months, the customer was unable to make a commitment until the last possible moment.

When the order was received, several problems faced the division and the works manufacturing management to enable them to handle a program of about two million dollars investment in new machines and tools. At the release date of the program a special task force was set up.

Steve Vail, manager of factory engineering, described the functioning of the original group organized to cope with these problems:

The initial plan was to set up a separate task force to do all of the coordination and planning of this compressor, independent of the rest of the plant until the processing, machines, gages, prints, tools, etc., were resolved, purchased, and brought into the plant. This group was to carry the program through to its preproduction start-up phase and transfer responsibility to operating management.

This group included members from factory engineering and industrial engineering headed up by a factory engineering supervisor.

Everyone was expecting a reasonable start-up and integration into the works with some adverse effects, but due to customer schedule demands and short lead time, the installation time schedule and output requirements in terms of production coincided. The start-up was anything but smooth. Pressures began to build which caused a lot of apprehensions and severe problems. We were afraid that the total compressor program would falter. Prestige, capital investment—many things—were at stake.

The initial task force was not getting the job done. The program lagged. The task force did a creditable job of planning, but when it came to transferring and implementation of these plans, decisions and actions were too slow. The lines of communications and the organization of the original task-force group were not adequate to cope with the new set of conditions in conjunction with the normal complement of manufacturing supervision.

Leo DiRuppo indicated how different the compressor was from other works products: "Compressors were completely different from what we were used to doing. We were shipping a finished unit that had to be 100 percent tested as a completed unit."

The addition of this product meant quickly finding space within the Euclid Works for this department (see Exhibit 3 for compressor department location). It also meant that there were numerous engineering and technical problems which had to be solved. Not the least of these was the installation within three or four days after delivery of the major piece of equipment—a $250,000 housing drilling machine. Other new equipment had to be installed, and new processes such as lapping and grinding had to be mastered. All of this had to be done quickly, as the order required Euclid to reach a volume of 1,000 pumps a day by early September 1964. As Bob Duncan said later:

This problem required extremely close coordination—much closer than we had to exercise before. We had to go through a learning curve to train people, try out tools and machines, make engineering design changes while accelerating our build from 0 compressor on August 1 to 1,000 compressors per day by September 1. We had to manage better, shorten the lines of communications, make decisions, and take action faster.

To deal with the problem, Donald Nelson, vice president and division general manager, asked Bob Duncan to get into the problem personally.

Steve Vail, manager of factory engineering, described this:

At the time, Bob Duncan tried to evaluate the problem to determine ways of getting faster decisions and action. He tried to deal with the problem by setting up an organization which drew on the total capability of the works. He corralled a total capability—an expediency on a temporary basis which he structured informally so as to get decisions and actions quickly. He got together a special group of experienced production supervisors and engineers who could deal with the preproduction problems. This group included members from manufacturing, factory engineering, industrial engineering, plant engineering, production control, quality control, and product engineering. The original task force, which had a basic function of planning the process, tools, machines, etc., got into trouble at the preproduction stage during the start-up. That's why Mr. Duncan structured the 24-hour effort in the initial phase.[1] It was quite a strain on everyone because there was so much to do and no time for grooming the machines. There were lots of problems which required communicating and analysis of many factors—tolerances, equipment capabilities, schedules, etc., so that everything could move ahead.

Leo DiRuppo, who was a member of this new group, recalled the stresses associated with the compressor start-up:

We got pretty close to this compressor. I came in at 7 A.M. on a Friday and left at 8 A.M. on Saturday because our production schedules were continuing to go up and we had to ship 1,000 compressors a day. We worked a lot of seven-day weeks of 7 A.M. to 10 P.M. Lots of times there would be six or seven calls waiting for me when I got home and I'd turn around and go right back.

By November 1964, many of the major problems were solved, and Bob Duncan and other members of the team became concerned with turning the compressor operation over to others. Steve Vail described this process:

All this time, Bob Duncan was keenly aware that we were discovering a new management technique and he kept notes and memos in a log, so that after we were over the hump (and it took a long time), we could pull out all the top-management group and turn the job over to an operating team. So, we decided that the way to do this would be to move in a capable general foreman, and we chose Walter Walenski and gave him his team which would continue to provide direct assistance on problem solving. Since the compressor was still hot, the compressor team had a privileged position in getting support from all departments in the works.

Thus, the compressor temporary team evolved into a manufacturing team for the compressor department with Walter Walenski acting as chairman. Other members were an industrial engineer, a factory engineer, a production control planner, a quality control engineer, and a plant engineer. This group met early each morning to consider immediate problems. Any problems which the group could not handle were taken up with higher management since Bob Duncan and the works manager were still very concerned about pump production capabilities and high costs.

---

[1]This was the procedure by which the group established priorities each morning as to what problems had to be solved within the next 24 hours.

Walter Walenski described how the compressor project team had improved the problem-solving process:

> With plant engineering—when shutdown schedules were necessary—it was easier to schedule machine repair and predict the impact of machine downtime. Likewise, since the factory engineering man was also there, he scheduled in his major fixture repairs or tool changes during the scheduled downtime. At the outset we had so many machines that were being modified and repaired that it would have been very hard to get things done without close coordination. For example, the quality control man would have to be scheduled to check parts to make sure that repaired machines could produce quality pieces.
>
> The compressor was more complicated and needed much more coordination than we ever needed before. It was impossible to do this with the old management methods. The problems had to be brought out in the open so that everybody could tie into them and get them resolved.

From many comments such as this and from his own firsthand experience, Bob Duncan was convinced that the team concept had played an important role in turning the compressor operation into a profitable one. His interest in extending the teams to the other parts of the Euclid Works was a result of an awareness among division and Euclid Works managers that a number of difficulties were being encountered in other areas of manufacturing in getting decisions and action on operating problems.

The Situation in 1965

Steve Vail discussed his view of these problems:

> I am very anxious to see if teams could work in the rest of the plant, because 24-hour problems are eating up so much of my time that I want more of these handled by lower levels of management. I am faced with a lot of long-range tooling and capital programs which I know have to be handled well, or they will be 24-hour problems next year. What we need is a means of giving the general foreman the service capabilities to correct 24-hour problems and to directly participate in longer range planning for his area.

Leo DiRuppo was also concerned about the role of the general foreman:

> They (the general foremen) spend a lot of time trying to get assistance from the services, and then following up. They spend time just expediting. Often there are conflicts with each other over the services of engineers.

John Walton, plant engineering manager, also was concerned about the situation:

> I spend one heck of a lot of time following up inquiries from people. We have no adequate measuring stick for assessing what actually is important.

... I spend 100 percent of my time on the "now" problems and have little left over for looking ahead.

Bob Timmons, a production planner, indicated that his function could be done better and could supply more information to those who needed it:

Most of our time is spent formulating a schedule based on customer requirements only, not considering the shop problems. We could do a better job if we knew more about which machines were down, where we were having quality problems, what purchasing deviations there were, etc.

Bob Duncan summed up his thinking:

I know we have many problems at Euclid and the other plants upon which action is not obtained quickly enough because decisions are too slow, due to long lines of communications and the limitations of the formal organization. However, we have learned something from the compressor experience. We analyzed our organization to improve the things that kept us from handling problems more effectively. My question is could this knowledge help in other areas of the plant and in the other plants of the division?

Torrence Industries (B)

In the fall of 1965, Bob Duncan, operations manager of Automotive Division of Torrence Industries, decided to begin extending the team concept throughout the Euclid Works. Subsequently, the concept was extended to the division's other two works, so that in the fall of 1967 manufacturing teams were operating in all three works. This case provides a brief summary of the team approach as it was developed in the Automotive Division, a typical example of the team's functioning at the Euclid Works, as well as a summary of the managers' reactions to the teams in the fall of 1967.

In a paper delivered to a professional association, Bob Duncan spelled out the team concept as it existed in 1966 and the ideas which had been used in its development:[1]

The Team Concept

We have three works of the division using the team method in an informal organizational arrangement. One of the major purposes of this approach is to get increased participation in making decisions at all levels of the organization. The concept is operated considering two time requirements for effective management:

1. Daily decisions required to get action on problems affecting production flow. The group effort is 24-hour action oriented.
2. Intermediate and longer range decisions which require greater planning and organization. The group effort concentrates on good planning.

The plants are divided into areas, or control centers, which have four specific team efforts:

1. *Manufacturing floor team.*
2. *Project team*—for each control center.
3. *Management coordinating team*—composed of department managers, manufacturing managers, and plant managers.
4. *Special teams*—which are designed to resolve specific problems.

---

[1] "Plant Management Practices: Organizing the Manufacturing Team for Results," Machinery and Allied Products Institute, Meeting, October 10, 1966.

The successful development and installation of our team method has been due to:

1. Clearly stated principles of operation which define what we are striving to improve with our team approach.
2. A good formal organization program at each works which is the framework for the informal team approach.
3. The recognition that the team method is an integral part of our total management improvement program and is tied into our objectives, formal organization, communications systems, controls, plans, and programs.

The major design principles used as the basis for the total plan of operation are:

Predetermined Objectives

Sound objectives are all important to the organization. Great emphasis is put on making our objectives clear, definitive, and feasible; and achievement is accomplished by organizing and motivating people. Objectives are used to determine the actual organization.

Decision Making

The requirement to make decisions is emphasized throughout the total organization. We indicate to all our people that decisions are the way issues are resolved at every level of management. The emphasis on decision making is encouraged to stimulate the request for authoritative knowledge on the subject involved. Decision making is considered the most important management responsibility which must be facilitated, recognizing that we compete with only approximately one-half dozen resources:

1. The workers and executives employed who make the decisions.
2. Information available to them for making decisions.
3. The money and finances available to them.
4. The equipment and processes in their plant.
5. The materials used to produce the product or service for the company.
6. External services which can be purchased from other organizations.

As these six basic elements are studied to see how profits can be made, the two most important factors for a substantial competitive edge are the resources of manpower who make the decisions and the information upon which decisions are made. While money, equipment, facilities, materials, and outside services are important, it is assumed that any one of these can be matched by a competitor since they are available externally and are physical in nature. Our basic competitive edge seems to lie in the hands of people bringing together, guiding, and allocating the company's resources for certain objectives, and the information upon which these people base their decisions. The critical edge in the total competitive marketplace is geared to the quality of the decisions made by the management and all employees of the organization and represents the reason for our designed approach.

Authority and communications are established to support decision making. Our objective is to channel and direct our abilities to make decisions by establishing planned objectives, and establishing an organizational structure through which rational decisions can be exercised by those concerned. *Since the decision-making ability of the people is considered the crucial element for efficient operation, it is the entrance of all levels of people within the organization in making decisions that is strived for and governs the participating aspect of the people.* Participation is considered a key to some of the human relation problems which arise from organizational limitation.

The extent to which problems and decisions move up and down is an administrative policy. We attempt to decentralize location of decisions at or near the place where the problems arise; in other words, limit upward referral. This policy increases the participation of people at all levels, and upward referral is geared to management-by-exception principles.

Organization

The organization and organizational relationships are set up to translate sound objectives into plans, then programs, then specific projects, and individual assignments.

The formal organization structure is planned, reviewed, and used similar to drawings that precede the construction of a machine, having circles or squares representing flow of materials, communications, and paths of authority and decisions. Our objective is to develop a dynamic organization on a well-planned basis, capable of adapting to change.

The oversimplification of the organization structure is recognized as a fundamental cause of poor management and poor employee relations. In the development of a formal organization, the number of different departments and subdepartments and the extent to which activities of both the individuals and groups are segregated considers investment, commodities, specialization, span of control, number of people, centralization versus decentralization, and unique area problems. There is uniformity of organization structure between works which permits the easiest application of the tools of management, of setting objectives, communication systems, controls, etc.

What I have said about organization so far relative to the formal organization is to stress that a good formal organization is required as a basis for the establishment of an informal organizational approach, such as the team method.

Our plants are instituting some important changes in patterns of organization by loosening the structure through the creation of a more informal arrangement. Among the devices being applied are project management, task forces, and management team concepts.

Four Distinct Levels

The team concept is divided into four distinct levels:

1. *Manufacturing Floor Team.* There is as great a need for effective decision making and efficient communications at the floor level, as there is at other levels of the total manufacturing organization. The floor level includes the hourly direct and indirect people and their immediate foremen.

The objective is to have a manufacturing organization that provides for effective decision making on the shift foreman level, coupled with an efficient communications system and well-conceived floor management techniques.

The approach used in the organization of the team on the floor is not as a *fixed* team but one that involves a team approach to any group of people involved with a floor problem. The people that can make up a "floor team" include an operator, a jobsetter, a floor inspector, an expediter, a project engineer, one or more skilled tradesmen, and the shift foreman of the department where a problem exists.

The shift foreman is the team leader. It is his responsibility to assemble a team of people to take action on a problem. The team is informal, and its identity as a team is limited to the problem at hand. It is dissolved as soon as the problem is resolved.

The minimum number of people in a "team" is three, and the maximum is seven. The maximum team is seldom used.

The meeting of the team is an on-the-feet meeting at the problem machine and lasts only long enough to get all the input into the problem, establishing direction, timing, and covering any other essential communications. The team may be called together several times before a tough problem is finally resolved.

2. *Project Team.* A project team approach is used at the next higher level of management and tends to optimize the ability to make decisions, take action, and produce results.

The nucleus of the concept is the establishment of a management organization designed for maximum effective delegation at the general foreman level.

A project team is assigned to *each major manufacturing control center* and supports the shift foreman floor teams. It corresponds to the areas of accountability of the general foreman.

Each project team consists of:

1. The general foreman who acts as chairman.
2. An industrial engineer who acts as secretary and covers industrial engineering functions such as work standards, layout, material handling, and budgets.
3. A project engineer who covers the factory engineering functions which include process engineering, tool and gage design, manufacturing development, and tool maintenance services.
4. A production control planner who handles specific machine scheduling and inventory control and part shortage problems.
5. A quality control engineer or quality foreman who covers the quality functions, particularly the analysis of quality problems.
6. A plant engineer or foreman who covers the general machine and plant maintenance services.

The goal of the project team organization is to make each manufacturing area a self-sufficient control center for problem solving.

A good organization in itself is not necessarily sufficient to produce the maximum results. A good management operating plan combined with a well-defined communications system is essential.

This is how the project team operates:

1. Each project team meets daily at 8:15 for 15 minutes. The meetings' purpose is to review the immediate floor problems so that decisions can be made at their level of management each day. Each project team member

makes his notes and reports to his direct-line supervisor on an exception basis, after the project team meeting.

2. Each project team holds a weekly meeting called the team planning meeting. The purpose of this meeting is to review longer range problems, set priorities, and plan corrective action. Specifically, the agenda of the meeting is as follows:

a) Organize action to correct the three most important problems in the control center.

b) Identify and review the action to correct the three most critical machine problems in the control center.

c) Identify the three problem tools in the control center and initiate corrective action.

d) Identify and review the action to correct the three highest cost variances in the control center.

e) Review capital items which are assigned to the area from the works capital program.

f) Organize and set priorities for other problems within their area of responsibility.

3. The project team concentrates on the top priority problems within the control center, applying the management-by-exception principle. The input to the planning meeting comes from the shift foremen, hourly people, other meetings, etc. It is their responsibility as a team to organize, identify, set a priority, assign responsibility, indicate action dates for each specific problem to get the greatest gain for the control center. Since the team planning meeting is rather comprehensive in scope, time is not available for intensive problem-solving which must be done outside the meeting.

3. Management Coordinating Team. Each department manager expedites his particular area of responsibility, based on information supplied by his members in the project teams. The input information covers such things as manpower position, critical production bogies, inventory safety banks, machine call-ins, major tool problems, purchased material shortages, etc. The key to the success of the meeting is the quality of the information used and the ability of the managers to bring forth decisions needed and the next action to be taken to move a problem. The meeting is conducted rapidly, emphasizing the decisions necessary to:

1. Designate the top priorities for corrective action of the major production flow problems of the last 24 hours.

2. Set priorities for corrective action of the major high-cost problems of the last 24 hours.

3. Isolate the potential downtime problems of the plant which need attention now.

4. Authorize money, projects, and overtime necessary to support the actions to be taken.

5. Assign problems which require follow-up and more detailed organization.

The daily management control meeting is held each day from 9:15 to 9:45 A.M. in the cafeteria conference room. The managers report in the following order, in three to five minutes each:

> Plant superintendent
> Factory engineering manager
> Plant engineering manager
> Quality control manager
> Purchasing manager
> Industrial engineering manager
> Production control manager
> Note: The product engineering manager also attends.

To facilitate the meeting, the following general rules of operation are used:

1. Items have a priority set by the manager reporting the problem. The priority can be changed at the meeting based on the total needs of the works.
2. If the problem is covered by standard service communications, it is not brought up in the meeting.
3. Items of a repeat nature are presented for decision.
4. Items which need immediate follow-up are discussed.
5. New problems are discussed.
6. If the manager has the problem in control, then he doesn't consume time in the meeting by presenting it.
7. The plant manager summarizes the top priorities of the plant, requesting each manager to call him by four o'clock if a problem has not moved satisfactorily.

4. Special Teams. On a number of occasions, such as a major capital program or a major manufacturing problem, a special team will be organized to handle the problem.

A prime department is assigned. An individual is designated as chairman, and the task force is organized around detailed objectives and a plan to complete the job. The efforts of this group are communicated and directed through the meeting system; but it is the individual contact of engineer with engineer, working toward a common, well-defined goal, which gets the results.

This type of team may work on the problem together, have weekly or bimonthly coordinating meetings for a period of six months. Then, when the need for emphasis diminishes, the group project effort can be dropped and normal control and follow-up take over.

Any team may schedule a "Special Action" meeting at any time. The action meeting is held as needed, possibly only once, and its purpose is to organize specific action on a problem requiring greater management emphasis or special technical expertise.

The teams may also set up a series of "Special Meetings" that are held at predetermined intervals to establish a continuous follow-up on an action program after the initial organization. The special meeting is discontinued when it has accomplished its specific purpose.

In Summary

1. The team organization establishes self-sufficient coordinating units for each major manufacturing area and coordinated emphasis on major problems.
2. It establishes participation of representatives from all major functions for solving the manufacturing problems (informal organization).
3. The team approach has demonstrated a significant improvement in decision making at all levels, but particularly at the floor management level.
4. The team approach has resulted in accelerating the response time for taking tangible action on immediate problems and has improved the planning of longer range problem corrections.
5. It tends to become a leveling factor where problems become "we" rather than "they" problems.
6. It has improved total management communications at all levels.
7. It has motivated team participants, improved morale, enhanced the status of the members, and improved the working relationship between the manufacturing floor and staff departments.
8. It has freed the department managers from some day-to-day problems, giving them more time to spend on longer range planning.

One recent addition to the team procedures at the automotive division was the emphasis on a formal procedure for setting priorities on maintenance, tools, quality, and other problems. Using maintenance problems as an example, all maintenance problems were to be given a priority designation based on a "number" and a "letter" system. The "numbers" listed below were to be assigned, primarily, by production control directly or by implication through the foremen of the area involved, according to the seriousness of the problem relative to production flow and customer demands.

Problem Type

1. *Critical (as soon as possible)*—There are no alternatives. Maximum action required to get production.
2. *Moderate action*—Very important; but by using overtime, other machines, or outside purchase we can live 4 to 24 hours. Any time the foreman or production control list a "2," they will also indicate a need time.
3. *Minor action*—Less important at the moment and, ordinarily, can wait for maintenance planning for the next weekend. Any time the foreman or production control lists a "3," they will also indicate a need time.

The letter designations, which were determined by plant engineering, indicated the estimated time required to make repairs:

Time
A. *Major* (over 24 hours repair time)
B. *Moderate* (4 to 24 hours)
C. *Minor* (0 to 4 hours)

All problems rated "1" were to be brought to the project team daily to assign action. All "1's" were also reviewed at the management coordinating meeting to make sure specific action was being taken. Special action meetings were called for all "1's" not satisfactorily under control.

Announcing and Implementing the Team Concept

While this was the established practice for team operations by the fall of 1967, the approach to introducing the teams to the rest of the Euclid Works and the other works (from 1965 through 1967) had been very gradual and almost on a trial-and-error basis.

Steve Vail described this approach:

The idea occurred to us to try out the team concept in the other manufacturing areas. The project engineers were already assigned by areas, and this facilitated the idea. The idea then evolved to form a team for each general foreman. Initially, we met for 15 minutes each morning on a very informal basis. We approached it on a "well-let's-try-it" basis.

Bob Duncan described his thinking about the teams:

We started with the team in pumps, then with other areas at Euclid, and finally in the other works of the division. I feel that it is very important that the team be considered by its members as an informal device—a device to be reevaluated and improved. We still have a lot of work to do to use our people effectively. I don't want to leave the impression that the system is complete. What is good today is not good enough tomorrow. This is a gradual approach to altering organizational practices.

John Walton, manager of plant engineering, discussed the introduction of the new maintenance priority system:

Ultimately, we want this [the priority system] to be used by the shift foreman on the floor. In this way, he will be able to indicate the degree of importance of his problem to my dispatcher. Our use of this is only 10 weeks old. We were hesitant to start with the shift foremen right off the bat. We elected to start off using it at the general foreman level first, so they would understand it.

Leo DiRuppo, manufacturing superintendent, also emphasized the gradual approach as he described the spreading of the teams and other new managment practices to all parts of the works:

We started first with the 24-hour problem meetings, then added the long-range meetings (such as plant layout, new orders coming up, etc.) on an every-two-week basis. Bob Duncan explained the whole setup to the other areas. He was the boss and he told us what he wanted. There was no question in our minds. He worked hard to sell it. The way you do this is a little at a time. For example, with the new priority system, it started in compressors, and when it got going it was started in the cold form area. It whet the appetites of the other people. It's like anything else; you've got to seed it. Another example —the Torrence maintenance program. We started in an area where there were good operators, proud of their work. It will be a success there. Now, operators come up to me and ask when they'll be starting it.

Finally, Steve Vail explained how the works coordinating effort had evolved:

The management coordinating team developed much later than the project teams. It developed because we had a need to communicate upwards and get decisions on problems which the project teams couldn't handle. The timing of the works management and the project teams just didn't fit in. The emphasis on improving our *total* operating efficiencies put pressure on the need for a higher level team to act faster on problems passed on to them, and to do for the total plant what the teams did for each area—set priorities, etc.

The Teams in Operation

In October 1967, on a visit to the Euclid Works, the case writer had an opportunity to watch some of the teams in operation. On a Tuesday morning about 7 A.M. he joined John Morse, one of the general foremen, on his rounds of the cold-forming manufacturing area. John walked directly to the shift foreman's office and checked the log (a record of critical events kept for all shifts). The shift foreman walked into the office and discussed with John a quality problem on turnbuckles (a component part) produced on the second and third shifts. John then continued reviewing the log, making notes, and asking questions of the shift foreman.

John then left the shift foreman's office and walked through the area. As he moved along, he was approached by people on the floor several times. All of these encounters were brief and businesslike. His tour took him to a cold header machine, which was down because of a burned-out cam bearing. John had earlier expressed concern about this machine, because it was a critical machine to keeping production flow going. At the cold header machine, John met a plant engineering shift and general foreman and discussed the difficulties they were having in removing the bearing. They had pulled half the bearing but could not get the other half free. From here, John continued his tour, discussing a number of other maintenance and similar problems, including the need to redesign the coolant system on a machine. In this case, he informed a plant engineer that since it was not a 24-hour problem, he would bring it up at the next project team meeting on longer term issues.

John then returned to the office shared by all the general foremen. He worked on paper work and talked over a mutual problem with another general foreman. At 8:10 A.M. John left his office and headed toward the cafeteria where all the project team meetings were held. Throughout the cafeteria there were clusters of men around tables. John joined his group, who waited a few minutes for the industrial engineering representative to arrive. The other members present were the production control, quality control, plant stores, factory engineering, and plant engineering representatives. John started the meeting by discussing what he felt were the major problems on the floor. He reported that the cold header was still not completely apart and asked Doug (the plant engineering representative) to bring the team up to date.

DOUG (plant engineering representative): It's still our number one problem. We're not sure why we're having trouble getting the bearing out. Our men are going over the prints a second time now. And even when we have it out, there might still be more to the problem than that.

JOHN (stamping general foreman): Well, when we do get it out, we should make sure that the entire unit is looked over to see if there are any other damaged parts which might have caused the noise we were getting on that diagnosis you had made before it broke down. The other thing that bothers me, Doug, is why didn't the fail-proof lube system work? Why didn't it shut the machine down before the bearing went . . . ?

RAY (factory engineering representative): Yeah, that's what I don't understand. That has got to be something we pin down before putting it together again. . . .

DOUG: Yeah, you're right. It shouldn't be hard to check it out for other damage once we get the other part of the bearing out. And the lube system should be checked out at the same time. [To the general foreman] I still can't give you a completion time on either of those items because I don't know how long it will take us to get the bearing out. But I'll get back to you by 10 on it one way or another. I think we should have a fix on the extent of the damage by then.

JIM (production control representative): Well, we can't move fast enough on it. It's a critical machine and it's affecting the production flow on one of our major components. I really think it should receive a number one priority all the way upstairs. I'd be really interested in keeping posted on the timing of that so that we can readjust the schedule to phase it in as soon as we can. Our stock position is still good for eight shifts, but we've been drawing off the banks for four shifts now and we'll reach a limit on it. So we can't stand still on it.

JOHN (stamping general foreman): Well, it's our number one priority. I'll talk to Leo [the plant superintendent] about it to see what we can do to push it at the management coordinating meeting.

The group then went around the table, with each man introducing matters about which he wanted to inform others and wanted to indicate what was happening to the problem. These included other machines which were down, the problem of getting a new die, and a quality problem.

John summed up the meeting: "To sum up, the hottest thing today is the cold header. Doug, you'll get back to me and production control on its status?" He then listed three other priority items.

DOUG: O.K., I'll get to that [the cold header] and give you its status by then.

JOHN: O.K. Thanks, gentlemen. Meeting's over for today.

After the meeting ended at 8:35, John met with Leo DiRuppo, manufacturing superintendent, and they discussed the cold header problem briefly. Leo's greatest concern was the lack of progress that plant engineering had made in pulling the bearing out, especially since they were not yet sure of the damage to be found inside and how long this might keep the machine down. He promised to start his report to the coordinating committee on critical problems with this issue.

At 9:15, the works coordinating committee met. It was chaired by John Einhorn, works manager, who asked Leo to start by giving the manpower status. Leo DiRuppo reported that they were currently behind 900 hours for the week due to a manpower shortage. A discussion of this followed. Leo then reported on quality problems; and John Einhorn, Leo, Steve Vail (manufacturing manager), and the quality control manager discussed the unusually high number of quality problems from the previous day.

Leo then brought up the problems he considered top priority by area:

In the stamping area our highest priority is still the cold header. It's still down, and we don't have the other part of the bearing out. This is something we've got to get a fix on today. We can't keep it in a torn-down condition. This machine operates three shifts and is one of the few machines in the whole plant that we operate on Saturday. This is a number one priority that we have to get some action on today.

[To John Einhorn:] I'm giving it a 1A. I don't think we should leave it an A because it's too critical. I'm not satisfied with it as it stands now.

STEVE (manufacturing manager): [To John Walton, plant engineering manager:] How about Universal Machine Engineering Service?[2] Can't we call them in to give us a hand? What's our problem? Is it jammed?

JOHN WALTON: I don't think it's jammed. We've got Alex Carson [an engineer] looking at it now and we're going over the prints again. Alex thinks we can handle it. We've gone far enough into it so that I think we should try to finish what we're doing now before we call Universal. Give me another four hours to get the second bearing out.

STEVE VAIL: O.K. That sounds O.K. Can you let me know your status by noon?

---

[2]A firm that distributed and repaired this type of equipment.

JOHN EINHORN: I agree we can't sit on this. John Walton, why don't you give Steve a breakdown on its status by noon. If we are not making satisfactory progress, let's get Universal in here.

LEO: That sounds good to me.

JOE DESCHAMPS (production control manager):   If we run into any delay on this work beyond a few more days, we have to make alternate plans for the parts, because we're into our banks for four shifts so far. We'll have to put one of the other cold headers on it. And this will be tight because they're all busy.

JOHN EINHORN: Steve, if this looks like a longer delay, let Joe know. Why don't you be ready [Joe] with some alternatives for tomorrow's meeting if the machine is going to be down for an extended period.

JOE DESCHAMPS: O.K. I'll get [one of his subordinates] on it if it looks as if we'll be delayed too long.

Leo continued to go over bogies on critical machines by areas.

JOHN EINHORN: [To John Walton:] John, what's your status today?

JOHN WALTON: We've had 136 maintenance calls in the last 24 hours. Ten of them were number ones. Of the 136 we have four which are not in control. The 7491 press is probably the hottest. [He then gave a description of its status.] The 3151 [the cold header] which we've already covered is our second one. The 3227 surface combustion furnace in cost center 36 is the third. These are new reports since 7 o'clock this morning. (A discussion on these machines ensued—taking about two minutes for each machine.) That's it for me.

John Einhorn then raised an issue with regard to another machinery problem. After this, the group discussed the scheduling difficulties raised by these machinery problems. In this discussion, Leo, Steve, and Joe took the most active parts.

The quality control manager then made his report and there was a discussion between Steve, Leo, John Walton, Don Wilson [product engineering manager], and the quality control manager, about the reject problem.

Next, Don Brown, the purchasing manager, made some comments about the effects of a steel hauler's strike, indicating that he foresaw no problems yet. Joe Deschamps then briefly discussed the manpower needs for starting up the pump department, which had been down because of an automotive strike. He also discussed areas where they had failed to meet schedules during the previous day.

At the conclusion of the discussion, John Einhorn raised an issue: "How about the surface combustion furnaces in general?"

JOE DESCHAMPS: We still have one operating though two are down. But if the last one goes down, I'm in real trouble, John.

JOHN WALTON: That's not reported.

JOHN EINHORN (checking on a page in front of him):   The second one's not reported as down. Why is that?

They then discussed, without reaching a conclusion, why this was not reported. Joe got up and used a telephone in the room to determine why the second furnace had not been called in. He asked his subordinate to make sure that it was down as reported.

After this, only 30 minutes after they had started, John Einhorn began to summarize the meeting:

I'd rate our number one priority the 3151 cold header. Did you check that second surface combustion? I'd give it second priority. With one down and one going down, these furnaces must get rolling again. The cold header needs action today. Give me a date as soon as possible on that, John [to John Walton].

He then gave directions to people around the table on items they should follow up for decision which had to be made that day. Joe Deschamps then briefed the group on assignments of people in his organization. At the end of this, John Einhorn said: "Thank you gentlemen, that's it for today." The meeting quickly broke up.

By the next morning the case writer learned that the other part of the cold header bearing had been pulled. No other damage to the machine was found. The new bearings were to be delivered the next day, and the machine was expected to be in operation within 48 hours.

Reactions to the Teams

All of the managers and engineers involved were enthusiastic in their support of the use of teams. For example, Leo DiRuppo pointed to the fact that the teams made everyone feel more involved:

Now we are able to take care of more problems because people are made accountable for them. Now, we have a factory engineer in each area who's flexible. He can handle design, methods for operations, and tool problems. They're also spending more time on the floor. We have much more immediate service on the floor. In many companies, the factory engineer comes in and reads a paper or does something which is nice but not necessary until he gets his first call, but our men go out on the floor to be ready for their team meetings. It makes them feel responsible, and services are where we need them on our problems.

The plant engineering or factory engineering guy makes a decision on the spot. People are more responsible and don't go running back to their boss for a decision. It's a good system. If I was 20 years younger, I'd go to other companies to start similar teams. We're getting more people participating in the plant on the problems.

Leo also indicated that the teams made his job easier:

It [team concept] has made my job much simpler because I find I now have all the information on the big problems coming right to me. The decisions are made by people who are capable of doing something to improve the situation. They identify the problems. They have experience and with the teams they're able to get all the answers. In the past, I was on the floor 95% of the time.

Steve Vail made a related point:

The teams permit action on the necessary decisions early in the day. This now frees my time because they've made these decisions, set priorities, and communicated them in less than an hour. They've got much of the routine out of the way to concentrate on planning and handling other problems.

The biggest thing to me about this team concept is the time that it's given me to concentrate on planning. It has freed me from the many, many things that tied me up before. Someone else is doing them and they're being done well. Sometimes I feel that I'm not needed, but that's a good position to be in because you can manage the bigger picture which will reduce the 24-hour problems next year.

John Walton made a similar point:

The teams reduced drastically the need I had for finding what the correct actions were to take on many smaller problems. Now other people do this. It's permitted me more time to do forward planning. Before the teams, 100% of my time was spent on the "now" problems and little was left over for looking ahead. Whereas before I spent a lot of time helping to solve and define the problems, now many subordinates are in a position (because of their contact with all of the factors involved through the team) to define the problems and move on solutions. The team has allowed them to get greater exposure that before only the managers had.

Bob Timmons, a production planner, indicated that the teams were enabling him to do a better job of planning:

Before, I was satisfying a scheduling requirement by formulating schedules based on customer requirements only. I am still very much aware of customers' needs, but I am doing a lot of things now which aren't part of the scheduling function per se, but things which affect the schedules in the plant. I am doing a lot more forecasting than before and assisting in planned machine downtime. I can do this better, because of a more intimate and immediate knowledge of the product, the process, the customer requirements, and the on-the-floor manufacturing difficulties.

The general foreman and engineers expressed the same enthusiasm as their superiors:

The teams are a mechanism whereby a general foreman can outline a problem, take action, and follow up the problem at his level.

. . . . . .

What the team does for us [general foreman] is it gets more help from the service areas because each of these guys participate in their team. They identify with the direct manufacturing area and try to get something done to help the team effort.

. . . . .

We've structured the informal organization so that we are crossing lines of authority to get the information and action that's needed.

. . . . .

Most of the teams take pride in their areas. For example, they meet to review their performance and to compare it with other teams' performances.

. . . . .

It saves time rather than uses more time because you commence with seven guys all at once rather than calling seven guys on the phone.

Bob Duncan stressed a similar point in indicating that the teams actually saved time:

Our bogie at the department manager level is to spend no more than 40 percent of our time in meetings of all types. We think this compares favorably with what goes on in other companies.

He also pointed to one unexpected benefit from the teams:

One of the things we got out of this approach is the ability to train other managers. Our division has supplied many management people to other divisions of the company.

Bob also indicated that the effects of the teams showed up clearly in division operating statistics and in the profit and loss statement.

Perhaps the most comprehensive list of the advantages of the teams which led to these results was provided by Bob Timmons when he wrote down the following list for the case writer:

TEAM ADVANTAGES

1. Instant communications with all team members.
2. Logical scheduling around specific problems—scheduled machine downtime.
3. Logical scheduling of special runs (new parts—alternate machining methods).
4. Concentration on most important problems (immediately affecting material flow).
5. Recognize upcoming problems and projects for sequencing.
6. Review past day's performance and potential problems for the upcoming day with emphasis on getting something moving.

Samantha Sportswear, Inc.

SAMANTHA SPORTSWEAR, INC. was a well-established manufacturer of women's clothing, with an annual sales volume of approximately $22 million. Samantha's two divisions—Junior Girls' and Women's—were organized as separate product lines and distributed on a nationwide basis. The sportswear items were manufactured at two locations in Pennsylvania and marketed through offices in New York.

In October of 1967 the management of Samantha Sportswear met to consider reorganization of their sales force. A decrease in sales volume, dissatisfaction on the part of several salesmen, and recent management changes had led them to question several aspects of their selling organization. One recent organizational change had involved the resignation of Jason Grant, who as manager for the Women's Division of Samantha Sportswear had directed the selling effort for that product line. Bernard Kasdin, who had previously done the merchandising for Grant's division, had been assigned to his position, and one purpose of the meeting was an attempt to clarify Kasdin's responsibilities. Present at the meeting were Sam Stein, president of Samantha; Carl Lowe, executive vice president; David Zweibel, vice president of sales; Dan Rubin, manager of the Junior Girls' Division; and Kasdin. (See Exhibit 1 for organization chart.) Kasdin began the meeting by asking:

What am I to do and how can I do it? Right now I've got both merchandising and selling. I can't handle both jobs. Let's start from scratch—how do we organize the division?

We have the most complex sales management in the world. Any temporary thing is bound to make it more complex. Primarily, I think these things should be clear-cut. We should be thinking about who do we want directing the sales force a year from now and start now. My own personal capabilities are in merchandising, and I think sales and merchandising should be split.

Another recent organizational change—the advent of "vertical selling" —had caused some confusion in the administration of sales. Historically many Samantha salesmen had carried only one division's products, but in the past year Zweibel had assigned several of the Junior Girls' salesmen to carry Women's as well, on the theory that greater selling efficiency would result from reducing a salesman's territory and giving him both divisions to carry. This new arrangement had involved a reshuffling of many salesmen-supervisor relationships. Dan Rubin was opposed to the vertical selling approach, since he felt that a division manager should push his own product line, and thus be responsible for sales in his division. Kasdin, however, was only concerned with the management aspect of this new selling strategy:

It's really the man, not the vertical or single setup, that spells out success. Should we have sales managers for singles or verticals?

Lowe spoke at this point:

This organization can't be done poorly, either. This is the fourth season in a row when sales are considerably less than the same period a year before. If this continues, we're in serious trouble. It's a matter not of conjecture but of necessity. It's hard to talk to a salesman when his income is on the downturn.

Lowe went on to describe the difficulties the company was having at that time with one of their salesmen who had suffered a great loss in income over the past year. He was now demanding a higher rate of commission and a position as regional sales manager. Lowe wondered if Samantha should have regional sales managers or not, and if so what they would contribute to the firm. Another question related to this was whether established, professional salesmen or novices should be used to break in a new territory. David Zweibel offered his opinion at this point:

I have a strong feeling that if you're investing money in expanding territory you do it with professionals, not amateurs. I think the question is do we go with the guy who will make us the greatest total profit and not worry about his rate of commission?

EXHIBIT 1

Organization Chart, October, 1967

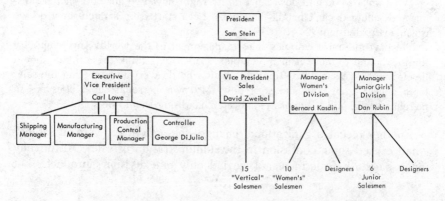

No one sales manager can control 40 salesmen. And that's what my job says I should do. We need regional sales managers.

Lowe then asked Mr. Zweibel who would represent management to the other parts of the organization—manufacturing, the distribution center, etc. Lowe stated his definition of the job:

The sales manager's duties should include sales promotion, managing the showroom, supervising new men in the field, reviewing the performance of each salesman and deciding what action to take.

Bernard Kasdin added to this:

He should also select the salesmen and work with promotions, with production, and he should set up administrative policies which will insure proper distribution.

Also, I think it is important in whatever we decide on to allow for getting feedback from the field. I'd like feedback on what's selling and what's not. It would help me merchandise.

Here George DiJulio, comptroller for Samantha, expressed a need that he saw for a strong marketing attitude in sales management:

We don't have a sales management which is oriented to retail needs. Sales does not have a sufficient voice in manufacturing. We must realize that Samantha can't sell everything the mill makes.

We need top marketing and sales management. We need a fresh approach. We should investigate all routes. Why do we lose accounts? Where is the retail business to be had? Should we have big store men and little store men?

DiJulio felt that a marketing-oriented manager who obtained feedback from the salesmen on current selling patterns could predict fashion trends more accurately than Samantha was at present able to do, advise manufacturing accordingly, and thereby enable the mill to produce more salable merchandise:

Could it be assumed that much of the knowledge about the direction of the new season was present at the retail level last season? Could the look or the color trend have been evident based on last season's retail check-out? I submit that it was there, and that we should have been aware of it.

Carl Lowe disagreed with DiJulio on this idea:

You can't escape the fact that this is a fashion business. Fashion means the public will buy something that's different, and feedback looks backward. What you're trying to do is say what happened yesterday is going to happen again tomorrow. You cannot forecast this way in the fashion business.

History of the Selling Organization

Samantha Sportswear, Inc. manufactured and sold both girls' and women's garments. When the firm was organized in 1947 around a knitting mill in Indiana, Pennsylvania, Samantha was primarily a manufacturer of wool sweaters, and the owners felt that as a manufacturer Samantha was able to control the quality of its product. As the company grew, other wool and synthetic items were added to the Samantha product line. Synthetic and woolen yarns were spun, dyed, and knit at the Indiana mill; cut and sewn wool garments such as skirts and slacks were manufactured at a factory in Wharton, Pennsylvania; and cotton and synthetic cut and sewn items were subcontracted. These garments were designed, marketed, and sold through offices in New York. In 1965, sales volume for Samantha Sportswear had reached $22 million.

Samantha Sportswear was organized as two divisions: (1) Junior Girls', including garments for junior sizes 5 to 15; and (2) Women's, consisting of items in ladies 8–18 sizes. The Samantha product line included wool and synthetic knit sweaters and swimwear, wool and cotton dresses, and sportswear (skirts and slacks); however, Samantha was generally described in the clothing industry as a skirt and sweater house. These garments were designed in basic and fashion styles, and generally in coordinated colors, that is, matching or complementary tops and bottoms.[1] Volume percentages of the two divisions for the 1967 holiday line were as follows: *Junior Girls'*—43.4 percent and *Women's*—56.6 percent.

Knitwear was produced according to three main buying seasons: spring, back-to-school, and holiday. Colors and fabrics were adjusted to seasonal weather and fashion; for example, swimwear and shifts were included in the spring line, and skirts and sweaters in fall colors were emphasized for back-to-school.

The Selling Organization

At the company's inception three salesmen, David Zweibel, Arnold Greenberg, and Robert Zimmerman, carried the Samantha line (Zimmerman carried only Samantha Junior Girls'). Dan Rubin, an early member of the firm, was largely responsible for the development of the Junior Girls' segment of the business. As Junior Girls' manager he handled marketing, merchandising, and sales for the division. Jason Grant was hired in 1960 as sales manager for Women's; Bernard Kasdin handled merchandising for this division. Salesmen, however, retained almost complete freedom in their operations. No formal sales training program existed, and both Rubin and Grant devoted considerable time to their marketing and merchandising responsibilities.

In June of 1965 management of Samantha settled on a new approach to the selling function. David Zweibel, who had been the company's out-

---

[1]"Basic" refers to the more conservative, timeless styles, such as crew neck Shetland pullovers and cardigans; "fashions" refers to more extreme styles in unusual knits and colors, such as fisherman knit sweaters or the "poor boy" sweater.

standing salesman, had offered his services as a market specialist for Samantha, to work with and train salesmen in the field. An arrangement was made whereby Zweibel would become vice president of sales and work in test areas with salesmen in an attempt to realize the full sales volume potential of a particular area. In addition he would evaluate salesmen, advise management on sales organization, territorial divisions, and commission arrangements, and make recommendations for future management in the area. It was agreed that once an area was assigned to Zweibel the salesmen would report directly to him. Prior to this all salesmen who sold Junior Girls' exclusively reported to Rubin and Women's salesmen reported to Kasdin.

As a result of his experiences in the test areas, Zweibel in 1966 decided to introduce the concept of vertical selling to the sales force. Although many Samantha salesmen had historically carried only one line, Mr. Zweibel felt that a more efficient system would be to reduce the size of a salesman's territory and give him both divisions to carry. George DiJulio explained that reactions to this arrangement had been mixed:

Through David Zweibel we have just had a year of "vertical selling." Women's salesmen were given smaller territories and the Junior Girls' line.

Perhaps one of these ideas [smaller territories] is good, the other not so good—maybe giving them two lines places a further limitation on how much territory they can cover.

Sales territories ranged from one to five states in size, and boundaries were usually consistent with state lines. Exhibit 2 shows the organization of the sales force in 1967 according to territory and division. Territories as they were assigned were sufficiently large that management felt there was a great untapped potential in many states. For example, Saul Hochman, who was of Samantha's top salesmen, was selling Samantha goods to 48 stores out of a possible 408 stores in his territory. DiJulio asked:

What is a manageable territory for a man? Territories respect tradition and state lines. Perhaps they should be broken down into trading areas.

The Samantha line was carried by 31 men in 1967: 6 Junior Girls' salesmen, 10 Women's salesmen, and 15 salesmen who carried both divisions. Records showed that Samantha depended on several high-performing salesmen for a large percentage of sales. Greenberg and Zweibel accounted for 25 percent of Samantha's total volume in 1966, and Zimmerman and Hochman added another 16 percent (out of a total of 23 salesmen). In several cases one salesman had control of a critical territory. DiJulio commented:

Take Greenberg—if he left, Samantha could stand to lose a large number of its accounts. Samantha has no backup salesmen.

EXHIBIT 2

Salesman Activities in 1967

Salesman Code Number	Territory	Percentage of 1966 Sales	Office	Assistants	Divisions
1	... Kentucky, W. Virginia	1.1	–	–	Junior Girls' and Women's
2	... Washington, Oregon, Idaho*	1.0	Yes	–	Women's
3	... N. Carolina, S. Carolina, Virginia	1.6	–	–	Women's
4	... Massachusetts (except Boston and Springfield)	3.0	–	–	Junior Girls' and Women's
5†	... Indiana	–	–	–	
6†	... Connecticut, Providence, R.I., Springfield, Mass.	–	–	–	Junior Girls' and Women's
7	... So. California	0.09	Yes	One	Women's
8	... W. Pennsylvania	2.7	–	–	Junior Girls' and Women's
9	... Montana, N. Mexico, Utah, Idaho, Colorado, Wyoming, Nevada*	1.5	–	–	Women's
10	... Delaware, Maryland, Washington, D.C., Virginia,* Pennsylvania*	12.6	–	Two	Junior Girls' and Women's
11	... Wisconsin, Iowa, North and South Dakota, Minnesota	6.8	–	One	Women's
12	... Alaska, Oregon, Utah, Montana, Idaho, Colorado, Washington, Wyoming	2.8	Yes	–	Junior Girls'
13	... Ohio	5.2	–	–	Junior Girls'
14	... Arkansas, Texas, Louisiana, Oklahoma	4.7	Yes	One	Junior Girls'
15	... Wisconsin, Minnesota, N. & S. Dakota, Iowa,* Nebraska	3.3	–	–	Junior Girls'
16†	... Texas	–	–	–	Women's
17	... Kansas, Iowa, Mississippi, Illinois	4.0	–	–	Junior Girls' and Women's
18	... Maine, New Hampshire, Vermont, Rhode Island*	2.3	–	–	Junior Girls' and Women's

EXHIBIT 2 (*cont.*)

Salesman Code Number	Territory	Percent-age of 1966 Sales	Office	Assistants	Divisions
19	... New Jersey, Long Island, Westchester County, N.Y.*	5.8	—	One	Junior Girls' and Women's
20†	... New York*	—	—	—	Junior Girls' and Women's
21	... Ohio	4.7	—	One	Women's
22	... N. Carolina, S. Carolina, Virginia	3.8	—	—	Junior Girls'
23	... Illinois, Indiana, Missouri, Kansas, Nebraska	1.8	—	—	Women's
24†	... Kansas, Iowa, Mississippi, Illinois	—	—	—	Junior Girls' and Women's
25	... Michigan	5.5	—	One	Junior Girls' and Women's
26	... Alabama, Tennessee, Mississippi	1.5	—	—	Junior Girls'
27	... Arizona, Nevada, New Mexico, California, Hawaii	9.0	Yes	Two	Junior Girls'
28	... New York,* Massachusetts*	12.9	—	—	Junior Girls' and Women's

*These states are divided between two or more salesmen.
†Salesmen who have been with Samantha one year or less.

And Hochman—his customers are Saul Hochman's customers, not Samantha's.

Although these "star" salesmen reported to their respective division managers or to Zweibel, it was generally conceded by management that the top four or five salesmen, who accounted for nearly 50 percent of sales, were not controlled by anyone.

Volume for a particular territory was projected according to the Buying Power Index.[2] (See Exhibit 3 for Samantha sales volume in relation to this index.) Salesmen were paid on a straight or sliding commission basis. The average compensation was 6 percent of sales, and this rate was considered relatively high for the industry. Although the majority of

---

[2]The Buying Power Index (BPI) is a composite index computed by *Sales Management* magazine from median family incomes broken down by counties and cities in the United States. The BPI was used as a benchmark for sales projections by management of Samantha.

salesmen earned 10 to 20 thousand annually in commissions, top salesmen earned up to $110,000.

The Salesmen

Each salesman operated in his own territory, working out of his home or an office. Salesmen with larger and more successful territories were encouraged by management to hire assistants, whom they compensated from their own funds. All costs involved in selling, such as advertising, travel, and entertainment, were met by the salesman himself. (See Exhibit 1 for a list of which salesmen had assistants and/or maintained offices.)

During the three main selling periods, which lasted approximately five weeks each, salesmen were "on the road," since accounts could be anywhere from 10 to 1,000 miles from their homes. The back-to-school line was sold from March 5 to May 30; holiday from August 25 to September 30; and spring from October 25 to December 10 and from January 2 to February 10 (the "split road" occurred in the spring line selling because the tendency was for stores to buy light initially and place heavy reorders).

Salesmen were concerned with two basic activities during these peak selling periods: (1) creating new business by selling new accounts, and (2) obtaining substantial orders from established accounts. Salesmen looking for new accounts in department stores called on a buyer or merchandise manager with samples or "bait" only after researching the store to ascertain which departments were not completely stocked with merchandise from a competing line. The following comment typifies the attitude of Samantha salesmen concerning this facet of their job:

I try to convince him [buyer or merchandise manager] that Samantha is necessary *after* I have seen that department. You have to use common sense to figure out why you should be in that department—your merchandise has to dovetail with what they have already.

After selling merchandise to an account, an order for the amount of goods desired was written up and sent to the mill in Indiana. According to their "first-in, first-out" policy, goods were delivered according to the earliest order date, regardless of the size of a shipment.

Between selling periods salesmen were free to service their accounts, counting stock and writing reorders.

Changes in the Business

Certain changes in the garment and retailing field seemed to affect the Samantha salesmen. Due to a tendency toward more specialized buying

EXHIBIT 3

Analysis of the 40 Primary Trade Areas of the United States

Trade Area	Women's Ready to Wear Percentage of U.S.	Department Store Sales Percentage of U.S.	Ideal Index Women's Ready to Wear and Department Store Index°	Percent of Samantha Sales
New York	16.2	11.4	12.2	10.8
Los Angeles	5.2	6.7	6.5	3.6
Chicago	4.5	5.5	5.3	2.4
Philadelphia	4.0	4.2	4.1	5.6
San Francisco–Oakland	3.5	3.3	3.3	2.9
Detroit	2.8	3.6	3.4	1.5
Boston	2.5	2.7	2.6	4.0
Cleveland	1.1	2.5	2.2	1.5
Washington	1.6	2.2	2.0	3.0
Pittsburgh	1.5	1.8	1.8	1.7
St. Louis	0.9	1.7	1.6	1.2
Dallas–Fort Worth	1.1	1.5	1.4	0.6
Minneapolis–St. Paul	0.8	1.6	1.4	2.9
Houston	0.9	1.3	1.2	0.6
Baltimore	0.8	1.4	1.3	1.9
Milwaukee	0.8	1.2	1.1	1.2
Seattle	0.8	1.3	1.2	0.9
Miami	1.3	1.1	1.1	0.1
Cincinnati	0.6	1.0	1.0	0.7
Kansas City	0.7	0.9	0.9	0.7
Buffalo	0.9	0.8	0.8	1.4
Indianapolis	0.4	0.9	0.8	0.8
Atlanta	0.8	1.0	1.0	0.7
Denver	0.7	0.9	0.9	1.4
San Diego	0.5	0.9	0.8	0.4
Portland	0.5	0.8	0.8	0.4
Columbus	0.3	0.8	0.7	0.5
Rochester	0.5	0.6	0.6	1.7
Hartford	0.4	0.8	0.7	1.3
Dayton	0.3	0.7	0.6	0.6
New Orleans	0.7	0.6	0.6	0.4
Toledo	0.2	0.5	0.5	0.4
Louisville	0.4	0.5	0.5	0.5
Providence	0.9	0.5	0.6	0.7
Charlotte	0.6	0.4	0.4	0.8
Syracuse	0.5	0.4	0.4	0.9
Phoenix	0.3	0.5	0.5	—
Albany	0.6	0.4	0.4	0.3
Oklahoma City	0.5	0.4	0.4	0.3
Grand Rapids	0.3	0.4	0.4	1.1
	62.0	69.7	68.0	62.4

°From *Sales Management* magazine.

in the stores, salesmen found that they could no longer depend as much on personal and business relationships which they had built up with buyers over the years. Individual store buyers were being given less authority, and merchandising managers became more involved in the buying decisions. Larger stores had become "number oriented" in their evaluation of sales performance, and salesmen were affected in several ways. Bill O'Mahoney's description typified the position of Samantha salesmen in this situation:

It used to be that buyers bought everything—one woman at [a large mid-western department store] bought all the sportswear. Today there are seven buyers and two merchandise managers.

The buyer today is strongly supervised. Samantha is correct in using me almost as a product manager in this situation—it enables me to talk more effectively on the merchandise level if necessary, rather than in a salesman-buyer relationship.

In Ohio [a department store chain] used to have one store—now they are spreading all over the state. They will probably have eight or nine locations within the next few years. I must have a larger sales concept.

Buying is centralized. The buyers are no longer on the floor. I get to know more about what's going on on the floor than the buyers. I now talk on a divisional level because of the dollars involved. The risk is greater, but also the opportunity for service is greater.

A more recent development concerned the "fashion" aspect of the industry. Department store customers were buying more fashion merchandise, and buyers discovered that the basic styles which had always been reliable sellers were providing less and less of total sales. Fashion and novelty numbers suffered the greatest markdown, however; and buyers were anxious not to be overstocked in these items. They tended to play it safe by placing smaller initial orders on fashion merchandise and reordering individual numbers which turned out to be best sellers.

The volatile nature of fashion trends made it almost impossible to predict what was going to retail most successfully. Samantha conformed to the new buying patterns by expanding its line to include fashion numbers; concern about end-of-season closeouts, however, caused Samantha to stop production of fashion and novelty items first. Because it took eight weeks to complete a sweater, Samantha had to anticipate reorders and manufacture sufficient quantities to fill them, but this production policy prevented Samantha from accommodating many reorders. The firm could not exist solely on its basic sweater business, and several people felt that there was a definite need for an ability to predict these trends. As was mentioned earlier, George DiJulio explained that he felt a salesman who was aware of the retail situation could feed back information to the design and merchandising staff at Samantha, thereby enabling Samantha to make "the right merchandise early enough to make timely deliveries with a minimum of closeouts."

DiJulio felt that Samantha's successful salesmen were successful because of their ability to inform buyers on fashion trends, and that they acquired this ability to predict fashion by observing the retail situation. He cited Arnie Greenberg as a prime example of this ability:

> In evaluating our sales force, if you will, I believe that you might agree that Arnie Greenberg has enjoyed very healthy increases in volume over the years; and I feel that these increases have been due principally to *his awareness* of retail check-out and his subsequent pressure on design and merchandising to come up with a style and/or color story which suits a retail trend.

DiJulio added that an ability to predict best sellers or "runners" would enable Samantha salesmen to convince buyers to purchase these numbers in greater depth initially.

Motivation of Salesmen

The case writer asked each of the salesmen interviewed what they enjoyed about selling and what satisfactions or frustrations they found in their profession. The following are comments from salesmen rated as above average by management:

1. Every season it is a new ball game. If you sell an item and it performs well, this is exciting. I love to sell—I don't care if it's shoelaces, I can sell it.
2. If I'm not a self-starter I shouldn't be in this business. I like the peaks and valleys approach of this kind of selling, the thrill of selling a lot and selling effectively. Busting it, and then really staying away when it's all done. The bit of smiling at them everyday is not for me.
3. The biggest hang-up most guys have is that they can't stay away from home. They can't force themselves to get away for a trip before Monday noon and they're back for the Thursday night card game.
4. I love people. This is the best business in the world for me. I love the entertainment part of it. You have to have a minimum amount of ego. I want to make it a success. This drive has worked out fabulous.

One of the newer salesmen rated by management as having above-average potential, said that he enjoyed being "a free agent":

> It's a great business because it is up to you. You don't have to go to your boss and say "I want a raise."

One of Samantha's salesmen, accredited by management as being "perhaps the best in the industry," explained his feeling to the case writer:

> I enjoy building stores—departments. I get satisfaction out of seeing the large sales—building a structure—getting customers excited about me and my

product. There must be personal incentive. I like to generate numbers—see the line moving.

Salesmen ranked as average made the following comments:

1. I enjoy meeting people and there is satisfaction in putting goods in a store and seeing them walk out—this verifies my judgment.
2. Working an account up from 10 to 40,000 is satisfying, and then going to a store and seeing your goods check out. Selling a store is an accomplishment, but it is not the fight when you go into a store and you are presold. People are glad to see you. The struggle is minimized when goods check out.

Salesmen rated as below average answered as follows when asked what motivated them to sell:

1. Money. The only reason for working is for survival. I work for security.
2. Dave (sales vice president) says I don't enjoy traveling on the road—he's right. I enjoy being home with my wife and friends. It gives me some satisfaction to sell, but my satisfaction is primarily money.

(See Exhibit 4 for background information on individual salesmen.)

Individual Selling Methods

When questioned individually about their selling methods, all salesmen agreed that although they could show their samples in a store, they preferred to set up their own showroom in a hotel. The selling process was more difficult when done in a store, since the buyer would be continually interrupted and samples had less eye appeal if shown in a dark, crowded stockroom. All salesmen were careful to sell conservatively to a new account. Arnie Greenberg explained this attitude to the case writer:

You don't take the shortsighted view—what you want to do is give them what they can sell. A store wants to invest the least amount of money possible and make the most profit. I would rather sell them a lot of one number that I think will go than several of a whole lot. I prefer to argue with the customer over this—it boils down to the performance of the thing.

Most salesmen, particularly the successful ones, felt that their ability to know a store's needs and advise buyers on fashion trends and merchandising matters was an essential selling point. Their success in obtaining reorders depended upon the store's success in selling Samantha. Bill O'Mahoney, one of Samantha's above-average salesmen, talked about his concern with merchandising:

I have developed the idea of myself as a Samantha merchandise manager to sell a total concept. . . . I take the merchandising view of selling. You must feel the needs of a store before you can actively fill those needs. This is the only way you can really establish a rapport.

One of Samantha's top salesmen was adamant on this point:

You must give the buyers the ammunition they need. I don't give them all the sales baloney—you should say logical things and have the customer's perspective constantly before you. You must be able to sell buyers things they can sell.

EXHIBIT 4

Background of Samantha Salesmen

Name	Age	Place of Birth	Number of Years with Samantha	Educational and Professional Background
W. Baker	40	Paris, Kentucky	3½	Boston College and University of Rochester; formerly with a major sportswear house.
Kenneth Burns	29	New York, N.Y.	2	Colgate College; formerly with two major women's clothing manufacturers.
Alan Caldwell	32	Portland, Oregon	3	University of Oregon; formerly with an electrical supply firm.
Edward Capello	51	Kansas City, Mo.	4	Washington University; formerly with a sportswear manufacturer.
Robert Edison	50	Bronx, N.Y.	1	New York University; formerly with a toy manufacturer.
Ray Folger	45	Camden, N.J.	3	Formerly with a major sportswear house.
Al Goldman	47	New York, N.Y.	17	Formerly with a dress manufacturer.
Joseph Gordon	47	New London, Ontario	5	Ontario Business College; formerly with a sportswear house.
Arnold Greenberg ...	39	New York, N.Y.	14	Columbia University, Bard College.
Saul Hochman	42	Bronx, New York	7	University of Wisconsin; formerly with a ladies' clothing firm.
Henry Isenstein	49	Knoxville, Tenn.	20	Formerly with Knoxville Deposit Bank.
Abe Kahn	49	Houston, Texas	10	Texas A. and M.; formerly with a sportswear house.
Mort Katz	39	Cleveland, Ohio	4	Western Reserve University and University of Florida; formerly with a sportswear house.
Albert Kievman	32	Washington, D.C.	8 mos.	Boston University and Georgetown University; formerly with a large eastern department store.
Stanley Laufer	56	New York, N.Y.	20	Formerly with a knitwear firm.
Reuben Levy	41	Manchester, N.H.	2	Harvard College; formerly with a knitwear firm.
Larry Litwin	58	Brooklyn, N.Y.	16	Queen's College; formerly with a knitwear firm.
Thomas McCoskry ...	43	New York, N.Y.	1	Hofstra College; formerly worked as an assistant to David Zweibel selling Samantha.
William O'Mahoney ..	42	Columbus, Ohio	7	Princeton University; formerly with a large midwestern department store.
Sidney Samuelson ...	56	New York, N.Y.	11	Formerly with a children's wear firm.
Barnett Sanders	38	New York, N.Y.	4 mos.	University of New Hampshire; formerly with a sportswear house.
Mark Simone	29	Pittsburgh, Pa.	3	Formerly with a major sportswear house.
John Starr	31	Michigan	4	University of Hawaii; formerly with a knitwear firm.
Ben Turner	31	Camden, N.J.	4	University of Florida; formerly with a ladies' shoe company.
Robert Zimmerman ..	40	San Francisco, California	17	Yale University, USC; formerly with a family-owned retail business.

The more successful salesmen all stressed the importance of special services in establishing a mutually beneficial relationship with a buyer. The following are typical comments on buyer assistance offered by salesmen rated as above average by management:

1. Show a buyer you have everything they need—become important in that department. Performance is the key to reorders. I take time to hold breakfasts and meetings with sales personnel, describe new yarns and workmanship, train sales help.

2. I write 99 percent of my orders—I give the buyer a full presentation, but I do the actual package they buy. Retail it for them when you write it up.[3]

3. In many cases they don't know what will be hot. You have to tell them. You have to know the reason for a look, a fabric, etc., and be the firstest with the mostest.

4. They [the buyers] have to believe you're looking out for them. Build up confidence—they know that if I say it's good it is.

One top salesman outlined his approach to the case writer:

We compete against every manufacturer for every dollar the buyer has. I'm competing for one third of her time with 1,000 salesmen. I have to be the most important salesman in the world. She has to see that I have something to give her.

You have to be concerned with the store's relations with customers, so I train salesgirls, run fashion shows, and check ads.

One salesman ranked as average by management described his method of servicing stores this way:

There is a lack of information between buyers and salesgirls—the salesgirl doesn't know what she is selling. Salesgirls have to be shown. I show them how to sell, and I give things away to them, too, as an incentive. You have to sell your goods to the salespeople first.

Salesmen ranked as below average by management put less emphasis on service. The following are typical comments:

1. Store management would like salesmen to do their nonproductive work—arrange fashion shows for them, train salesgirls, etc. This is a waste of my time. They want free help.

2. In regard to meetings with salesgirls, merchandise managers, etc., lots of guys do this but I don't think it helps. Anyone can tell a pink sweater goes with a pink skirt—salesgirls don't need to be told all this. Just get them to sell your merchandise.

---

[3]Although the usual practice was for buyers to make their own decisions on the composition of a merchandise order, some Samantha salesmen preferred to "write the orders" themselves—that is, make the decision for the buyer on what and how many numbers to buy for their department.

Several successful salesmen talked about how they differed their approach to dealing with smaller stores:

1. The small specialty store buyer wants performance—he has the payroll to meet. He worries about the little reorders, not about having lunch with you. When you are good he is more loyal, but when you are bad he hates you.
2. Small store operators are very different. With him you don't pussyfoot. You have to handle all the little things so they don't feel small. You have to be smart enough to dance with all of them.

Role of Entertainment in Selling

Salesmen for Samantha admitted that entertainment and personality were a definite part of selling activities. John Starr, a top salesman, stressed this point in his interview with the case writer, explaining how he established good relationships with his customers:

The whole game is personality and getting close to them [buyers]. A good 75 percent of them are personal friends of mine, and with this kind of relationship you can work weekends with them. I also go back after the selling season and bullshit with them.

A big portion of my business is entertainment. Always have a customer to lunch. I don't care how much he does. I give gifts—men's alpaca sweaters, pens, desk sets—during the year, not at Christmas. You've got to be ready to lay down $2 to make $5.

I love the entertainment part of it. You've got to be a good time Charlie. If you don't have this kind of personality you'll have problems.

Reputation is very important. To make a reputation you have to be a sport with new guys in the territory. For example, you have to help a new salesman carrying a noncompeting line by giving him help in finding a house, directing them to possible accounts, etc. It all gets back to you because they will put in a good word for your line with buyers.

A salesman thought to be ineffective by management gave this opinion of personal contact:

It doesn't hurt to put some interest in a buyer, but you shouldn't get too friendly with them. It just takes up time.

The Buyer

The case writer interviewed five buyers in large metropolitan department stores to establish their impressions of the salesman's role, and more specifically to find out what influenced them to buy a particular line. Miss Morgenstern, buyer for the size 5–15 girls' department in a major store, had been buying for 30 years. She commented:

The main reason I buy a line is the merchandise—this is number one. A salesman might influence me in a situation where I was considering two lines of equal quality, but I like to keep myself open.

Mrs. Shore, buyer in the same department in a competing store, concurred: "My buying starts with merchandise."

Miss Fernald, buyer for the preteen department of a very progressive, fashion-oriented store, had been a buyer for three years. She was quite adamant about her reactions to a "sales pitch":

I don't like a salesman who comes in and starts talking—telling me about his firm's incentive plan, markdown, etc. I want to see merchandise. And if it is not the right merchandise for my store, I don't care about their delivery system, how they will pay 50 percent if we run an ad, or any of these things. This annoys the hell out of me.

Miss Morgenstern explained that she did not rely on salesmen but shopped in New York in March, September, and January for her merchandise:

I buy in New York at the shows—I shop *all* of the lines—I cover *every* resource. During these days I shop from 9 to 9—this is a very valuable opportunity for me to see everything that is available. It is also a good chance for my assistant buyers to meet all the salesmen.

Mrs. Shore and Miss Fernald both stated that they did not accept assistance from salesmen in making a buying decision. Miss Fernald explained that she accepted help in this regard from only one salesman that she had known a long time, and whom she felt had helped her a great deal in her profession:

I look at all the merchandise and then I buy. I decide how much stock I want to start and end with. Dave Zweibel is the only salesman who helps me decide how much. I know the percentages I want, and he figures out how much of what merchandise should go to which store. Essentially he helps me with the arithmetic.

Mrs. Shore, who bought for the same store, explained how she did her buying:

I work on a plan basis—I figure out the numbers and break them down by stores.

I don't rely on a salesman's advice on what to buy. Often they don't know market trends. They know their own line but not the whole market. I might ask him what he is booking best in other stores, just to get an idea.

The case writer asked the buyers if they had felt any changes in the industry, and if so, how these had affected buying patterns. Miss Morgenstern explained:

Today everything is fashion. It used to be that everything was basics—we could carry 10 styles. Now we have 40–50 styles.

Our main line is Samantha—we have carried it for 20 years. There is customer acceptance with a brand name, and we know it is good quality. However, buying patterns have changed. We no longer buy 80 percent of our stock early—we reorder.

We find that a large house like Samantha can't deliver. We have to order Samantha eight weeks in advance, but smaller firms which carry fewer items are quicker. For novelty items we use small houses.

Miss Brodie, a ladies' sportswear buyer in the same store as Miss Morgenstern, had been at her job for two months. She concurred with this approach:

We get novelties from other houses. It takes eight weeks to knit a sweater, and with a big company they stop cutting their fashion items first and we can't reorder them. So we use other smaller companies for this fashion resource—they can deliver reorders.

All the buyers interviewed agreed that this situation existed, but several dealt with it differently. Miss Fernald explained how she met the problem:

Eighty-five percent of our stock is fashion merchandise—it turns over very quickly. By the time you reorder an item and get delivery on it, it is too late and the customer doesn't want it anymore. Instead I am always looking for something new from the market.

Mrs. Shore explained her attitude about fashion and reorders:

I realize that I can't reorder from a big firm like Samantha, so I place the initial order in depth. They made up a kilt skirt out of a certain plaid especially for me, and I know I can't get any more of them.

You only sell something once. In a branch store, especially, if you have the same customer coming in once and twice a week, she has seen a coordinate group and bought it. The next time she comes in she is looking for something new. I reorder basic items and *types* of things—for example, striped knit dresses.

One change in retail operations which was brought to the case writer's attention was the new "numbers" approach to buying. In past years buyers were able to choose quite varied items for their departments, knowing that everything would sell eventually. However, in recent years stores had begun to evaluate the retail check-out rate on a day-to-day basis, with an objective of fast turnover. Because of this system, buyers had to acquire the merchandise which was currently in greatest demand; the more unusual, slow-selling items were relegated to specialty stores and boutiques. Miss Fernald explained the system at her department store:

There are nine stores involved in my buying decisions. I have a book here, with one column for last year's sales and another column for this year's. I have the figure for November 27 last year and I will fill in today's sales figure next to it. As you can see, some days I am over last year's figure, other days we go in the hole. Also, every two weeks I get a breakdown which shows my department's sales, profit, gross intake, markdowns, etc., for this two-week period this year and last year. This year I am behind—business is bad in skirts and sweaters, and all the sales are in the dress department.

You can't buy off the top of your head—I have to have a plan, some solid basis for my buying decisions. Then I can start buying.

The case writer asked buyers what influenced them favorably in regard to a salesman. Miss Fernald explained her attitude:

I like a salesman to be interested in the store, to ask about our problems with deliveries, to give me information I can use in meetings—for example, new ideas and techniques for selling.

One of our salesmen is a young man who puts on shows for the buyers and salespeople. Instead of just showing his merchandise in the traditional way—holding it up and saying this is such and such—he is very imaginative. One time he brought out a model who was wearing a pair of slacks, seven skirts, seven sweaters, and a blue blouse. He proceeded to undress her, and everytime he removed something, her outfit was still well coordinated.

The following are typical comments from other buyers:

1. I like to get a salesman's advice on what to buy—they know what's what, and it behooves them to tell you because they make their money on re-orders. Also I need the salesman to count inventory—I expect that. I can't be on the floor all the time—I can't keep track of everything.
2. Every little bit helps.
3. The main thing I expect of a salesman is that he be well informed. I don't want him insulting my intelligence with his sales pitch.
4. A salesman has to have my confidence. A large metropolitan department store has buying power—we are a big store, and manufacturers know we will display their merchandise in the best possible way.
5. I don't like the pushy kind of salesman, either, who sells you all he can and then you don't see him again until next season.

When asked about the role of entertainment and personality in selling, Miss Morgenstern said quite frankly that she did not believe in the practice of "wining and dining":

Salesmen have heavy expenses, they work a full day, and they have wives and families. I don't believe entertainment is part of the process. Once in a great while I will have lunch with someone, but I don't want to feel obligated. You should keep free.

Miss Brodie commented:

When you are new you get everyone approaching you. Some of the salesmen are obnoxious, but personality does enter into your buying decisions after
a while.

Miss Fernald told the case writer that she thought being entertained
in the evening by a salesman was ridiculous:

Entertainment? Who needs it. I never expect anyone to take me to lunch
or dinner. I have my own circle of friends, and I don't need to be entertained
in the evenings. If I go to lunch with someone, it is because they are people
I enjoy, not because I want a free meal. Salesmen are people with wives and
families—why should they have to spend their income entertaining me?

It would never influence my buying—the merchandise has to be good for
this store, no matter what. It is the same with gifts—if I am going to buy a
line it doesn't matter whether the salesman gives me a Christmas gift or not.

It might be different for someone if the store were their whole life, social
life included.

A sportswear buyer from a large New York department store expressed
his opinion:

My first responsibility is to the store. . . . I never allow myself to feel
obligated.

I'm not interested in being entertained, unless it happens to be a day when
I feel like a free lunch and all I have to do is find a salesman. But this is New
York—farther away from the city they are probably more impressed by this.

Current Issues at Samantha

When questioned about their reasons for coming to work for
Samantha, the majority of salesmen noted (1) a respected brand name,
(2) the high quality of the Samantha product, (3) a reputation for
ethical and stable management, and (4) perceived growth potential. At
the present time, however, various salesmen mentioned dissatisfaction
with one or several of these points.

Robert Edison, who had been selling Samantha for one year, explained
that he had joined the sales force after working for another clothing
manufacturer because of Samantha's reputation for stable management
and income potential. At the end of the year, he found his commissions
to be much lower than expected, and the pleasant working relationship
he had anticipated with management had not materialized:

When I came with the firm, I was given no training, briefing . . . the
product was new to me, but they just sent me samples and left me completely
on my own.

Lines of communication to New York are very fuzzy—I don't know quite
what function Dave serves. I sense a lack of direction at the top—this lack of
direction affects my confidence in management's stability.

When an organization is harmonious this is felt—it used to be a point of strength with Samantha. Now I sense antagonism, conflict. At the sales meeting I noticed a complete lack of fire—salesmen sat on their hands. Management has become impersonal.

My territory is too small—I used to have all of New England.

Ben Turner, another new salesman, expressed a similar disillusionment with the firm's management:

There are too many chiefs and not enough Indians. Everybody is running in different directions. There are no clear-cut areas of responsibility. I can't say definitely, but I think Dave Zweibel is my boss.

Stanley Laufer, rated as an average salesman, complained about the lack of security regarding hospitalization and pension plans and stated that Samantha "needs to straighten out the confusion on top."

All salesmen interviewed criticized Samantha's delivery system and the lack of flexibility in production.[4] Often salesmen felt these problems to be a serious detriment to their selling success, and to Samantha's public reputation. Typical comments were:

1. No matter how good our number is, and even if the store is willing to wait the length of time required to deliver it, they still must buy someone else's sweater in the meantime.
2. Our ability to deliver on time has been our biggest enemy. I'm having a tough time maintaining good relations giving excuses.

John Starr criticized the "first-in, first-out" policy:

I think we have to vary from this policy now and then because it costs us big accounts. For example, a buyer [large midwest department store] whom I've tried to sell refuses to do business on two sizes with me because I won't promise her delivery preference.

One of the firm's most successful salesmen talked at great length about the problems he saw with sales management at Samantha:

Samantha used to be a three million business. With a present 40 million potential, the digging instrument must be more complex. No one human can watch 32 men. They spend all their money on machinery for the mill—what they need is a capital investment in the sales area. Samantha is no more salesman-oriented than it is customer-oriented. Samantha doesn't even know it has salesmen—doesn't know their needs.

They don't think about the stores, that is, markup. What can we do to help them with markdown? Now we wash our hands of the whole deal. Our competition uses consignment.

---

[4]Samantha Sportswear's delivery policy was that goods were shipped according to the order date only. Many other clothing firms gave delivery priorities to more important accounts, but Samantha management felt that an impartial delivery system was fairest to all concerned and less complicated in the long run.

We are getting a smaller and smaller share of a bigger and bigger market. Look at the sales meeting today—no pep talk. They don't give the men tools to sell. The salesmen should leave the meeting anxious to get their samples and sell. They should send those men out with their hair standing on end.

We give customers the impression we are not interested in them and their needs. We put salesmen in a position where they are not being used effectively. My resource is time. This company is unbusinesslike because they don't make the maximum use of me.

I've talked to Sam and Carl, but nothing is ever done. They have no sales supervision and no realization of growth at Samantha resulting in growth of sales force. How will they handle it? They don't do anything about training their salesmen. Our salesmen don't even know the fundamentals of *retailing*— I was dismayed at this. As you increase your sales force you increase turnover —you have to have someone who knows what is going on.[5]

I have no sense of security. Nobody says, "You've got a big future here." So if someone waves a bigger check I'll go. Running faster and faster to stand still is disillusioning. This company is going backwards.

Dave Zweibel, one member of Samantha management who favored a regional sales manager setup, explained why he thought this would benefit the firm:

Regional sales management is a good idea because it is impossible for one man to watch 24–30 salesmen. If it were done on a regional basis, you would deal with one regional manager representing five or six men instead. And this is how it is usually done.

Another reason—for the best interests of the corporation, the office in Chicago should be owned by Samantha, not the salesman. If there is a disagreement and the salesman quits, people are still used to coming into that one office.

The argument against this is that it is too costly. I can't see it. I think we can start with three regional sales managers—in Chicago, California, and the South. This alone would relieve the man at the top of 15 men.

Samantha spends $50,000 on a machine that may be obsolete in four years, but they won't spend a dollar on their sales force. Without sales, the firm doesn't exist. Without the machine, we might have three to four less numbers in the line but we could still exist.

Vertical Selling

Zweibel, who had introduced the idea of vertical selling to the Samantha sales organization, explained to the case writer why he had promoted this setup:

---

[5]Earlier in the year Greenberg had run a marketing arithmetic seminar for Samantha salesmen, and he discovered that some salesmen present did not even understand markup and markdown.

The most successful men in the sales organization are carrying both lines—Starr, Greenberg, and me. If a salesman doesn't carry both lines he ends up with a sideline—your income is not sufficient.

If a salesman carrying both lines is doing a million in business and grossing $50,000 in commissions, when he decides he wants to change he has to replace Samantha with two firms. No one else has our setup. If a salesman does only a quarter million in business, carrying one line, he can say O.K., I'll be satisfied with a quarter million from Samantha and take on another line.

He gave one reason why a salesman might have some difficulty adjusting to vertical selling:

It takes a little more talent to sell Women's than Junior Girls'—we are a byword in Junior Girls', but we do not have this reputation in Women's wear. Also, selling is a faster game—fashion moves faster, changes are more frequent.

Salesmen differed in their opinions concerning the vertical selling plan. John Starr had just completed a year of selling both Junior Girls' and Women's. He told the case writer he felt certain that he could handle even three lines by adding assistants to count stock and sell small stores. Mark Simone, an up-and-coming salesman, said he would be happy to carry both lines as well. Bill O'Mahoney, another successful salesman, preferred to carry both lines:

I like the idea of representing Samantha, not a range of sizes. Also I like the total merchandising concept of constantly working with and servicing the stores. To me, two men selling a store is ludicrous.

Arnold Greenberg, who had always sold both Junior Girls' and Women's, expressed his feelings about vertical selling:

If you have a lousy salesman, better have him responsible for as little as possible. With a good salesman, have him carry as much as possible.

With a smaller territory, you can spend more time with the customer. Suppose you are a merchandise manager or top executive with a large department store—you have to think in the total store point of view. If you have two salesmen for two divisions, he says what will each of you do for the Samantha concept in the store, instead of being able to talk to one specialist in Samantha. You have to have someone who can talk with authority for all of Samantha.

Jack Schultz, rated by management as an average salesman, thought that selling two lines would be an impossible task. Sid Samuelson, who carried Junior Girls', also felt it was better for a salesman to carry just one division:

I have fought this tendency for carrying both divisions at Samantha. The buyer is looking at Women's while you are showing Junior Girls', and the cost of two sample rooms is prohibitive. Too many people to work with. Also, all my friends and acquaintances are in the Junior Girls' field.

Other salesmen did not feel strongly about carrying both divisions but preferred one particular division to another because they were already acquainted with buying patterns in that field and did not want to pioneer another division. Several salesmen felt that the Women's division offered a better volume potential than Junior Girls'.

Carl Lowe was not sure whether the vertical setup should be continued:

It reduces time and expenses. By concentrating on a smaller area, the salesman should be able to provide better coverage and service to the department stores.

However, some salesmen who have been carrying one line don't like this. They think of themselves as specialists who can give fashion advice. They feel it is impossible to show a lot of samples properly.

Also, a lot of salesmen do their selling on a personal contact basis, and they really know this area. If this area is cut and they have to take another line, the salesman has to do a lot of pioneering.

The methods of merchandising Junior Girls' and Women's are different. Samantha Junior Girls' is high priced, usually the better line in a department. In the ladies' line they are more low priced. This may not be compatible with the way a man sells.

Often there are marketing shows which would necessitate a salesman being in two places at one time. Sometimes selling seasons don't coincide—Junior Girls' may go out earlier than Women's.

Rockford Containers (A)

ROCKFORD CONTAINERS was a division of the Rockford Paper Company, one of the larger and more diversified manufacturers and retailers of paper and paper products in the United States. The Containers Division designed, manufactured, and sold a wide variety of corrugated shipping containers and related packaging systems, utilizing in the process a large percentage of the total output of the corporation's paperboard mills. The division's function was to receive rolls of paperboard from these mills and to convert the rolls into sheets of corrugated board and, subsequently, into corrugated shipping containers made to customer specifications. Geographically, its operations consisted of a large number of widely scattered local plants in 18 states and a division headquarters in suburban Chicago, Illinois.

Since the division's beginnings in late 1956, its executives had been concerned with their inability to find and implement an organization structure that fit the division's tasks and management capabilities, and allowed for profitable performance. They had tried a number of different structures but in 1967 still wrestled with the problem expressed by the division's chief executive as: "What would be the organization that we should function under for the best overall performance? And, once we find the structure, how do we get to it?"

Rockford Containers (A) describes the division's work environment and the requirements for effective operations. The (B) case gives the history of the Containers Division through 1961, while the (C) case brings that history up to 1967.

THE INDUSTRY ENVIRONMENT

Until the middle 1940s, the corrugated box industry had made a distinction between mill and converting operations, the former producing the raw paperboard used by the latter to manufacture the corrugated containers. Each was run as a separate business with separate owners. But, by the end of World War II, a definite trend toward vertically inte-

154

grated operations emerged, with mills buying up converting plants or vice versa. The objective in either case was to insure an outlet for mill tonnage or to control a source of raw materials. This trend progressed so strongly that in 1967, 75 percent of the total corrugated container industry was fully integrated. This extensive integration posed special problems for the industry. On the one hand, integrated firms had the option of taking their profits at the mill level or the converting level, while, on the other hand, the firms were in good measure responsible for maintaining stability in the industry by at least broadly matching converting capacity to mill output. This latter problem was all the more complex because although both converting and mill operations were capital intensive, the latter was by far the more so. Thus, because the cost structure of building and running a new mill was such that the larger the facility the more economical it was, integrated producers always had the constraint of operating so as to maximize machine utilization in the mill.

Division executives said that competition in the corrugated industry was "fierce." Rockford Containers ranked in the top 10 in absolute size in the industry. The largest competitor enjoyed only 6 percent of the domestic market, while Rockford's share was only slightly less. The division's most prominent integrated competitors in the corrugated container business included Weyerhaeuser, Mead, International Papers, Owens-Illinois, and Union Bag, but as one of Rockford's local salesmen said, "There is really no one leader in the corrugated industry . . . no one company is strong enough in every area to be a leader in them all." Competition in the industry was sharpened by the existence of independent, or nonintegrated, companies. These firms were generally classified as "sheet plants" and "regional corrugator plants." The former did not have a corrugator[1] in their plants but bought corrugated sheets from their competitors to fabricate in small quantities for smaller customers demanding rapid, responsive service. The latter were the much more threatening competitors, operating in direct competition with the regional plant operations of the integrated companies. These independently owned corrugator plants usually had the advantage of buying their basic raw material, paperboard, below the published price because a local mill was often ready to bargain on price to get needed volume.

Rockford Containers' managers said that profitability in the industry was largely a function of highly efficient manufacturing operations and local pricing and product mix decisions. The division's vice president and general manager was even more explicit when he suggested:

---

[1]The corrugator was the focal piece of conversion equipment in the corrugator plant. Running about half the length of a football field and costing about $800,000–$900,000 in 1967, its function was to convert rolls of paperboard into corrugated sheets for further processing. There was usually only one corrugator per plant.

For every $0.10 an efficient manufacturing operation can save per thousand square feet of product, the sales end can save $1 by its pricing and mix decision. And yet, what have they got to sell. Only manufacturing's time and ability.

Another division manager said:

The activity of the sales organization is 80 percent of the key to profits in the industry, but they can sell only the quality and service that manufacturing gives them.

This same manager saw "the sales manager's ability to accept a proper mix of accounts at the right price" as any firm's major competitive advantage. And a third manager in the division headquarters succinctly summed up the thoughts of a number of the local managers in stating:

The key to making money here is in selecting your business. You need the right price and the right accounts, that is, the right mix for your particular plant.

For an integrated converter in particular to be successful, it had to offer at least the quality of services of its integrated competitors and, in many cases, also had to possess the competitive flexibility of the independents.

THE MARKETING ENVIRONMENT IN THE INDUSTRY

All orders in the corrugated container industry were produced to meet definitive customer specifications, with no containers produced in anticipation of future orders. The industry was, therefore, of a job shop nature, with a customer's order invariably being used to satisfy his immediate usage requirements. As a local Rockford manager observed, "No one wants to inventory air. He orders a box because he needs it *now*." In addition, the high cost of transporting the finished product served effectively to limit the market radius, usually to approximately 150–175 miles. Both the job-shop character of the industry and the high transportation costs made the industry's markets highly localized.

And because the markets were local, they were highly diverse. As an example, the industry's Florida markets consisted primarily of seasonal fruit and produce growers with fairly standard box requirements, while the Detroit or Chicago markets contained a wide variety of nonstandard industrial customers with much less seasonality of needs. A local manager expressed his feelings concerning the diversity of markets this way: "Corrugated markets are really autonomous. The concerns of the customers are entirely different. A person schooled in one market would have to learn another market all over again."

Although the characteristics of the customers in the local market in general determined the sales mix available to the local corrugated box firm, local box managers had a good deal of latitude for selecting a particular mix of accounts for their plants.

There were for the most part no published price lists in the industry and each customer order was a separate order requiring a separate price. Therefore, pricing became a vital marketing decision. A local manager recognized this by saying: "You've got to be in the ballpark on price before anything else can happen."

Prices were quoted on a "delivered basis," highlighting the import of transportation charges in limiting a market area. Division executives indicated that not only prices but also delivery, quality, and service were fairly uniform among the major producers in a particular market. No one firm could greatly influence these factors, and it was therefore ultimately the market itself that effectively determined the levels of price, delivery, quality, and service. One executive said: "The market tells us what to do about pricing and service. We don't tell it what to do. And different local markets tell us different things."

Because of the uniformity of the sales factors among firms in a particular market, the competitive edge was often decided on the reputation of the producer for especially good service or, more important, on the personal relationship between the producing box firm's personnel and the customer. A local manager called a firm's reputation for service and its personal relations with a customer "our lifeblood, when we don't open the gates for competition on price." Another executive recognized: "If an account is ready to give you some business because he likes you, he'll see that your price is competitive by telling you when it's not and letting you bid down. If he doesn't want to give you any business, you won't get it at any price."

Although the industry's markets were localized, many of its customers were not. The industry sold and serviced both local and national accounts, the latter defined as "an account with a central purchasing office and multiple shipping points." Rockford managers felt though that in practice the distinction between a local and a national account was not as precise. Often what was defined as a national account would be handled on a face-to-face basis between the local corrugating company and the local office of a national firm. A trend toward centralized purchasing and, therefore, more national accounts was evident. Quoting a divisional manager: "Where purchasing is already centralized for economic reasons, it is rarely, if ever, decentralized. It's usually the other way around."

But, one local manager was quick to point out that "Lots of central purchasing agents say they have complete control over the assignment of local box business, but they don't. They'll give in if the locals complain enough."

National account business was generally considered to be high-volume business, where price was a much more important factor than in local accounts.

THE MANUFACTURING ENVIRONMENT IN THE INDUSTRY

The technology by which mill paperboard was converted to a specialty corrugated container was relatively simple. (See Exhibit 1 for a diagram of the typical conversion process flow.) Throughputs were short, usually in terms of hours; but because of the job-order focus of the industry and the price competition, setup costs, waste, and overtime costs had to be carefully controlled.

As in most capital-intensive industries, volume was a critical element in the manufacturing cost structure of the corrugated box business. The converting plants aimed to operate at capacity, or at least well above the break-even point, to get the leverage advantages of capital intensity. In general, it was only at capacity that rigid account scheduling priorities had to be observed. Otherwise, plant scheduling was a relatively flexible process, only limited by a particular market's delivery requirements and individual customers' delivery expectations. A division manufacturing executive summed all this up by stating: "We could care less what we run in the plant as long as we satisfy sales and the customer. When we reach capacity, then substitutions must be made."

And a local manager pointed out the scheduling constraints imposed by customer expectations by saying: "If a customer is used to getting 10 days' delivery, he expects it in all kinds of weather."

Division managers indicated that their business was, in general, sales oriented. Manufacturing was, therefore, as one local plant manager said, "trained to operate and run on whatever sales has produced in orders." Nonetheless, a particular plant layout or a particular piece of conversion equipment was often more conducive to one type of customer order than another. For example, a particular corrugator may have been able to produce only one or two of the three standard size flutes,[2] or a plant layout may have lent itself to longer and faster runs, or higher volume orders, than another. Thus, the mix of accounts that sales provided and the nature of the machine layout and capabilities in large measure determined the efficiencies available to manufacturing managers. A local manager called sales ability to provide the proper mix "a grossly underestimated industry problem" in determining a particular plant's cost structure and profitability.

---

[2]"Flutes" were the ridges in the corrugated paper. They were the "corrugating medium" referred to in Exhibit 1.

EXHIBIT 1

The Conversion Process Flow

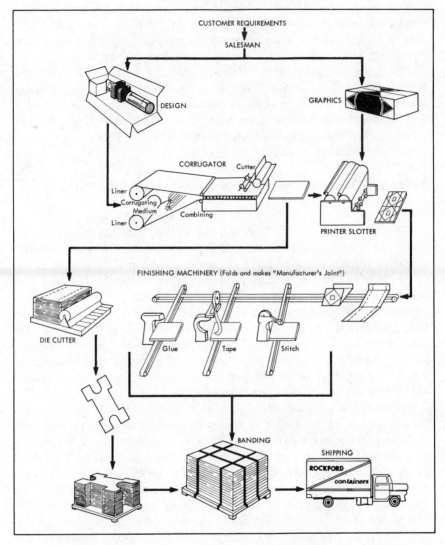

The plant labor force in the box business was semiskilled and plagued plant managers with an unusually high turnover rate. Rockford Containers' 52 percent turnover rate among hourly workers in 1966 was indicative of the overall industry rate but was believed to be far better than the worst competitor's showing. In markets located in industrial areas, wages for unskilled workers in other industries were generally higher than those for the semiskilled box workers, thereby compounding the turnover problem. Local managers in the box industry were reluctant to shut down a shift in a low-demand market situation because the laid-off trained help rarely returned. Training in the plant was for the most part on-the-job. The printer-slotter was considered the piece of equipment requiring the most skill, but a new man could be trained to run this in a matter of six to eight months.[3] Union bargaining for the labor force was typically on a plant-by-plant basis, even for the largest of the integrated manufacturers. The two most important unions representing the industry's hourly workers were the International Brotherhood of Pulp and Sulphite Workers and the United Papermakers and Paperworkers, both strongly centralized unions.

OPERATING TASKS IN THE ROCKFORD CONTAINERS DIVISION

Marketing Tasks

Division executives felt that because of the job shop and predominantly local nature of their marketing environment, "the key marketing decisions concerning price and mix must be made daily and even hourly in the division." As the managers quoted earlier indicated, the rapid pricing and mix decisions that had to be made in the face of strong, local competition to a large extent determined a firm's profitability. Thus, sound judgment on such decisions was seen as calling for strong, local sales direction. Invariably, local sales managers listed pricing decisions as their major concern, as typified by the statement of one: "Pricing decisions are my major decisions. But these decisions also include mix considerations to maximize the plant's capabilities."

Another local manager stated that "at least 80 percent of the sales business is pricing." The number of pricing decisions was large. For example, with an average order size of $300, Rockford Containers in 1966 entered 300,000 orders and quoted on 600,000–700,000 more. Rockford salesmen in the field did not quote prices but instead referred an order to the local sales executive for pricing. It was this latter executive, then, who, by his decision to quote a price or not or by his decision as to what price to quote, was able to screen incoming accounts and ultimately determine the firm's mix. In the industry, according to a local sales manager: "You do not tell a customer you do not want his order if it's a tough one for you to handle. You either don't quote, or you quote high enough to make some money on it for the plant, even though that price may be over your

---

[3]The printer-slotter, in one pass through this equipment, transferred printing from a dieplate to the corrugated sheet and removed small strips from the corrugated sheet to make it easier to fold to customer specifications. See Exhibit 1 for its position in the process flow.

competitor's." Obviously then, Rockford Containers' managers felt that although the total volume of orders running through the plants was an important profit variable, the contribution obtained from individual order-pricing decisions was just as important.

Salesmen in the division were for the most part college graduates, many recruited right out of their graduating classes. Sales trainees went through a six-month formal training program at division headquarters. This training in selling was supplemented by later local on-the-job training in the basics of the manufacturing process and the distinguishing features of the local market. Turnover among the salesmen was described as "high . . . that's an industry and professional characteristic," with a number of reported instances of a salesman's taking profitable accounts with him when he left. Rockford salesmen felt in general that they were evaluated on "results," which they defined in terms of volume, contribution, and the generation of new accounts. But some local managers saw as a continual problem some salesmen's lack of selectivity in accounts. One said:

It's difficult to make a salesman selective. He wants to sell everything he can. He'll sometimes go overboard on promises. He never looks at it from a profit angle.

With the exception of one plant in the division, the sales force was on straight salary only. In the exception, salesmen were paid a base salary plus commission. The salary level in Rockford Containers was defined as "competitive . . . maybe a little higher."

Sales managers and salesmen alike distinguished between "cracking" a new account and servicing an existing account as the two major concerns of the sales force. (It should be noted that local Rockford sales managers often personally handled a few key accounts.) Although there were some differences in the art of "cracking" an account as opposed to servicing an account, the basic sales function was the same. This function was succinctly phrased by one especially personable sales manager as "earning a position with the customer." Continuing, he said:

What's earning a position? It's knowing when a customer really needs the order in the 24 hours he says he does, and when he is crying "Wolf," or when the customer will accept the plus or minus 10 percent of the amount ordered that is the normal order understanding, and when he won't. In general, all this adds up to putting yourself on the customer's payroll without charge.

His definition of this phrase also included calling on a customer a number of times before even beginning to talk about orders, and learning the customer's business, his needs, and his problems. The character of the selling function was further defined by a number of other executives as:

. . . building a long-term relation with the customer, moving him a little bit each time you call on him . . . a build-up of low pressure . . . and . . . selling the salesman before you sell the product.

One local executive used a rule of thumb for evaluating new box business, a rule expressive of his view of the selling job: "That which comes easy, goes easy."

Salesmen in the Containers Division often showed the all-important personal interest in their customers by inventorying the customer's stock to be able to anticipate his needs and by aiding in his design of a more attractive package or more efficient packaging system. A local salesman reasoned: "Markets change from hard to soft. If you've done your job in one type of market, you can have the edge in them all."

Another took the other side of the coin and suggested: "You've got to stay in with a customer. Once you're out, you're out and it's really tough to get back in."

According to division managers, selling a national account required as much a personal selling effort as did selling local accounts, but this high-volume national business was much more price-sensitive. Such accounts in 1967 brought in about 20 percent of Rockford Containers' sales volume. Because these accounts involved a number of shipping points and were concentrated in the largest of the industrial areas, a separate sales force had been established to handle them, even though the local box plant was ultimately responsible for production. A national accounts executive saw as his task "to put desired footage at desired prices in the desired local plants," and viewed himself as "a tool to put large-volume business where it's needed at the local levels." The pricing of national accounts was done by this same executive, not by the local manager.

Manufacturing Tasks

Although each customer order carried its own specifications regarding size, folding characteristics, printing, etc., Rockford manufacturing executives felt that in general, meeting these specs did not pose major problems. But, problems did often arise in the plant's scheduling of orders to optimize machine utilization and to meet rigid delivery commitments. A local manufacturing manager estimated that "95 percent of our day-to-day problems center on scheduling for delivery requirements."

The general manager of the division himself emphasized: "When the customers want a truckload of boxes at 7:30, they mean 7:30."

Manufacturing managers preferred a ten-day to a two-week lead time on delivery, but they readily admitted the contention of one local executive that "although we like the lead time, we have done some pretty unusual things to satisfy customer delivery requirements." Another recognized that "if a customer needs the boxes and has a high-speed assembly line, he can't shut down; so we'll go to overtime to get the product for him." And a third more generally suggested: "In this business, you can't sit down on Friday and make out a firm production schedule for next week."

Division managers recognized that rush orders frequently interfered with production schedules and that order priorities depended on the customers and their needs. A local man said: "With General Electric or Procter and Gamble it would be suicide to say, 'We can't take the rush order.' We would almost turn the plant upside down for them."

Manufacturing personnel indicated, therefore, that the scheduling problem was a daily one of substituting orders, consolidating orders, and asking for extensions on orders, all to satisfy customer delivery priorities and optimize machine time.

Because margins in the industry were small, manufacturing managers indicated that control of manufacturing costs was a major issue. Most saw themselves evaluated on their budgets and the variances from them, and many expressed specific goals of improving their performance on the manufacturing budget. Typical of this attitude was the local manager who had as an objective "to go into the plant and find one job a month to process better and more effectively," and who listed as his current objective "to improve my setup to running-time ratio by 20–25 percent." A local executive summed up the importance of manufacturing costs by stating: "There are two ways of making money at the plant: raise your price, or lower your costs."

The manufacturing plant was charged with meeting the quality requirements set by the market. Invariably, manufacturing managers recognized the value of a quality product. A headquarters manufacturing executive said: "Quality has benefits out of proportion to what you might think. We sell to a commodity market. What has the salesman got to sell? He can sell the best box. So I attack quality with some missionary zeal." And a local man added: "Every box is different, it's not just a box. It's got to be a masterpiece."

Because of the high turnover among hourly plant workers, training and advancing employees became a key manufacturing function. Both local and division manufacturing managers listed this task as paramount, and one local executive incisively pointed out the impact of this task on the already recognized task of maintaining quality standards: "One reinforces the other. With a lousy quality product, the attitude of your plant people is lousy. And with lousy people, you get lousy quality."

Joint Marketing and Manufacturing Tasks

Rockford management spoke often of "crossover tasks," referring to decisions that required the participation of more than one functional unit, and especially to those decisions that required a joint marketing and manufacturing effort. They indicated that local sales and manufacturing information must be combined most often in significant aspects of mix, scheduling quality, and budgeting decisions.

Because it was the mix of accounts selected by the sales organization that in large measure imposed scheduling and cost constraints on the plant, both sales and manufacturing managers expressed an acute awareness of their part in that selection. Sales was seen as being fundamentally responsible for the mix, but statements such as the following from local sales managers indicated the real "crossover" nature of the task:

My goal is to keep a constant flow of product through the plant that will utilize the equipment we have here. I look for a product mix that will do this. . . . I have to consider that the number and type of orders running through the plant determines the cost structure, the setups, the overtime, and the like. And I must consider that the layout of our plant now tailors itself to longer runs and larger volume orders. The more the orders, the more the number of die-plates and setups. That's not for us. We're taking a hard look at small accounts. If they pay the price to make some money for the plant, we'll take it, otherwise not . . . and. . . .

My prime objective is to go after accounts that *this* plant can handle.

In the same vein, various manufacturing managers expressed themselves:

We get together with sales a lot on the acceptance or rejection of an order. If it's a dog that would ruin the schedule, we talk it over and decide whether or not to take it. . . .

If I see an order in the plant that's really costing us money or ruining the schedule, I'll come back to the sales office and ask, "Are we getting a good price on it?" . . . and. . . .

On new business and additional accounts, sales and manufacturing will sit down and decide whether we want it or not. We talk about the future prospect of the account, the manufacturing time available, the overtime we might have to run, and whether or not it would jeopardize other accounts.

The customer's demand for rapid delivery was a special aspect of the scheduling problem. With two-week lead times being the practical maximum in the industry, sales and manufacturing regularly got together to juggle the production schedule or to decide the fate of a rush order to provide for the customer's delivery requirements. A local sales executive set up the following hypothetical situation:

Suppose an account unexpectedly finds himself in need of a box. He wants it, oh, in four days. I'll ask the plant manager what he's running now. Can he slip the order in without too much interruption? Could we run it with a similar order already scheduled? Could we use idle equipment? Or would it cause him a real problem? If he says he really can't run it in four days, I may check back with the customer. You know, most purchasing agents lie by a couple of days.

A manufacturing manager was in general agreement with the above statement:

I try to see that both manufacturing and sales have a voice in scheduling. Our planning and scheduling is done subject to change for the customer's benefit, but it's done without disrupting the entire plant. If an order really has to disrupt the schedule, then I'll get together with sales and decide if an order now scheduled can be delayed on delivery.

And a second manufacturing executive specifically touched on the "crossover" nature of both delivery and quality problems in:

We sit down with sales to make sure customers are satisfied, deliveries are on time, that the product is a quality product. Sometimes sales comes in with a carton and wants it run one way for the customer's quality specifications. I want to run it another way. We talk about the pros and cons and try to work it out together if we can.

A less frequently encountered, but equally important, local "crossover" task was the budgeting function. Manufacturing and sales relied on each other both in annual forecasting and budgeting and in capital equipment budgeting. It was marketing's sales estimate on which manufacturing built its annual cost budget; and as one manufacturing manager said, "The validity of that forecast can really affect the way your performance turns out and how closely you meet your goals." Conversely, manufacturing's estimates of the manpower situation and the plant costs and efficiencies set parameters on the sales forecast. For deciding on initiating capital budget requests, marketing and manufacturing came together to discuss the character of the accounts and the sales potential in the local market, and the plant equipment and layout best suited for the desired mix.

Interdependence between Separate Marketing Areas

In Rockford Containers, managers in separate local markets felt that they had to coordinate with other local managers for interplant transfers and for national account sales. Because a plant serving a market usually did not produce all three standard flute sizes as indicated earlier, and because certain specialty items were produced only in one or a few specially equipped plants, interplant transfers were common occurrences. The two basic types of transfers involved (1) products sold in one market that had to be produced and delivered directly to the customer from another market's plant; and (2) products produced in one area for delivery to a plant in another area, rather than directly to the customer. In either case, the two market units concerned coordinated on the basic questions of accepting or rejecting the order and the pricing of the order.

The large-volume national accounts which usually involved putting business in more than one plant, posed the need for national account representatives to consult with representatives of the local plants. Their joint tasks centered on the acceptance or rejection of an order, a problem all the more difficult because as a national accounts executive said: "In some cases, we have to talk to a local manager about taking a lousy piece of business if taking it makes the difference in getting good business for other plants and a profit for the overall division."

Rockford Containers (B)

HISTORY OF THE DIVISION THROUGH 1961

RAPID GROWTH THROUGH ACQUISITIONS

ROCKFORD CONTAINERS DIVISION executives said that the Rockford Paper Company, with primary interest in "white" paper in the post–World War II period, was slow to react to the vertical integration trend in the "brown" paper portion of the industry. Finally, on June 10, 1956, the corporation, with the purchase of the Manassas Containers Company of Chicago, Illinois, initiated a separate Rockford Containers Division. Following that first move and during the next five years through 1961, the division added acquisition upon acquisition in the container field. Specifically, in 1957, the division acquired corrugated containers plants in Baton Rouge, Louisiana; Toledo, Ohio; Cleveland, Ohio; Trenton, New Jersey; and St. Louis, Missouri. Acquisitions in 1959 totaled four, one plant each in Tacoma, Washington; Springfield, Massachusetts; Detroit, Michigan; and Eugene, Oregon, while in 1960, the division purchased two box plants, one in Orlando, Florida, and one in Dallas, Texas. Finally, 1961 saw acquisitions in Utica, New York; Jackson, Mississippi; Fairfield, Connecticut; and Pawtucket, Rhode Island.

Rockford management's reasoning behind the development of a separate container division was similar to that of its competitors: the division would guarantee an outlet for the corporation's mill output and give the company the option of taking a profit at the mill or the converting end. More important though, Rockford's executives recognized that the company, as only a producer of paperboard, was subject to the strongest of competitive pressures since paperboard was essentially an undifferentiated commodity product. When pricing pressures became intense, the firm that just produced paperboard and did not convert it either had to lower its price or see a large part of its tonnage lost to a lower priced

167

competitor. As a specialty converter of paperboard though, a company was able to build an important customer franchise through its service and price. Rockford management said that although customers were not easy to develop, once the franchise had been won, they were not likely to run away.

DIVERSITY OF THE ACQUISITIONS

According to division managers, the box companies that were acquired were highly diverse, differing in policies, procedures, markets, plant characteristics, management talent, etc. Mr. David Burns, the division's young director of planning and a graduate of Harvard Business School's Program for Management Development, said:

With each acquisition, the company acquired a new policy, a different business philosophy, and unrelated compensation program and treatment of employees' benefits and differing labor contracts. In a few instances, Rockford acquired as well competent management who either remained as managers of individual plants or assumed divisional management positions. In many instances, though, former owners retired from active business and, in all too many cases, were not backed up with capable replacements.

The vice president and general manager of the Containers Division, Mr. Roger Cunningham, a dynamic gentleman raised in the box business, added:

We had to contend with plants with miserable cost systems and plants with no cost systems. There were differences in accounting practices, foreman training, and the like.

Mr. Cunningham liked to refer to the problem posed by this diversity as "the great digestion process."

Some examples will illustrate that the markets served by the purchased firms and the characteristics of the acquired plants were as separate and distinct as were their policies and procedures.

The Springfield acquisition was a "sheet plant"[1] catering primarily to a small number of large-order customers such as General Electric, Colgate-Palmolive, and Procter and Gamble. Originally, the plant obtained its corrugated sheets from the division's Trenton plant; but in 1960, Rockford purchased a one-story building in Springfield, installed a corrugator, and revamped the plant's operations to include all the services of a completely equipped corrugator factory.

The Baton Rouge firm had two corrugators in its plant (a rarity in the business) and was therefore better suited to the large number of smaller volume

---

[1] A "sheet plant" operated without a corrugator, as indicated in the "Industry Environment" section of *Rockford Containers* (A).

orders that its market provided. The sales manager of the Baton Rouge plant estimated he had 25,000 separate specification cards for his multitude of customers.

Hand-crafted, nonrepetitive display containers made up a sizable portion of the Tacoma plant's product. The sales job for those displays necessitated special skill, for, as the Tacoma sales manager, Mr. Bill Marshall, said, "Point-of-purchase displays require a knack for design, consumer buying habits, and creative marketing. The language of our display customers is completely different from the usual box business. It sounds more like Madison Avenue."

The Orlando operation, according to division executives, was "unquestionably a world of its own." The majority of its sales was to fruit and produce growers and was highly seasonal; published price lists were adhered to; and the fruit and produce boxes had to conform to the Florida railroads' specifications and quality standards if the railroad was to be held liable for damage to the perishables in transit.

A local executive in St. Louis tersely summed up this diversity of operations by warning: "When you're trying to compare our district with any other, you're comparing apples and oranges because of the markets, the mix, and the plants." To reinforce his perception, it was only at this executive's plant that division salesmen were paid a commission on sales as well as a base salary.

Division executives said that the managers that came to Rockford Containers with the acquisitions represented a wide spectrum of experience, ability, and background. Manassas Containers, the first acquisition, supplied the new Containers Division with its chief executive, Roger Cunningham; and the Cleveland, Ohio, acquisition gave the division so many excellent executives at both the local and headquarters levels that it was known as "the West Point of Rockford Containers." Production managers ran the gamut from Mr. Les Williams in the Baton Rouge plant, who "came up from the bottom" and wanted to see his hourly workers have the same opportunity, to Mr. Dick Gerber in the St. Louis plant who formerly sold insurance and whose grandfather designed Memorial Hall at Harvard University. Sales executives included Baton Rouge's Marv Winman, who had been with the plant's sales organization for 32 years; Tacoma's Bill Marshall, who started in the plant's shipping room and moved up through administration to sales; and young Mike Devlin of Orlando, a crusty former paratrooper who swore he became one by virtue of the Army's computer error and who was reputed to do some of his best selling in Bermuda shorts and sandals.

SIMILARITIES AMONG THE ACQUISITIONS

Although the acquisitions did differ markedly from one another, managers noted that nonetheless a general orientation seemed to characterize them and their managers after their incorporation into Rockford. Mr. Ken Eddy, a former management consultant who was the sales manager at the Cleveland, Ohio, plant, reasoned:

The top executives of the acquisitions in many cases became fairly disinterested in Rockford after they got their money out. Some left immediately. Others went up to division jobs, but they were relatively unsophisticated on staff functions and, just as important, were generally unsympathetic to central direction. Some Rockford central policies came out, but they were not universally effective. Pockets of resistance to central direction sprang up.

The case writer himself noted that one 1961 acquisition in 1967 still answered the telephone identifying itself by its former name and that another had its magazines and newspapers sent in care of its preacquisition name.

Division managers said that those chief executives that did remain after consolidation to run the local operations, instead of functioning as general managers as intended, became more sales oriented. Mr. Cunningham recognized that "normally the presidents became the general managers, but they were also pretty sales oriented." A local sales manager said: "Most of those top managers in the acquisitions were sales happy, with volume goals only." And a division manager proposed: "It was as if the executives in the acquired firms felt that their superior knowledge of the essentially local market ought to be used to prove themselves to division people."

THE INDUSTRY CLIMATE DURING THE PERIOD OF RAPID GROWTH: THE "BLOODBATH"

From 1959 through 1961, at the height of Rockford's acquisition program, mill overcapacity jolted the industry. General overproduction of paperboard at the mill level was made intolerable when a major integrated producer brought on-stream a huge mill in 1960. A Georgia Tech–trained salesman in Baton Rouge incisively pointed out the effect of the increased industry integration in such a situation:

Independents had been a stabilizing force in the industry in that they tried to and had to make a profit at the converting end. With more integration though, the tendency was away from this because an integrated firm could make its money at the mill instead.

Mr. Cunningham reflected on the 1959–61 overcapacity period, which the industry had dubbed the "bloodbath":

The integrated manufacturers began marketing their excess paperboard by depressing the price of their converted product rather than the board from the mill. Box prices really dropped. This put a lot of pressure on reducing manufacturing costs and on accurate pricing. The local general managers *had* to become principally sales managers. Pricing became a 16-hour-a-day job. But they also had to cut their factory costs to survive in that environment.

STRUCTURING THE CONTAINERS DIVISION

The Initial Organization Plans

As each new acquisition was incorporated into the growing division, its chief executive reported directly to Mr. Cunningham, who talked about the reason for such a move and its effect on the organization:

With acquisitions, the natural thing to do was to have the president of each company report to me. This was necessary from an acquisition point of view. We had enough problems without complicating the organization. It would have been tough to tell the president of any acquisition that he was to report to anyone other than the vice president and general manager of the division. Besides, we consciously and deliberately wanted to move into the acquired companies very slowly. We recognized that they were all pretty small and had their own policies and operating procedures, and we didn't want to disrupt their operations. So out of all this, an informal organization evolved. People tended to report to one of three people, even though the organization chart showed them all reporting to me. People tend to relate to people they can get the answers from, particularly to people whose answers they like. One of the three was me; the others were my administrative assistant and the general sales manager. It rocked along informally on this basis. There were supposedly 16 or so different operating managers reporting directly to me. This just couldn't work. That's when the consultants came.

In late 1959 and early 1960, a major and well-respected consulting firm that had been maintaining a relationship with the Rockford Paper Company was retained by the Containers Division to make recommendations concerning the division's structure. (*See the Appendix following this case for significant excerpts of the consulting team's 1960 recommendations, the plan for implementation, and the organizational concepts on which the consultants based their recommendations.*) The gist of the consulting report was to establish regional and district managers solely responsible for both selling and manufacturing operations, and, ultimately, for profits in their geographic areas.[2] A divisional general sales manager was to have line authority over the field in certain aspects of pricing, scheduling, and interplant transfers.

Mr. Cunningham's observations on this first consulting report were:

---

[2]For all practical purposes, the "district" managers were to be equatable to "individual plant" managers.

The consulting firm's recommendation was, as you know, for regional general managers and district plant managers. We acted on their recommendations and looked for the strongest sales managers to make regional general managers. The rest were made district managers.

Mr. Cunningham also reported that it was sales managers who were put into these positions because selling was considered the more important operating task given the industry climate imposed by the "bloodbath."

Roger Cunningham then spoke candidly of his perceptions of the structural problems his division experienced after implementing the recommendations of the first consulting report:

Originally, also following the consultants' recommendations, we had a staff production manager at the regional level, and the district general manager was also supposed to function as the district sales manager. Well, that theory eroded and eventually regional general managers set up separate district sales managers. This was done because the general manager usually wanted to promote somebody. There was also in the division in general a strong motivation to take care of everybody. Who ended up in different spots depended much more on who they wanted to take care of than on who was needed to occupy the spot. There was something less than perfect objectivity in placing people in the division.

After a year or two of working under the consultants' regional and district manager setup, sales volume and prices went down and manufacturing costs went to hell in a hand basket. What was happening was that the sales-oriented managers who were now general managers didn't know how to be general managers and nobody was telling them how. They were spending a lot of time in manufacturing—their rationale was, I guess, they didn't know anything about manufacturing, so they should straighten it out. Besides, they had formerly worked in sales, and they were sure they had done a good job in sales, but sales went to hell because they spent no time at it. They confused the manufacturing situation considerably. What also happened initially was, with their training and orientation, they were interested in serving the customer, and they did this without regard to manufacturing costs. None of this was helped by the continuing "bloodbath." We started three programs to get manufacturing costs back in line. One was a waste program, the second a labor cost program, and the third an overhead reduction program.

So when the costs went up, we quickly developed those programs I mentioned to get them down, but we couldn't get them implemented. To get these programs accepted, we had to get the regional general manager to agree to them, then the regional manufacturing people, and then the plant people. This was a hell of a lot of people. And this was extra tough because the philosophy of the plant was still, "Let's not do anything to interfere with the customer."

In trying to implement the manufacturing costs programs, we weren't getting anywhere. The structure and the kind of people made it unworkable. Even the consultants recognized that the structure wasn't doing what it was supposed to.

The Decision to Functionalize Management

In response to the situation in 1961, Mr. Cunningham had the same major consulting firm do a second, quick study. The consultants' oral report recommended a functional organization for all levels, a recommendation adopted by the division that same year. (Exhibit 1 is an organization chart for the 1961 functionalized Containers Division prepared by the case writer.)

As described by Rockford Containers' executives, the division's functional organization dissected the overall task of the division into its marketing and manufacturing elements. Thus, at the divisional, regional, and district levels, separate marketing and manufacturing managers were established. And at both the regional and district levels, the two functional managers were made jointly responsible for profits. District functional managers reported directly to their regional counterparts, and these regional functional managers reported respectively to a general sales manager and a general manufacturing manager. The individual plant remained the division's basic profit center; and although a centralized national accounts organization was established, it was not designated a profit center of its own.

Division managers indicated that a fundamental reason for going to the functional organization rested in the diversity of the acquisitions. The functional structure allowed division management more effectively, as one headquarters manager noted, "to go from a helter-skelter approach to an integrated punch." Mr. Bud Nathanson, the head of the national accounts section, who was at division headquarters during the decision making that resulted in the functional structure, said:

We had a lot of diverse plants. We had a problem in bringing them together to evolve an overall company policy that would meld them all. The centralized functional organization allowed us to do this.

The director of planning, Dave Burns, reasoned:

We had to functionalize because of the differences in the firms acquired. That is, we had differences in managers, differences in systems, etc., all in an environment that required a cost-cutting effort and more overall control.

Ken Eddy, Cleveland's sales manager, pointed out:

With the existence of pockets of resistance to central direction among the old-time owners that I mentioned earlier, the division went to a functional structure to achieve consistency in policies and operations.

Mr. Tom Barry, the division's director of industrial relations, confirmed:

EXHIBIT 1

The Functional Organization in 1961

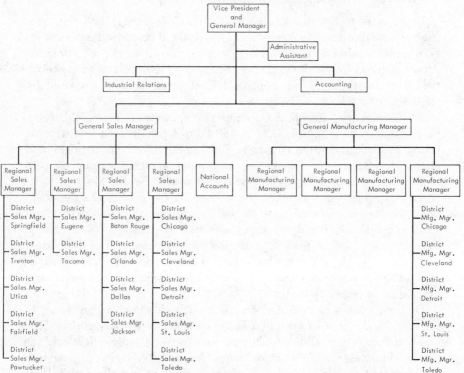

The diversity of the companies we acquired was focal to the development of a centralized functional structure. We had a number of different managers acquired, a number of different policies, a number of different control systems. We had to have more coordination than we did.

And Springfield's sales manager, Mr. Wayne Landry, tersely reckoned:

We had to specialize when we were building the division because of the differences we found in the acquisitions.

Executives reported that Rockford's new functional organization continued the trend that was started by the 1960 consulting report toward highly centralized accounting and budgeting practices and personnel and salary administration. Concerning the latter, Tom Barry, the industrial relations director, said:

This centralized salary and personnel administration extended all the way through the regional and district levels. I would have to go through Roger [Cunningham] and Roger through the corporate level to get any change here.

Even in hiring a man, a manager couldn't just hire anyone. He had to work through industrial relations. There were deviations from this on an individual basis, but there was a strong tendency to preserve the strictly central control.

The functional structure also gave more centralized control over inter-district transfers and the national sales effort. Mr. Cunningham said:

We had to have more coordination in sales across the country. The role of the regional sales manager and the general sales manager in the functional organization helped us do this.

Bud Nathanson of national accounts indicated that:

The national accounts show was a direct result of the move to functional management in 1961. If each plant ran its own show, it would have been chaos. So we had to have more centralization so that we could have all the plants' capabilities theoretically available to us. I work through the regional managers in placing this business. I'll ask the regional managers if they're willing to take the business at a specific price, and they ultimately decide where it should go on the local level.

With the wide spectrum of management backgrounds and abilities in the acquisitions, Rockford's functional organization was also intended, according to division executives, to make better use of the specialty skills of the acquired managers. A local manufacturing manager reasoned:

About the split management in 1961—top management felt that professionals in each function could devote all their time to their specialty. You know, we had some general managers who were too sales oriented and really weren't acting like general managers anyway.

Mr. John Jakowicz, a regional manufacturing manager, was even more specific:

The company felt that if managers concentrated in areas in which they're best suited, we'd maximize profits.

Regional functional managers invariably saw as part of their role the application of specialty skills. Most succinctly, one said:

After 1961 my job included helping my district people in aspects of their functional job in which they're weak.

Mr. Cunningham indicated that the specialization of the task was also expected to help the Containers Division more effectively to focus the required skills on the critical manufacturing cost-cutting effort.

In summary then, in 1961, Rockford Containers went to a split or functional management structure at all levels of the organization. At the regional and district levels, the single general manager with overall operating and profit responsibility was replaced by separate manufacturing and sales managers jointly responsible for profits. Division executives hoped that the new structure would eliminate or checkmate many of the management problems they faced.

APPENDIX

EXCERPTS FROM THE 1960 CONSULTING REPORT

PLAN OF ORGANIZATION

The revised organization structure of the Rockford Containers Division is designed to meet the division's immediate organization needs and to provide a sound base for continued growth. Rockford Containers is a group of 14 plants, many of which were independent, privately owned companies only a few months ago. These individual plant organizations must retain their local entrepreneurial aggressiveness and enthusiasm but at the same time work within a coordinated national program following a common division policy. The new organization is a major step toward achievement of this objective.

The basic concept and principal features of the new organization are summarized in six points.

1. *Establish Regional Managers to Direct and Coordinate Operations of Appropriate Groupings of the Division's 14 Plants.* The nature of the corrugated container business and the large number of Rockford Containers' markets and plant locations confirm that the division should organize its 14 plants and sales operations on a regional basis. Although only four regions are presently required, this number can be increased to meet the needs of further expansion.

The regional manager is a line executive having direct responsibility for all selling and converting operations within a broad geographic area. He controls, through district managers, the selling activities within his region and, with the aid of a regional manufacturing manager, provides overall guidance to the region's manufacturing operations. He carries complete profit responsibility for his assigned plants.

The regional managers will report directly to the vice president and general manager. Not only does the importance of the position warrant this organizational level, but the regional managers will benefit from a close personal relation with the top executive of the division. Conversely, this reporting relationship will permit the vice president to maintain a firsthand knowledge of the business's operating problems by working directly with the regional managers.

The regional manager has full authority over the organization and operation within his assigned area. He is, of course, limited by divisional policy in regard to such things as the approving of capital expenditures, sales of company assets, or the expenditure of funds in excess of established budgets. In addition, he should take full advantage of divisional staff executives by reviewing with them and getting their prior approval of changes in key personnel or major revisions in operating methods.

It is of the utmost importance, however, that the regional concept of organization does not detract from a strong plant operating foundation. Each plant must be relatively autonomous and be staffed with competent executives capable of operating without close supervision from the regional office. The regional organization should be kept small with only a regional manufacturing manager and, where necessary, a staff assistant to assist the regional manager. Development of a large regional staff would tend to produce excessive supervision of the district activities and, as such, would only weaken the effectiveness of plant-level personnel.

2. *Full Authority and Responsibility for Operations and Profitability of Each Plant Should Be Assigned to a Single Individual.* District organizations will be aligned in accordance with the basic concept of a single individual being in charge of each plant operation. The district manager (as this individual will be called) will have complete responsibility for the sales, manufacturing, and service functions necessary to produce a satisfactory return on the corporation's investment at each individual location. He will report to the regional manager and will be, for all practical purposes, "Mr. Rockford" to his customers, employees, and community.

3. *The General Sales Manager Shall Have Line Authority over the Field Organization in Certain Specified Sales Functions.* The container business is fundamentally a sales business, and the decisions that affect profits most are predominantly sales decisions. Since, as a practical matter, the vice president and general manager do not have the time to direct most day-to-day functions involving selling, pricing, and interplant scheduling, a strong home office sales function is essential. The vice president and general manager, therefore, will delegate to the general sales manager the responsibility and authority for directing and controlling the field organization—that is, regional managers and district managers—in regard to these specific sales functions. This is a practical method for relieving the vice president and general manager of the bulk of the day-to-day operating decisions without reducing their overall control of regional operations.

The line-staff responsibilities of the general sales manager must be clearly defined to insure effective working relations with the regional managers. The regional managers will still report directly to the vice president and general manager, but they will work closely with the general sales manager on all sales and pricing problems. The general sales manager must not attempt to supervise personally the sales activities of individual plants. His primary job will be to initiate overall marketing programs and to administer and coordinate the execution of these programs. He will get involved in the "firing-line" details only in emergency or unusually critical situations.

4. An Expanded Program of Marketing Services and Sales Staff Functions Will Be Provided by a Home Office Marketing Staff.

5. All National Accounts Activities Should Be Grouped into a Single Organization Headed by a National Accounts Sales Manager. The national accounts sales manager should be responsible for selling the required volume at satisfactory price levels to the accounts under his jurisdiction. He should be responsible for the division's entire national accounts program and should maintain local offices in whatever cities are necessary to provide adequate coverage and service. He should develop plans and programs to aid the national accounts salesmen in selling this volume business on the most favorable contract terms. He personally should maintain contacts with principal accounts to place Rockford Containers in a position where it can obtain large volume orders when needed. With the knowledge and approval of the general sales manager, he should work with the regional managers on the proper pricing and scheduling of these orders.

6. A General Administrative Manager Will Direct All Staff Planning and Control Activities. The general administrative manager should be in charge of all administrative and control activities of the division. He should be responsible for the overall planning of the division's volume and profit goals, and for measuring performance against these goals. He should direct all staff and general office personnel and should assist the vice president and general manager in carrying out specially assigned projects.

BENEFITS OF PLAN OF ORGANIZATION

The organization briefly discussed in the preceding paragraphs represents a sound forward step for Rockford Containers at this time. It provides six major benefits to this Containers Division.

1. It Limits the Number of People Reporting to the Vice President and General Manager. As shown in the organization exhibit, only four regional managers plus three home office positions would report to the vice president and general manager under the recommended plan. This is in contrast to the 14 district managers and much of the home office staff that report to him at the present time.

2. The Delegation of Selected Line Responsibilities to the General Sales Manager Clarifies His Relationship with the Regional Managers. By specifically delegating direction of the selling and pricing functions to the general sales manager, the vice president and general manager can be relieved of much of the day-to-day operating details of the business. At the same time, by retaining control over personnel, capital expenditures and sales and operations policies, the vice president remains in complete command of the division's total operations as its chief executive officer.

3. *The Consolidation of All Accounting, Control, and Nonsales Staff Functions under the General Administrative Manager Will Provide More Effective Control and Administration of the Division's Operations.* The expansion of the Containers Division has created the need for more extensive planning and control throughout the division. The consolidation of these home office functions under a single top-level executive will provide the management strength necessary to develop these functions into effective management tools. This in turn should be reflected eventually in the division's sales and profit performance.

4. *It Provides Several Profit Responsibility and Decision-Making Points.* The regional managers will be able to provide on-the-spot coordination and direction for all operations within their area of responsibility. They should be able to assist the district managers, sales managers, and manufacturing managers within their regions in the appropriate pricing and acceptance of orders. The regional form of organization, therefore, provides points of profit responsibility and decision making at the district manager, regional manager, and the vice president levels.

5. *It Provides the Framework for Scheduling Orders at the Most Appropriate Plant in Each Region.* Plants differ enough in their size, capabilities, and profitability of operation so that at any one time one particular plant may be able to handle a specific order more easily and more profitably than can the other plants. By having a regional manager in charge of several plants, the scheduling of orders should be improved and greater teamwork developed within each region. The general sales manager will coordinate the scheduling of orders between regions.

6. *The Recommended Home Office Staff Organization Should Be Adequate for a Considerable Period of Further Growth.* The recommended home office staff is adequate for the size of the business today. Further expansion and subdivision of the staff functions can be accomplished over a period of time as the need arises, without changing the basic organization concept.

THE NEXT STEPS

The plan of organization outlined in the preceding section provides the basic organization framework for Rockford Containers Division. The plan should be expanded in certain areas and a program of installation undertaken as soon as possible. Five steps should be taken.

1. *Indoctrinate All Key Container Division Executives in the Concepts and Operating Relationships of the Proposed Organization*
   a) The recommended plan of organization should be reviewed with the Container Division's key executives to assure understanding and agreement.
   b) This indoctrination process should continue over a period of four to six weeks and will be coincident with the development of more detailed organization plans for the general administration manager, general manufacturing manager and regional managers.
2. *Appoint the Regional Managers*
   a) Any questions or differences of opinion should be resolved and final decisions reached on proposed regional territories and regional managers.
   b) The regional managers should be appointed and the proposed organizational plans discussed with them.
3. *Establish the Organization Structure for Each of the Four Regions*
   a) The consulting firm should work with each of the newly appointed regional managers in developing the organization plan and staffing for each region.
   b) The proposed regional organization plans should then be reviewed with the general manager and the necessary revisions made to obtain general agreement on a sound plan.
   c) Division managers and other key personnel should be appointed.
4. *Establish the Organization Structure and Scope of Responsibility for the General Administrative Manager and General Manufacturing Manager Positions.*
5. *Announce the New Plan of Organization for the Division and Establish the New Reporting and Working Relationships.*
   a) Publicly announce the new organization plan for the entire Containers Division.
   b) Hold a series of plant meetings with sales and other key personnel to explain the new organization and discuss changes in operating procedure.
   c) Distribute new organization charts and written descriptions of the duties and responsibilities of all key positions.

BASIC ORGANIZATION CONCEPTS

This section of the report provides additional material on how the organization should function. Some of this discussion gets into the basic principles of organization, but it is felt that the inclusion of this type of material will help to provide a more thorough understanding of the concepts and workings of the new organization plan.

1. *The Division's Effectiveness Is Dependent upon Strong Individual Plant Sales and Manufacturing Operations.* No amount of staff services or divisional control can substitute adequately for capable and aggressive executives at the operating level. The individual salesman, the district sales manager, and the plant supervisors are the men who in the final analysis produce the division's volume and profits. Proper organization and top-management planning, direction and control is, of course, essential in achieving maximum operational effectiveness and continued growth and profitability. However, extreme care must be taken to assure that this management structure does not discourage or dilute the effectiveness of the men on the "firing line."

The basic concept should be constantly kept in mind as the division's organization is realigned to meet the expanding needs of the business. Top management's role must always be to plan, direct, and control—but not (except in special or emergency situations) to do the job of its line subordinates. Capable aggressive managers must be developed for each plant and regional position, with top management's time being devoted primarily to providing overall guidance and to preparing the division for the future.

2. *Internal Working Relations and Channels of Communication Should Be Based on Common Sense and Organizational Courtesy.*

3. *All Organization Planning Should Be Built upon Proved Principles of Organization.* In developing the new organization plan, certain principles of organization have been observed. Although each organization must be tailored to its specific situation, basic organization principles provide general guideposts toward the establishment of effective organizational relationships. As listed in the following paragraphs, these principles of good organization should prove helpful to Rockford personnel in understanding more fully the reasoning and purpose behind various features of the new plan. In addition, an occasional review of such principles should help the division maintain sound perspective in its future organization planning.

a) *The Organization Structure Should Be Simple and Economical.* The plan of organization should be divided into the minimum number of units and levels consistent with recognition of major functions and effective distribution of work loads. Every unit of the organization should be worth its cost. This principle holds the organization to the fewest practicable groupings and to the smallest practical number of people commensurate with attainment of objectives.

b) *The Organization Structure Should Be Built around the Functions of the Business Rather than around Personalities.* The division's organization should be developed around the several major functions of the business. However, it is necessary to give full recognition to individual strengths and weaknesses and to provide a practical balance between the ideal functional organization and the abilities of its key people.

The organization should provide for the assignment of similar or directly related activities to one person insofar as possible. It should encourage management teamwork.

c) *The Plan of Organization Should Be Sufficiently Flexible to Meet Changing Requirements as Business Conditions Change.* Rockford Containers' organization should be flexible and capable of expansion or contraction within the original framework as the need arises and without loss of effectiveness.

d) *The Plan of Organization Should Provide a Continuous Supply of Qualified Management Replacements to Assure Perpetuation of the Company.* Top management has the responsibility for successful perpetuation of the company. Rockford Containers' plan of organization should provide for subordinate positions of sufficient responsibility and authority so that at all times there are replacements in training for each key position.

e) *The Number of Subordinates Reporting to a Superior Preferably Should Be Limited to No More than Six or Seven Whenever Direction, Control, and Coordination Are Involved.* Whenever direction, control, and coordination are involved, the span of control should be limited in order to provide for adequate planning and for the attention subordinates deserve. The number of reporting subordinates, however, should be large enough to achieve maximum use of the superior's abilities.

f) *Authority Should Balance Responsibility.* Full administrative responsibility for each major function should be delegated to specific executives together with the commensurate authority necessary to undertake such responsibility successfully. Men should be held accountable for conditions within their control. The responsibility of a superior for the acts of his subordinates should be absolute.

g) *There Should Be a Clear Line of Authority from the Top to the Bottom of the Organization.* The chain of command should be continuous and complete from the top to the bottom of the company's organization structure. Application of this principle is essential to attainment of purpose, to efficiency, and to firmness of decision.

h) *Reliance for Making and Carrying Out Decisions Should Be Placed on Individual Line Executives.* Staff and committee units should not be permitted to dilute the responsibility and authority of individual line executives. Except in unusual situations where for practical reasons staff units are required to have limited line authority, their work should be confined to counseling and advisory functions. Line executives should have the responsibility for decision and action.

i) *Key Managers Should Be Free to the Greatest Extent Possible of*

Minor Operating Details and Routine Matters. Managerial ability can be fully used only when the manager is relieved of all matters which can be reduced to a routine or can be handled through approved plans or policies.

j) The Power of Decision Should Be Placed as Closely as Possible to the Point Where Action Originates. There should be a decentralization of responsibility so that the ability to decide and act within the scope of approved plans and policies is placed as closely as practicable to the point where need for decision or action originates.

k) The Responsibility and Authority of Members of the Organization Should Be Definite and Clear-cut. Each member of management should have, in writing, a clear-cut description of the responsibilities, authorities, and reporting relationships of his job. Whenever changes in responsibility are made, all persons concerned should be informed.

l) The Creative Efforts of Individual Executives Should Be Encouraged. Each individual executive should be free to think, plan, and create new policies and initiate improvements within the scope of his assigned responsibilities.

Rockford Containers (C)

THE DIVISION IN 1967

ROCKFORD CONTAINERS continued its high rate of domestic growth from 1961 through 1967, using a combination of acquisitions and original construction.[1] A 1966 examination by the Federal Trade Commission of Rockford's container plant acquisitions had resulted in a consent order under which Rockford agreed to divest itself of a number of corrugator plants and to refrain from acquiring any container plants for 10 years. The order did not, however, prevent the company from building new plants wherever it chose.

Thus, by the end of 1967, the Containers Division operated 24 plants, built around a nucleus of 19 acquisitions. The division was expected to expand at the rate of about two plants a year over the next five years, doubling the number of exempt personnel during that period.[2] In addition, the division's vice president and general manager, Roger Cunningham, estimated that by 1976 international operations would be giving Rockford a sales volume equal to 50 percent of the total sales volume in 1967.

Three newly developed products—Picture Pak, Cold Pak, and Twist Pak—had helped Rockford Containers to service its customers' specialty needs. Picture Pak was a process which preprinted corrugated board in a wide variety of colors to customer specifications and designs. Because this product required a special knowledge of graphics and printing, a separate divisional product manager and "technical sales specialists" had been established to assist local salesmen in selling it. However, only the Springfield, Massachusetts plant had the capability of processing Picture Pak, so that an interplant transfer was required if another plant was to use this increasingly effective competitive tool.

---

[1] For review of Rockford Containers' growth from the birth of the division in 1956 through 1961, see *Rockford Containers (B)*.

[2] Exempt personnel included sales and manufacturing managers, general foremen, salesmen, etc.

Cold Pak, a plastic wax container developed especially to handle the shipment of poultry in ice, and Twist Pak, a spirally wound tube that could be cut and folded, were sold only by the regular sales force. Cold Pak was manufactured in the Orlando and Macon plants, while Twist Pak was manufactured only in a separate manufacturing facility in Chicago. Both specialty products therefore added to the interplant transfer problem for the division as a whole, but the problem concerning Cold Pak was at least partially offset by the geographic concentration of poultry markets around the Orlando and Macon plants.

The Containers Division, in the mid-1960s, developed a number of computer-based controls for its operations. Because, as Mr. Cunningham said, "the industry is plagued by the lack of adequate cost systems and costing is of tremendous import in the business," the division formulated a computer standard cost system called CAVEAT.[3] The system was described by managers as providing each plant with definitive cost data concerning an incoming order, considering current work loads and existing equipment in the plant, and with the most efficient and economical routing of that order through the plant. The inputs to the model were the budgets and cost estimates submitted by a plant's managers; the outputs included the order's "actual" cost CAVEAT estimate, based on the budgets, and the order's "opportunity" cost CAVEAT estimate, based on predetermined costs for a hypothetical, proficient plant. Thus, managers could use CAVEAT in their costing and scheduling decisions and could compare their plant's "actual" costs with the hypothetical costs of a proficient plant. In 1967, all of Rockford's container plants had access to this system.

The CAVEAT printout, generated in the Chicago division headquarters, normally went only to the local sales function, where it was used by sales managers primarily as an aid in the multitude of local pricing decisions. Local managers for the most part indicated CAVEAT was only a guideline and not a solution for their pricing problems.

Although most managers found CAVEAT helpful, one divisional executive was less optimistic about CAVEAT's value:

CAVEAT is beautifully intellectual, but there are a lot of problems with it. Some plants used only the computer to price and didn't take into account other key factors such as volume. And it gets the managers playing with marginal economics that they often don't understand.

A second analytical computer model developed in the division was CIRCE[4] which enabled division managers to review each customer's orders and profitability for a given time period on the basis of actual

---

[3]The initials stood for costing and variable economics advanced techniques.
[4]The initials stood for computer indications of relative contribution effects.

orders and deliveries. The CIRCE output went to the sales offices and was used to decide whether certain products should be adjusted in price or eliminated from the line, or whether a particular customer used only lower contribution containers and should be phased out. As with CAVEAT, CIRCE was available to all the plants in 1967 and was viewed as primarily a management guideline. One local sales manager commented on the overall control aspect of the models: "CAVEAT and CIRCE make it easier now for one man to make overall decisions. Before these programs, it wasn't that way."

In 1967, the division was also experimenting in computerizing the scheduling of the container plant's complete operations. Executives reported that the process was being set up in two pilot plants to determine its effect on improved customer service, the reduction of inventories, and additional efficiency of operations and decision making.

NEW CENTRALIZED STAFF SERVICES

Containers Division executives said that the decision to functionalize management in 1961 immediately brought centralization to the accounting, budgeting, control, and personnel functions, and that by 1967 certain marketing and manufacturing services had also been centralized in the Chicago division headquarters. (See Exhibit 1 for a partial organization chart of the Chicago headquarters in early 1967 as prepared by the case writer.)

In the marketing function, the new product development that had resulted in Picture Pak, Cold Pak, and Twist Pak, all mentioned earlier, was centralized under Mr. Peter Rice, while certain marketing services had been centralized under Mr. Lyle Townsend. In 1967, both Mr. Rice and Mr. Townsend reported to the general sales manager in Chicago, the latter through a director of market development. Mr. Townsend's marketing services office performed five major functions. His graphics group existed to satisfy the division's creative graphic needs, while his audiovisual group made up presentations for new products like Picture Pak, or for a sales demonstration to a new customer. His office also included a staff structural engineer concerned with the shape and stress of the box, but Mr. Townsend reported that because each district had its own structural lab, only when a local project was too large for the local level to handle would it be sent up to marketing services. His advertising and sales promotion group functioned primarily to filter advertising and promotion information up from the districts to the Rockford Paper Company advertising manager, the latter executive handling Rockford promotions on a corporate basis. And, finally, his marketing services coordinated "key account planning" for the local level. This planning was described as essentially "a good sales program for now and the future to sell accounts

EXHIBIT 1

Rockford's Chicago Headquarters Organization in Early 1967
(certain staff functions not mentioned in case are omitted)

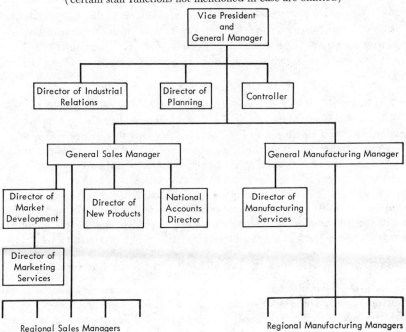

that are particularly valuable because of the volume or price they bring in." The program would include the customer's present and estimated future needs, a description of his industry's characteristics, the perceived best way for selling the customer, etc. Mr. Townsend felt that for him and his staff to be of value to the division, they had "to be seen as doers by the line." He continued: "Our goal is always to improve and supplement the district's sales abilities. But sometimes the local old-time sales managers are afraid to use our services. They want only the face-to-face contact with the customer."

The centralized manufacturing services office, reporting to the general manufacturing manager, aided the plants in designing more efficient layouts and plant construction, in setting production standards, and in formulating and submitting capital budgeting proposals. The manufacturing staff, according to one Rockford Containers manager, was also "to keep abreast of the technology of the container process so they can pass this knowledge on to the district plants." In 1967, the primary objective of manufacturing services was defined as "supporting and assisting the line manufacturing management in meeting the conditions and assumptions incorporated in the CAVEAT cost estimate based on the use of a hypo-thetical, proficient plant."

Rockford's operating managers had mixed feelings and attitudes con-cerning the value they saw in centralized staff services. Although most considered the new product development staff and the centralized ac-counting and control procedures, especially CAVEAT and CIRCE, to be major competitive advantages, one sales manager had less positive feelings:

This innovative stuff that comes from marketing services in Chicago is won-derful. It's imaginative and grabs the customer's eye. But I've got to pay not just for the stuff I feel I can use but also for the stuff that's of no value to me. I have no need for a centralized graphics service. Another thing is the time it takes to get one of these services when I request one. It takes so damn long to get some graphics work for a customer that I get the graphics done locally. It's quicker, and sometimes cheaper. . . . And the reports and forms we have to fill out because of the centralization of personnel and accounting, etc.! The reports are all standard, and they can't always apply to my specific plant and my market. They don't highlight the real intangibles of a good sales effort.

Two managers questioned the practicality of the forms and reports:

I have my own informal data and gauges to keep a current handle on the plant operations. The divisional figures are often of no practical use to me, so I develop my own. The standard division forms and reports appear to assume that all plants and all markets start with the same inputs and serve the same needs. But the markets and plants are as different as night and day.

Since our acquisition by Rockford, paper work and details have risen enor-mously. I'm taking a good hard look at the forms and reports we turn out so I can estimate their value.

The Industry Climate 1961–67

Mr. David Burns, the division's director of planning, while talking about industry conditions between 1961 and 1967, said that the container industry's profitability had always been extremely sensitive to operating capacity, and continued:

With a prevalence of continued significant overcapacity from 1961 to 1965, operating losses were common in the industry as prices continued to fall at the converting level.[5] Since 1965, though, the capacity within the industry has been more in balance, and profits, to a degree, have been restored.

Roger Cunningham spoke of the effect of the 1961–67 industry climate on his division in relation to the development of CAVEAT:

---

[5]See the "Industry Climate" section of *Rockford Containers* (*B*) for the develop-ment of industry overcapacity from 1959 to 1961.

The period required careful pricing. But some of our people didn't know how to price. They didn't know how to use cost information to price. During this period, prices went down like a bomb, and we felt that as much as our competition did. We developed the new cost system, CAVEAT, to help our managers. By 1966, though, even its effect had deteriorated because some sales managers used only the cost estimates to make pricing decisions. But the pricing decision should be based on more than just these cost estimates. Managers got so concerned with cost estimates that they forgot about the other variables like schedules and volume.

Although Rockford executives in 1967 noted that industry overcapacity of paperboard production was a continued possibility because of announced mill expansion, Mr. Bud Nathanson, the national accounts director, was optimistic about the industry outlook:

There is the possibility of oversupply again in the industry with more mills coming on line. But the industry has reached a certain stage of maturity. We've gone through too many "bloodbaths" . . . the industry has consolidated a lot of family businesses, making business in general more stable. And I'm optimistic about sales abroad. Per capita consumption of containers abroad is far below the U.S.'s. So, I feel that the industry will be able to assimilate intelligently the increase in productive capacity in the foreseeable future.

THE PROS AND CONS OF THE FUNCTIONAL ORGANIZATION

The Organization's Effectiveness

Except for the addition of more plants and more centralized services, the functional organization initiated in 1961 remained essentially the same in 1967.[6] After six years of experience with functional management, division executives reported that the structure proved to be highly effective in achieving consistency in the policies and procedures of the acquired firms. Ken Eddy, Cleveland's sales manager, said:

The functional structure really helped in getting better implementation of the division's overall programs. In achieving consistency in our acquired operations, we were very successful with this type of structure.

Tom Barry, the director of industrial relations, reported:

We had to get all the acquired firms to do the same thing. This required the strong central control that the functional organization gave us.

Roger Cunningham believed that the functional organization had also been a success for the manufacturing segment, since manufacturing costs

---

[6]See *Rockford Containers* (*B*) for a description of the 1961 functional structure and management's reasons for instituting it.

had come down 8 to 12 percent for the six years after 1961, the period of intense price cutting.

Immediately after the 1961 decision to functionalize management, strong overall profit goals seemed to be prevalent in the division. One manager said:

For a while after 1961, functional managers were pulled together by some pretty strong profit objectives. In some cases that's all they had to tie them together. The functional managers were new to their positions and new to each other, so they felt they had to work together for the overall profit goal.

But, division executives noted that gradually separate functional goals at both the plant and the regional level began to take precedence over a joint profit goal. Mr. John Jakowicz, a regional manufacturing manager, said:

In 1961, we had rising overhead and falling industry prices. So we went to functional management and made tremendous profit progress. But, slowly, goals began to be set for manufacturing versus sales and vice versa. Each function learned how to make itself look good on the figures even though overall profitability may have been suffering as a result.

A local manufacturing manager commented:

Some managers in the division were too budget oriented. They tried to meet their separate budgets instead of aiming for an overall result. Lots of friction at the plants arises from the budgets and variances from the budgets. I'm held accountable for efficiency in manufacturing even when sales takes on difficult orders. Sometimes I have to take the attitude "the hell with the variance report" when profit is at stake, but there are some manufacturing managers who wouldn't look at it that way.

Another local manager added:

Sales often only wanted the orders. They thought only in terms of their own goals, that is, volume and price. They didn't consider manufacturing. Both functions came to have separate goals, and these were performance goals, not necessarily profit goals.

Another executive explained that while one reason for functional management had been to upgrade manufacturing talent, manufacturing people had only become number oriented:

They felt they were evaluated only on the numbers, so they learned the tricks that made their budget and variance figures look good.

Several other managers commented that sales and manufacturing were thinking in terms of their own objectives and subgoals, such as meeting budgets rather than an overall profit goal. One regional manager reported:

> Manufacturing wants quality, no waste, etc., and sales wants volume. . . .
> Each feels it is being evaluated and promoted on its own separate objectives.
> That's the way it is all up the line, so that the profit center really becomes
> Mr. Cunningham at the top, not the individual plant.

In general then, manufacturing managers in the division felt they were evaluated on plant operating efficiency while sales managers felt they were judged on volume and contribution, although both stated that their major goal was "profitability."

Decision Making and Problem Solving in the Functional Organization

Division managers emphasized that the functional organization specialized in decision making: sales managers considered themselves responsible for pricing decisions and relations with customers, while manufacturing managers felt responsible for plant operations and efficiency. However, as Dave Burns stated:

> Real success at many locations has been more dependent upon the ability
> of individual sales and manufacturing managers to cooperate in a joint endeavor involving functionally divided authority and responsibility.

Rockford Containers' executives indicated that this relationship between the sales and manufacturing managers was a crucial variable at all levels. Mr. Vic Bradley, a regional sales manager, said:

> We operate a group of local businesses that have local problems and local decisions to be made. We have plants where the functional team works effectively. But where it doesn't, we really have problems. And where there's a lousy relationship down in the district and it goes upstairs, the relationship at the district becomes all the worse. In functional conflict at the district over a decision, often the strongest man wins, and often that's to the detriment of the company. In some plants, the functional team works, but where it doesn't, we really go in circles.

Other managers in the division made the following comments on functional organization:

1. With functional management, each manager has a full-time job, and no one really has the overall picture. Sometimes you need one man who could look at the total organization and make decisions on that basis.
2. I'm convinced that ultimately split management and split decisions will strangle us. You just can't throw two people together and expect them to make love. Hell, even with couples that are really in love, statistics show that one in five will be divorced.

3. In the functionally oriented plant, when there is a difference of opinion the stronger man takes over. It doesn't matter if he is sales or manufacturing.
4. What we really have with functional management is fragmented management . . . in many cases a man doesn't know how much responsibility he has or where that responsibility lies.

One divisional executive felt that having a general manager as a common boss would definitely improve the critical relationship between sales and manufacturing and make their decisions more company oriented. A local sales manager also felt strongly about the importance of the relationship between function managers for profit-generating decisions:

Not having a general manager or some one person responsible for profits at the plant is like not having a policeman at the scene of a crime. You've got to rely on a close, informal rapport between manufacturing and sales and rely on their both really feeling their profit responsibility when they make their functional decisions.

Some local managers, however, indicated that they were quite satisfied with decision making in the functional management structure and that the addition of a general manager at the local level would be superfluous. (The case writer observed that this view was generally expressed by managers who had extremely good relations with their functional counterpart.) One manufacturing manager said that his efforts were combined with those of the sales manager to make a profit, and that the two of them were sufficiently experienced in the business that they did not require the services of a general manager. He also commented:

The manufacturing manager and I can't live without each other. He needs sales, I need manufacturing, and we both know this. . . . I accept the split responsibility now and I feel it works quite well.

Other comments were made in favor of the functional setup:

1. With a general manager all you have is a third party, an arbitrator who makes decisions based on both manufacturing and sales, but still just a third party.
2. For efficiency the present structure is good. We're both experts in our decisions and we respect each other.

Rockford executives reported that functional managers were often rotated within the same function to gain broader experience or to solve a particular district problem. This system appeared to make the relationship between the functional managers less stable. Tom Barry, the division's director of industrial relations, reported that out of 20 districts, 13 district managers had been in their jobs for less than 1 year.

Although problem solving between managers was at times based on the personalities of the executives involved, Rockford managers also indicated that the relative status of the two functions played a key part in problem resolution. One manager said that the status of manufacturing versus sales differed from plant to plant and from time to time. Roger Cunningham explained the status situation in the division in the early 1960s:

An unfortunate thing happened just after 1961. The manufacturing organization really had stronger leadership than sales. This didn't work because the power structure got out of balance. If one group should have more influence, it should be sales, but in this situation we had just the opposite. Sales improved after the change to functional and specialized management, but it didn't improve as much as manufacturing, and didn't have the power that manufacturing had in the organization.

Managers in the Containers Division said that the most prevalent method of resolving differences between managers at both the regional and district levels was face-to-face problem solving. A regional manager reported that "98 percent of the conflicts my counterpart and I have are solved across the table," and Springfield's sales manager said:

My plant manager and I have a good day-to-day relationship, so that conflicts are resolved early and are resolved here. This hasn't been a problem for us because I understand him and he understands me. It's a simple relationship.

A regional manufacturing manager stated that manufacturing and sales managers should solve their conflicts together, on the local level, but that resolving any problem face-to-face took time. One manufacturing manager complained that he was always away from the floor and that the sales manager was always away from his desk and his customers, and added: "If there's a lot of pussyfooting, competition gets the business."

The same executives that indicated the prevalence of face-to-face problem solving recognized that the functional structure quite often lent itself to a second method of problem solving: sending the conflict "up the line." Managers were concerned that too many problems were being pushed up the line and that the nature of these problems was often operational (e.g., overtime and vacation schedules) rather than policy, and therefore impeded Rockford's ability to respond quickly to a competitive situation.

The complaint against this method of problem solving was summed up by one local manager:

The length of time it takes to get some decisions made around here is unbelievable. Once you have to work up through the functional hierarchy, you've had it. So we try to solve most of our problems on the local level, but when we can't and have to send it up, we've had it.

A third procedure for resolving conflict and solving problems in the division was, according to division executives, "no procedure at all." There was some avoidance of decision making; and Roger Cunningham, the division's chief executive, was particularly concerned with avoidance at the top level:

What was happening immediately after 1961, regardless of the structure, was that there was a strong centralization of decision making, or maybe I should say of no decision making. Top management really didn't tell people down the line that decisions were supposed to be made by them. As a result, the word got around that the decisions were to be made at the top only. When the decisions got there, especially those involving both functions, there was a lot of avoidance of these decisions. They just sat there with no decisions.

A local manager reported on a problem in his plant when a difficult situation arose and no one would accept responsibility for it: "No one was in charge of the whole operation so we just sat on our fannies and didn't do anything."

Two separate organizational units had evolved to help coordinate manufacturing and sales on the local level. The first, commonly called "sales service," would usually participate in initial pricing and scheduling decisions, insure that delivery commitments were kept, expedite an order through the plant, and handle routine customer telephone orders and complaints. In general the sales service unit reported to the sales manager of the local district, and experience in sales service was seen as a natural step to becoming a salesman. One local manager said that "sales service has to know the customer and his needs almost as well as the salesmen do." There were a number of sales service representatives in the plant, each responsible for certain salesmen and accounts. Sales service acted as a buffer between manufacturing and sales, as one manager explained: "Salesmen never talk to plant people and vice versa. We talk to sales service. The sales service manager has under him order writers, expediters, etc., all to satisfy the customer. He should know where an order is at all times in the plant."

The second of the two units, production scheduling, usually reporting to the manufacturing manager, formulated plant schedules for the orders that the sales function had produced. But, because of the numerous rush orders, substitutions, delivery delays, etc., that had to be considered, the unit's critical task was more often to juggle an already established schedule to meet delivery dates and customer requirements as communicated by the sales function, and to insure optimum utilization of plant machinery and personnel as communicated by the manufacturing function. Production scheduling therefore consolidated orders, substituted orders, moved orders ahead or back, etc., all to satisfy sales' indications of customers' requirements and manufacturing's indications of plant requirements.

Together the two units were day-to-day intermediaries between the sales and plant functions, each providing information to both functions. More important, however, the two units exchanged information about customers' orders and plant requirements, and, on the basis of that information, *jointly* established routine delivery priorities, reworked schedules, and insured that customer requirements were met. This joint effort relieved the local sales and manufacturing executives of much routine daily operating coordination over specific customer orders and plant schedules.

The Management Development Gap

Operating under a highly functional and centralized organization structure had taken its toll in failing to develop general managerial talent in the division. To many executives, this managerial gap was the major frustration of the functional structure, made all the more frustrating because much of the box industry was already operating under, or in the process of implementing, the general manager concept of organization structure. Mr. Cunningham spoke frankly about this:

We made a mistake. We carried functional management too far. We have created a group of specialists in sales and manufacturing but no one to pull it together. We don't have enough people with broad backgrounds. We have functional specialists, not general businessmen . . . and practically all our competition is working on the general manager basis.

This opinion was echoed by other executives, who used phrases like "penny wise and pound foolish" in referring to the management gap. One regional manager explained: "We never thought about bringing along people who were just plain good businessmen."

THE SEARCH FOR THE OPTIMAL STRUCTURE

External and Internal Recommendations for Change

In early 1966, Rockford Containers engaged a second large and well-respected consulting firm to make recommendations concerning the division's structure.[7] (See Appendix A for excerpts from this consulting report.) The consulting firm advised the division to continue with its functional centralized organization, with some clarifications of reporting relationships and job description, but with no essential change in the

---

[7]In 1959, a first national consulting firm reported on the division's organization. See *Rockford Containers* (B) Appendix for portions of this report.

structure itself. The alternative of setting up general managers at the regional level was rejected.

Late in 1966, a task force of three Containers Division executives, headed by David Burns, the division's director of planning, was given the following assignment by Roger Cunningham:

Determine the organization structure best suited for a large integrated producer of corrugated shipping containers presently and for the foreseeable future. Determine the management responsibilities to be performed at each level of the recommended structure and define the main specifications necessary to fill each position.

In January of 1967, the task force submitted its report. (*Excerpts from this report appear in Appendix B following this case.*) The task force's fundamental recommendation was for a decentralized structure. Dave Burns described decentralization as "pushing the operational and profit decisions and responsibility back down to the action level." The task force also recommended that the decentralized structure be based on the use of general managers at the regional level, defining a "region" as a "manageable marketing area," that is, as a geographic sector that could be feasibly handled on an operating and profitability basis by a single manager. Thus, according to the task force, a "region" could encompass the area of more than one manufacturing unit, especially if the units served overlapping markets, even though only one sales manager was to be responsible to the general manager for sales in the region. Division managers indicated that it was important to distinguish the task force's definition of "region" from the division's traditional use of the term in referring to the level in the functional organization hierarchy above the district or plant level.

A number of other task forces were set up in the following months of 1967, with instructions to make recommendations concerning such issues as incentive compensation for salesmen and hourly workers, long-range planning, interplant transfers, etc. Most of the members of the task forces were regional managers, all of whom had their offices in the Chicago headquarters. Roger Cunningham commented:

Some managers were saying that our policies made it impossible to function. And the January report had recommended a decentralized structure. So, the task forces, as I see it, are first to examine our traditional policies, many of which have never been written down, to see how we need to change them to decentralize decisions, and second to give the people at the regional level initially an opportunity to do work in a general manager environment. I don't know how to measure whether people could be good general managers unless you have an environment where you can see them using these skills. The task force reports should be submitted to corroborate or modify the recommendations of the January report before we decide to effect a move to decentralization. It allows people to be committed to the idea before we try it, and it lets them participate before the move so that we won't have to work by edict.

One of the task forces (also headed by Dave Burns) had the assignment of identifying decision makers. As Mr. Cunningham put it:

We are trying to get several inputs from this task force: first, to identify all the types of decisions that have to be made in running this business and to be sure the responsibility is assigned to someone under our present structure; second, to find out in this process which decisions are not easily assignable in the present organizational structure and thus get a better feel for the importance of a general manager and at what level.

The Regional Team Approach

In the summer of 1967, the division's existing functional organization was modified to initiate a team approach at the regional level only. (The region here was defined in the traditional manner as the level in the organization above the local or district level.) Under this approach, top management assigned profit goals to the two functional managers in charge of a particular region, emphasizing that the managers were to work as a team. As one manufacturing executive said:

Mr. Cunningham made it clear that concerning the profit goal he would not speak to just one functional manager of a region—he must speak to both because both are responsible for the goal.

Regional teams were to report directly to Mr. Cunningham. The general manufacturing manager and general sales manager became his staff assistants and were primarily responsible for line salaries and promotions. (Exhibit 2 is an organization chart depicting the regional team

EXHIBIT 2

The Regional Team Approach, Summer 1967

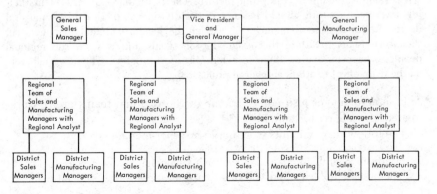

structure, drawn for the case writer by a regional manager.) The regional teams would assign profit goals to the local level, but local managers would be free to develop their own plans for attaining these goals. A regional analyst was assigned to each regional team to determine the optimal product mix for each district by using a combination of the computer-based controls discussed earlier and the knowledge of district and regional managers. Roger Cunningham further explained the new structure:

> I set it up so that all regional managers report to me as general management teams. I wanted to get close to the action and I figured I could handle 10 or so people myself. We set new profit goals for the division, the regions, and the plants, and the timing to reach the goals. I wanted to give the regional managers the experience of working toward a definite profit goal. And I wanted to see if we could make this general management team work. If we can make it work at the regional level, then we can try it at the lower level. We might decide, though, to make the regional level a level of single general managers and set up teams below them on the local level. But, we can experiment a little bit and see which works best.

Many regional managers agreed with the managers who said that the team approach was "merely formalizing and emphasizing the relationship and goals we should have had all along." Some managers were very enthusiastic about the new arrangement. One regional executive said that he and his functional counterpart were for the first time seeking an overall regional profit goal together:

> I had very little to do with my counterpart before we became a team. The only time we got together was in disputes, otherwise we'd write each other notes. We used to send a lot of disputes up the line, but solve them together now. We'd keep records on what the other fellow was doing wrong. Now that we have to work together for the profit goal, we've both decided that the other guy is not such a bad fellow after all. But we have to be able to identify false performance, that is, where a functional manager looks good on the figures but is really screwing up the profit picture. The particular expertise of marketing and manufacturing should be kept in the division, and we can do that and do it without a general manager if we let the local functional managers set their own plans to attain the assigned profit goals and rely on the regional people to keep an eye on them to avoid false performance. Then, we can rely on the team effort to attain an overall profit goal.

This same manager also noted: "Some of the regional teams aren't working half as well as our team is."

The following comments were made by other managers:

1. With an overall profit goal now, each functional manager has to look at the other's problems and you don't need an umpire or a general manager.

2. Now I've got something in common with my counterpart. We've both got to hit that profit goal.
3. The sales executive and I are supposed to be a team, but I'm still production oriented and he's still sales oriented and we just don't think the same.

The General Manager Problem

The initiation of the regional teams with an emphasis on cooperation toward overall profit goals and the inception of task forces to make recommendations concerning crucial division issues were listed as signs of an improved climate in 1967. Managers also said that a new program of "cross-fertilization" of functional managers was under way; sales managers were taking manufacturing managers' positions, and vice versa, on the regional and district levels. One sales manager who had been assigned the job of a manufacturing manager said: "The cross-fertilization is to let us become more acquainted with both functions so that we can see problems, not from a parochial view but from an overall manager's view."

Rockford executives in general seemed to feel that in the long run some variation of the general manager type of structure would be most effective for the division right down to the district level. Their reasons centered on the difficulty of holding two managers responsible for profits at any level and on the excess time it took to get decisions made without an executive with overall responsibility. Wayne Landry, Springfield's sales manager and a former regional manufacturing manager, listed his major reasons for preferring the general manager approach. His reasons were similar to those given by other division managers:

I believe the general manager concept would work best for Rockford. First, decisions in this business must be made quickly, so it's better to have one man responsible. Second, I think the decisions would be better ones because the general manager would have the whole picture to consider. With split responsibility, the sales manager is constrained to be customer oriented and can't give too much thought to manufacturing, and manufacturing is constrained by the plant and can't give too much thought to sales. Third, I think having a general manager would result in a better relationship between manufacturing and sales. There'd be less possibility of conflict and strained relations or morale within the functional suborganizations if you had one man who made the final decisions. And, last, there would be better overall control of the organization because you would have one man who was responsible for maintaining this control and planning for the future.

Division managers recognized that implementing the general manager approach posed a fundamental problem: six years of functional management had developed specialty skills but little general management talent.

Tom Barry, the director of industrial relations, talked about the possibility of hiring general manager capabilities outside the firm: "It's unrealistic to feel that we can bring in managers from the outside. We've got to get them internally or it would destroy the organization. The word would get around that a man can't move up in the organization."

Some Containers Division executives saw an effective general manager in the box business as a combination of sales and manufacturing skills, a blend of the expertise in both. Most executives, though, expected a general manager to be first and foremost a good businessman. As a divisional executive described it, "He should be a professional, not a specialist." The division's chief executive, Roger Cunningham, listed the characteristics he felt an effective general manager must have:

These following things come to my mind because they seem to be weaknesses in the current people:

1. I think he needs self-discipline in making risk-taking decisions. There are lots of these kinds of decisions in this business. The whole industry is unskilled at this. We don't get at the pertinent facts and evaluate them unemotionally.

2. He has to be willing to fire people. This is important because if a man can't face up to this kind of decision, he'll never really be able to get people to work toward high performance goals. Subconsciously, he will always be circumventing the problem of setting high goals because he'll see the risk of having to fire people who don't perform, which he won't be willing to do.

3. He has to be good at planning, organizing, integrating, measuring, etc. He has to be able to get ahead of the problems rather than waiting for them and then reacting to them.

4. I think he has to be really able to encourage supportive relations, 9–9 instead of 1–9 or 9–1.[8]

5. He has to be able to set high performance goals for himself. He's got to want to reach his goals.

6. Lots of managers say he would have "to know the territory," that is, know the market, the customers, and the plant inside out. I don't know whether he would really have to know the industry that well or not. I feel the other things I've listed rank higher. If he knows about these other things and can handle them, he can learn the business. Our business is changing— knowing the old business may be a disadvantage.

---

[8]Mr. Cunningham here was referring to the scaling on Robert Blake's management tool, the "managerial grid." According to the measurements on the grid, a 1–9 manager or leader had a low orientation toward the accomplishment of the task but a higher orientation toward people. A 9–1 manager was just the opposite; while a 9–9 manager had a high orientation toward both the task and his people. For more information, see Robert Blake's and Jane Mouton's, *The Managerial Grid* (Houston, Texas: The Gulf Publishing Co., 1964).

Mr. Cunningham indicated that one way he hoped to improve the development of future managers in Rockford was by recruiting at graduate schools of business:

One way to get MBAs started in the division is to give them some kind of analytical job under the regional manager here in headquarters, something like our regional analyst role. I think this is an ideal spot. We can get them really involved here. Then, after some period of time, we can put them in as plant managers or sales managers. Some of our people in the districts say this wouldn't work because the young fellow wouldn't know the box business. I don't believe this. I think we've got a challenging role for MBAs to play in the division.

Management Development at Rockford

The division had been participating in the Rockford Paper Company-sponsored Executive Development Seminar held annually in Suffern, New York. For eight weeks selected managers attended lectures and took part in discussion groups on such subjects as leadership, planning, organizing, finance, motivating workers, communications within the organization, and problem analysis and decision making. In 1967 the division sent 10 managers to the seminar, all of whom were from division headquarters. The group included seven regional managers and three staff men.

Another factor which seemed to indicate a healthier management development climate was the division's interest at this time in taking part in a three-year program conducted by a well-known behavioral scientist. This scientist was a proponent of "participative management,"[9] and he proposed to use seminars, training, the exchange of ideas, etc., to help the division "move to more participation to tap and develop more talent in the organization." His program included making a survey or profile of the division's environment regarding participation in 1967, and then periodically updating the profile to measure the move toward more participative management.

The director of industrial relations, Tom Barry, said about this program:

The division wants to hear more about the participative management program. This is a healthy sign concerning management development. Only

---

[9] "Participative management" was most simply understood as the sharing of decision making by all levels of an organization. For more on this approach to management, see Douglas McGregor, *The Human Side of Enterprise* (New York: McGraw-Hill Book Co., Inc., 1960); Rensis Likert, *New Patterns for Management* (New York: McGraw-Hill Book Co., Inc., 1961); or Chris Argyris, *Integrating the Individual and the Organization* (New York: John Wiley & Sons, Inc., 1964).

limited ideas are being fed up the line now. We need more input from the managers than we're getting. We've got to get people to carry more of the load themselves.

The Dilemma in 1967

By 1967, after two national consulting firms and an internal task force had made recommendations concerning the division's optimal structure, division executives in general favored a move to some form of decentralization. One local manager said he thought that a change to decentralization would be met with a great deal of relief. An executive in Chicago commented that "the centralized approach was necessary to weld the division together, but it's not needed now." The managers did not, however, want to return to the "helter-skelter" organization that characterized the division before the move to functional management, and did not want to lose the functional expertise that had grown in the division. Neither did managers want to lose the advantages of some central control over sales, especially national accounts sales, since more customers were centralizing purchasing, and since interdistrict transfers were increasing for Picture Pak, Cold Pak, and Twist Pak. Division executives felt that plant coordination on national accounts and transfers was essential.

Roger Cunningham summed up his opinion of the situation:

I'm not prepared to say yet that we will go to general managers and completely forget about functional management. There is a temptation to go to general managers because everybody in the industry is doing it. I am concerned that although we have enough talent in the organization to make regional general managers, we do not have it at the plant level. Besides, I wonder if there isn't a better way than just the choice between a functional organization and a general manager organization. I'm convinced that decentralization of decision making is important, but an organization structure doesn't insure that.

APPENDIX A

EXCERPTS FROM THE CONSULTING REPORT OF 1966

LONG-RANGE PLAN OF ORGANIZATION

This section of the report evaluates the advantages and disadvantages of the functional and general manager concepts of organization, reaches conclusions regarding a proposed long-range plan of organization, and sets forth recommendations for taking advantage of the major opportunities for improvement.

Alternatives Considered

Two major alternatives merit consideration by Rockford Containers Division in selecting a sound long-range plan of organization. These are: (1) functional plan of organization and (2) regional general manager plan of organization. The present organization structure is based primarily on the functional concept.

Functional Plan of Organization

The advantages of a functional plan of organization for Rockford Containers Division includes:

1. Major decisions having broad effects on the long-range business activities would be made from an overall point of view.
2. Functional specialists could be developed on the job with minimal difficulty, and such specialists are more easily recruited than personnel with general management experience.
3. Within each function, optimum utilization of manpower and physical resources would be facilitated and a high level of efficiency could be achieved.
4. Maximum use could be made of specialized functional experience, both in daily operations and in the analysis of major investment opportunities.
5. The division would have greater flexibility in achieving its integrated profit responsibilities and in pursuing opportunities of advantage to the overall business.

The disadvantages of a functional plan of organization for Rockford Containers Division include:

1. Top management would have to coordinate major operating decisions and resolve differences of opinion between functional department heads; thus, some involvement in daily operations would be necessary and delegation of decision-making authority to lower levels of management would be somewhat limited.
2. Delegation of profit responsibility is complicated and may not be possible below the top operating position in the organization; responsibility must be fixed and authority delegated in terms of specific objectives, the achievement of which is within the control of the individual.
3. Assessment of the impact on, or contributions to, profits of key managers is difficult; and proper responsibilities can be evaded without prompt discovery unless satisfactory controls are established.
4. Special programs and unusual efforts would be required to develop

managers who can think and act in broad rather than specialized terms; sound preparation for top-management succession would be necessary.

Regional General Manager Plan of Organization

The advantages of a regional general manager plan of organization for Rockford Containers Division include:

1. Major operating decisions could be made at lower management levels, thus freeing top management from involvement in daily operations.
2. Effective communication and coordination on matters affecting regional operations are more easily achieved.
3. Profit responsibility would be fixed more clearly and would constitute a strong management incentive for effective performance.
4. Many of the advantages of small company operation would be realized; key managers could readily see and appreciate the effect of their positions on costs and profits; and it would be difficult to evade responsibility.
5. Means for developing a larger number of general managers would be available, and succession to top-management positions of qualified general managers is inherent in such a system.
6. It is somewhat easier to develop and implement an effective management information and control system with this organizational concept.

The disadvantages of a regional general manager plan of organization for Rockford Containers Division include:

1. Individuals with general management capabilities required in a large corporation (as contrasted with the small company entrepreneur) are difficult to find; on-the-job training requires the willingness to accept a certain number of costly mistakes and an unusual amount of effort to foster the development of such general managers.
2. Successful operation requires that there be few major functional problems calling for the attention of highly experienced functional experts.
3. Unusual efforts must be made to develop an overall, rather than regional, viewpoint in making major decisions.
4. Flexibility is reduced for promptly relocating resources to achieve optimum usage on an overall division basis.
5. Overall facilities planning for achieving the future growth and development objectives of the division might be hampered by the strong incentive for regional profit as compared with integrated profit for the overall business.

Conclusion and Recommended Choice

While strong arguments can be presented supporting either of the alternatives, the following considerations should weigh heavily in the selection of the best plan for Rockford Containers Division for the foreseeable future:

1. The division is relatively new and long-range plans for its growth and development are still in the formative stage.

   a) Overall plans regarding the kinds of facilities required and where they should be located to best service the market over the long range have not been made. Studies now under way may have a profound effect on the selection of facility plans, methods of operation, and identification of regions.

   b) Functional specialist attention is required to develop and implement long-range plans for the division. Particular attention is required in the facilities planning and marketing and new product development areas of the business.

2. The increasing importance of national accounts in the future development of the business would have the effect of diluting regional general management responsibility for profits and hamper achievement of overall divisional goals.

3. Systems for handling the products from the end of the manufacturing line to the ultimate consumer will become more important in new product development and marketing of containers in the future. Such systems require coordination of all phases of the business, unusual staff support and cooperation between functions to ensure that these needs are met.

4. The development of the division has been through acquisition of small businesses with entrepreneurial management. The transition from this type of management to that required in a large corporation takes considerable adjustment in the outlook, habits, practices, and relationships with others on the part of individuals involved. This transition was started only recently and development for some may be slow.

In the light of the division's recent pattern of development, the uncertain nature of its future facilities plans, the composition of the markets served, including the increasing portion to be obtained from national accounts, and expected changes in serving these markets in the future and the need for expert functional specialists to take advantage of opportunities for improvement, we believe that for the foreseeable future the net advantages of the functional plan of organization far outweigh those of the regional general manager concept.

APPENDIX B

EXCERPTS FROM THE JANUARY REPORT OF THE TASK FORCE

REQUIREMENTS FOR SUCCESS IN CORRUGATED CONTAINER BUSINESS

. . . A sound understanding of the business and its objectives, with timely decision-making ability and authority at the point of action.

. . . Secure superior sales position through a disciplined selling effort which seeks, recognizes, and satisfies customer needs at a profit.

. . . Maintain a high level of manufacturing efficiency and control of overall costs, consistent with the quality and service requirements of its customers.

. . . Attract and maintain an adequate supply of competent people in key positions, working in a team effort toward the common objective.

ALTERNATE ORGANIZATION POSSIBILITIES

An organization structure provides for the orderly classification of all of the work of the business. It should also facilitate the carrying out of the work in an effective, efficient manner. The alternate types of organizations available need to be evaluated in terms of the corrugated container business. From a careful evaluation of the different types of organization that might be considered, it was concluded that both the centralized and the decentralized types of organization should be given consideration. Their respective advantages are as follows:

ADVANTAGES OF CENTRALIZED (FUNCTIONAL) ORGANIZATION STRUCTURE

1. Provides more rapid response to changes in goals and strategies.
2. Provides easier implementation of uniform philosophy, policy, and procedures.
3. Provides opportunity for high functional efficiency.
4. Tends to make problems involving functional activities highly visible.

ADVANTAGES OF DECENTRALIZED ORGANIZATION STRUCTURE

1. Provides a framework for timely, sound decision making at the point of action.
2. Provides better opportunity for broad personal perspective and growth throughout the organization.
3. Provides clear delegation of profit responsibility and authority to the point at which decisions affecting profits are made.
4. Easier to establish effective and meaningful control systems.
5. More responsive to demands of local environment.

6. Provides a reservoir of well-trained candidates for management succession.
7. Promotes team effort toward common objectives.

The relative value of any one of these objectives is dependent upon the particular needs of a given organization at a specific point in time.

RECOMMENDATION

After objective appraisal of alternate organization possibilities, we have concluded that a decentralized organization offers the best opportunity for success for an integrated manufacturer of corrugated containers.

1. The nature of our business is such that decisions affecting profits can best be made at a point close to the point of action.
2. Ours is a business of small orders of nonstandard products in which imperfect measurements of functional performance often conflict with the overall profit objective.
3. Decentralization promotes greater breadth of thinking and better functional decisions at the profit center, as a result of the greater teamwork inherent in concentrating on the common profit objective.
4. Decentralization will enable us to attract and retain an adequate supply of competent people for key positions, because of greater opportunities for broad personal growth.
5. Decentralization provides for operating decisions being made at lower management levels, thus freeing higher management to develop, coordinate, and implement long-range business plans and strategies and review performance against approved plans and budgets.

ORGANIZATION

In conjunction with the recommendation that a decentralized organization is best for the corrugated business, the committee has several thoughts with regard to how to make such an organization more effective. (See the recommended organization chart following this report.)

Of prime importance is the necessity of having competent personnel at the regional and area general manager level. These positions have total profit responsibility for their respective portion of the total business of the division. Their competence in making sound business decisions will play the decisive role in the division's success. If the merits of a decentralized philosophy are accepted, the difficulties in achieving the necessary level of competence in these positions is not a valid reason for post-poning its implementation. It will, however, require special efforts to provide the necessary training at the earliest possible moment.

The committee recommends decentralization to a profit center which encompasses a manageable marketing area. While in some cases this will be the area served by only one manufacturing location, it could also encompass the area of more than one manufacturing unit. The manageable marketing area has been designated as a region. All sales effort throughout the region is coordinated by one sales manager, and one regional general manager oversees the entire region as a single profit center. Many advantages derive from this concept of a profit center built around a marketing area.

The concept of organizing around "manageable marketing areas," rather than individual physical manufacturing units, represents a unique feature of the committee's recommendation. It was developed to capitalize on situations wherein several small manufacturing units are located in generic overlapping markets. Inherent advantages in organizing around more realistic profit centers include:

1. The flexibility afforded the sales organization in being able to direct its effort to the capacity and capabilities of several manufacturing units.
2. The practical elimination of inappropriate and damaging competitive activity between individual components, that is not in the overall best interest of the division.
3. The ability to realize manufacturing efficiencies through more effective scheduling of business.
4. The larger sales base of regional profit centers permits upgrading the qualifications and effectiveness of key regional management personnel.

The regional general managers will report to a vice president and area general manager. The vice president and area general manager will serve as an extension of the arms of the president and division general manager, largely relieving him of responsibilities for the short-term operation of the division. He will possess substantial responsibility and authority to deal with all short-term aspects of the business. The vice president and area general manager will also work closely with the president and division general manager to keep him in touch with the market and to assist him in the important future planning effort.

The president and division general manager, supported by competent staff, can devote necessary time and effort to overall divisional planning, including provisions for future growth and development, and integration of divisional plans into those of the corporate board group. In addition, he will give overall direction to the entire work of the division and review performance against approved plans and budgets.

Staff departments have been structured to concentrate their strengths in areas of greatest potential benefit. In as far as possible, like skills have been combined into one department so as to effect greatest efficiency. Responsibility for each significant part of the total work has been assigned to one individual, thus minimizing confusion. Where practical, staff activities have been moved closer to the line function they are servicing so as to maximize their effectiveness. Remaining at division level are those staff activities which require a divisional point of view, to afford overall economies through location at the division.

Recommended Organization Chart

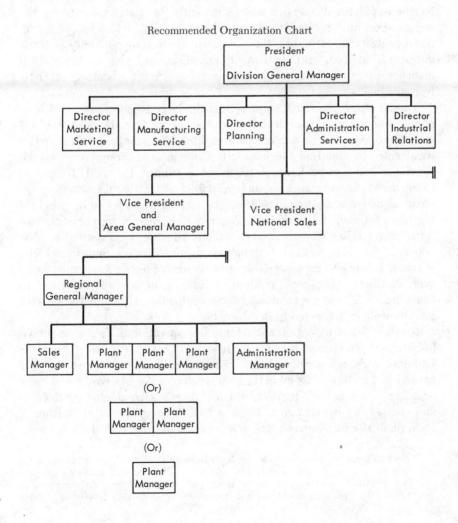

Northern Electric Company, Ltd. (A)

IN JANUARY of 1964, an ad hoc study group of managers from the Northern Electric Company was faced with the task of designing the organization of a proposed semiconductor devices plant.[1] In specifying the organizational structure, the group had the rare opportunity of starting afresh with an entirely new organization, and also of having top management's consent to apply the newest and most advanced concepts from the behavioral sciences.

The Northern Electric Company was the largest manufacturer of telephone and other communications equipment in Canada, and its 1964 sales were expected to exceed $300 million. The company's head office was located in Montreal and it had 10 plants located throughout Canada. Northern was a subsidiary of its major customer, the Bell Telephone Company of Canada and, as such, supplied all of Bell-Canada's equipment needs either by manufacturing the required articles or by purchasing them for Bell from outside companies. The parent-supplier relationship between Bell-Canada and Northern Electric was similar to that between the Bell System Companies in the United States and the Western Electric Company; unlike the Western Electric Company, however, Northern also sold equipment to a number of independent Canadian, U.S., and overseas telephone companies, although the bulk of its sales were still directed to Bell-Canada.

Northern Electric was organized into five operating divisions, as shown in Exhibit 1. The semiconductor devices works was part of the Apparatus Division. Although semiconductor production was not yet extensive or housed in a facility of its own, the semiconductor devices works had been organized during 1963 to unify the existing semiconductor production and engineering departments. These activities were housed in Northern's main plant site in Montreal. The temporary semiconductor devices works

---

[1]Semiconductor devices are electronic components made from semiconductor materials such as germanium and silicon which are designed and made to perform specified electronic functions. For the most part, these devices are considerably smaller than the equivalent traditional electronic devices which they replace in circuits.

EXHIBIT 1

Simplified Organizational Chart

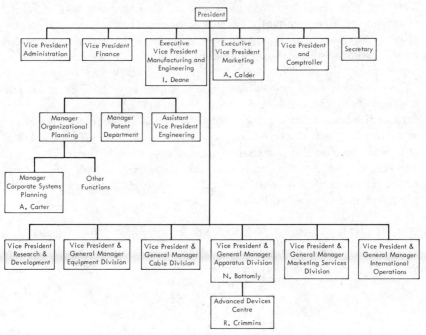

organization was made up of a works manager and superintendents for engineering, accounting, and personnel (as shown in Exhibit 2). This temporary organization was responsible for managing the previously separate semiconductor activities and for doing the detailed planning of the new plant.

The Proposed Plant

The proposed plant involved a large increase in the scale of Northern's semiconductor operations, and therefore represented a major commitment on the part of Northern Electric to the future of semiconductor devices. Sales volume was expected to increase from $2 million annually to $8 million or more by the time the new plant reached capacity. Productive floor space in the new facility was planned to exceed 150,000 square feet, a sizable increase over the 20,000 square feet utilized by Northern's existing semiconductor facilities. The semiconductor works also anticipated that the 1963 employment of 200 employees would probably be doubled.

Although it was hoped that the new facility might compete in the outside market for semiconductors, its main objective was to provide the Northern Electric Company with semiconductor devices needed for its communications equipment. Whether a semiconductor device was purchased from the outside or made by the semiconductor works depended upon a comparison of design, quality, and cost. If an outside manufacturer could meet Northern's design and quality requirements and charge less than the semiconductor works' transfer price, Northern would normally buy that component from the outside. As a result, the more standardized and simple components were generally bought from major semiconductor manufacturers whose economies of scale enabled them to sell these devices cheaper than Northern could make them. The more specialized, complex devices or those which were in small volume and hence not attractive to outside suppliers were generally made by the semiconductor devices works.

EXHIBIT 2

Temporary Organization—Semiconductor Devices Works

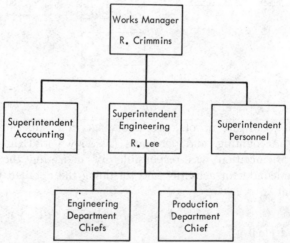

The new semiconductor plant had additional limitations when compared to outside semiconductor manufacturers by virtue of its charter as internal supplier of Northern's semiconductor device needs. The plant's primary focus in producing semiconductors would be on making a device which would optimize the performance of the communications system for which it was intended, as compared with a focus on parameters which would optimize the process and hence the ease of manufacture. An independent semiconductor manufacturer, however, could design a product which would meet the general needs of the market and concentrate on process parameters to improve yields and reduce cost, with relatively less concern for its final application.

Design of the New Organization

The design of the organizational structure for the new plant was in the hands of an ad hoc group of managers made up of the temporary works management team and two men from outside the group who were experienced in organizational planning. The key personnel involved in the effort were Mr. Anthony Carter, manager of business systems planning for Northern Electric Company; Mr. Robert Crimmins, semiconductor devices works manager; Mr. Raymond Lee, superintendent of engineering in the new works; and Mr. Paris Townsend, a psychologist on retainer as a consultant by the Northern Electric Company.

Mr. Carter, though not a member of the works management group, had actively helped win top management's approval to allow the group to base the organization design on a "system's approach" utilizing modern organizational concepts. Mr. Carter had taken part in the planning of several organizations within Northern Electric and had done a great deal of work in planning large-scale business systems, first in the communications equipment division and later on the corporate level.

Mr. Crimmins, the recently appointed works manager, had considerable experience in manufacturing management, although he was new to semiconductors.

Mr. Lee had been superintendent of semiconductor engineering before the formation of the new works and continued in that position with the added responsibility for production and materials management in the new organization. Mr. Lee also had engineering and manufacturing experience in Northern's more conventional products.

Mr. Townsend was a well-known Canadian behavioral scientist who had been affiliated with several Canadian universities and the Systems Development Corporation as senior human factors scientist. He was also a partner in Ross Townsend Associates, a group offering psychological services in areas related to the "design and development of man-machine systems."

The group differed on the extent to which the new organization should be untraditional and experimental. Mr. Crimmins felt that the organization should be different from that of Northern's other plants, and that this was an excellent opportunity to apply new management concepts. He also felt, however, that the group should proceed with an element of caution. Mr. Carter and Mr. Townsend, on the other hand, saw the new organization as an opportunity to apply the findings of the behavioral sciences in "an integrated organization system which would integrate the goals of the organization and the individual so that common purpose can be shared." Mr. Townsend elaborated on these goals in a paper which he had prepared for a psychological journal by describing the philosophy behind the aims in the design of the organization:

This attempt to integrate personal and organizational goals implies a need to consider all aspects of the situation so that no one element is enhanced at the expense of others. In other words a "system" view is required in which all elements of a system are specified and their relation to and dependence upon all other elements of the system are clarified and made explicit.

To this Mr. Carter added that it was essential "to emphasize 'system' values as opposed to departmental barriers" in making such an organization work. Carter also felt that the semiconductor business and technology was one which lent itself naturally to the application of these new concepts, especially in view of its rapidly changing product line and its complex manufacturing processes.

Semiconductor Industry and Technology

The expansion of semiconductor activity undertaken by Northern Electric reflected the increasing value of semiconductors to manufacturers of communications equipment. The major advantages which semiconductor devices offered in 1964 were substantial reduction in size (when compared to the conventional electronic components which they replaced) and the potential for better future reliability and cost reduction.

Semiconductor devices could be designed to perform many different electronic functions and to replace conventional components. These devices were made from semiconductor materials, so named because they could be classified neither as conductors nor insulators in electrical conductivity. They were useful as electronic components because their ability to conduct electricity could be changed by introducing precisely controlled amounts of selected impurities (a process called "doping") into semiconductor material. By the appropriate location of the areas to be thus doped, a tiny piece of semiconductor material could be made to perform functions such as rectifying or amplifying electrical currents.

Semiconductor devices which performed a single electronic function were called "discrete devices." Semiconductor devices were also made which included the electrical functions of an entire circuit and were thus small circuits in themselves; these were called "microcircuits" or "integrated circuits." Although often smaller than match heads, microcircuits could, in some cases, replace large conventional circuits several hundred times their size.

The developing semiconductor industry was characterized by an almost continual improvement in product design. The nature of the product was such that the design of a device was very interdependent with the processes required to make it; the device was therefore designed in conjunction with the process.

The industry was dominated by several major electronics companies, most of which were located in the United States, but it also included hundreds of small companies. Many of these smaller companies had been founded by one or two engineers who had developed a new process design. The volatility and rapid obsolescence of processes and designs, especially in microcircuits, made many of these ventures short lived. The developing nature of the product line and price competition by major manufacturers made competence in research and process development and responsiveness to industry changes a necessity for survival.

The Manufacturing Process

Northern's semiconductor line included transistors, diodes, and varistors, all components which performed a discrete electronic function. Northern had not yet developed a line of microcircuits but was involved in development activities and expected to have microcircuit production by the time the new plant was completed.

The discrete semiconductors made at Northern were grouped into two general product lines: planar products and nonplanar products. As can be seen in Exhibit 3, most of the nonplanar products were made from germanium crystal and some from silicon crystal. All of the planar products were made from silicon. After the material growing, both the planar and nonplanar products went through similar materials preparation processes of slicing, polishing, and etching. From this point on, the methods of forming the semiconductor junction and the assembly steps became fairly different for planar and nonplanar products. Most of the planar products went through the assembly process shown in Exhibit 3, while the nonplanars went through five parallel but different processes.

All of the devices being produced were extremely small. The actual elements of some devices were so small that they could easily be lost under a person's fingernail. In addition, the manufacture required a dust-free environment and the immediate vicinity of the element had to be closely controlled during processing. The combination of these two factors required careful, sometimes painstaking, attention on the part of the production operators, who handled the product with micromanipulators and who could not see the element except under a microscope.[2]

As shown in Exhibit 3, the manufacture of semiconductor devices involved a long, complicated series of operations using sophisticated tech-

---

[2]Micromanipulators are instruments used for manipulating parts which are too small to be handled manually. The actual manipulation of the parts is viewed through a microscope.

EXHIBIT 3

Flow Diagram of the Semiconductor Production Process

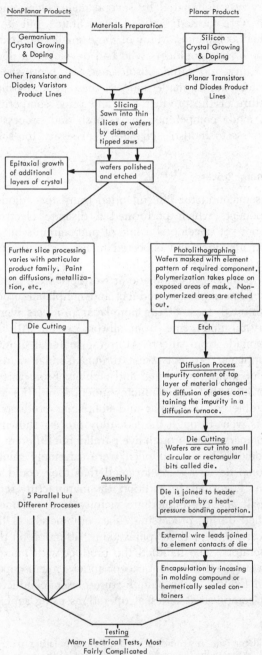

nologies such as the crystal growing and diffusion processes. The nature of the process involved many separate and difficult operations, and an error in any one of the intermittent operations was often not detected until the final testing, making the role of the individual operators very important. The operators' personal sense of responsibility, care, and awareness could greatly influence production yields.

There was considerable "art" still left in semiconductor production since operations were often affected by minor changes in environmental conditions, materials, etc., and required frequent intervention and assistance by engineering personnel. Hence, the technical expertise of process engineers and their ability to work with production personnel also influenced production yields. This added complexity had sometimes resulted in semiconductor manufacturers losing their "skill" for making a particular device because a process engineer who had a "feel" for the process had left.

Process problems often required the efforts of a number of different specialists, and the continuous appearance of new devices required continual coordination with research personnel during the introduction period.

The important factors in the successful manufacture of semiconductors were described by Mr. Charles Kimball, chief engineer of the Apparatus Division. Mr. Kimball was not directly involved in the planning effort but he had been a supporter of the plan to experiment with new organizational techniques and as chief engineer of the division was interested in the new plant.

The three key factors in the success of semiconductors production are the processor, or operator, who is performing the work, the process itself, and the facility.

Because of the nature of the product, the processor must have the manual dexterity and mental awareness to pick out unusual situations and problems. And finally he must have integrity. If the operator is not with you, you are not apt to find out for a long time because there are so many steps to the process. Their commitment to making good products is very important as is their ability to constantly monitor the process. Although you have as many in-process tests as possible, there are 98 operations before the final testing, and that's a long way for feedback in correcting a problem.

The second important factor is the process itself, because the product and the process are so completely interdependent. When one is changed it affects the other. We have many parameters in the process which can change, and one variable is often apt to affect several others, and of course the product. This means that the ability to understand process parameters and our knowledge of the process determines our ability to control it, which in turn influences our yields, the quality, and our ability to manipulate the process to meet new customer requirements. What's needed, then, is a process engineering capability to work out the process parameters, good data collection, and feed-back loops in the manufacturing process.

The third important factor is the facility itself—not only in the cleanliness of the building and the building itself but especially in the processing and testing equipment. Our competitors such as [a large semiconductor manufac-turer] can develop highly specialized machines because their large volume al-lows them to make big investments. But Northern can't afford that. Our equip-ment must be designed to be economical and versatile. It has to be clever enough to be specialized yet adaptable to new uses. Our engineers who design the process and the test equipment must be extremely clever and know the processes.

The Shearer Street Facility

The importance of adequate facilities suggested above was one reason for the recommendation to build a new plant. The existing semiconductor activities were housed in Northern Electric's huge Shearer Street works in Montreal. The Shearer Street works was a large eight-story building built in 1914 which covered a city block in the heart of a French Cana-dian low-rent area. The building had over a million square feet of floor space and housed the activities of nearly 6,000 employees.

The semiconductor activities were dispersed throughout this large building. Exhibit 4 is a plan view of the building showing the locations of the various activities. Semiconductor production occupied about 10,000 square feet of space on the third floor of the main wing of the eight-story building (except for painting and finishing, which was located on the same floor in an adjacent wing). Semiconductor engineering was located

EXHIBIT 4

The Shearer Street Works—Showing the Locations of the
Semiconductor Operations
(plan view)

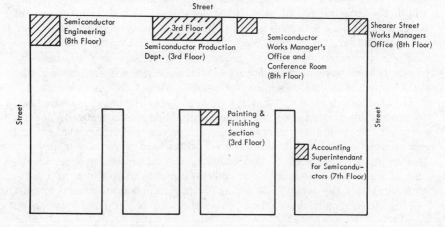

on the eighth floor, two wings away from manufacturing. The semiconductor works manager and his conference room were also located on the eighth floor, but on the opposite end of the main building. The personnel superintendent used the conference room as a temporary work area. The accounting superintendent and his section were housed in a wing adjacent to the works manager on the seventh floor. Both accounting and the works manager were two wings and several floors away from the production department.

The facilities at Shearer Street were managed under the temporary organization referred to earlier, with the superintendents of accounting, engineering, and personnel reporting to Mr. Crimmins, the works manager. The production department and the three engineering departments reported to Mr. Lee, engineering superintendent, as shown in Exhibit 5.

EXHIBIT 5

Semiconductor Engineering Group

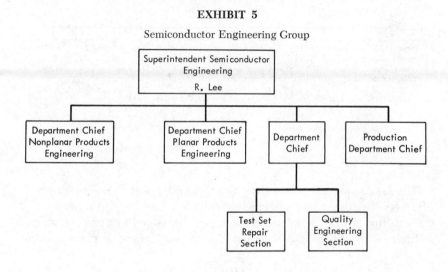

The department chief for planar products engineering had engineering support responsibility for the final processes in planar assembly and also for the material growing and material preparation processes for both planar and nonplanar products. This arrangement existed because the material preparation processes (slicing, polishing, etching, photolithography, diffusion, and dicing) were essentially the same for both planar and nonplanar products. The department chief of nonplanar products engineering was responsible for the assembly processes of nonplanar products (which made up the bulk of Northern's semiconductor production) and the diffusion process used for a small number of nonplanar products which could not be processed in the main diffusion furnace.

The production department was organized as shown in Exhibit 6, with six section chiefs reporting to the production department chief. The production department was divided into sections geographically rather than by process. Roughly 130 employees worked in the production area, the majority working in nonplanar assembly as shown in Exhibit 6. Although some production personnel were skilled technicians, most were women who were housewives or young high school graduates. All production workers were paid on hourly rates.

EXHIBIT 6

Organization of the Production Department

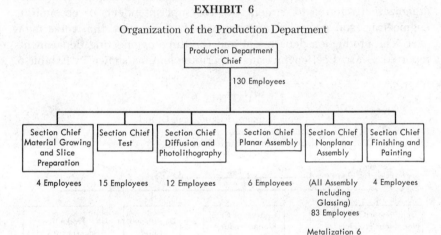

The semiconductor production area was laid out as shown in Exhibit 7. Mr. Lee, superintendent of semiconductor engineering, pointed out that the existing layout had many faults which he hoped would be corrected in the new plant. The materials flow in the production area was not con-

EXHIBIT 7

Layout of the Semiconductor Production Department

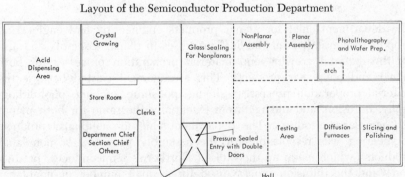

ducive to efficient materials handling, especially in view of the many operations involved. He added that the considerable art still left in the business required frequent assistance by engineering personnel, and the distance which separated engineering from production made such inter-action difficult. This seemed especially important since no one person had a "corner on the expertise" needed for successful manufacturing.

Mr. Lee also felt that the coordination with research needed for the constant stream of new devices was hampered by the geographic separa-tion between Shearer Street and the corporate research and development laboratories located in Ottawa. In addition to the lab, Northern had historically located branch laboratories of central research in each of its plants and one existed in Montreal for the Shearer Street works but not for semiconductors. The branch labs normally designed new products, handled applications engineering, and conducted the initial process de-velopment of new products.

Mr. Lee went on to add that the Shearer Street environment was not conducive to the high standards of cleanliness needed to make semicon-ductors. Although a pressure-locked entry of double doors separated the production area from the rest of the building, people tended to dress roughly in the Shearer Street plant and carried dirt into the area. This problem was caused in part by the distance between the locker room and the production area. Mr. Lee explained that the Western Electric Com-pany had minimized this problem by locating the locker rooms close to the parking lots and the production areas close to the locker rooms. In this way the dirt tracked into the locker rooms was kept to a minimum, and the operators were able to move directly into the dust-free produc-tion areas after changing into clean work clothes.

Mr. Lee felt that the freedom given to the group to design the new organization, including layout and spacial relationships, would allow Northern to eliminate many of the present problems. Mr. Carter and Mr. Townsend also envisioned the design and allocation of area as an im-portant part of an integrated approach to the new organization.

Background on the Present Situation

Mr. Carter pointed out that the interest of several managers in new management techniques had influenced the decision to base the new or-ganization's design on concepts from the behavioral sciences. Northern's two executive vice presidents, for example, had both given considerable thought to the question of organizational growth and to the changes tak-ing place in the industrial environment. Mr. Ian Deane, executive vice president for manufacturing and engineering, and Mr. Aaron Calder, executive vice president for marketing, had both been strong proponents of new methods in their previous assignments and were still generally supportive of innovations. Several outside management consultants had also played active roles in introducing behavioral concepts. A third influence was Northern's "Factors in Growth Program," a series of management development courses which exposed Northern's managers to modern management techniques, such as materials management, quantitative methods, and sensitivity training.

Mr. Carter elaborated on this background by saying that both Mr. Deane, when vice president of the Communications Equipment Division (CED), and Mr. Calder, when vice president of sales, had acquired reputations for having shaped major changes in these assignments. Mr. Calder had completely reoriented Northern's market focus from the sole supplier to Bell-Canada to an aggressive competitor in domestic and overseas markets. Mr. Carter described the atmosphere which existed in CED when Mr. Deane was its vice president:

There was a marked difference between CED and the other divisions. Ian Deane was always pushing for new management techniques, explorations of new ideas, decentralization, etc. We always had management development courses going on, and it was an exciting environment with a lot of learning. Deane was an old-timer and had been brought up in a very traditional, hierarchical, and autocratic era when Taylorisms and work measurements were at their heyday. In fact, he established many of the traditional practices which still exist at Shearer Street when he was works manager 20 years ago. But he also had the foresight to realize that times were changing and he gave much thought to adapting to these changes through innovation.

One of the first outside consultants to question the established methods of organization was Mr. William Durneen. In 1958, Mr. Durneen was introduced to Mr. Deane, then vice president of the Equipment Division. Mr. Carter described Durneen's influence by saying:

Bill Durneen was a management consultant who had formerly been a professional engineer but who was dissatisfied with engineering and read quite a lot. He read philosophy, psychology, everything. He joined with a fellow named DuBarry who was an industrial psychologist and general semanticist, and they formed a partnership in management consulting. Durneen questioned the assumptions of management and the purpose of business organizations. "Why are we doing things this way?" "Is it the best way?" Ian had him hold seminars with the top-management team of CED.

Durneen had us do various things—wine tasting, oil painting, etc., to show us that we're limited by our assumptions and that we needed to increase our perceptions and our assumptions. This triggered a series of management discussions about the traditional ways of doing things.

In 1962, Northern Electric was introduced to Mr. Paris Townsend, the consultant currently working with the group designing the new organization. Mr. Carter described the beginning of Mr. Townsend's relationship with Northern Electric by saying:

At that time our major problem was getting new ideas implemented and that's where we brought in the behavioral sciences and Paris Townsend. Durneen had met Paris in 1960 and suggested that we talk to him about implementing change. The approach Townsend articulated was the "man-machine" concept which was an integrated system approach. His presence added a good deal of support to those of us interested in change because he offered psychology and the system approach. He also had a lot of status because of his psychological background and because he had been a human factors scientist looking at large-scale systems at Systems Development Corporation (SDC). He and Ross [his partner] came back to Canada to head up an activity similar to SDC's study of the U.S. defense system. This naturally lent him stature among Northern's top management.

His first project dealt with studying relationships at Northern's general committee level (vice presidents and higher). One of his reports recommended a junior chamber which would be an integrative, multidisciplined group of junior executives who were on the way up and who would look at the functions, goals, values, missions, and misunderstandings of the company. They would then recommend programs of change to correct these problems. The recommendation was not accepted by the general committee, however.

In 1963, Deane and Calder were promoted to executive vice presidents of manufacturing and engineering and marketing respectively. Subsequently, Mr. Carter was assigned to his current assignment in corporate business systems development.

By this time, strong interest existed at the Northern Electric Company in applying current organizational theory on a pioneering basis to one of the branch plants. Mr. Ian Deane gave a speech to the annual company conference in August of 1963 (which became widely quoted in Canadian business circles) entitled "The Factory of the Future." This paper was felt by many to articulate top management's views on the need for change. The highlights of this paper are given in Exhibit 8.

A second major event occurred in November of 1963, when Anthony Carter and Paris Townsend, with the assistance of several Northern managers, prepared a presentation (to outline organizational alternatives for the proposed semiconductor plant) for Mr. Niel Bottomley, vice president of the Apparatus Division. Present at the initial meeting were Mr. Bottomley, the management group of the newly formed semiconductor devices works, and several interested Northern managers, including Mr. Kimball, chief engineer of the division. Mr. Carter explained the purpose of the session in the following way:

We knew that Niel Bottomley was very supportive of innovation by virtue of his background. Niel had moved up the systems engineering hierarchy but

EXHIBIT 8

NORTHERN ELECTRIC COMPANY, LTD. (A)
The Factory of the Future

The key to approaching the factory of the future is to determine what philosophy of management we wish to follow and, by synthesis, build up situations so that the goal can be reached. The two main factors are knowledge and cooperation. We should perhaps assume that each employee knows more about his own task than anyone else and is, or should be, best at it whether he is a janitor or a department head. In an ideal organization there would be feedback from all to all. We don't *make* the growth, we can only establish the environment . . . [but] as a goal, we would expect substantial growth in the group. We would expect to note a continued increase in our intangible assets (of much greater value than the tangible of "book" assets). The growth should be, in particular, in *the capacity of the group to learn and cooperate.*

One might almost go further and state that the ultimate goal of such a business group would be to develop the people and ideas, with service and profit being an important but secondary role. A big jump in performance and therefore a new profit level should develop which in turn would mean that prices could be reduced toward the international level.

The organization, in a sense, would be something like a play and all the group would be the actors, each doing his best. No one in such an organization should need to be discharged. Mistakes would be made and would be expected but scapegoats would not be needed. Growth implies some waste and decay.

. . . .

I would not want the following to be considered as rules or regulations but points to be considered in establishing this new pilot plant. First of all, it could be considered as a paying research project, but the man who is to run the plant should work out the details and the following suggestions are only to give some idea of how far we are prepared to go and, incidentally, not to imply that we are limited by these points. We want to tell the leader of the plant what we want to accomplish and not exactly how we wish to accomplish it.

Minimum of paper work. For example, no layouts, notices, instructions, piecework rates, time clocks, hourly rates (all on salary), grades (but higher salaries for higher skilled tasks), shop orders, work tickets, department numbers, manuals.

We should not need a personnel department with the 85 responsibilities they presently have. Out with the miserable and antiquated "blue book" given to all new employees, containing a list of "infractions of regulations" and which says that people may be discharged for fighting, gambling, immoral conduct, etc.

There are approximately 300 general instructions from general accounting and 100 from Industrial and Public Relations. Some would be needed. They might all be deposited as a guide without the necessity of all the reporting involved. The plant could build up suitable simplified data for themselves.

We would need to determine the minimum amount of corporate interference, as for example, W. E. Technical Information Agreement payments, auditing of accounts, inventory, insurance, taxation, deductions from pay, the Pension and Sick Benefits Committee, quality assurance.

. . . .

There would probably be no formal inspection group.

The leader would hire each person and carefully explain the fact that we were running a cooperative unit where everyone would contribute their best to the project. New employees might be considered temporary for six months and be approved by the rest of the group. It would be clear that there were to be no walls between "management" and the "workers" as in the normal organization and that there was no hierarchical structure of supervision. There would be only one group—those engaged in the enterprise. This almost presupposes that there would be no union as there would be no group to be represented "against" management. The leader

The problem is nobody tells you how to do it. The model which Paris and I are most comfortable with is the man-machine systems model. We've also been influenced by the communications systems models coming out of Bell about designing integrated telephone communications systems. Also literature on group problem solving, understanding personal growth, and on the systems approach have intrigued us.

Many alternatives existed in designing the organizational structure for the new plant. Among those being considered were the project management type of organization, the matrix organization (in which task-centered units called on the resources of different functional departments), the product management type of organization, and a traditional functional organization with coordinating teams. Mr. Townsend amplified on the need for an appropriate structure:

> The structure of an organization affects the sociological groupings of people, and many alternatives can be taken. The work done by Rensis Likert at the Institute of Social Research of the University of Michigan and his publication, *New Patterns of Management,* indicate different types of performance characteristics for different organizational structures.
>
> For example, the authoritative type of organizational structure tends to develop attitudes which are usually hostile and counter to organizational goals and produces communication patterns that are mainly downward throughout the organization, with control coming from outside of the individual.
>
> At the other extreme is the participative group structure, which tends to develop attitudes that are favorable to the integration of individual and group needs and provides powerful stimulation to behavior that is supportive of organizational goals. The communication pattern is improved, and self-control is facilitated.

Even after the issues of philosophy and structure were resolved, a number of specific decisions had to be made by the group. One of the problems foreseen was how the organization would relate to other parts of Northern, such as marketing, R & D, and the plants using the devices.

A number of specific organizational design issues also existed. For example, the new plant would have a more extensive need for quality control. The group had to decide how the expanded quality control functions, which would include finished parts testing, in-process testing, environmental testing, the design of testing equipment, and test methods, should be organized.[4] All or part of these functions could be included in a single control organization, they could report separately to works management, or they could be included as part of process or product departments.

---

[4]Test methods were the procedures used for testing devices, including the quality criteria to be used; they were an important part of semiconductor quality control.

Similarly, purchasing and inventory control could be separate functions or could be included under a material function.

The organization of the engineering function also raised questions. Engineering could be organized around processes (such as crystal growing, diffusion, assembly, etc.) or around products. The functions could also be under an engineering head, or they could be separate, reporting to product departments.

Device design, initial process development, and applications engineering had always been performed by the central research lab. The group had to decide how best to integrate these activities with the semiconductor plant.

Given an organizational structure, the study group was then faced with the problem of how to implement the design and what, if any, organizational development activities might be appropriate. The new plant, presently under construction, was a two-story building located in Ottawa adjacent to the research laboratories. The group had the opportunity to

EXHIBIT 9

First Floor Plan Showing a Possible Allocation of Space

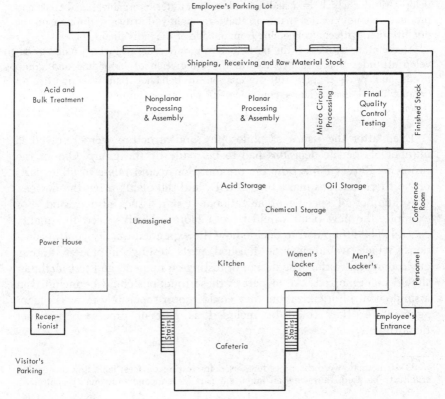

EXHIBIT 9 (*continued*)

Second Floor Plan Showing a Possible Allocation of Space

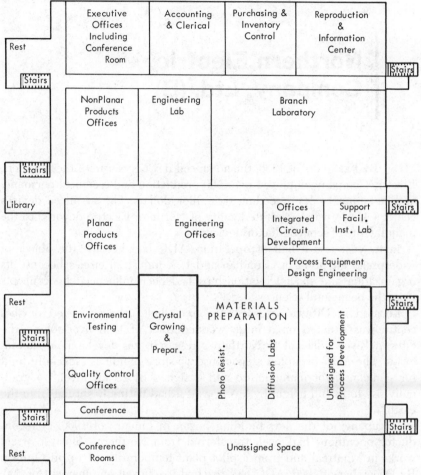

Heavy lines indicate parts of building which, under this arrangement, would be dust-free.

design the spacial relationships and location of activities within that building. Exhibit 9 is a hypothetical layout of the two floors in order to show the relative amount of space required by each activity.

The study group was aware that all of these decisions had to be made by December 1964, at the latest; and they were committed to having at least a detailed proposal for Northern's top management by midyear.

Northern Electric Company, Ltd. (B)

By February of 1968, the advanced devices centre of the Northern Electric Company employed over 500 production and technical personnel and had annual sales exceeding six million dollars. The advanced devices centre (ADC) was a separate facility of Northern Electric devoted to the manufacture of semiconductor devices.

In its year and a half of operation, ADC had become the object of widespread attention in Canadian and U.S. industrial circles because its organization and spacial relationships had been influenced by concepts from the behavioral sciences.

Located in Ottawa's residential "green belt," the advanced devices centre was situated on a large wooded tract of land overlooking the Ottawa River, adjacent to Northern's research and development laboratories. The ADC occupied a spacious two-story building, especially built for semiconductor manufacture and designed by its architect "to gradually rise to its full height by levels, as if it had naturally sprung from the earth."

Occupancy of the new building began in January of 1966. Semiconductor operations had been transferred from Northern's Shearer Street works in Montreal and from a pilot plant temporarily set up in Ottawa. By December of 1966, ADC had reached its current employment of 500, and the majority of this number had joined without any previous experience in either the semiconductor business or the Northern Electric Company.

The organization was designed using a "man-machine" concept which attempted to identify all of the resources needed to operate a business. Once identified, an organization was designed as a "system" to integrate these resources. Strong emphasis had been placed on developing "human resources" and the "environment" for the resources in the system. Participative management was recognized as an important element in the functioning of the ADC organization.

The resulting centre was in many respects unconventional. All employees, whether production operators or professionals, were salaried and were called "members." No time clocks existed. Members were expected to contribute a full day's work, but the time or duration of lunch or coffee breaks was not specified. All new members went through a one-week orientation which included technical product information, "human factors" material, knowledge of business systems, and management philosophy. ADC was operated by teams at all levels of the organization.

The centre did not have a union except for five stationary engineers in the powerhouse. A "participative representation council" (PRC) existed in which all occupational categories, from operators to top management, were represented. No "labor contract" existed between members and the company. A "statement of intent" was agreed upon each year by the PRC and ADC management, specifying such things as salary rates, job levels, etc.

For example, the PRC instigated an arrangement whereby the ADC shut down for a Christmas vacation between Christmas Eve and January 2. The lost time was made up by operating several Saturdays on a centrewide basis. Similarly, in early 1968, the PRC had proposed the adoption of a policy which would allow members to take an extra week of vacation without pay, so that members' vacations could coincide with the longer vacations of relatives employed by the federal government in Ottawa.

ADC had employed social workers to counsel employees on personal problems and people skilled in "group dynamics" to develop team process skills.

This unconventional organization was in great part due to the efforts of several men: Mr. Anthony Carter, formerly manager of corporate business systems and subsequently assigned to ADC's top-management group in 1965; Mr. Charles Kimball, presently in charge of ADC and formerly chief engineer of the Apparatus Division; Mr. Raymond Lee, formerly superintendent of semiconductor engineering and production; and Mr. Paris Townsend, a consulting psychologist who assisted in the design and implementation of ADC.[1]

Mr. Robert Crimmins, works manager of the temporary organization in 1964, had for personal reasons preferred to remain in Montreal and was replaced by Mr. Kimball in early 1965.

A number of other changes had occurred between early 1964 and the move to the new plant in 1966. The planar devices part of Northern's needs had increased much more than expected. The nonplanar product line had also increased substantially and was now referred to as VAGAS (short for varistors, glass diodes alloyed, and straight-cut diode devices). Northern Electric had decided to develop and manufacture both integrated and thin film microcircuits which it had not planned on doing in

---

[1]See Northern Electric Company, Ltd. (A) for background on this effort.

1964.[2] ADC's product line in 1968 included discrete devices, integrated microcircuits, and thin film devices.

The ADC Organization

Kimball, Lee, and Carter held three of several key positions in ADC's unorthodox organizational structure. They were members of the "planning and resources group," which was the senior committee of the ADC organization. As seen in Exhibit 1, ADC's management group consisted of a system operations council, which included the planning and resources group and 18 "administrators" arranged in a "matrix" relationship.

The role of the planning and resource group was described by Mr. Paris Townsend in a paper published by the Canadian psychological society:

The planning and resource Group is comprised of individuals who are responsible for consulting and advising in the four principal areas of the operation. These are resources environment (the organization and philosophy), manufacturing resources (technology), human resources, and resource accounting (business). The responsibilities in these positions are very broadly defined, and the occupants are required to be generalists rather than specialists.

The [position] of chairman of the SOC (system operations council) carries the responsibility for integrating and facilitating the efforts of the planning and resource group and all administrators.

The responsibilities of these five senior managers were summarized in the following way:

PLANNING AND RESOURCE GROUP

Chairman, systems operations council: Responsible for the successful growth and performance of ADC. Responsible for facilitating and integrating the efforts of the resource group and all administrators.

Manager, resources environment: Provides guidance and assistance to team members in the development of environmental conditions for effective team action to achieve both business and human factor growth. Records the historical development of ADC.

Manager, manufacturing resources: Provides guidance and assistance to team members on the design, procurement, operation, and development of manufacturing resources.

---

[2]Unlike the silicon monolithic integrated circuits being developed in 1964, thin film circuits are not made by doping silicon crystals. Thin film circuits are made by depositing a metallic resistive film on a substrate which is then selectively etched away. Electronic elements such as small transistors or capacitor films are affixed to the thin film circuits to provide the needed circuit functions. Thin film circuits are generally larger than integrated microcircuits but still much smaller than conventional circuits, and they serve in many applications where integrated circuits alone would be inadequate.

EXHIBIT 1

Organization Chart, Advanced Devices Centre

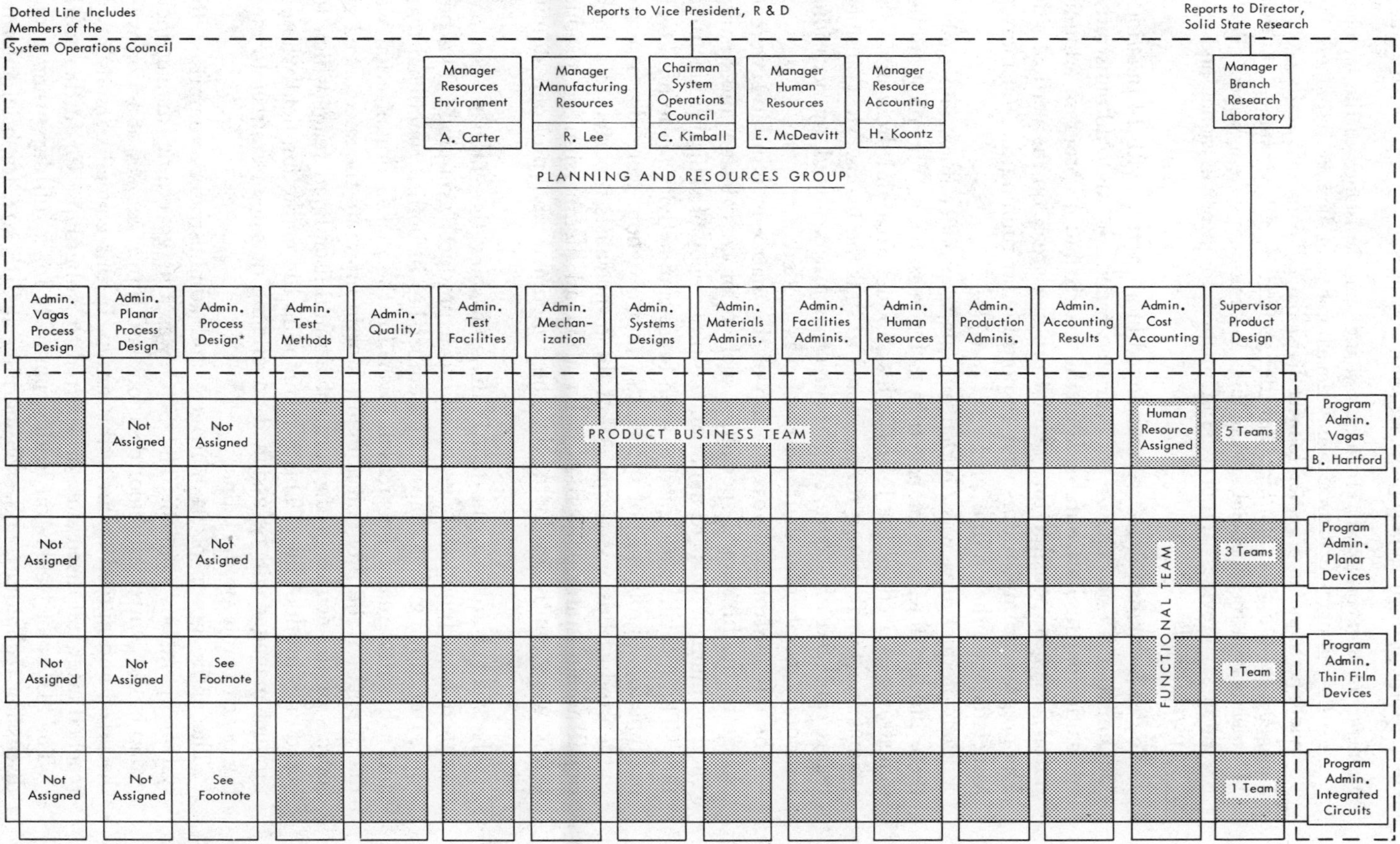

Reports to Vice President, R & D

Dotted Line Includes Members of the System Operations Council

Reports to Director, Solid State Research

Manager Branch Research Laboratory

| Manager Resources Environment — A. Carter | Manager Manufacturing Resources — R. Lee | Chairman System Operations Council — C. Kimball | Manager Human Resources — E. McDeavitt | Manager Resource Accounting — H. Koontz |

PLANNING AND RESOURCES GROUP

Program Admin. Vagas — B. Hartford — 5 Teams
Program Admin. Planar Devices — 3 Teams
Program Admin. Thin Film Devices — 1 Team
Program Admin. Integrated Circuits — 1 Team

FUNCTIONAL TEAM

PRODUCT BUSINESS TEAM

Human Resource Assigned

Column headings (left to right):
Supervisor Product Design · Admin. Cost Accounting · Admin. Accounting Results · Admin. Production Adminis. · Admin. Human Resources · Admin. Facilities Adminis. · Admin. Materials Adminis. · Admin. Systems Designs · Admin. Mechanization · Admin. Test Facilities · Admin. Quality · Admin. Test Methods · Admin. Process Design* · Admin. Planar Process Design · Admin. Vagas Process Design

Cells noted:
- Vagas row: Not Assigned (Process Design*), Not Assigned (Planar Process Design), Not Assigned (Vagas Process Design)
- Planar row: Not Assigned (Process Design*), Not Assigned (Planar Process Design), Not Assigned (Vagas Process Design)
- Thin Film row: See Footnote (Process Design*), Not Assigned (Planar Process Design), Not Assigned (Vagas Process Design)
- Integrated Circuits row: See Footnote (Process Design*), Not Assigned (Planar Process Design), Not Assigned (Vagas Process Design)

*Program administrators for thin film and integrated circuit programs served as process design administrators for their groups.

Manager, human resources: Provides guidance and assistance to the members on the hiring, engagement, and development of human resources. Provides personnel information to meet divisional and corporate needs.

Manager, resources accounting: Provides guidance and assistance to team members in the financial, accounting, and business systems aspects of the business. Provides accounting information to meet divisional and corporate needs.

The 18 "administrators" were arranged in a "matrix" with 14 functional "administrators" in charge of various technical and administrative specialties on the horizontal side of the matrix and 4 "program administrators," each responsible for one of 4 product areas, on the vertical side. The program administrators were responsible for running the "businesses" associated with the product areas.

Each product area was divided into major product lines, and each of these product lines was managed by a business team. The program administrator chaired all the teams in his product area and drew upon the various functional groups for personnel to staff the teams. Most business teams consisted of a core of permanent members joined by occasional temporary members as their assistance was needed.

The administrators across the top of the matrix in Exhibit 1 were in charge of the functional specialties such as process design and quality. Their assignment was "to maintain the proficiency of skills in their function." The specialists assigned to each functional activity made up a team or "functional grouping" of specialists, most of whom were also assigned to the product business teams. All of these specialists reported to a functional administrator, but those who also had membership on product teams were jointly evaluated by the functional and program administrators.

The shaded areas in the matrix diagram show the "human resource" assigned by a functional "grouping" to a product "grouping." The person(s) occupying that space had membership in both a functional team and a business team. The reason given for the matrix organization was that it enabled the program administrator to integrate the specialized resources of the centre in the form of a multidisciplined team which focused on a product line. "This is common in the marketing field where a product manager will be assigned advertising or sales resources to meet the needs of his product line."

The entire group of 24 managers and administrators comprised the system operations council. The SOC was the governing management group in the centre. All major decisions and future courses of action were discussed and agreed upon by this group. In this council consensus was reached after full discussion, or referred to "subgroups" for further work.

The SOC met weekly on Friday, normally for a full day, using group discussion techniques, and each morning at 8:15 A.M. for brief information exchange. The purpose of the system operations council was described as threefold:

The introduction of the system operations council as the main management body is intended to—

a) Increase the perception of all administrators in the centre in regard to the overall business requirements.
b) Reveal and resolve interdepartmental and interprogram conflicts before they create frustrations and loss of energy in the organization.
c) Bring to bear more specialist knowledge from all areas of the business on the overall management decision-making process.

It was the planning and resource group's responsibility "to remove as much detail as possible from council concern, to anticipate future developments, and keep the council informed of new events."

As can be seen in Exhibit 1, no formal reporting lines existed between the administrators and the members of the planning and resources group. Administrators were responsible to the entire SOC, and hence did not formally report to any one resource manager. They were expected to seek advice and assistance from all of the resource managers as the need for their expertise arose. All of the administrators, however, were evaluated by the P & R group annually.

Summary descriptions of the various functional and program administration functions were given as follows:

FUNCTIONAL ADMINISTRATION

Process design: Concerned with designing and developing manufacturing processes for ADC products, and for performing the methods engineering function to the product lines.

Materials administration: Concerned with procurement (purchasing), inventory, and distribution of all materials, products, and services. Receives and fills customer orders.

Systems design: Concerned with designing and developing business and information systems. Prepares supporting information for use by other departments in their operations such as yields, comparison to budgeted, efficiency, etc.

Test facilities: Concerned with designing, building, and repairing all testing facilities.

Mechanization: Concerned with designing and building processing and materials handling equipment.

Facilities administration: Concerned with plant maintenance, power plant operation, and supporting services.

Production administration: Concerned with production supervision, scheduling and control. Thirteen "process leaders" supervised the functions of the production personnel (called "processors") and reported to the production administrator.

Accounting results: Concerned with reporting accounting and performance results.

Cost accounting: Self-explanatory.

Human resources: Concerned with personnel administration and the development and growth of members and teams in ADC.

Quality: Self-explanatory.

PROGRAM ADMINISTRATION

1. Concerned with planning and scheduling product business team activity.
2. The role of the program administrator is seen as a business manager working with multidisciplined specialists as their team leader.
3. Business teams will generally consist of permanent representatives drawn from process design, facilities design, quality, materials administration, resource accounting, business systems design, human resources, and process administration (the process leader concerned).
4. The program administrator will lead the team in achieving business results in the areas of customer service, quality, cost, and growth towards the overall ADC objectives, both social and economic. In performing this role the program administrator would be concerned with functioning guidance, counsel, and training of team members on establishing the business team objectives, evaluating progress towards these objectives, and communicating results.

Organizational Philosophy

The organization described above reflected the organizational philosophy implicit in ADC's total system concept. This philosophy was articulated in a paper prepared by Mr. Kimball and Mr. Carter for a business journal.

It had been planned that the new plant would have the latest equipment for the manufacture of some of the most advanced devices being produced in the electronics field today. The product would be produced by a long sequence of operations where cooperation between individual processors and between them and the technical staff would be extremely important.

What better circumstances could be found for creating an environment conducive to increased commitment and participation of all those involved?

It was agreed then that in this unit, in addition to meeting the normal economic targets of a manufacturing unit, there would be a concerted effort to modify the industrial environment in order *to create a self-renewing system more capable of adjusting to socioeconomic changes.*

In order to create such a system, it was necessary that the value system of the organization recognize both social and economic value. This belief was embodied in the statement of management philosophy which was formulated to guide the group as the program began.

> *To provide, by purposeful and deliberate change, a social and economic environment that will stimulate the growth of both the individual and the centre.*

It was agreed that effort would be focused on—

a) *Increasing the rate of learning* by improving communication, creating new roles, and by job enlargement.

b) *Integrating the needs of people with the needs of the business* by striving for increased participation of all, for individual treatment, for goal setting, and for elimination of class barriers.

c) Emphasizing *"system" values* as opposed to departmental barriers.

A number of supporting activities were found to be helpful.

1. The use of a *matrix structure* of organization with the formation of a system operations council, and a number of multidisciplined *business teams*.
2. A functional approach to *physical layout*.
3. Introduction of techniques including *team problem solving* to achieve effective *group operation* and increased participation.
4. A program of joint *goal setting* for both business teams and individuals.
5. The use of *change agents* to stimulate the development program.
6. A *human resources approach* to achieve full utilization of the work force.

This philosophy was based on assumptions which were clearly identified in the early planning stages of the ADC organization. These assumptions were stated by Mr. Carter in a video-tape presentation used in orienting new members to the ADC:

People are our most important investment and we have to create a climate which allows them to work in comfort without excessive anxiety so that they can cope with a rapid rate of change.

1. We assume people have different attitudes, intelligence, and interests and grow at different rates. Men are individuals and we want to enable them to apply individuality in their work by building their goals into the company's goals.
2. People change. We want to help the individual understand his progress as an individual.
3. People are purposeful and like to work for the attainment of well-defined goals.
4. The way that people interrelate is very important. Trust, confidence, free communications, and openness will help people interrelate.
5. We should encourage people to move from the old ways where no one moved unless the supervisor told him, to one where he is productive and willing to take responsibility.

Spacial Layout

An important aspect of the "total system approach" taken in planning the ADC organization was the designing of the spacial relationships in the new building. The plant was laid out as shown in Exhibit 2. The approach taken was described by Mr. Carter in the following way:

Before moving into the centre each of the functional groups was asked to look at their departmental area and challenged to innovate in terms of providing a layout which met the functional needs rather than the status needs of the group. The group discussed their job functions, then interaction patterns, and the facilities needed to enable them to fulfil these functions.

As a result, there is considerable departure from the traditional rows of offices and physical barriers between one department and another. Furthermore, in the overall layout, the process area is entirely surrounded by the support areas. Only the glass partitions, required for the control of the air conditioning, separate those members of the centre who perform process activities from those members performing the supporting and administrative activities.

The concept of "product centres" was used to support the matrix organization. Those members who spend most of their time relating to a particular product team, are grouped together physically with the program administrator.

All members use the same parking lot on a first-come, first-served basis, the same general locker area, and all members are paid on salary.

A floor plan of the VAGAS product centre is shown in Exhibit 3. The product centre included a program operations room where the five VAGAS business teams met, and where production and cost data for all of the product lines were displayed on wall charts. The operations room could also be used for impromptu work meetings of subgroups. Two discussion rooms also existed for such meetings or for private counseling or discussions. All personnel working in the product centre were in the open with their desks situated to facilitate interaction. In general, administrators and managers did not have private offices, since their desks were located in their activities "centre" in the open. There were certain exceptions, however, dictated by specific needs for privacy in such positions as the chairman, the manager of human resources, and the resource accounting manager.

The planning and control centre shown in Exhibit 4 served as the "centre" for the planning and resources group. Although the managers of resource accounting and human resources were located with their groups, Mr. Kimball, the chairman, occupied a study in the centre, and Mr. Lee, manager of manufacturing resources, and Mr. Carter, manager of resources environment, had desks in the area. Carter and Lee generally used the discussion rooms adjacent to their desks for private discussions, or the informal discussion area behind their desks. The system operations room, where the system operations council and other centrewide groups met, was also located in the planning and control centre.

Group Participation

Participation was considered a necessary part of the ADC organization. Teams were viewed as the principal vehicle for decision making, and the operation of ADC was accomplished through a hierarchy of

EXHIBIT 2

First Floor Layout—Advanced Devices Centre

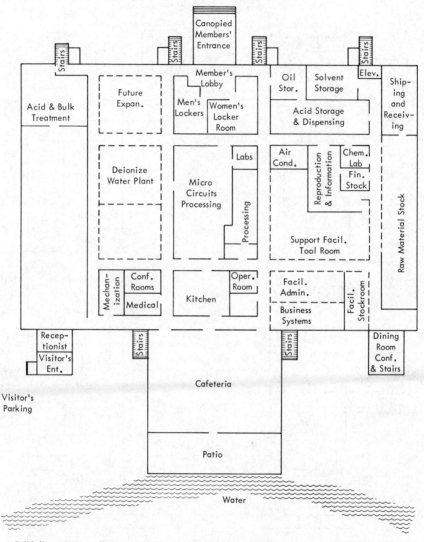

Solid lines show walled areas. Heavy lines enclose dust-free areas. Dotted lines demark non-walled areas.

teams outlined by Mr. Carter in the diagram shown in Exhibit 5. The SOC was responsible for operating the "total business" of the centre, or the total ADC system. The various "businesses" associated with each of the product lines were operated by the product teams. As shown in Exhibit 5, the program administrators were the "linking pins" or integrators between the SOC and the business teams; the functional adminis-

EXHIBIT 2 (*continued*)

Second Floor Layout—Advanced Devices Centre

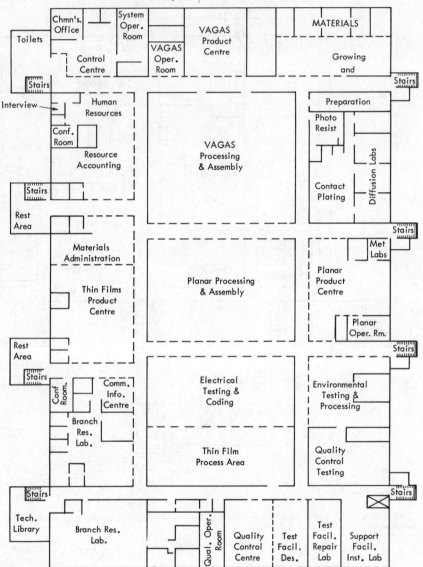

Solid lines show walled areas. Heavy lines enclose dust-free areas. Dotted lines demark non-walled areas.

EXHIBIT 3

VACAS Product Centre

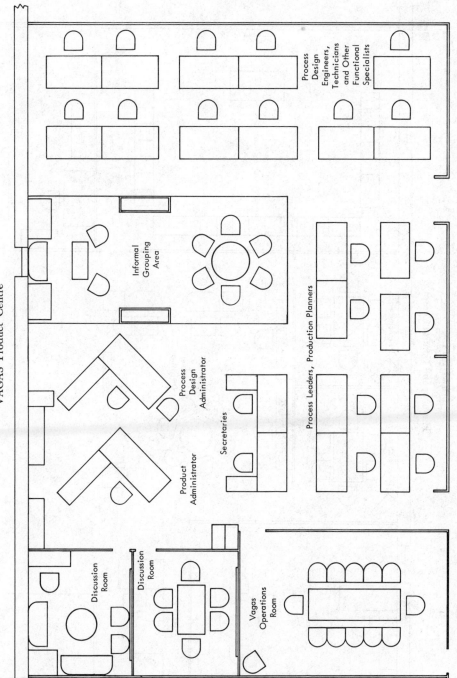

EXHIBIT 4

Planning and Control Centre

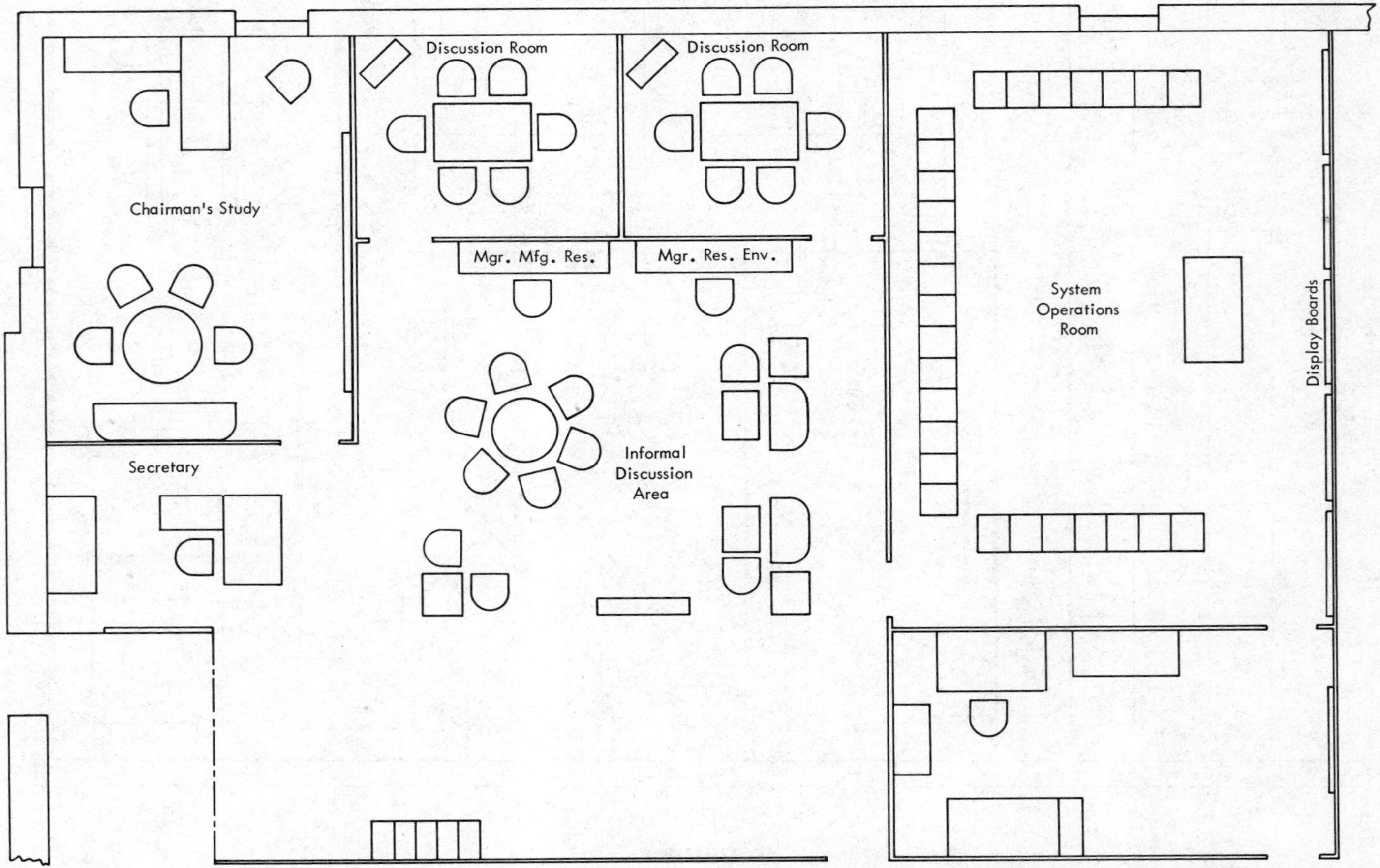

EXHIBIT 5

Hierarchy of Operating Teams
(showing "linking-pin" members)

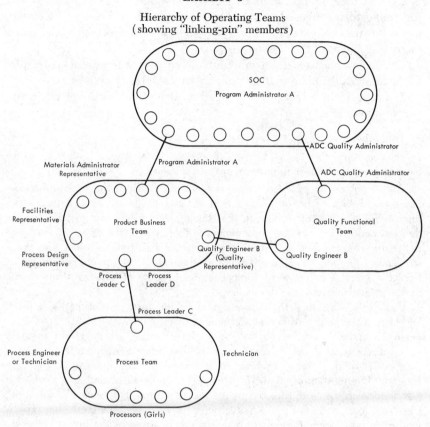

trators were also members of the SOC and their own functional teams, and hence were linking pins.[3] These functional teams were concerned with the growth and implementation of their expertise. The functional representative to the business team was the linking pin between the functional and business teams.

The lowest level group was the process team (which was concerned with operating a process), comprised of the process leader, the processors (or girls operating the process), and a technician or engineer as needed. The process leader was a member of both the business and process teams and was their linking pin; engineers or technicians might also share that dual membership.

---

[3]The expression "linking pins" was originated by Rensis Likert of the Institute of Social Research at the University of Michigan. "Linking-pin" members belong to more than one group and provide integration and information exchange between the two groups.

Each of these teams met once weekly. The SOC and the business and functional teams focused on decision making and information exchange, while the process teams, comprised of roughly 15 processors, discussed the requirements of the coming week.

The technique used for team problem solving was described by Mr. Carter and Mr. Kimball in the working paper referred to earlier.

Team problem solving brings together all individuals involved in the problem in order to:

1. Identify problem areas.
2. Devise solutions.
3. Determine actions to implement or test the solutions.

This is not easily achieved and is the principal task of the problem-solving discussion leader. First of all, there is a need to differentiate between the three different types of leadership that takes place within the group. There is the *assigned leader* who has the nominal authority over the group. Then there is the *discussion leader* who helps the group as they proceed along the problem-solving process, and finally there is the *expert leader* whose comments have the greatest influence on his colleagues because of his expert knowledge in the particular area under discussion.

Usually it is assumed that the assigned leader must play all of these roles. We have attempted to differentiate among them, at least to the point of having a discussion leader who is *not* the assigned leader of the group engaged in the discussion. In fact, wherever possible, we have tried to assign a discussion leader who is not caught up in the needs of the moment as brought about by the question at hand. He is usually a "generalist," and as a leader his task is to keep the team directed to the logical order of problem identification, then solution, and finally action decisions. In this role, therefore, his task is neither to govern nor to mediate disputes but to listen to the group "process" and keep the team directed toward the problem. He relates comment to comment, redefines, seeks clarification, and summarizes until consensus is achieved.

We have found that the discussion leader should be *very authoritative* concerning the use of the technique of problem solving; that is, the group first identifies the problem to the satisfaction of all the members present, lists alternate solutions, selects criteria against which these alternatives can be weighed, and programs a plan of action in accordance with the solution selected. On the other hand, there is a need to be *very permissive* with regard to the material that is put forward by any member of the group as long as it fits into the format that the group is following.

We have found it useful to try to differentiate between various portions of a meeting, particularly those business meetings which tend to occur regularly; that is, to select *information exchange* items and separate them from discussion items, because the mode of operation is radically different.

The group problem-solving process is not the same as the democratic process; that is, there is no chairman following a set of rules in order to obtain a majority of votes in favour or against a proposal. Rather, there is the objective of trying to identify a problem, which is a satisfactory summation of the views of the group, and there is an agreement to use the technique of team problem solving in arriving at a solution which has consensus of the people present. It is not always possible to obtain consensus in the time available and at times we have been forced to depart from the ideal.

In order to assist the leader in performing his role, a group member is chosen to act as a reporter. The reporter provides short-term immediate and long-term permanent memory for the group. In providing the first service he usually makes running notations of the discussion, taking care to use "objective" language. These rough notes can be kept on a pad or flip sheet as preferred. This immediate memory can be used by the leader or any member of the group, to review or to verify points covered.

The long-term memory consists of the record of the problems, the solutions and actions agreed to by the group. It is intended to be available to all members at all times as a reference or guide to those assigned to actions. It is also used by the leader to begin subsequent meetings. It helps the group evaluate its progress and ensure that each step in a problem-solving technique has been adequately completed before passing on to other areas.

The role of members in such a group is expected to shift from one of personal defensiveness or status seeking to that of group goal-directedness. He may be assisted in this reorientation by the rotation through the roles of leader and reporter. In the performance of these roles, the participant is required to abstract himself from the "content" in order to listen to the "process." Practice and skill in these roles will have a positive effect on his future behavior as a regular member.

Northern Electric Company, Ltd. (C)

NORTHERN MANAGEMENT cautioned that it was too early to draw conclusions about the advanced devices centre's effectiveness as an organization after only a year and a half of operation, but most indicators were favorable. By early 1968 the advanced devices centre (ADC) had met its 1971 target for rate of return on investment and in the words of Charles Kimball, chairman of the systems operation council, "was doing as well as most other operations in Northern Electric." ADC's labor turnover averaged less than 2 percent per month, or roughly 12 percent per year, a low average for the semiconductor industry.

Mr. Kimball was quick to point out that ADC was still far from achieving its full organizational potential and that the centre was not yet operating as a completely participative organization.

One of the problems is that we have people who are convinced *intellectually* about the concepts we're trying to apply but just can't yet do it *behaviorally*. And others don't yet believe it deep down. For example, it means that an administrator of an engineering function must accept his role not as the best engineer in the department but rather as a motivator of his engineers to get the best job done.

To do this he has to relinquish his dependence on the authoritative role. It requires a change of role—he must be a facilitating leader rather than an authoritative leader. If our administrators don't really believe, they don't really behave.

For example, we had a process leader who suggested we close the cafeteria because he had a hard time keeping people on the job.[1] The object of the process leader's concern was a worker who took a 20-minute coffee break rather than 10 minutes. But further discussion revealed that she was the top producer in the department and that nothing should be done.

These new roles are difficult to fulfill because of the expectations which people have about how the various specialists, leaders, and managers should react based on their experience in traditional hierarchical organizations. When peo-

---

[1]A process leader's function was similar to that of a production foreman in a conventional organization. See Northern Electric Company, Ltd. (B) for a description of the various titles and functions in the ADC organization.

246

ple don't react according to these expectations, anxiety and frustrations build up.

It's necessary to continually observe the levels of anxiety within the organization and the progress people make toward fulfilling their new roles in order that an effective operation can be maintained.

A fairly long interval of time is required for people to learn and apply new roles in an organization. Because of conditioning in the traditional roles of specialists, supervisors, and managers, there is periodic reversion to the older styles of behavior and to previous roles while the incumbents are struggling to fulfill the new roles.

Mr. Carter, manager of resources environment, amplified on the difficulties that some members of ADC were having in adapting to the new organization and its philosophy:

Not everyone can adjust to the lack of such status symbols as private offices. We want status to be reflected in achievement, not in status trappings. We've tried to reduce the number of offices while at the same time giving people the space they need because space is needed by some people as a compensation for walls. It isn't one universe yet. For example, the technicians don't want to be on the line. But we all share the same parking lot, the same locker room, and the same office areas.

Another problem is that people are not yet comfortable with undefined roles. People need definitions. My response is that definition restricts, but not everyone will accept this kind of free-wheeling operation. We want our emphasis to be on the goal rather than on a designed relationship which may no longer be appropriate with time.

We've tried to tease these problems out in meetings. All of this is a process of learning. It takes quite a while for people who weren't used to thinking in systems terms. It takes a while to digest, but it's growing slowly. The manager's role should be to facilitate and ascertain that the best decisions are made rather than making the best decisions.

The new roles which managers, leaders, and specialists were expected to play were described in the article prepared by Kimball and Carter. See Northern Electric Company, Ltd. (B).

An acceptance of the new roles within the organization was required:

1. To facilitate the operation of the matrix structure of organization,
2. To use more knowledge from the behavioral sciences, and
3. To facilitate the introduction of the management philosophy throughout the centre.

These new roles are concerned with a movement from authority concepts towards concepts based upon facilitative counselling and educational relationships. For example, in regard to various specialists throughout the organization, their acceptance by the team or a group is based not only on the personality of the individual but his ability to provide results for the group that can be understood and appreciated in the practical operation. In regard to leaders, a greater understanding of interpersonal and intergroup relations has been necessary and a deeper knowledge of behavioral science, as it applies in these areas, has been desirable and necessary.

With regard to the specialist and the technical expert, some have had difficulty in accepting the team concept, particularly the possibility that someone less skilled in their specialty now has the opportunity of questioning their decisions.

The case of the nonspecialist seems to be quite different. Many people of limited academic background are now tackling broad problems with the interest of the overall operation in mind.

Administrator's Feelings about the Organization

A nontechnical functional administrator elaborated on the difficulties inherent in implementing the new organizational approach:

A lot of people felt it would be automatic, just by changing the structure. The weakness was the assumption that people would be highly motivated in this kind of environment and they're not. There's a threshold value of personal maturity or outlook, and below it people are more effective in a hierarchical, not an open system. The (ADC) system doesn't take into consideration the differences in basic behavior of people. Some will accept the freedom and thrive in team organizations. But others are just not responsible or self-disciplined enough to make this work. These differences are not divided according to disciplines or education. It's a function of personality and it's in all areas. I'd say that there are about 25 percent who truly respond properly in the participative sense. The other 75 percent don't.

But I don't want to condemn this system because there have been massive gains coming out. Information flow, for example, is excellent; and I'm able to do things here which the hierarchy in (another works) would have stifled.

A program administrator added to the above comment on members' maturity: "The goals here have been preestablished rather than coming about through evolution. This is one of the problems. Human growth has not been equally rapid with all people."

This administrator compared ADC with his previous organization by saying:

In traditional terms of customer service, costs, and profitability, I would have to put (the other plant) ahead. But in human values, ADC would be ahead, and it certainly offers greater potential. But even the term human values has to be defined because for people who need direction ADC is not as satisfying. People with those needs suffer a great deal of anxiety here.

The manager of the branch research laboratory located in ADC amplified on the above:

If you really needed a "directive" environment you'd have problems here. Some people have opted out. But you can get conditioned to it and roll with the punches.

Some people have difficulty in relating to a group of people for decisions rather than to a single boss. It takes longer and is less clear-cut. The decision-making process in ADC takes much longer than elsewhere because so many people are involved. In most places the manager gathers the inputs he thinks are adequate and makes a decision. Here there are many inputs, sometimes resulting in a data glut. But when you do convince a large group of people and your ideas are accepted, its very satisfying. The final decision is usually an evolution of your original idea with the ideas of others and is usually better.

An administrator in charge of a technical function felt, however, that the organization often caused many frustrations:

Life inside the ADC is very confusing. There's much more engineering effort diffused and wasted than in a traditional organization. Engineers are involved in many things which are not an appropriate use of their effort, which keep them from doing valuable work and frustrate them. For example, if you talk to an engineer at Western Electric and ask him how the rest of the groups on his program operate, he doesn't know or care. He's only interested in doing his engineering work well.

Our engineers get involved in many things not directly related to engineering. While this helps the program as a whole in a marginal way, it decreases his ability to do his own job.

I feel strongly that participation is needed in running the business, but not the way it's done here. Members don't really make decisions, don't understand goals or accept responsibility. All they have is an endless series of meetings. Maybe it's just a phase, but I would try to get away from this "cult of the team" and view it more as a group of individuals working together, each with competence and playing his part as needed.

A program administrator involved with a developmental program not yet in production elaborated on limitations he felt the participative philosophy imposed:

My biggest problem with the ADC philosophy is that it requires people to conform as much as any hierarchical type of organization will. Our mode of operation seems to be working well right now, but I'm concerned that when we go into production we'll lose flexibility and that our teams will have to be run as formally as the others. For example, we have separate meetings for problem solving and for information exchange. We don't make technical decisions at the business team meeting because it would be tying up people who don't have the technical competence to input into these discussions and it would interfere with getting the routine scheduling done.

If you get a guy whose main contribution is technical and is worth his weight in gold but doesn't want to broaden out or be concerned with other areas, you have to make a place for him. That's why the participative thing can be too inflexible and carried too far if you try to force people into doing things they don't want to do.

My concern is that there are certain people who in their makeup are missing certain desires, or needs, or personality traits, who are incapable of being the "whole person" that Anthony Carter talks about. In our present situation we have the flexibility so that there's room for these people to be productive and satisfied.

The focus and extent of participation in the business teams and their effectiveness was elaborated on by a process design administrator:

Not all of the programs look at participation in the same way. For example, the program administrator and I agreed we wanted results through participation, but results are more important. We felt that it was bad to legislate attendance at team meetings especially if members did not feel it would be a valuable use of their time. So we told the technical men you must be here when we need you. We invite you to attend any time, but no one is forced to come.

They (another program area) say participation will bring results; let's focus on participation. But they're forcing people, and if members don't feel it's a valuable use of their time they fight it. In fact, it's become a game, and I've heard guys say, "so and so is proposing something; let's block it." To (the other program area) participation is an end not a means. To us it's a means to a result.

The benefits of the participative philosophy in reducing traditional barriers were described by the quality administrator:

In another works, QC was organized as another line department, up through the hierarchy. There were terrible interfacing problems between manufacturing and QC. I don't feel that applies here because I identify much more closely with the manufacturing departments than in the old organization by virtue of my connections with them at SOC. The manufacturing organization has postured itself to realize that quality is not a policing organization, performing a control function and not an end in itself, but another part of the total organization effort.

Also, disputes don't go up the line. They're resolved before going up the line between administrators—most of the time before going up to SOC.

Business Team Members' Feelings about the Organization

Like the administrators, most business team members were in agreement with the concepts on which the ADC organization was built (if not always with their implementation). A materials control programmer described his reaction to the ADC climate:

I've liked it here from the start. I've had a feeling of freedom and feel that I've been looked on as an individual. People are interested in me as a person, and I feel I've been able to contribute to ADC. Here your job is flexible enough so that you can look for things to improve and make comments without fear of repercussions.

There are some things, however, which could be improved. For example, everyone is treated the same whether he's a person who works hard or an individual who doesn't. People overlook a bad job in the hope they will improve themselves. This can sometimes be discouraging to the guys who work hard.

For example, four of us are programmers. Two are paid more than me—one because he has a degree and the other because he's been here longer. I'm doing a better job than the guy who has a degree but he's paid more. The new concept doesn't change methods of remuneration. It doesn't reflect performance.

The other thing is that there is a tendency for people in responsible positions to hold back until after a decision has been made. I feel they do this because they want the others to have the experience of working out decisions. But this leads some people to fear that the reason they're not being led is because the people in charge are not confident enough to be leaders. Some people need direction and don't understand when they don't get it. I've been in other places where people have disliked a boss but respected him. Sometimes in ADC it's the reverse. People like a boss but don't respect him.

ADC is sometimes too much of a contrast with life when you go home—where the fellow up the street has a $30,000 house and you have a $20,000 house; he has two cars and you have one. It's almost like being a split personality.

It would be good for someone around here, once in a while, to be mad. Life outside is not a bowl of cherries. For no one to be mad about something is strange. You feel, in a sense, that you're being ignored.

A team member from a nontechnical function described the differences he perceived between ADC and other organizations in which he had worked:

The biggest difference between ADC and the other places I've worked is that I've had a lot of ideas about problems in the past but I never had the opportunity to *do something* about them.

But here I *can do* something about these things and help in correcting them. Instead of just having the responsibility of the end results, I also have the opportunity to do something about it. Honestly, I feel more responsibility here for my results but without feeling more pressure.

A process design engineer who was also a member of several business teams disagreed:

When I came here I was told I should feel individually responsible and this irked me because it's unfair to give a person responsibility without commensurate authority. They have prostituted the work responsibility which to me meant the duty and ability to implement my function. In the past it was a fair course to run. I had the positional authority to implement what I needed. I now read the work responsibility to mean "concern."

I don't feel that management here gives you the commitment to follow a definite course of action.

This same engineer commented on the effectiveness of the business teams:

They have a philosophy here that before they can get anything implemented they have to get everybody together to nod their heads. This is often awkward and unproductive. The team does not have the competence to make a reasonable decision on most technical problems. They're embarrassed as I am when someone brings something in that I know nothing about. It's demeaning to have to seek the approval of people who don't know enough to understand. Even in Parliament, the representatives of the people, not the people, make the decisions. It's a sign of not trusting the people charged with each function.

I think more leadership should be shown in the team by the administrators who have management and technical skills and the specialists in their specialized skills. For example, the program administrator sits in on the team and has the skills but suppresses them. He has a right to show his feelings and speak up on issues.

They're all such good guys they won't tell you what they really feel. They don't square with you on whether you should be doing something—whether you're doing it well or not, or wasting your time.

A recent university graduate described his feelings in acclimating to the organization:

At first I just sat in team meetings as a lot of guys do, and I was really disillusioned from a professional point of view. I was eager to get into technical discussions, but this was really discouraged at business team meetings. Another new guy who came in with me, who's very professionally oriented, also found it frustrating. He had a product line which did involve him in team meetings but he sort of rejected the whole idea. But after I began participating in the team meetings I found it very satisfying.

He elaborated on how some technical members viewed the business teams:

In a way the ADC is not a satisfying place for the (technical) professional. You seem to have to go through a lot of red tape and coordination to get something technical done. Although ADC is very progressive in an organizational and administrative sense, it seems to be very conservative in a technical sense—not receptive to new technical things and in getting them through the organization.

A lot of the functional people feel that the team meeting should be a place where you go to give your inputs and leave. They feel frustrated because they spend a lot of time on issues they don't feel concerned with.

The technical guy is principally interested in technical things and the business team in economic problems. There's a certain type of research-oriented person who would be completely frustrated in the team. He's not interested in business or human relations, unless they have a direct bearing on what he's doing.

This same member added, however, that he had grown to derive satisfaction from team meetings:

A lot of guys in the functional area tend to see the team assignment as a punishment—a drag. I think it's because they don't try to participate. I sort of felt that way at first. Interestingly, the thing that changed my attitude was that I was forced to act as recorder for our team and that required me to listen. I started taking a greater role in the team and I've found it more satisfying. I feel much more a part of the team now.

One process design engineer summarized his feeling by saying: "I'm basically a scientist. Scientists are individualists and you appreciate freedom in your thoughts and action. And this basically goes across the grain of the business team."

Mr. Dale Adams, a process design engineer, described his feelings concerning the extent to which the team should become involved in technical decisions:

I agree with the concept of teams in principle and that they can be useful. But the team should respect that functional specialties exist and acknowledge differences in judgment on technical problems and rely on the specialists to be responsible.

The team should be able to judge the competencies of each individual and grant him that much trust.

The 400 Diode Team Meeting

Closely related to Mr. Adams's comments was a technical decision he made which had been challenged by the 400 diode team, a team of which he was a member. The issue arose in a regularly scheduled meeting of the 400 diode team. These meetings were held in the VAGAS operations room located in the VAGAS product centre, which was also used for the meetings of the five VAGAS business teams and contained flip charts showing performance data for all of the teams' product lines.

The meeting format was set up in two parts: information exchange and problem solving. It was customary to have a "process" session at the end of the meeting.[2]

Present at the meeting were:

1. Baird Hartford, VAGAS program administrator.
2. Tom Norman, programmer, materials administration, and discussion leader for the meeting.

---

[2]"Process" discussion consisted of critique of the interpersonal behavior of a group meeting.

3. Jerry Hayes, representative from business systems.
4. Ann Jackson, a new representative from business systems. (Jerry's work load had prevented him from attending meetings for several weeks, and he introduced Ann at the meeting as the person taking his place.)
5. Dale Adams, process design engineer.
6. Art Handy, quality engineering representative.
7. Andre Beauchamp, product engineer.
8. A technician.
9. A process operator attending in place of the process leader.
10. Mrs. Jeanne Lovell, a specialist in group dynamics with considerable experience in government and volunteer groups who was on retainer by ADC.

Mrs. Lovell had been working with the 400 diode team for several months and more recently with the participative representation council. The 400 diode team was generally acknowledged to be one of the better functioning teams in ADC. During the information exchange part of the meeting, Dale Adams announced that the original estimates on a process improvement would cost more than originally budgeted. The question was raised as to whether the improvement should still be made. When it became apparent that a problem-centered discussion was evolving, Tom Norman, the discussion leader, suggested that the item be brought up under problem solving. The information exchange was conducted in a rapid, business-like manner, taking about 30 minutes.

When the question came up in the problem-solving part of the meeting, Dale explained that only four magazines would be tried instead of 12. (The magazines were used for loading parts.)

JERRY: Will four be enough?

DALE: Yes, because it will give us a chance to see whether the magazine will reduce costs. We don't yet have enough data on how it will work to calculate an exact savings; and with the magazines being more expensive than we thought, four will minimize the cost risk.

ANDRE: Is the reason for only four, then, because of uncertainty of the magazine's performance or because they're more expensive than you thought?

JERRY: . . . We (in business systems) never learn about these things until the decision to do something is made. We'd like to get into it sooner. Also, get the team behind you; it's easier to influence the expenditure's approval.

(At this point there was considerable discussion about when in the decision process Dale should have gone to the team with the change.)

DALE: Well, I thought that since I had made the trip on it and have the expertise, I could make these judgments without coming to the team. The money is in my functional administrator's budget. They make it up and spend it. (Functional budgets were not made up by the business teams.)

BAIRD: One of the problems is that we're responsible for the capital invested but we're not yet able to spend the money.

ART: I don't really think that the team should be involved in making the decision because it's reasonable enough to trust the technical experts who have the ability, which we don't have, to make the decision.

JERRY: But one of the principles of work simplification is that you bring a proposal to a group of people and the decision is better because there are more inputs.

ART: Yes, but we don't have the technical ability to make this decision.

MRS. LOVELL: In a way it's similar to Parliament where the Minister of Agriculture, for example, can't be an expert on an agricultural proposal. Nor is Parliament. But they consider the technical aspects and build on what the technical experts say.

JERRY: I don't need technical expertise when I go into an area to consider a cost reduction proposal. Many times I can see very simple problems that are overlooked because I'm not technically involved.

TOM NORMAN: I think that what Jerry is saying is that it wouldn't do any harm if you kind of kept us posted—had briefed us on your trip to Western, so it doesn't hit us wild.

ART: I think he did this. He gave us a report when he came back from Western!

JERRY: I think it would be more convincing if you had put together a cost proposal; even though you've done a lot of work on the outside, we're not aware of what you did. I think it would be better if we had the team's participation in the decision.

DALE: I think we're making a lot out of nothing. Supposing I had just gone out and done it without telling the team anything. I'd have done it; you'd not have known it; and I'd have my magazines! You'd have to trust my judgment. It would be expedient.

JERRY: But if we're going to control our budget we have to start going through the team and considering each proposal. We can't do it expediently.

ANDRE: It appears that we're discussing both principle and the problem. I suggest that we discuss them separately.

(At this point Mr. Hartford entered the discussion to clarify and assist in separating the two issues of principle and problem aspects.)

MRS. LOVELL: Well, what we should do is consider them separately and consider the problem first today.

BAIRD: Let's put it down then—the principle involved in this as a separate issue—and discuss it later.

(They then discussed the specifics of the problem.)

DALE: The reason I didn't give more detail is that I felt it was a traditional system, or problem, and I went to my functional administrator to do this. If you want me to explain it to you, I will do it. (. . . discussion on the merits of having the technical details explained.) O.K., to make everybody happy, I'll come in next week and formally present it to all of you.

JERRY: All we want is to get more participation into it!

DALE: O.K., I'll bring it here. The reason I didn't is because—to be honest—let's not be hypocritical—Jim (the functional administrator) has the money. We don't have it in the team (*laughter*).

JERRY: O.K., good. You're a good team member!

TOM: Should we spend the remaining five minutes on discussing the principle involved?

VARIOUS MEMBERS: No. . . . We don't have time . . . next week.

TOM: Well, I'd like to put in my own thoughts on it anyway. It's short, even though I'm not supposed to do this as a discussion leader.

JERRY: Well, that's O.K., but we should discuss that next week.

TOM: The problem is that the team member can't be blamed. It's his boss who has the purse strings. His boss should be in here when something like this comes up.

BAIRD: How many problems do you want (*laughter*)?

(The group then moved on to its process discussion of the meeting.)

JERRY: Well, at least we can still talk to each other and still laugh about it.

DALE: A couple of weeks ago we brought up the need for better definition of the team's role, responsibility, etc. I think that this is a very eminent need, and we should clarify it right away.

BAIRD: Well, that's what the morning meetings have been for, Dale.

DALE: Oh, I see, I'm sorry I didn't realize that. The other thing I've wanted to bring up is about your role in these meetings, Baird, now that we have a rotating discussion leader. Should you be a participant now in the role of program administrator? There are a lot of things in which you could help the team by letting us know your own feelings on problems.

BAIRD: Yes, I think that would be appropriate.

The meeting ended with a discussion on the tenure of the rotating discussion leader and the recorder.

Problems Facing Management

Mr. Charles Kimball, chairman of the system operations council, realized that the ADC organization and philosophy were not infallible, and that in fact some new problems had arisen. Several concerns for the future stood out in his mind:

I think we should be looking at our organization structure to see where it can be improved. There are too many creaks and groans from the matrix. For example, the production administrator has 17 process leaders reporting to him. Some people say that it should be a higher powered job. Others say he's overworked. Also, Ray Lee (manager of manufacturing resources) has 12 people relating to him. Is this too many people for one man to relate to? Some people feel there should be two Ray Lees, one for on-going, conventional products, and another for the developmental product lines.

Also, the two developmental programs (thin films and integrated circuits) will be coming on stream soon, and I'm sure that they're not operating as business teams yet. Right now the program administrators also double as process design administrators for these two developmental programs. Should there be one program administrator for development programs with two process design administrators, or two of each?

By 1971, our present development programs will account for more business than our conventional lines. Will our present organization be able to adapt? What will happen when we have a thousand people working in ADC? What would happen to our operation if Ray Lee left ADC for another assignment?

How do we get more participation from the line? The process leaders each do it in their own way, but they have to be emotionally mature to let the group run itself. They have to be self-sufficient enough to give up their status.

I feel strongly that we should be beefing up human resources to develop the teams. We have to make the distinction between effective participation and laissez-faire because the difference between them is not apparent to many people. We need more development effort in improving the effectiveness of the teams, talking to people about how participation works, and the techniques of achieving effective participation. I think we can't be self-satisfied. We must be flexible and self-critical of our progress.

Hickman Associates

In the spring of 1971 the management of Hickman Associates were reviewing the appropriateness of the organizational arrangements of the firm and were wondering what changes in the structure and procedures of the firm they should adopt. Hickman, an international accounting firm, was facing organizational problems similar to those of the other of the "top 13" firms in the industry. Diversification in terms of tasks and geography, resulting from both internal growth and growth through acquisitions, had placed increasing strain on Hickman's organization; and the firm sought to develop an organization that would meet its current needs as well as lend itself to modification required by continued growth.

The firm, which was a partnership, had a group of one dozen senior partners chosen by the partners to serve on the senior partner committee (SPC), a body that had significant influence on the direction of the firm. Early in 1971 the SPC stated that the firm's two most pressing organizational problems were:

1. To meet the organization's need for both a strong geographical organization and strong functional organizations;
2. To develop viable career progressions for partners through the functional and administrative organizations.

The History of the Firm

In its recent history Hickman Associates grew from a relatively small accounting organization into a large international firm providing a broad spectrum of financial services and advice. In 1970 the firm had over 250 active partners and nearly 3,000 professionals, with offices in all major U.S. cities and in over two dozen countries. The firm's growth reflected increasing client demands for more and broader services and an aggressive approach toward practice development[1] by Hickman, as well as billings from clients obtained through acquisitions.

A significant aspect of the firm's growth was an expansion in client services to include wide departures from opinion audits, such as consulting assignments in marketing, production, and organization. These management services were offered in response to client demands for advice in areas other than the traditional accounting and financial control systems. The largest portion of the firm's management services billing derived from major information systems implementations with industrial clients, governmental agencies, and trade associations. Less than half of the 1970 management services volume was done with audit clients.

The firm's audit and tax practice was characterized by a widening scope of services which evolved to meet management's requests for general reviews of operations, assistance in merger evaluation and resultant reorganizations, and estate planning. The new diversity, intensified by Securities Exchange Commission (SEC) requirements, increased complexity in the tax code, and special governmental requirements on many clients resulted in the development of specialized staffs and services. Contrasting with this functional specialization was the development within accounting and auditing of a broader based set of integrated consulting services which provided a range of financial services primarily for small companies. An office providing integrated services to a client usually had very close formal and informal relationships with the client, and services between Hickman and the client were usually limited to contacts through a single office. Much of Hickman's integrated consulting services practice originally was brought to the firm through mergers.

Pressures in the environment leading to functional specialization pushed upon the firm's geographic organization. Traditionally, the main contact with a client was the local office, which would be in contact with the client three to four times a year in addition to the intense contact required during an audit. As client firms grew and demanded a broader range of services, they also necessitated the establishment of contacts through several local offices. Functional reporting relationships were added to the basic geographical organization to make better use of specialized resources including personnel, to provide a national level of coordination for planning and for operations, and to provide for stricter "quality control" of the services offered. Hickman's clients expected the firm to meet high standards adhered to by the large national firms, and strong functional reporting relationships assisted the firm, especially in those offices that were obtained through acquisitions and which were accustomed to different operating procedures.

---

[1]Practice development in a professional organization such as Hickman included activities leading to developing new or additional services for existing clients as well as acquiring new clients.

The changing scope of the firm's services was also reflected in important changes in staff composition. The number of new staff who were not accounting majors was increasing, a reflection of the new hires who were engineers, lawyers, general business graduates, and mathematicians, and those who were experienced in data processing, personnel services, and in specific industries.

The Tasks of the Firm

In several written documents the firm had outlined its basic objectives and tasks. In a broad sense, the major task of the firm was to provide a broad range of quality services to its clients. This included basic opinion audits and attendant requirements performed each year in a relatively routine manner and a variety of nonroutine engagements which occurred to fulfill specific client needs. These nonroutine engagements included services in connection with SEC registrations, special tax matters, mergers and acquisitions, and consulting engagements in a variety of financial, tax, and management areas.

In providing these services the basic contact with the client was between the client's management and Hickman's professionals in the local office in the same geographic area. Providing a variety of services to a client required continuing coordination by the local office of the service groups. Often, however, more than one office would be required to become involved in meeting a single client's needs. For example, the Chicago office would audit a Chicago plant of a New York–based firm, which would be the immediate client of the New York office. Quality assurance and setting of quality standards required the participation of a national functional organization. National functional responsibilities also included the development of new services for clients and participation in developing and performing complex, nonroutine engagements.

A second set of tasks for the firm were its practice development activities. At the local office level these tasks concerned establishing and maintaining a favorable community image and reputation, retaining clients through service and contact, and implementing specific potential client practice development programs. National considerations included developing industry or service programs and providing specialists with specific backgrounds from various locations to achieve maximum results.

The Organization in 1971

The organization in 1971 could be viewed as being composed of three major components: a top-management group, a geographical organization, and a functional organization. The top policy-making body in the firm was the senior partners committee. Operating responsibility was handled by the senior operating partner (SOP) and the operating committee (OC) which was composed of directors of the geographical and functional organizations. (Refer to Exhibit 1 for an illustration of these top-management groups.)

EXHIBIT 1

Top Management and Geographical Organization

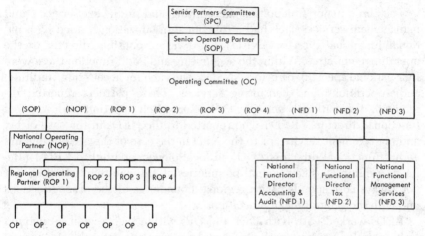

The Geographical Organization

The basic organizational unit of the firm was the office, a geographical or territorial dimension. The office unit was headed by an operating partner (OP), who had profit responsibility and fairly autonomous authority in operations.

Each office typically had functional people and functional operations; accounting and auditing, taxes, management services, and, in some offices, consulting services. Functional operations within an office were departmentalized in varying degrees. In larger offices, the functional operations were large, formally departmentalized, and partially autonomous, with a director of operations (DO) for each function. These larger departments operated as profit centers. In smaller offices departmentalization was informal, if not nonexistent. People with functional skills were utilized in corresponding operations but did not operate as independently as in the larger offices.

Operating partners each reported to one of four regional operating partners (ROP). The country was divided into four regions each headed by a ROP who reported to the national operating partner (refer to Exhibit 1). It was the responsibility of the ROPs to coordinate the activities of the offices in their regions. The ROPs did not have profit center responsibility, however.

The Functional Organization

The three major functions of accounting and audit, tax services, and management services each had a functional organization headed by a national functional director (NFD) who was responsible directly to the operating committee. Within the accounting and audit function there were four national specialty directors (NSD), one each for accounting, auditing, audit operations, and consulting services. These partners reported directly to the national functional director. Each function had regional functional directors (RFD) who reported to the NFDs in the case of tax and management services or to the NSD in the case of the accounting and audit. Functional directors (DO) in local offices reported to RFDs. (Refer to Exhibit 2.) The regional boundaries of any one function often but not always corresponded with regional boundaries of the other functions and with the geographic organization.

RFDs worked with both DOs and OPs within their region. Function's tasks included working with offices and departments on problems, gathering and disseminating information, interviewing management personnel, forming operating policies, and reviewing departmental operations. No

EXHIBIT 2

Functional Organization

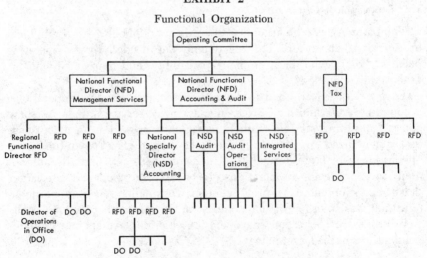

operating responsibility was given to the functions, and each function approached its operational responsibility somewhat differently.

Each function had a technical responsibility (in contrast to an operating responsibility) for setting standards and determining technical operating procedures, quality assurance, and new service development. This technical responsibility was carried out in several manners varying from national staff, regional technical directors, or in combination with operating responsibilities through the RFDs.

The NFDs were responsible for providing promotion and compensation guidelines and procedures to the OPs and RFDs, and they reviewed promotion and compensation recommendations made by OPs and RFDs. They were also responsible for long-range (over 12 months) planning of the individual function and the coordination and long-term direction of the operating, technical, and other elements within each function.

Interviews with Partners

Several partners spoke with the case writer about the firm, its organization, and what they felt were good recommendations for changes in the organization. One commented:

It may appear obvious, but we must not overlook the importance of maintaining professional standards and a highly motivated well-trained professional staff. This is complicated by the size of the firm, its geographic dispersion, the pace of advances in technology, and the fact that our breadth of services requires us to deal with several professional groups.

The professional must maintain his competence in a rapidly changing environment. As important as technical competence is for the firm, it is equally critical for the professional himself. He is to us a scarce and expensive resource, and we must be able to identify, develop, and rapidly advance the most capable professional staff. This includes the talented client-oriented individual as well as the highly competent technical professional.

There is a conflict that naturally arises between providing integrated client services with proper control and coordination and maintaining the professional, specialized aspects of the firm.

Another partner said:

What we really have here is a matrix organization—but we have not recognized it and it is not working smoothly. We need to iron out the operational problems of working with a matrix—that is, who has primary responsibility for a specific decision or activity, the function or the office? What we need is something like I saw in another organization—a set of rules to sort out primary and secondary responsibilities in a matrix.

Primary responsibility for maintaining and coordinating services to clients, recruiting and developing professional staff, and obtaining new clients is essentially a geographic consideration. The departmental organizations within each office are required to provide proper service to clients and are also the pivotal point between geographic and functional organizations. It is these functional directors (ODs) who report to both OPs and RFDs, although traditionally the relationship with OPs has been considerably stronger than the one with RFDs. The first thing we must do is strengthen the functional reporting relationship—we can begin by giving ODs and RFDs profit responsibility.

In establishing working rules for the matrix, responsibility and authority must first be clearly spelled out. The basic client and personnel focus should be the office, which should have the primary line authority in client service and personnel attraction and development. Responsibilities assigned solely to the offices should include:

a) Routine client service.
b) Acquiring, retaining, compensating, promoting, and terminating staff below the level of manager.
c) Engagement practice development.
d) Facilities planning.
e) Shared services such as typing, etc.

For technical matters the basic responsibility and concomitant authority to set policies should be delegated to the functional organizations. They should also have the responsibility to monitor adherence to policies. Responsibilities assigned solely to the functions should include:

a) Setting technical quality standards.
b) National-level industry practice development.
c) New service development.
d) Functional planning.

Certain responsibilities have to be assigned dually to the office and function. However, in many cases, it is possible to define primary and secondary responsibility. For example, the following responsibilities should be assigned primarily to the office and secondarily to the functions:

a) Complex, nonroutine client service. This would occur more often in MS than in audit or tax.
b) Observance of technical quality standards
c) Development and training of staff below manager.
d) Retaining and developing partners and managers.
e) Geographic office planning.

One of the most complex areas requiring dual authority is transfers of partners and staff. Temporary transfers should be made by the offices with functional operations providing communications and liaison between offices. Permanent transfers should have equal involvement of both offices and functions.

In dealing with the inevitable conflicts that arise, the conflicts should be resolved at the lowest level possible. If they cannot be resolved at that level, they should be taken one level higher, until resolution is achieved. To avoid having conflicts unnecessarily escalated, it should be spelled out that the organization having sole or primary responsibility has the right to make decisions or take actions within its area of responsibility—should the other organization feel differently about a given decision, the burden of proof lies with it. For example, tax should set and enforce technical policies. If an office feels that one of these policies is inappropriate for a given situation, the burden of proof lies with the office to show that the policy is inappropriate.

A senior partner commented upon the organization:

My feeling is that we should have four national functions and run them however is convenient—their organizations need not be similar. The functions would be the three we have now plus administration as the fourth. Although a regional form of organization works well for all but MS, the sizes and boundaries of the regions should vary from function to function depending upon the distribution of clients relevant to the particular function. For MS, a core city approach to organization would be more appropriate. In this way, we could have strong offices in several core cities which would serve clients in satellite offices as well. This is needed because in MS you can't have a viable function with one or two people, which is all some of our offices can support. The technical content of MS is much more amorphous than auditing and accounting. There is no repetitiveness and a limited number of competent people wherever the job is.

I can't see why it's so unique to have the functions operating rather independently. Take some major conglomerates for example. They have suboperating groups within larger groups. For us, it's all right as long as you stay at the "technical-technical" level, but when you cross functions you get into trouble. Automatically, you have an accumulation of functions and product lines at the office.

One of the problems that I'm worried about is providing viable career paths for partners. What happens to a partner after he has been an OP? Not everyone can move up to be NOP. You could move an OP or a DO to a larger office as a promotion. But it's hard to develop administrators for operations or for technical functions. When partners become OPs and when they should be working as administrators, they still hesitate to give up their clients. They somehow feel there is a power base associated with keeping their clients. . . . By and large, a recruit is hired into a function and he stays there. The major problem on personnel is getting people out of an office and into a super-structure—whether administrative or functional. A good theorist should go through the technical side to the national staff—a good operating man should go from territory to territory to the national office or to NOP, but these groups can't do it if they don't let go of their client bases, and so far they won't.

Urban Development Corporation

URBAN DEVELOPMENT CORPORATION, specializing in lower income, multifamily housing, anticipated in April 1970 a continuation of its rapid growth. The company believed it had a practically unlimited market, which would provide for most of the company's growth to be internally generated. Mr. Roger Hamilton, newly appointed president of UDC, considered one of his top priority tasks to be a review of the company's organizational arrangements as they had evolved over its two-year history, resulting in possible revisions which would allow UDC to meet its performance and growth objectives.

The Company

Urban Development Corporation had been created as a wholly owned subsidiary of a diversified, worldwide corporation with sales in excess of $1 billion. The parent corporation had experienced rapid growth in the past decade, having expanded 30-fold by a combination of acquisitions and internal growth. The growth in size had been accompanied by consistent profit increases at the rate of 20 percent compounded annually. The corporate image could be best described as innovative, exciting, entrepreneurial, and youthful. Many highly skilled young men had been attracted to the corporation as a result of this image and had subsequently been promoted through the ranks, reaching high-level positions at an early age. The corporation's operations had been based on a philosophy of decentralization with each division or subsidiary being left alone as long as it was meeting corporate expectations. (These expectations were formalized in strategies and budgets developed by the operating entity and approved by top management.)

Urban Development Corporation had been conceived primarily as a response to the crisis in urban housing in the United States. The parent corporation believed that UDC could play an important role in solving the social problem of inadequate housing and at the same time earn a "fair profit." With corporate experience in related fields as well as

266

corporate financial resources, the new venture was considered to be a natural extension of the parent's diversification program. However, all key personnel had been recruited from outside the corporation.

Description of Operations

UDC staff generally explained their function as that of creating real estate values. Within that broad description, most of UDC's efforts were focused on developing federally insured and subsidized low- and middle-income housing on urban renewal sites. One official described the work as follows: "We acquire the land from the local renewal agency, arrange the financing, designing, and construction of the buildings, and obtain the tenants. We then sell the value we have created, or the bulk of it, to investors who can better utilize the long-term investment potential."

The first step in the process was to find potential "deals." This function had received top priority in the early life of UDC, with the premise being that more potential deals meant a greater likelihood of completing more deals profitably. Information about prospective developments came from numerous sources, varying from formal solicitations received by mail to "tips" passed on by trade contacts. Any city in the United States was considered a prospect.

Once the initial contact was made, an investigation of the prospective project was the next step. In this stage, which took four to six months for a full-scale investigation, the critical factor was accurately determining the feasibility of the project. During this period negotiations for the right to undertake the project and guideline discussions with the local FHA office were held, area income levels and expectations thereto were determined, as were basic rents and mortgage constraints. Preliminary construction plans were developed, construction costs were estimated, and contractor negotiations were begun. Coordination was often required with model city groups, neighborhood committees, and various other private, civic, and governmental organizations. Decisions were made throughout the investigation which could significantly affect the project's feasibility, such as type of construction and selection of contractor. For UDC, the most critical task of its operation was to develop the "package" which optimized the combination of construction and operating costs and tenant satisfaction within the constraints of financing guidelines. Tenant satisfaction was reflected in rental income as well as maintenance costs (which tended to soar with unhappy tenants). Thus, a successful "package" required consideration and coordination of many subjective factors along with the analytic financial analysis.

If UDC decided the project was feasible, the investigation stage was followed by the FHA processing stage, in which applications were submitted to FHA for a financing commitment. As soon as the firm commitment was received, UDC sold (by private placement through investment bankers) 95 to 99 percent of its interest in the project to high-income individuals as limited partners. These individuals were guaranteed a high return on their investment because of quick tax write-offs applicable only to this type of housing.

Two primary functions remained to be performed: First, the construction itself had to be completed; this required a coordinated effort of the contractor and UDC personnel. Since the construction was contracted for at a fixed amount, proper previous planning was critical in insuring a minimum number of problems during the actual construction. UDC personnel required extensive construction experience to properly supervise the construction and to make decisions on modifications that might arise during that phase. Second, the rental and operation of the buildings were obviously important functions. UDC had guaranteed its partners that it would retain its ownership interest and operating control for at least 20 years. In addition to the danger of incurring losses on operation of a low-occupancy project, the company was very concerned that the corporation's reputation could be tainted with a "slumlord" label from a poorly developed project. Therefore, the long-run maintenance of good quality in the projects was deemed important by Mr. Hamilton.

UDC Organization and Employees

Mr. Hamilton had the following supervisors reporting to him: eastern operations, western operations, construction, property management, community development, finance, and accounting.

There were two primary offices—neither near the parent company headquarters. On the West Coast, the president and his financial and secretarial staff were located in one suite of offices, while the western region operations personnel were across the hall. The construction personnel were located at a construction site nearby. On the East Coast, the eastern regional operations were located in the same offices as the FHA manager and the Center for Community Development. Travel was extensive, both to project sites and between offices.

The Center for Community Development had recently been formed to provide expertise in the more intangible aspects of community development. It was anticipated that this group would provide a competitive edge for UDC in getting new projects and making them successful in the long run by a community development orientation.

The Construction Division personnel could best be described as the "old pros" of UDC. They worked closely with the architects and contractors throughout design and construction—doing none of the actual construction themselves. Most of the staff (10 to 12 people) had several years' construction experience and exhibited considerable expertise in their specialties. Several of these people joined UDC in anticipation of operating fairly independently as a separate profit center, assisting UDC projects but also developing their own construction projects. Recently, the parent company had curtailed UDC's power to engage in construction projects as a separate operation, and this decision had resulted in disappointment for the construction personnel.

The bulk of the project work had been performed by the 10 project directors. Each director was responsible for three to six projects in various stages of investigation.

The directors had acquired the nickname of "young tigers" to denote their energetic and youthful attack on project problems. They were bright, educated men in their twenties and thirties who had a particular interest in the real estate development field. Most had MBA degrees from leading universities, with limited experience in fields related to their present experience. Generally, they were attracted to UDC by the opportunity to learn about this new field within the parent company's reputed framework of entrepreneurial freedom. Some anticipated going out on their own after a period of experience with UDC, hoping to make for themselves the "packaging profit" they were making for UDC.

The rental and operation of completed projects had been handled by independent property management firms. Mr. Hamilton had already decided to develop a property management department to supervise these functions, as well as to assist on the original feasibility studies. Financial operating statements were prepared for UDC as a whole, considering it to be one profit center. This concept was adopted in order to encourage a team spirit and mutual assistance.

Mr. Hamilton believed a greater degree of communication and coordination between the project directors and the remainder of the staff was needed. He believed that some costly errors in the past—particularly in construction—could have been avoided with more input of technical expertise. Exhibit 1 shows Mr. Hamilton's conceptual model of functional interdependence. The width of the lines in his diagram reflect the relative importance of each function at different stages of the project. For example, he believed the project directors should have the major responsibility through the investigation phase, the construction department through the construction phase, and the property management department through the operations phase.

Plans for UDC Growth

Mr. Hamilton was replacing the "founder" of UDC, who had received a promotion to the parent company. The operations of UDC had been considered successful, although only three projects had been completed. A small profit had been recorded in UDC's second year of operation, and

EXHIBIT 1

Project Execution

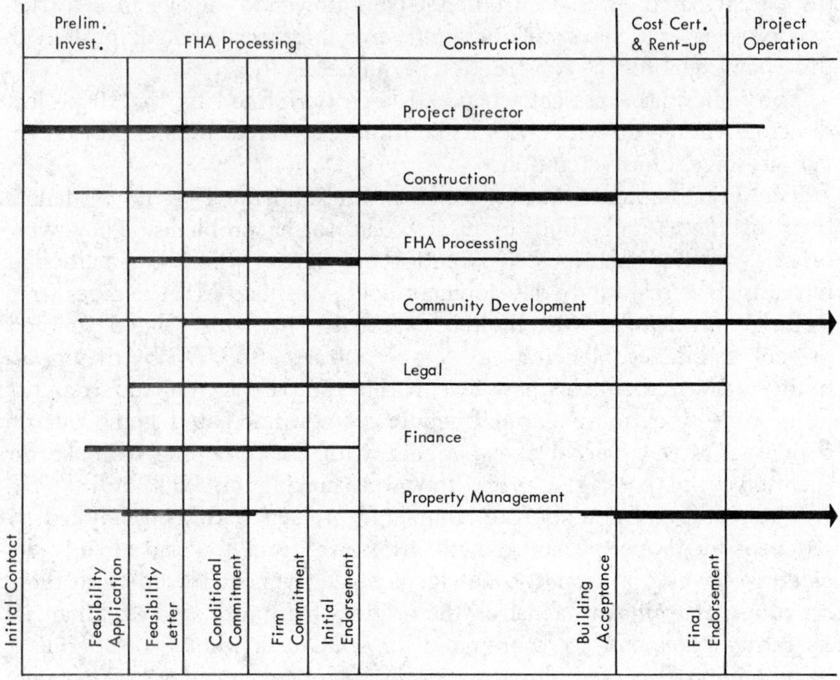

Prelim. Invest.		FHA Processing				Construction		Cost Cert. & Rent-up	Project Operation

Project Director

Construction

FHA Processing

Community Development

Legal

Finance

Property Management

Initial Contact | Feasibility Application | Feasibility Letter | Conditional Commitment | Firm Commitment | Initial Endorsement | | Building Acceptance | Final Endorsement

pre-tax earnings were budgeted to increase to $4 million by 1974. Seven new project contracts were budgeted for 1970, and two had been signed by mid-April.

As to competition, the 1970 strategy expressed the opinion that UDC had a head start on its competitors. This document stated "our increasingly proficient young tigers will keep us up front" and recommended that UDC be expanded as rapidly as economics and staff permitted, in response to an unlimited market and a stronger national commitment for federal subsidies in low-income housing.

The Rouse Company

EARLY IN 1970, James W. Rouse, president of the Rouse Company, committed the company to a thorough review of its organizational arrangements and of its organization development process in the interests of better achieving its goals. This case presents data relevant to this review and change process.

At a company assembly on May 26, 1970, that formally inaugurated this review and development process, Mr. Rouse spoke, in part, as follows:

There are 974 people in the company, or thereabouts, today, and 219 of those people were with our company this time three years ago. We actually had 432 people in the company then, so we have grown about 125 percent in those three years. . . . Together these figures say a lot about the company and why we are here. They point out growth and a trend of growth, which causes us to think that the 974 is somewhere in the middle and not in the end. They point to the opportunities that are available to us in the company and that have caused us to grow—really at a faster rate than we planned. They point to considerably less experience in our task than we really would like to have to do our jobs in the best possible way, and they point to inexperience in working together as people and knowing how to form a team and how to go about a job in the most effective way. There's got to be a lot of rough edges existing among us from 219 three years ago to 974 today.

These figures also hold out warnings for us. They hold out warnings about organizational congestion and the red tape likely to come with this, about inefficiency, about loss of the importance of the individual as an especially important person wherever he may be. They hold out warnings about creativity, and about views, and about excellence; and these are things that have mattered to us and still do. It's because of this combination of growth and opportunity on one hand and the clear warnings on the other that we are here today, to talk about where we're going, where we want to go, and how to get there.

We are in the business of city building. We say that over and over again and we really mean it. It's true. Not necessarily always building a whole city, but we are either financing for others or developing for ourselves all over the

271

country the bits and pieces of a city. Sometimes, as in Staten Island, we deal economically and with the feasibility of a city on a very large scale—450,000 people. Sometimes we deal on a regional scale, as we are now doing in Hartford—700 square miles, 700,000 people. There's an odd fact about this business that we are in and that we have got to hold up there as a reminder, and that is that no company in the history of this country has ever grown big in the business that we are in. Not many companies have ever gotten as big as we now are. Furthermore, big corporations—big insurance companies, GE, Alcoa, other big industrial corporations—that have come into the city building business believing that there is a sitting duck that they can take over and fire in their talents and capability, have left with their tail between their legs, whipped by the task of trying to build communities.

Why has this happened? I'm not sure we know, but we have good reasons to suspect some of the reasons. There are certainly messages for us in this, and the message really relates to bigness. Big departments and elongated processes force the point of action back from the decision making. People can't get heard. This is why we have to find new ways to do our job. We've got to be aware of the fact that there has been some stubborn condition out here that has caused the bigness not to operate in the field in which we are involved. There seems to be a process for city building, a process which calls for so much in the way of ad hoc decisions, and meeting crises, of making decisions at the point of action, that it just doesn't submit to the routine disciplines that seem to be a part of bigness. All signs say now that we are a huge success, and we are, by all the indexes that we apply. . . .

. . . But you and I know that we can do what we are doing a lot better than we are, much better, and that we need to. At one time or another we are finding it too hard to get a decision, and it's not always clear who is responsible. We see signs of things costing more than they should. Some people feel lost in the company, can't get in on what is going on, don't feel part of the show. The training and development of one another is not systematic and not well organized to grow. We are not each in this company realizing the fulfillment, the joy that we ought to be able to experience in the exciting work in which we are engaged. . . .

. . . This is an enormously talented company—there is not a comparable group of people in the world engaged in the task that we are engaged in. People on the outside world say to us that we represent in individual talents the spectrum of capabilities across the whole range of needs to deal with the problem of the city. We are the most remarkable group of people organized in this country and probably in the world. We represent an enormous resource for effective work and have therefore an enormous responsibility for using it and using it well. . . .

. . . But bit by bit people are coming to see that you can build a good city— that it is really possible to produce a good community in which to live and raise a family and work and run a business. We're coming closer everyday, and there's not a doubt in our minds that we will soon reach a day that convincingly proves what we set out to do: that is, it is more profitable to build an environment for the best. And that is the thing we must prove, and we can't prove that by just barely making it. We have got to really show America that it is a more profitable thing to do this job well than to do it with sprawl and clutter and aimlessness, the way our cities grow. . . .

. . . Our company is 31 years old, and it seems sometimes (I remember saying this about a year ago at a company assembly) that up to now we have really been preparing ourselves for the greatest opportunities that we now face. With the rising prices and rising demand we yearn in the American city for a better answer than our society has been able to provide. We have reached a point at which we clearly have the ability to do things that we haven't yet attempted, and we have the ability to do better in the kinds of things that we have done. The cities are crying out for help—they cry out at the market, and in business terms it is both an opportunity for us and responsibility for us. . . .

. . . The mission in our company is to prove that we can build communities, real communities that can work for people in new lands outside the cities and in the old, worn-out areas of the cities, and that the whole urban center can be reverted into places where it fits people to raise families. . . .

. . . We have corporate objectives, we believe they are meaningful, and they influence the decisions we make, continually. . . . These objectives were adopted almost two years ago now, and they have had a marked influence on the company during this period. They are relatively simple. There are four of them:

1. Provide maximum opportunity for personal performance for people working in the company and for the participation in working in the company's growth.
2. Improve the quality of life available to people in the United States.
3. Create through superior planning and design and development maximum values in land development. (You could say that 3 and 4 are the same.)
4. Create thereby an annual increase in earnings of 25 percent.

If this sounds flabby or unreal, it isn't. This is the fundamental discipline for which we need to plan as a company.

Each of us as individuals in this company has gifts and capabilities that are underdeveloped. Now, as in relationships with one another, we are incomplete; we need to develop to the fullest extent. We must bring forth our self-respect, our pride that can emerge from self-respect, and our service to others. We need to each enjoy the satisfaction of the pursuit of the highest standards which we can make today in this company in our relationships with one another, in our relationships with people outside the company, in duty, equality, service, and excellence in everything we do. There should be a basic move within the company toward that kind of action. We should be intolerant of low standards wherever we see them, whether it is in our personal performance, the way something is built or operated or managed, or the way any aspect of the company runs. We need to build such an intolerance of doing less than we know how to do well that we are continually exerting a pressure on the company to lift up, to grow, to be best. We can begin, and we do begin with trust, that each of us is here to work, to grow, and to be a better person. Our job as a group, as a company, and as a corporation is to find a way to enable us to bring about, to train, to develop, to create opportunities, to create the kind of ability that is in this company and which people are growing and moving and excited by.

By the quality of life we mean the physical environment, the ecology. We mean the economics of the region sufficient to support the life of people. We mean the institutions of the community. We mean the way institutions relate to one another. We mean a basic circumstance that supports the growth of the individual and the family.

And profit—we don't shrink from it, we understand profit as being the legitimate and anticipated reward for effective service. If we are not making an adequate profit, we are not doing the right job or we are doing the right job badly. Profit is the measure that society pays for something it wants to have done, and society is willing to pay for it if it is done well and efficiently. Profit is not today suffocating the business you are in; it's an invigorating system. The profit system is the democracy of the working place, working all the time, not the arrogant judgment of a group of people who decide for someone else what is best. Profit strips out waste, and waste is a loss to everyone. It provides a measuring rod for efficiency. Bad things happen in this country. The profit system has allowed itself to be degraded and misunderstood. I spent a weekend defending the profit system against the capitalism imperialism charges of my 19-year-old son. But it is an understandable judgment because the American business system has revealed not a concern for service with profit as the reward but a belief that profit is a right that it has, and that business has a kind of arrogant expectancy that profit is good for the country and profit a legitimate reward.

. . . How do we organize to fulfill these objectives? What kind of a company do we best become? What would this company really be like if it worked—if it worked in the best possible way that we know how? How do we take these resources, and talented people, capital, organization, reputation, and put them to the task of the American city, old cities, new cities, in the best possible way? How do we do that? That's what we are really about.

. . . We have got to learn to marshal creativity and create circumstances under which creative people (which just doesn't mean architects and planners and draftsmen but also creative people in the construction field, creative people in the finance field, creative people in the field of community and institution) are able to work together, feeling that their maximum creativity is being put to work.

We need to bring the decision closer to the actions; we need to examine and persistently attack the elongation that tends to grow as the company gets bigger between what's got to be done here and who's going to say what should be done back there. We need to establish clear lines of responsibility—who has the ball, who's really responsible—and then we need to establish clear systems of accountability by which that person and that team, and that group, and that whatever it is, reports back in relationship those responsibilities in such a way that is measurable, and understandable, and that decisions are facilitated and things move ahead. . . . We need to have a more systematic review of the results that are occurring in the company, in relation with the objectives, how to improve the efficiency of what we are doing, how to im-

strong and rationalize the conflicting tension under which we must operate prove the quality of what we are doing, how to improve the humanity of what we are doing, how to improve the beauty of what we are doing. We need not believe that we have to hold up everything until we have the perfect answer, but believe we have brought together a system in which creative people can go at a task, can take a risk with them and bring about a result. We need to feed out data to the people who are taking the action on how it can be done better. We need to improve communications through the company. We need to develop a greater openness of giving and receiving information, information that hurts sometimes. We need to knock down our defenses and really be open. We need to trust others and to give ourselves and what we know to others.

We need to create an openness for change. We need to expect change. We want to resist finding comfort in the settled and the rigid. We have got to expect in the work ahead of us that change is going to be such a constant part of life and growth and activity within the world, our country, within a community and within a company that we expect it, anticipate it, have processes to accommodate to it and to move it. We need to be able to hold high and and never drop any of the forces that bring about those changes.

Those fundamental forces are beauty, community values, and arithmetic. They fight one another in every decision that is made, and they always need to be held up, and they always need to be understood, and they always need to be compromised, one with the other, to bring about the results to justify what we are doing. We need to understand and respect whole new techniques that are unfolding in our times for improving interpersonal and intergroup relations, and all of the new science and capability that can open up to us the ability to become more open as people and to deal more effectively with others. We need to enlarge our sense of service. When you go into a great store, you really see a great sense of service. The old idea that everybody is a customer is a concept that we all can afford to have. If you really could see everybody else as a customer and our living depended on serving him, attitudes would change among all of us.

We want to be conscious of being the best we know to be as individuals, as a group, as a company. We want to avoid the straightjacket of "it has to be the way it is," of "it's no use," of "can't change," of "give up." We want to believe that the best can be and to make it be throughout the company, throughout what we do—beauty, service, efficiency, and humaneness. These are the questions and the purposes and the direction of the world today.

Moving in this mainstream of concern, we have to become a part of it. It is important to business that we do. American business today is losing the ball game; American business today sits as perilously in its seat as the chancellor at Berkeley or the president of Columbia sat a few years ago and didn't know they were in peril. We are going to see a great transformation. We have to hope that we don't throw out the baby with the bath water, but we deal with a reaction in our nation to the excesses of the independence and the self-interest of business. We have got to be careful that we don't lose the vitality of the marketplace seen as a process to deliver service effectively to people. . . .

THE COMPANY'S TASKS

The Rouse Company (TRC) started in the mortgage banking business and extended its activities into the general areas of commercial development and community development. The mortgage broker acted as an intermediary between real estate developers and lenders. The broker represented the borrower in the sense that he sought financing for the borrower's project and technically he was paid a commission by the borrower for this service. He served the lender in finding opportunities for the use of his funds and in ensuring that the proposed investments were sound. The mortgage broker in many ways was the lender's representative in a given city, and the continuing relationship between the lender and the broker was based upon the lender's trust that the broker would bring him favorable, well-analyzed investment opportunities.

Walter F. Terry III, vice president of the commercial operations home office (which served as mortgage brokers for the Rouse Company itself) commented, "The key to the success of the mortgage broker is to be a real estate man. You have to know what is going on in the market and why, and you have to know who is a good developer. To do this, the broker knows 75 percent of what he needs to know to be a good developer."

Commercial Development

TRC's beginnings and its largest activity in commercial development was developing regional and large shopping centers. The company later began developing office buildings—principally located in its shopping centers—and apartment buildings located in the communities around the centers. Development of the three types of commercial property was similar in that they all included the basic activities of making the deal, determining feasibility, arranging financing, selecting sites and arranging rezoning if necessary, planning the use of the land, designing the structure, buying and supervising the construction, obtaining tenants, and managing the completed building or center. In addition to size, there were several differences among the three types of projects, however.

The first and most critical task in developing a shopping center was making a deal with one or two major department stores. Proper selection of the department stores was critical to the total success of the center. Often a department store would acquire land and come to TRC to develop it into a shopping center, but reaching agreement on the proposed center had to be accomplished before the project could proceed. Retail stores locating in the centers generally leased for relatively long periods of time and considered store location and the potential of the center for generating business to be critical factors that could outweigh somewhat higher rents. Within the shopping center individual stores had to be designed and constructed to meet the needs of both the tenant and the over-all character of the center. The proper mix of tenants and their placement within a center also affected the success of the center. The task of management of the center included selection of new tenants and management of promotional efforts, as well as maintenance and other routine activities. The developer's reputation for being able to develop and manage profitable centers which generated good revenues for their tenants was important for obtaining new opportunities, making new deals, obtaining financing, and obtaining tenants.

Although the developer's reputation was important in helping him obtain financing for office buildings, it was not as critical a factor there as it was in shopping center development. Development of office buildings required the same types of skills in design and construction, but differed greatly from shopping center development in leasing and marketing activities. Whereas tenants in shopping centers tended to be chains of retail stores, and the developer's reputation and the personal relationship between the leasing agent of the developer and the site selection personnel of the retail chain were influential factors in the leasing activity, these factors were not relevant to obtaining occupants for office buildings.

In apartment buildings the developer sold directly to the public and thus had a quite different marketing task. For both apartments and office buildings there was little product differentiation among buildings, and there were many more competitors than in the field of shopping center development. Management of the completed developments also differed in tasks such as releasing and in the type and amount of continued marketing effort that was required.

TRC constructed the first closed mall shopping center in 1958, and the company developed a skill and a reputation for the quality of centers it developed. One of TRC's corporate goals, which was expressed by several members of the company's management, was "to improve the quality of life." The company first worked towards this objective by building better shopping centers, such as the closed-mall centers. It then began community development activities.

Community Development

TRC applied its skills at developing multiuse urban areas through several different channels. It developed residential areas around its shopping centers, as in its Echelon development. It contracted to analyze the needs of an entire urban area; and it developed complete new cities, such as Columbia, Maryland. Required among these different types of activities were many similar types of skills, but the focus of the activities and the required combination of skills differed among activities.

The analysis and formulation of recommendations for an urban area was carried out in what best could be described as a consulting relationship with a city. In May 1970 the company was working on a study for Hartford, Connecticut, and it had submitted a proposal to the City of New York to perform a study of Staten Island. Among the skills required for this activity were those in basic disciplines such as sociology and economics as well as the ability to interrelate the effects of political, social, and economic factors. The task involved the understanding of the economic potentials of an urban area, alternative uses of land, trends in population, institutional requirements—hospitals, schools, etc.—as well as the mutual interaction of these factors. The thrust of the company's involvement in this type of project could last several years (in the case of Hartford) or up to 10–15 years (in the case of Staten Island), and the relationship with the client could last several years beyond that.

The actual development of communities included the activities of research similar to those described above but perhaps smaller in size and shorter in time span, as well as activities in economic planning, physical planning and construction of roads, community facilities (such as parks, schools, and hospitals), and commercial and residential developments. The complexity of the community development process was greater than that of either pure residential or commercial development and had to deal with subtle interactions between these areas as well as with a broadened project size and scope and generally a much longer duration. The institutional development components of the multiuse urban development were most different from commercial development activities. Institutional development included activities such as determining placement of schools and libraries, convincing the local authorities of the merits of the proposal, then actually developing the institution. Institutional development, although critical to the total development of the urban area, did not as a separate entity yield favorable monetary returns.

Development of a whole city such as Columbia, which had a planned population of 100,000 for 1980, represented a task of an even larger magnitude. It had a longer time span and required more different types of skills than any single other commercial or community development.

A TRC advertising brochure described the company's objectives in Columbia. The article, entitled "A New Quality of Life—The Emphasis Is on People and How They Live," stated:

> From quiet residential neighborhoods to a downtown which is coming alive, Columbia is becoming a city full of opportunity and hope for today, as well as for tomorrow.
> Seven villages, each with three to five neighborhoods, will make up the new city. Each village will have the stores and shops needed most frequently in day-to-day living. Schools will be close enough so most children can walk to them.

Diversified housing already includes townhouses, ranches, split levels, colonials, and contemporaries, and midrise and garden apartments. More units are being added each month in price ranges suitable for the executive as well as the industrial worker.

In the midst of the villages, but not detracting from their individual identities, Columbia is developing an alive downtown with the entertainment, shopping, and business opportunities which make downtown an exciting place to go. An air-conditioned shopping mall planned for 5 department stores and 200 other stores by 1980 is being built in Columbia now. Columbia Mall's first phase with 2 department stores and about 70 stores is scheduled to open in 1971. Around this downtown retail core, office buildings containing more than 2 million square feet are planned.

Throughout the new city's limits more than 20 percent of the land is designated as permanent open space and cannot be used for other purposes. This means that parkland, lakes, golf courses, riding trails, and places to stroll or cycle will always be close to home.

Roads and pathways are arranged so that cars and children do not have to mix. Most wiring is underground. Trees have been left standing. Careful landscaping adds emphasis to the hills of Howard County in and around Columbia.

THE COMPANY'S ORGANIZATION

TRC's organization structure generally reflected its basic areas of activity (see Exhibit 1). The Mortgage Banking Division consisted of approximately 100 people in 8 offices located in key cities across the country. One office, located in TRC's headquarters in Columbia, Maryland, handled the financing for projects being developed by TRC itself.

The Commercial Development Division handled the development and management of all of the company's commercial properties (except for some in Columbia). The division employed nearly 200 people of which nearly 100 were in the construction department, 80 were in the planning and design department, over 20 were in the leasing department, and nearly 50 were in the property management operations department. In addition to these functional departments in the division, 3 senior project directors, assisted by 10 project directors, were handling the development of the 8 different centers in various stages of development in May 1970. The senior project directors reported directly to the senior vice president who was the head of the division.

The development process began when a project director consummated a deal for the development of a shopping center. The project director then called upon the different functions in the Commercial Development Division to perform the functions of planning and design, construction, marketing, and leasing. He also called upon other divisions of the company for financing and legal functions, and sometimes he obtained services from other companies. The procedure for shopping center develop-

EXHIBIT 1

Organization Structure, May 1970

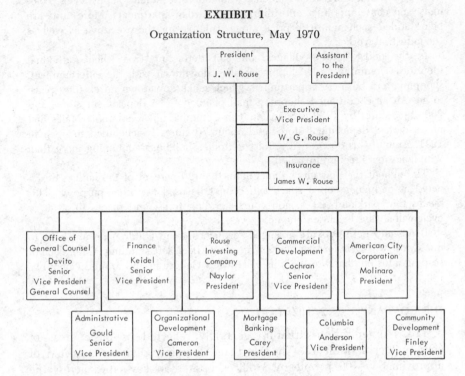

EXHIBIT 1

Organization Structure, May 1970

ment had been formalized into a written document, which is shown in Exhibit 2.

Functional specialists reported to the head of their functional area and not to the project director. The assignment of functional personnel to any particular project was handled by the functional manager, who had the authority to reassign his personnel among the various projects. In practice, a continuity of personnel was achieved on the project, although assignments were not permanent and were sometimes changed. Functional specialists were evaluated by their functional managers, and project directors provided feedback to the functional managers on performance on their projects.

Project directors had much influence in the division. Skip Cochran, senior vice president of Commercial Development and the man to whom both functional department heads and project directors reported, had previously been a project director. The company's history in developing shopping centers started with Jim Rouse pulling together the elements needed for the development, with the company later building its own capabilities in the functional areas.

Upon completion of a development, it was formally assigned to the

EXHIBIT 2

Shopping Center Development Procedure, 3/7/69

Function	*Responsibility*
1. Conceive building project	1. Project director
2. Examine and evaluate site	2. Construction VP and planning and design VP
3. Set schedule for development	3. Project director
4. Site survey, borings, and local conditions	4. Construction project manager (use site inspection check list)
5. Prepare development program and development budget	5. Project director
6. Develop project feasibility drawings	6. Construction project manager, planning and design and project director
7. Prepare construction budget	7. Construction project manager
8. Revise development program (if required)	8. Project director
9. Revise construction budget (if required)	9. Project director
10. Approval of development program, development schedule, and budget	10. Commercial Development Division VP
11. Revise development budget (if required)	11. Project director
*12. Obtain original budget authorization	12. Construction project manager
12A. Begin utility negotiation	12A. Construction project manager
13. Prepare architectural program and leasing plan	13. Construction project manager and leasing department
14. Obtain department store approval	14. Project director and Commercial Development Division VP
†15. Complete schematic drawings	15. Construction project manager, planning and design department (outside A & E if required)
16. Complete schematic cost estimate	16. Construction project manager
17. Revise schematics (if required)	17. Construction project manager and planning and design department
18. Revise cost estimate (if required)	18. Construction project manager and planning and design department
†19. Written approval by project director, planning and design and construction of schematics and cost estimate	19. Construction project manager
20. Department store approval	20. Project director and Commercial Development Division VP
21. Plan approval by the design committee	21. Project director
22. Select architect and engineer (may be accomplished at start of schematics)	22. Construction department VP, project director, planning and design department
23. Execute architectural contract	23. Legal, planning and design, Finance Division project director, construction department
24. Prepare schedule "B"	24. Construction, planning and design, leasing, legal, project director

EXHIBIT 2 (*continued*)

Function	*Responsibility*
25. Complete leasing plan	25. Leasing department
†26. Prepare preliminary drawings and outline specifications	26. Construction project manager, planning and design department
27. Lease tenant spaces	27. Leasing department
28. Prepare preliminary cost estimate	28. Construction project manager (general contractor, if required)
29. Review preliminary drawings and cost estimate	29. Construction project manager, project director, planning and design, marketing and leasing
30. Revise preliminary drawings (if required)	30. Construction project manager and planning and design department
31. Revise cost estimate (if required)	31. Construction project manager and planning and design department
32. Written approval by project director, planning and design and construction of preliminary plans and cost estimate	32. Construction project manager
33. Obtain department store approval	33. Project director and Commercial Development Division VP
34. Plan approval by the design committee	34. Project director
35. Arrange permanent financing	35. Project director
36. Obtain construction loan	36. Project director
37. Select general contract (may be accomplished at completion of schematics)	37. Project director and construction department VP
38. Execute general contract	38. Legal, planning and design, Finance Division, project director, construction department
39. Complete design input	39. Planning and design
†40. Start working drawings and specifications	40. Project director and construction project manager
41. Establish guaranteed maximum construction price (GMP)	41. Construction project manager
42. Complete working drawings and specifications	42. Construction project manager
43. Review working drawings, GMP	43. Construction project manager and planning and design department
44. Revise working drawings	44. Construction project manager and planning and design department
45. Revise GMP	45. Construction project manager and planning and design department
46. Written approval by project director, planning and design and construction of working drawings and GMP	46. Construction project manager
‡47. Prepare final estimate and detailed construction schedule	47. Construction project manager
†48. Obtain construction start approval	48. Construction project manager and project director
49. Obtain building permit	49. Construction project manager
50. Start shell construction	50. Construction project manager

EXHIBIT 2 (*concluded*)

Function	Responsibility
51. Approval of site architectural samples (as required)	51. Construction project manager (planning and design)
52. Obtain and approve tenant drawings	52. Construction project manager
53. Start tenant construction	53. Construction project manager
54. Complete shell construction	54. Construction project manager
55. Complete tenant construction	55. Construction project manager
56. Obtain use and occupancy permits	56. Construction project manager
57. Open center	57. Construction project manager

°Project manager submits standard form "Original Budget Authorization" for project director's approval.

†Project manager submits standard form "Request to Proceed with Project" for project director's approval.

‡Project manager submits standard form "Authorization for Change to Budget" for project director's approval.

APPROVED BY:

_____   _____
Commercial Development Division—Senior Vice President   Date

_____   _____
Construction Department—Vice President   Date

_____   _____
Planning and Design Department—Vice President   Date

property management department. This department performed the basic functions of running the ongoing center, and it was organized geographically according to the location of centers across the country.

Most of the personnel in the division were located in a complex of buildings approximately three miles from TRC headquarters. Both construction and leasing specialists had to do extensive traveling, however, to inspect sites or contact prospective tenants. Legal and accounting functions were handled by departments located at corporate headquarters.

Several members of TRC's management commented on the tasks of the Commercial Development Division and on the functioning of project teams and the role of the project director. Woody Beville, director of corporate planning, commented:

The project director is the key man in the overall coordination and management of a shopping center. When we first started developing centers, he was a real entrepreneur; he did the work from the feasibility all the way through the construction. Now he is more of a coordinator.

Initially, we established close relations with chains of department stores, and they bought property and came to Rouse to develop it as part of a center. The chains learned they were the key to the success of the center. Now they are competing for the hot trading area sites.

When we started building office buildings, we found the experience of our leasing people wasn't too valuable to us. It's a totally different client and set of problems.

Aubrey Gorman, a senior project director and vice president, commented:

The key to the commercial shopping center is in the "percentage rent." Rent payments are based upon a minimum monthly payment or a percentage of the tenant's sales—whichever is greater. This rewards the successful entrepreneur-manager who builds better, runs better, and keeps customers coming to the center.

In residential development, you're competing with hundreds of competitors. There may be 10 other apartment buildings that shine and that you're competing with directly, but it's not this way for shopping centers.

James Montague, director of construction, commented:

Presently, I am personally responsible to the project director for the construction of every project, and I assign my people to the projects. The project director has responsibility for the project, but none of the people he must rely on work directly for him. The project director knows who in construction is the project manager for his project, but he doesn't necessarily know the specific engineers working on it. . . . Also there's the problem of the specialists getting too specialized and becoming bored with the job—like the architect who does nothing but store fronts. Sometimes they get more excited about one project than the others, and they work on that one at the expense of the others.

On the other hand, what if you permanently assign functional specialists to project teams? I have a real hang-up with the team concept. Two years ago I was firmly against it. Now I still see some problems. Where does a guy go on a team? An architect wants to be an architect; a financial man wants to be a financial man. How do you tell a guy he's done a good job and move him up to more responsibility? A project manager from a functional area can move up to project director, but that's all.

Skip Cochran, senior vice president of commercial development, commented:

The main concern of the project director is getting a center built on time and on budget—calling on the resources of TRC. But he doesn't have very much to do with the details after the initial phases. We assign the construction project manager out of the construction department, etc., and these guys work pretty much 100 percent of their time on the project. When we had weak departments—back when I was a project director—I did much more in legal, architectural, leasing . . . myself. Now with strong departments, they work much more independently.

The Community Development Division had the personnel to perform the research activities, economic modeling, and institutional development for urban development projects. Community developments which included both development of a regional shopping center and development of the surrounding community were in their preliminary stages the responsibility of this division. After the preliminary stages of the project, however, it historically had been assigned to Commercial Development. In addition to its own employees the Community Development Division utilized specialists from other parts of the company. Of the division's 40 employees, 20 were assigned to market analysis and project evaluation and 14 to Columbia Community Development. Nearly all of the division's employees were located in the Teacher's Building, adjacent to the American City Building, which was the location of corporate headquarters.

The American City Corporation analyzed the needs of the urban area and made recommendations for its development. Nearly one third of the division's 30 employees were working on site in Hartford. The division called upon personnel from other areas of the company as needed.

The development of Columbia was the responsibility of the Columbia Division. Of a total of over 40 employees about 15 were assigned to business and industrial sales and residential sales. Columbia had its own institutional development department of three people, its own property management department of nine, and its own land and facilities development departments which together contained five people. Most of the personnel in the division were located in the Teacher's Building, although all sales personnel were in the Exhibit Building, and a few land planners and planning and design personnel were located in the same building as most of the Commercial Development Division personnel. The Columbia Division utilized the services of the other divisions of the company and relied heavily on the Community Development Division and on the Commercial Development Division for design and construction personnel.

INTERVIEWS WITH TRC EXECUTIVES

Several TRC executives were asked what the differences were in building shopping centers and in building larger scale projects like Echelon or Columbia. Jim Montague responded:

Developing shopping centers is fairly well established. One of the problems with an urban center such as Echelon is a personnel problem within the company. There are a large number of skilled shopping center developers in the Commercial Development Division, but there are none in Community Development. There is the temptation to let the shopping center "wag" the community development project. The problem is to find a guy or group of guys to do the whole process.

Phases of bringing a project into construction are: first, nonphysical planning. That's done by people like Mike Spear (director of market analysis and project evaluation in the Community Development Division). They will get sociological factors and political factors and take about two months to do the research. The proposal then goes to the Community Development policy board for two to three more months. It then goes to the land planner, who is in planning and design, and from there to the engineer in construction. This can go on for several months since the planner and engineer work back and forth bringing the ideas up to meetings and modifying their proposals. At the meetings, which are held about every two weeks, are members of the project team for the preliminary study. This team includes an urban planner, landscape architect, engineer, residential planner, and leasing man. . . .

In another interview, Mike Spear commented:

We've probably mastered the business of building shopping centers. We've probably almost mastered the business of building office buildings, and we're pretty good at building apartments. We're good at all things—we have or are in the process of getting—all parts of building a city. But to do a whole town you have a new problem. You're starting with raw land; you have to create an infrastructure into which all these projects should be built. Financially it's different because the arithmetic keeps changing where an individual project is fairly static and requires only monitoring. You have a different problem in physical planning—relating whole uses one to another requires a staging process. Marketing is different. You build a building and lease it with 5 percent or less turnover; but not here. You don't have a complete project. Try to market a notion with the city only one-tenth finished. The legal problems are more complicated. The organization is much more difficult; you're dealing with people over a longer period of time. You make all the decisions in a building in two years or maybe three. On a building, you have a team that's informal, but it's intact over the period of the project. With a city, the longer time frame means a changing team and a changing company behind it. What we do in Community Development is the front end of projects. There are several development groups. We're responsible for projects until they're accepted by management—that's the Community Development policy board. We rely on other departments—construction, etc.—then go outside the company. We put together plans, programs, and the economics. Community Development is a lot more involved and takes many more disciplines than a commercial development project. Choice of the man to head up a project depends on the individual more than on his specific background.

William Finley, vice president of Community Development, commented:

I have responsibility for people who are responsible for institutional development—concerning hospitals, schools, churches, etc. The total community is what is important to Rouse. Most developers do only what they are forced to do by the government agencies. We're usually way ahead of the agencies. This adds value to the land, every foot of it. But this requires a broader education. If you don't have knowledge of sociology in America, you can't even answer the questions intelligently or deal with citizens' groups.

Zoning is an example of the differences between Commercial Development and Community Development. In Columbia we have a long-term relationship with the county. In a shopping center you can take a short-term view and try to get the most favorable zoning right away—you don't have to go back for several changes over the years. Zoning for Columbia is completely innovative in that there is nothing else in the United States like it. We have complete freedom in zoning.

We opened Columbia from inception to initial occupancy in five years. One thing we underestimated was the continuing predevelopment process—that means getting the blob on the map to recorded land to the sales department. . . . It was our responsibility to maintain the integrity of the project. But the sales department, in their eagerness, commits parcels for uses different than we specify. In Columbia 10 percent of housing is subsidized for low-income families, and sometimes the sales department commits that land for other uses. For example, right now in the fourth community we're trying to make up for the deficit in low-income housing because the marketing department oversold land for other uses in the first three villages. . . .

I couldn't take control of the shopping center guys because they had been making shopping centers for years, and they still think Columbia is a flash in the pan—some of them. The policy board is meant to ride herd to make sure all programs are planned and financed under the overview of the policy board. Everything larger than shopping centers has to come under the policy board. That way we know that the institutional and community development aspects of the project are given proper consideration.

He elaborated on differences between shopping centers and larger scale developments:

We're not asking engineers to do anything different; they're still laying out roads, etc., but we're asking them to avoid trees, give lots with views. For the manager there is a balance between the community life you're trying to create and the business decisions all the way down the line.

Aubrey Gorman, the senior project director in the Commercial Development Division who was responsible for the Echelon project, commented on his experience with commercial development and community development.

We in Commercial Development have an organization that can build shopping centers and commercial developments. But we can't build true communities, and we are getting into that. As a company we are attracting the best talent in the country in community development. But these guys are in a separate organization. It's difficult to integrate that kind of talent into our projects, but we severely need it. We're living with this kind of agony.

Echelon started as a normal shopping center. We picked up the adjoining land—we knew at that point as a company we were going to get into more than regional shopping centers. It was our responsibility to assemble the various uses of land and bring them together. Echelon's advantage was that it was at the terminal point of a new transportation system. We were motivated really to do something. In this project guys like me, who are really commercially oriented, were making decisions on location of schools, how much land we should give away, the transportation link to the high-speed line, what kind of buildings, decisions on the community center, and how to tie it to the shopping center. We had no organization to deal with those questions. We had people but no organization, and that's where we are today. It's a hell of a lot easier to assemble the real estate acquisition for the smaller 300–400 acres than to get a Columbia-sized piece of land—it crosses so many borders. In Echelon we were able to tap Columbia-type talent on a crash basis only. Under pressure of deadlines we got planners—mostly Columbia planners—to do things. But first they played around for eight months. The functional guys knew they were not going to be in on the whole development process, and therefore their interest could only be a passing interest. It's a terrible problem just having personnel to stay with the project—the men are dancing for a different piper. There's also the problem of getting continuity of personnel. Different guys would come to meetings and wouldn't know what had gone on before. There were less problems with construction and others who were under the Commercial Development Division; but on residential development, where people were reporting to Columbia, it was more difficult. But you can't separate the commercial venture from the residential venture. The problem was magnified by the fact that residential guys, who were busy as hell, had a different kind of building schedule than we had. You can build a shopping center in 18 months and an apartment in only 6. The residential guys couldn't see why to start the apartment development as soon as the commercial people wanted—so they wouldn't always make the decision we needed.

Dick Anderson, vice president and general manager of Columbia, and Skip Cochran discussed the development of shopping centers, Echelon's and Columbia's:

COCHRAN: In an Echelon—and it didn't work this way—we should have assigned a general manager. He has to handle land acquisition, improvement, etc. He would then sell a piece of land for the development of a shopping center. In the case of Aubrey Gorman, who was a senior project director for Echelon, he did it out of his hip pocket.

ANDERSON: Size is not the only difference between Echelon and Columbia. First, in Columbia we have a partner. There is a difference from a shopping center, where the partner just gets the cash flow. Here partners are on the board. The reason for that is they have more risk and exposure.

COCHRAN: We might just get an equity partner from the word go on the next Echelon.

ANDERSON: The projects have different objectives. We're concerned with the environment—this brings new skills. We're also concerned with developing and selling land. There is an ongoing relationship with the county. The time span is different—for Columbia it's 15 years; for Echelon, 7; and for a shopping center, 3. Next, the key to a new town is that from the beginning we must have projects going—shopping centers, apartments, office buildings. . . . In the short run the return on these "pre-service" projects will lower our average return, but we must have them. You need the capacity to build these things.

COCHRAN: Looking at it in the short term, the last thing we want to be in is the development of these individual buildings in Columbia. What we're looking for there is critical mass and momentum. . . . The way of looking at it is different. The shopping center or office building is not going to give returns immediately, but it fits into the longer development financial picture.

Peter Wastie and Peter King of the institutional development section of the Community Development Division commented on their jobs. They indicated that they or other members of their department worked on things other than Columbia, but they were starting to extend their role to things like Echelon, where there was a requirement for an institutional component—relooking at shopping centers and their impact on the community.

WASTIE: A lot of people think we're a great waste of time and money up here. Projects that we work on cost money. But the powers that be don't think this, because it adds something—a texture to the developments. . . . This is the only company in the country where I can do what I'm doing.

One of the things we're working on is the problem of kids hanging around the shopping centers. You get hot-rodders there, and the adults have problems with there being so many kids around. The kids look bummy, the adults get jostled around, and there is a problem with shoplifting. The merchant feels these kids are clowns, but often the kids have real problems.

In Echelon we hope to have an "Earth Station." It will be 20,000 square feet with multiple levels. It will have light shows, and groups will perform there. The shops in the Earth Station will be for the kids—selling beads, clothes, etc.—maybe the kids' own bank and a hip doctor.

We deal with this kind of stuff. Then when it gets to the economic stage, we hand it *very carefully* to the project director.

If a guy from Antioch [Antioch College had a "field center" of about 100 students in Columbia] comes in with the idea for an inflatable building; when I find it OK I put him in touch with land, construction, the architectural review committee, planning and design. . . . We put people together. Now once we get something going we bow out. I'd like to be able to keep on it.

KING: Quite often it takes us a long time to find the right guy in Commercial Development to act on some of our proposals. We ought to be able to do something about that.

Woody Beville and Bob Cameron, vice president of Organizational Development, spoke of the changing directions of the company and the need for organizational change.

BEVILLE: The momentum of the company is changing from shopping centers to larger scale projects, but we need to change the guts of the company to do that.

CAMERON: Even in the shopping center side of the house the organization is frustrated because of the slowing down in getting decisions the growth in size has caused. The key in our business is the entrepreneur, the guy who pulls it all together. . . . We look at Rouse's philosophy as a mission. If we don't do these things, the country is going down the drain. We could double the amount of money we make if we concentrated on only the most financially attractive commercial developments, but that doesn't fit with our direction.

We have to institutionalize—that may be a bad word—the development process. The young people are telling us something. We must push decisions down; we must find a way to allow younger employees to develop faster.

Change in the task emphasis is increasing the scope and the time span of the project. Projects larger than shopping centers require more formal techniques —such as the use of CPM. The project directors are the intuitive types. The planning directors and community development people are more junior, but they are up on CPM. It's a real selling job. The entrepreneurial project directors can do the CPM kind of stuff on the smaller scale in their heads, but when they see it on paper they think it's too much to comprehend. I hope we have enough of those rare birds who can stand in the position between the entrepreneurial types and the CPM types. In changing our organization we don't have to do anything conventional. We're willing to start with no givens, but we've got to believe that what we come up with will really work.

In closing his remarks to the company assembly on May 26, 1970, Mr. Rouse introduced the company's executive committee and the newly appointed organization development task force. He then concluded:

. . . It is my hope and the hope of each of us on the executive committee and on the organizational development committee and in the whole company, that it will never be the same again, after today. I expect change to begin now and to keep growing towards a more efficient and a more humane enterprise. I expect your work to change and your performances to change, and I expect my work to change and my performance to change. By this fall I hope to face a different set of responsibilities, different set of goals, different set of schedules, a different way of working. I expect to be more effective. I expect to contribute more and have fun doing it. Good luck to you too.

New York City
Project Management Staff

"FOR A TIME, in the late fall of 1968, it seemed that the city might not survive. Perhaps there would cease to be a New York, and the city's 8 million residents and the 500,000 outsiders would have to find some new form to bring civic order into their lives. . . .

"What happens to New York is, of course, tremendously important in its own right. The city's metropolitan area shelters 8 percent of the total population of the U.S. and the Borough of Manhattan serves as the economic and cultural capital of the nation, if not the world. But what happens to New York is also important because, as New Yorkers are perversely proud to forecast, ills that cripple the nation's largest city to-day are likely to hit other urban centers in a very short time."

The above statements by A. James Reichley in "A Nightmare for Urban Management" in the March 1969 issue of *Fortune* indicate some of the external manifestations of the problems of New York City government. Five years earlier, in the September 1964 issue of *Fortune*, Richard J. Whalen stated in "A City Destroying Itself," "New York is a miracle. . . . The truth is that serious-minded voters have given up all hope of having responsive, efficient city government. They believe they live within an unfathomably complex system, which mysteriously runs on momentum and periodically collapses into anarchy. . . ."

Organization of the Government of the City of New York

Several bodies have direct responsibility for determining the direction of the City of New York. The city council consists of councilmen from each of 27 districts and 2 councilmen-at-large from each of the 5 boroughs. The board of estimate is composed of the 5 borough presidents, each having 2 votes, and the comptroller, the mayor, and the council president, each having 4 votes. The board of estimate must approve actions of the city council in the fields of administration, finance, and charter changes; and it has thus established considerable power.

291

The comptroller, who in addition to the mayor and city council president, is an elected official, is the chief financial officer of the city. The comptroller's organization, which is separate from the bureau of the budget and other line agencies under the control of the mayor, has among its powers the ability to investigate and to preaudit and postaudit all city accounts.

The mayor directs the executive arm of the city and has powers in executive and legislative areas. He can recommend legislation to the city council and veto legislation passed by the council. (The veto can be overridden by a two-thirds vote of the council.) As the chairman of the board of estimate, the mayor has considerable influence over administrative and budgetary matters. Subject to the approval of both the city council and the board of estimate, the mayor has the power to allocate $6 billion in yearly expenses.

The operating agencies, shown in Exhibit 1, are staffed with over 300,000 people and are responsible for the actual development and delivery of services. Agencies with similar programs are grouped into super-agencies under an administrator. The agencies often have narrowly defined responsibilities and are highly dependent upon each other. For example, the personnel department handles all hiring for the city agencies.

One of the most powerful agencies is the bureau of the budget. Having the responsibilities of preparing the expense budget, working with the planning department in preparing the capital budget, and administering the budget through pre- and postaudits, it has considerable contact and influence over other agencies. It established a programming, planning, budgetary system (PPBS) where budget bureau program planners work with other agencies to analyze city problems.

The functioning of the executive arm is described in *Fortune:*

Many of the roadblocks that now make city government inefficient are the perverse byproduct of the various reform movements that have swept through City Hall during the past fifty years. In order to forestall corruption, the reformers installed a series of rigid fiscal checks through the whole network of government. Political jobholders were replaced with career civil servants, who were insulated from political pressures. Minute administrative procedures were prescribed by law. . . .

Until recently, this system was partially redeemed by the quality of the men who ran it. During the depression years of the thirties, talented young men were attracted by the security and relatively high pay of city jobs. Most of them stayed on through the forties and fifties, gradually locked in by accumulating retirement benefits. But now they are reaching retirement age, and their replacements are not up to their standards. "I call them mules," says a key member of Lindsay's administrative team. "They carry the government on their backs, they know how to do the job but aren't very anxious for change,

EXHIBIT 1

Organization of Executive Department, City of New York

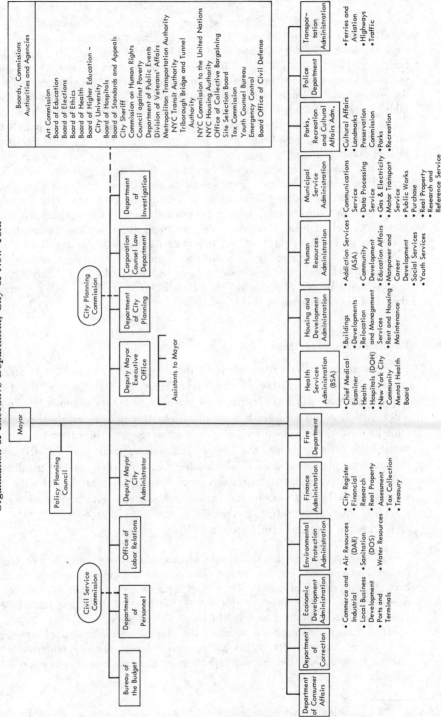

and they are mules . . . because they produced no successors. . . ."
. . . Lindsay's strongest administrative weapon—more important even than his right to hire and fire department heads—is his control over the city's operating budget. . . . Increasingly, Lindsay has used his power over the budget not only to control expenditures but also to impose administrative changes on the departments. . . . Under (Budget Director) Hayes' direction, detailed time-tables have been set up for every project in the city's capital construction program, and a single man has been made responsible for completion of each step in construction. Agency heads have been given more flexible authority over salaries and purchasing.

In the bureau's newly created division of program planning (PPBS), headed by Peter Goldmark, twenty-eight, about thirty recent college graduates work at developing more efficient administrative systems for the departments. Not surprisingly, contact between them and the veteran city employees has often been abrasive. "We sometimes think we can measure our effectiveness by the degree of our unpopularity," says Goldmark. But gradually, particularly in agencies like the police and fire departments where the bureaucracy is weak, the new systems have begun to take hold. "There is no way to make people like change," Hayes tells his staff. "You can only make them feel less threatened by it."[1]

Project Management Staff

Through executive order, Mayor Lindsay created the policy planning council (PPC), consisting of the mayor, the budget director, the two deputy mayors, and the chairman of the city planning commission. The PPC, which acted as an advisory group to the mayor, established two staff groups, one to consider issues for analysis and the other to implement high priority programs. The project management staff (PMS) was the implementation arm of PPC. Headed by Carl Allen, a 1964 graduate of a well-known eastern business school, the group was staffed with 20 professionals having various backgrounds and experience. Most of these men had extensive consulting experience.

Carl Allen described the function of PMS:

. . . responsible for the application of program/project management techniques and concepts for the timely management and implementation of the mayor's top-priority programs. These programs cover a number of areas and a wide range of city agencies. (A list of the projects PMS has undertaken along with a description of each can be found in Exhibit 2.)

The group's responsibility involves the design and planning of projects, assigning of responsibility within the agencies, design of the monitoring and control systems, and the regular reporting to the mayor and other top city officials.

---

[1]"A Nightmare for Urban Management," *Fortune,* March 1969, pp. 99, 170–71.

EXHIBIT 2

Projects Undertaken by the Project Management Staff

Project	Description
Hospitals renovation program	Begin renovations on 12 city hospitals by October 1969—reducing the cycle time for the first stages of this project from the normal 24-month cycle to 12 months.
Addict rehabilitation program	Increase the number of addicts in voluntary treatment by 2,000 by October 1969.
Police man-on-the-street program	Add 3,000 men to the department by June 1969. Review the assignment and use of scooters. Acquire 286 additional walkie-talkies and install 50 repeater stations by June 1969. Establish a special events squad of 630 men. Establish 280 one-man patrol sectors by early 1969. Fill 520 civilian vacancies in the department.
Swimming pools project	Open 46 mini-pools for the 1969 swimming season. Complete as many of the 14 vest pocket pools, for which sites had been selected, by the summer of 1969. Complete one large pool by the summer of 1969.
Community playlots project	Convert 50 city-owned vacant lots for use as fully equipped playlots by August 1969.
Pilot bus shelters project	Install 50 bus shelters throughout the 5 boroughs to test the utility and desirability of bus shelters and to test the adequacy and durability of various shelter designs.
Air pollution abatement NYCHA	Comply 2,652 NYCHA incinerators in 145 locations with Local Law 14.
Air pollution abatement board of education	Bring 814 public school incinerators in compliance with Local Law 14.
Air pollution abatement municipal hospitals	Bring 30 incinerators at 19 municipal hospitals into compliance with the provisions of Local Law 14.
Central Brooklyn model cities program —interim cleanup and rat control project	Programs designed to reduce unsanitary conditions and resulting rat infestation in the central Brooklyn model cities area. Set up management structure of field coordinators. Sidewalk sweeping program. Yard and lot cleanup program. Rat stoppage program. Rat extermination program.
Clean streets project	Hire 850 new sanitation men by June 1969. Test the use of plastic bags to determine the feasibility of changing the health code that required metal cans for garbage. Reduce the number of abandoned cars in the streets to 500 by June 1969. Provide the department of sanitation with various containerized equipment. Replace 547

EXHIBIT 2 (*continued*)

Project	Description
	sanitation men with civilians. Develop and test programs to lower the backlog of bulk refuse. . . .
Safety surfacing project	To reduce physical injury to children, install safety surfacing material in 295 playgrounds by September 1969 at a cost of $2 million.
Taxi driver licensing project	Study the taxi driver licensing procedures in use by the NYCPD to enable the processing of 200 applications per day and reduce the backlog of drivers awaiting licenses. (Five thousand additional drivers were needed to get all of the taxis out of the garages and onto the streets.)
Brooklyn Navy Yard	Set up a project management function in the department of commerce and industry to achieve the objective of commercially developing the Brooklyn Navy Yard.
Parks special cleanup program	Obtain improvements in the state of repairs and cleanliness of selected parks and playgrounds.
Air pollution program pre–WW II incinerators	Close 4 pre–World War II incinerators and implement new procedures to handle the 600 tons of garbage burnt in each incinerator each day.
Air pollution program post–WW II incinerators	Upgrade seven post–World War II incinerators to comply with the provisions of Local Law 14.
Sanitation maintenance operations project	Improve the management of the department of sanitation's vehicle maintenance operations.
Lead poisoning project	Accelerate the design and implementation of the lead poisoning control program.
Air pollution control	Design and accelerate the installation of a control and information system for use in enforcing private-sector air pollution program including on-site incinerators and oil burners.
Parking violations bureau	Establish the parking violations bureau and insure that it is fully operating by July 1, 1970, removing the handling of parking violations from the criminal courts.
Central Brooklyn model cities program including the day care/early childhood education program	Accelerate the implementation of these programs.
Operation main street program	Economic revitalization of 25 shopping streets throughout the 5 boroughs.
Rent stabilization enforcement program	
Development of a prototype urban action task force district organization for middle-class neighborhoods	
DOSS day care center program	

In the original plans for the group, the PMS project coordinators were given the functions of providing to the line agencies:

1. Technical assistance regarding the concepts of project management, including techniques of planning, scheduling, task definitions, and project control.
2. Staff assistance to do work where and when required. For example, in the beginning, considerable effort will most likely be required just to define the objectives of the projects and to identify the tasks necessary to accomplish these objectives.
3. Assistance in expediting the progress of projects:
   a) By coordinating interdepartmental activities and helping to remove roadblocks.
   b) By pointing out early signs of slippage in the project schedule.

Allen outlined to the case writer why in his judgment project management would be the best approach to the identified projects of critical priority (shown in Exhibit 2):

1. All are one-time projects with tight time schedules.
2. Each has a definable single goal.
3. Such projects involve activities/efforts different from ongoing continuing operational activities. As a result, existing agencies are not as well accustomed or staffed to handle projects.
4. Most of the projects are more nebulous and harder to define than capital programs with which the agencies become involved.
5. Each is complex, and the relationship between activities and results is hard to predict.
6. Most importantly, each requires significant participation by many agencies at a number of levels.

The following sign in the office of PMS indicates the philosophy of the group:

The difficult we can do immediately
The impossible will take two hours
... PPC

Hospitals' Crash Renovation Program

A crash renovation program was undertaken by the department of hospitals during the spring of 1966. The purpose of this program was to make 13 hospitals adequate for another 4 to 6 years until permanent rehabilitation or replacement could be accomplished.

The PPC project management staff became involved in February 1969. At that time, only one hospital was completed and 10 of the remaining hospitals were without a list of the renovations to be undertaken. The objective of the crash renovation program was to begin renovation of 11 of the 12 uncompleted municipal hospitals by the late summer of 1969 and of the 12th in December 1969.

A PPC report describes the approach:

In order to meet the above objective, it was necessary to reduce the time required for preconstruction activities from the normal two years to less than one year. The major obstacle to accomplishing this was the lack of clear-cut authority for construction decisions within the department of hospitals. . . .

As shown in Exhibit 1, the department of hospitals (DOH) was a part of the health services administration (HSA). Each of the city hospitals was headed by a hospital administrator, who was a deputy commissioner in DOH. The HSA planners were responsible for hospital construction and renovation. Under city charter, however, the department of public works (DPW) was responsible for hospital construction. As with any project in the city, the personnel department was responsible for hiring all staff, expenditures had to be approved by the bureau of the budget, and the budget itself had to be approved by the board of estimate. DOH was responsible to the board of estimate for expenditures on the crash program. When DOH asked for the responsibility to renovate the first three hospitals, DPW demanded "cognizance" over the renovating and they were given responsibility for renovations on five of the hospitals. (Eventually, they gave one of these up to DOH.)

Within DOH a task force was set up under the chairmanship of Deputy Assistant Commissioner Frank Starvel. The case writer first met D.A.C. Starvel while his secretary was reporting some trouble in getting results from another agency. Starvel told her, "Everything you do in this city, you do it yourself. Otherwise, you have to shove it (your request) so far into the machine, it comes out the other end." He later described his task and role:

I came here in July 1967, but we didn't get the architectural contracts for the first three hospitals signed until March 1968. It is difficult to cope with the city administration. It took a year and a half for the personnel department to decide on the qualifications and titles of the people to manage these projects. If you don't wait for their decision and make provisional appointments, you risk the possibility of them getting bumped. There was the complication with DPW which created a coordination problem between DOH and DPW. And there is an ongoing conflict between DOH and HSA. . . . [He elaborated later.]

Frank used the diagram on page 299 to describe his position.

He continued:

The bureau of the budget felt each commissioner should have a deputy for the management of capital projects. They didn't include secretarial staff or

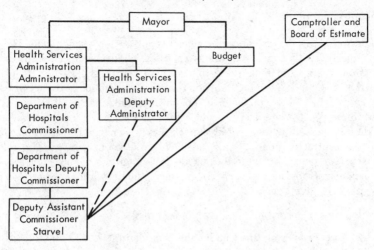

even the guy's salary. I started with the same problem my boss did—no staff, no budget. . . . You wouldn't believe how long it takes for the bureau of the budget to recognize that you have a position to be filled. It was also difficult to negotiate architectural contracts because the comptroller wouldn't accept their fees.

Frank described the role of PMS:

In February 1969 Dave Anderson was assigned to the project. He was going to spy on us for the mayor, I thought. I promptly dubbed him the "mayor's fink," and I introduced him to people that way. He showed a capacity to grasp the problem and conducted himself with unabashed self-confidence—but in no way overtly suggesting his power. He would set up meetings with commissioners, the budget bureau. . . . He had no fear of these people, and this helped move the project along.

I explained why I couldn't move—my role wasn't clearly defined. I wasn't in the position of telling hospital administrators anything, and there was inter-agency friction between HSA planners, the commissioner of hospitals, and the hospital administrators. In HSA there is a belief in the autonomy of the hospital administrators. I can't tell anyone anything in planning, either. And with DPW we had to fight a battle for the renovations to stay in DOH.

The fundamental question was to decide what renovations should be done in each hospital. I suggested to Anderson that for each hospital there should be a planning unit or task force of hospital administrator, architect, health facilities planner, and myself. Anderson wanted me to be in charge but I told him it couldn't work that way because of the status of the hospital administrator by law. I didn't think there was any point in being a czar—what was important was that the three participants agree. Anderson was able to move things through agencies as the mayor's priority project. That miraculous effect can't continue long, because after a while the mayor is even ignored.

Frank also commented:

Anderson is the biggest single beneficial input in this organization. He provided objectivity that reduced things to essential elements. Then he and I worked on trying to manage these things. We discussed CPM—he's all caught up in this modern B.S. But CPM won't work on alteration jobs because you don't know what work you have to do until you tear the wall down. It occurred to me . . . (maybe I think it was my idea and it was really Anderson's) that the simplest thing we could expect was a bar graph with milestones. Then if a contractor doesn't make an event, you know it. . . . The role of Anderson can never be underestimated—he brought it to an analysis. The commissioner of hospitals never gave me any guidance, and no one else here was capable of giving any.

A PPC report described the involvement of PMS:

A task force was established under the chairmanship of the deputy assistant commissioner. This task force consisted of individuals with essential technical skills as well as individuals who participated in assignments connected with hospitals under their direction.

The chairman of the task force had the necessary technical experience to manage a construction project. However, a problem developed in that he was at a lower organizational level than some of the other members of the task force. As part of the mayor's office, the PPC project management staff lent its authority to that of the chairman and enabled him to exert sufficient authority to achieve the coordination necessary for successful renovation of these hospitals.

A project-oriented task force coupled with a chairman having sufficient authority provided the basic organizational element for utilizing other project management techniques. These include the development of detailed schedules with which to monitor the progress being made toward completion of the project. In addition, project status reports were prepared monthly so as to inform all responsible parties as to the progress made and problems incurred in achieving the project objectives. . . .

Dave Anderson described the problems that Frank Starvel had encountered in a manner similar to Starvel's account. He elaborated:

Starvel was hired by the deputy administrator of HSA. For several years the project bogged down and Starvel was frustrated—not knowing to whom he was reporting. He is a very able construction man and capable architect. He came from outside the city organization and was not a bureaucrat. He had no real managerial ability, but a willingness to accept help. DOH didn't know PMS. To them we represented the mayor . . . but the amount of clout was unknown.

I established good relations with Starvel. He used me as a political commissar —I could do things he couldn't dare—I could tell other departments and DOH to do things. I also offered a managerial approach. I talked through ideas with him with an idea of the solution but let him conceive of the solution himself. Over six months he developed administrative and managerial skills.

There was also the question of DPW. At one time, they had responsibility for the renovations of five of the hospitals. They could hire the architect but they could effectively contribute nothing. When we set up the task forces, I told them that they (DPW) would have to accept the fact of the functioning of the task forces. This was hard for DPW to do. Previously (and still) they will not work with DOH. Effectively, we removed DPW from the planning phase.

The bureau of the budget was important for acquisitions. There we straightened out Starvel's problems with the budget examiners. We helped the examiners and developed a relationship between them and Starvel. The bureaucrats over there can't be fired, so it is a question whether my being from PMS was of any importance. By making the examiners feel we were assisting, personal relations developed. I've been lucky in terms of working relations. . . .

Addiction Rehabilitation Program

In September of 1968 PMS began working with the addiction services agency (ASA) in an effort to increase the number of addicts in voluntary treatment by 2,000 by October 1969. In April 1969 this target was revised downward to 1,078. A PPC report describes the approach to the project:

In order to focus sufficient management resources on the project objective of providing treatment for 1,078 additional addicts by October 1969, ASA established a task force to design the project. The task force analyzed the cycle of activities required to bring an addict into voluntary treatment, considering the steps required to open additional physical facilities as well as those to recruit addicts into treatment and the probabilities of addicts dropping out of treatment at different stages of rehabilitation. From this analysis a schedule was developed which showed the activities required to open the treatment and re-entry houses required to accomplish the project objective. . . . From this schedule, a milestone chart was prepared which provided a basis against which to measure ASA's expansion of its treatment capacity. Progress made in achieving these milestones was reported in biweekly status reports. These reports also identified serious problems and suggested a means of resolving them when this was appropriate. . . .

In September 1969 PMS terminated its relationship with ASA. The project was considered by PMS to be a complete failure, with only 130 additional addicts in treatment in that time. The PPC report describes the problems they encountered:

ASA did not accept basic project management concepts, such as focusing on one identifiable project with well-defined goals and monitoring progress against these goals. Rather, they wanted to monitor the whole agency in a general way. Midway through the project at the suggestion of PMS, ASA contracted with a management consulting firm to provide an experienced, qualified person to act as project manager. The outside consultant adapted ASA's approach of monitoring the entire agency, diluting his effectiveness on the PPC-defined project.

At the same time, they regarded project management personnel as merely additional staff rather than viewing the project manager as responsible for coordinating the agency's efforts around a particular project.

The task force set up by ASA did not include individuals at a high enough organizational level. Consequently, the agency's commitment to the project objective was not as strong as it might have been. If the commissioner and his assistant were members of the task force, the agency's commitment might have been more assured. . . .

James Warner, a younger member of PMS, initially worked on the ASA project. He was later assigned to a project to develop neighborhood playlots. The playlots project involved working closely with the department of highways and was considered by PMS to have been successful. Jim commented on ASA:

Agencies dealing in "hard stuff" (things) rather than "soft stuff" (people) are better organized. By pushing hard, you can get things done. Sure, there's red tape and bureaucratic screw-ups, but things can get done. In agencies with soft stuff, they are not organized to think in a way that gets things done. They are also less receptive.

On ASA I could call meetings and suggest approaches and that's it. . . .

Chuck Homer, a more experienced member of PMS, also commented on the ASA project:

When the addict rehabilitation project started, Carl Allen and PMS had little credibility. They could get no support from PPC or the mayor. If it would happen today, it would be a different story.

There are a lot of people who can go into the agencies and say they are from the mayor's office. The people in the agencies don't know how close you actually are to the mayor. Most assistants to the mayor are young, intelligent, and from Ivy Schools. But they get the hairs up on your back right away if you're a typical bureaucrat. They look at the assistants like chipmunks running around a tree. Everything to the assistants is priority—you have to make the agencies know you're not doing the same thing to them. . . .

Air Pollution Abatement

The department of air resources (DAR) was responsible for the enforcement of Local Law 14, which stipulated pollution emission standards to which incinerators in the city had to conform. By law, incinerators in multiple dwellings had to meet these standards and be issued a certificate of operation by December 20, 1968 for dwellings having 20 or fewer units (category 1) or 101 or greater units (category 2) per incinerator; October 20, 1969 for dwellings having 61 to 100 units (category 3) per incinerator; and May 20, 1970 for dwellings having 21 to 60 units (category 4) per incinerator. The New York City Housing Authority (NYCHA) operated housing units throughout the city which had incinerators not meeting the standards of Local Law 14. The options open to NYCHA on these incinerators were (1) discontinuing operations of the incinerator, resulting in increased raw garbage placed on the streets to be picked up by the department of sanitation (DOS); (2) compacting, or pressing, the garbage into a smaller volume before placing it on the streets for pick-up by DOS; and (3) upgrading the incinerators to burn the garbage while meeting the standards of Local Law 14. The following table describes the distribution of NYCHA incinerators and their condition as of April 1969:

Category	Locations	Total Incinerators	Discontinued	Upgrading Requested or in Design	Upgrading in Progress
I.......14		564	44	520*	
II.......93		550		335	145
III.......33		191		153	38
IV.......55		1351		1343	8

*NYCHA had previously changed its decision to discontinue these incinerators.

Major steps in upgrading an incinerator were assessment of the condition of each incinerator, approval by the bureau of the budget, approval of funding by state and federal lending agencies, engineering design, granting of building permit by the building department, securing equipment from manufacturers, construction, and granting of certificate of operation by DAR. NYCHA projected that once funding was approved it required 12 months to upgrade a typical incinerator. Some NYCHA incinerators were in violation of Local Law 14, and it appeared that most of the others could not be upgraded in time to meet compliance dates. Many groups were pressing the mayor on the subject of air pollution. It was impractical for DAR to summons NYCHA for its violations, since both were part of the city government. A PPC report listed key problems cited by NYCHA as affecting overall progress on the project:

1. Limited authority—(in-house) engineering manpower requires that considerable design work must be contracted outside.
2. Delays occur in receiving funding approval from state and federal lending agencies.
3. Delays occur on equipment deliveries from manufacturers.
4. Equipment installation delays occur due to the limited number of qualified installers available.

The air pollution abatement project was ongoing in NYCHA since March of 1966. Carl Allen commented that the key reason for the lack of progress was that the officials of the housing authority didn't want to make a decision. The commissioner was having difficulty deciding between the alternatives of compacting and upgrading, and no one within the housing authority was assigned the responsibility of having the incinerators comply with the law.

In September 1968, Jerry Johnson of PMS became involved in the project; and in March 1969, Tom Hamilton of PMS joined Johnson and was given principal responsibility for the project.

Assistant Commissioner Kenneth Coleman of DAR commented on PMS:

If there is a central group—which is the project management staff—coordinating and keeping track of all the agencies, our job—the enforcement of Local Law 14—is much easier.

The only way to get other people to move is through the power of the mayor. They (PMS) also had to coordinate external sources such as large manufacturers, but the key to their success is their power.

Initially they came in and said "I'm going to help you." Some people look at them as coming in and usurping authority, but to me they were a great help —how you look at it depends on your personality.

My initial contact with PMS was actually in a meeting with the mayor. Carl Allen was introduced as someone coming on to help. His power wasn't spelled out, but the fear of unknown power is more effective anyhow. Carl's approach has been to come in and say he was going to help; and if that doesn't work, exert pressure.

Both Tom Hamilton and Jerry Johnson were experienced engineers, an asset which they felt helped them work with the engineers in NYCHA. Hamilton commented:

Prior to the involvement of PMS, NYCHA did have an ongoing program to comply with Local Law 14. But their organization left much to be desired. It was poorly designed and poorly implemented. The housing authority wanted to comply (to the law) but had headaches doing so. For example, they initially chose to discontinue incinerators in category 1. This was an unpopular decision with the tenants, most of whom previously had come from tenements. They were happy having incinerators and didn't want to come down and put garbage in containers. The kids played in it, and it put more burden on DOS. The tenants organized politically against it. They said they would "air express" the garbage—out the windows. Then the snowstorm hit and the garbage piled up. The housing authority had to reopen the incinerators and start burning. Their enthusiasm for the pollution abatement project went way down.

In other areas, they couldn't decide whether to use compactors or to upgrade. As with many agencies, they have a lack of in-house technical capability. You have to go to outside consultants, and that slows things down.

When PMS first got into the picture, PMS was just getting started and was unknown and didn't have anyone's respect. By February (after Jerry was there for nine months), PMS was beginning to move. We went to the chairman of the housing authority and told him we were a project management team assigned to the project. He referred us to his number 2 man, who gave us a car and two or three of his men. We first went to all the 20 or under (category 1) locations. We were met at each location by the local supervisor. We interviewed him, walked through the facility, met maintenance people, talked to tenants, and saw piles of garbage.

We decided that they were pursuing the wrong course. Upgrading was the best alternative because it didn't leave any raw garbage on the street. We wrote a report describing our findings. The housing authority was enthusiastic, but DAR wanted discontinuance. We didn't think that was good, and we sold the alternative of upgrading to the mayor.

We did surveys with people from the housing authority and set up milestone charts. We offered to help them and promised not to release our reports without first letting them see them. We didn't have any authority with them except implied authority. If you use clout it takes twice as long. If you do it right they feel it is their project, and it lasts after you leave. Jerry and I felt we should not manage the project for them. They agreed that they needed a coordinator and took an engineer from the field to fill the job. We taught him to use his field inspectors to report project status and contractors' actions. We still help him on his status reports, but by the first of the year we won't have to. Part of the coordinating job was to call meetings with tardy contractors. By having bigwigs there you could get them moving. Often the problem was with the city itself, such as waiting for approvals. In the beginning we spent time introducing contractors to the people in the agencies that they had to work with—that happened three to four times a week.

As far as the housing authority is concerned, it is an ongoing project. They have learned to run a project of this size. They don't love us because we got in their hair, but the reaction to our group is favorable.

We did the same thing for other agencies—the board of education, city hospitals. . . . Our approach there has been the same—start with the top guy, set up the control system. . . . Part of our effectiveness is that the system maintains pressure. You have to get things done or you start looking bad.

Now our influence stems from our past record. Initially the HA had to deal with us because we were an arm of PPC. I don't think any of them felt they would lose their jobs because of us. We were just a couple of other guys from the mayor's office. We developed a relation with them—with the engineers; our engineering backgrounds helped.

Observations on the Functioning of PMS in the Government Structure

The bureau of the budget was involved in virtually every project in the city. Deputy Assistant Director of the Budget Paul White commented on the city government and PMS:

There is a multiagency setup for almost every project in NYC. Because of the reach of the budget bureau, they are in almost every project, and almost always a regulatory agency such as the department of buildings is in.

One of the projects of the Lindsay administration was to form many departments into superagencies. There are long histories of the separate agencies, and many people in these organizations don't recognize the superagencies. New York City has a great shortage of middle management types. Many came up through the ranks of civil service. Many are bright and hard working but older than they ought to be for their position. They know how things are done but are not ready to change. They have a feeling of responsibility, but they stick to old traditions—their mental image is not in keeping with the changes. Anyone who introduces change into the system should do so with trepidation. The systems now operate—take them apart at your peril. Classic concepts of management don't work—especially when most of the employees are both members of strong unions and civil service.

When asked what key elements made PMS effective, White commented:

1. They have managerial talent—both innately good and trained.
2. They have the influence of the mayor's office—it is rarely called upon but is significant.
3. The bureau of the budget is not independent from the rest of the mayor's office, although it looks like it to some. The bureau can deter or delay things from happening. Carl's (Allen) group is close to but not part of the bureau of the budget. They have the power as insiders to move things through here.
4. There is an esprit among Lindsay's appointees. Carl's group is able to tap into that to get cooperation.
5. They also tapped a desire for accomplishment among civil servants who feel things should work and suffer frustrations. These people see PMS as an opportunity to get things done.
6. PMS is able to shortcut bureaucratic routines—cutting lines of communication to go direct. They can do it because they are outside the chain of command. If you get lots of this (say as PMS grows), it would become a monster. There are questions of how it fits into the system. The solution is to develop a PMS group within each superagency.

The two deputy mayors would each say Carl works for them. Actually PMS is paid by the budget bureau. Not all of the budget bureau would say they align with PMS—I do, but many of the old-line bureaucrats see themselves in the review function only and not in running programs. New York City has no tradition of orders being given and carried out. (This is not true in Chicago.) Here nobody gives orders. The New York tradition is that people meet and reason with each other—sometimes at unbelievable length. If you convince a civil servant rationally that something is good, he'll do it. You don't need line authority over him.

An agency can be a tremendous obstruction to a project. You need the support of the commissioner to break roadblocks. He could set the project as low

priority, simply disagreeing with the mayor. There are fights for resources between the project approach and the normal functions of a department. In
many ways PMS has not had the resource allocation problem to face.

Chuck Homer of PMS also commented that the biggest stumbling
block on projects from the point of view of the agencies was the bureau
of the budget. He also commented on the importance of getting the support of the commissioners involved in the project. When asked why PMS
was successful he commented:

We made them (the people in the agencies) see they could do it. They
never stopped to analyze but only thought of reasons why they couldn't get
projects done. Also they're scared they'd be shown up in front of the mayor.
We can use our reports as a wedge to get them to do things. Carl is harder in
his dealings with people than others here—we call him in only when there is
no other way.

Jim Warner, who considered himself the devil's advocate in PMS, did
not agree with Chuck Homer:

Status reports are useless as anything other than a reporting device. Status
reports, as a way of providing clout in my experience, hasn't worked. Going
to Carl to put pressure on a personal basis has worked. All the while we
operate through other agencies. When we go in as the mayor's representatives,
it doesn't work—personal contacts in the agencies are important.
    The real cancer, the real evil, is the lack of well-defined organizational
structures in agencies; and, secondly, the lack of real good people. Project
management reflects a certain amount of John Rosefield's (assistant director
of the bureau of the budget) outlook in assuming that agencies and commissioners can be told what to do by a bunch of bright young p . . . . s.
While many commissioners are poor managers and administrators, it's really
arrogance to assume that we can run their lives—even if it's only on one
project that's been selected out of the entirety of an agency's activities. The
cancer is the old guys who are commissioners and upper-level civil servants,
and of course the complexity of the system—the number of steps necessary to
get anything done. It's true you can't revolutionize the whole agency. Project
management is the best way out of a poor situation. We go in there and learn
the agency and make them think they're doing the project. The oversell is the
use of PERT and status reports. The only guys who know the system are the
civil servants. It is important how responsive the agency head is—power is the
name of the game, and project management doesn't have that much clout. All
you have is the assumption that you're working for the mayor and if you (the
agency head) show up bad, it shows up to the mayor—that's not enough.
    We've brought together at meetings people who wouldn't otherwise have
thought of getting together for projects that cross agency lines or lines of departments within agencies. We've also hand-carried paper to the guy who had
to sign it. In trying to cut red tape, you know the city mail will take five days.
The guy who puts it in the mail ends his responsibility there. You are the only
one to move it faster, but should you? I don't think I'd throw as much money

into this operation as the mayor does. I'd get a lot of management experts as assistants and commissioners.

In an informal discussion Chuck Homer, Jerry Johnson, and Tom Hamilton commented on the functioning of PMS:

HOMER: We do a hell of a lot of coordinating. If you ask people, they'll say it's our most important role.

CASE WRITER: Is that within or between agencies?

HOMER: Both. In one department people two doors away wouldn't talk to each other. You have to get them together by calling a meeting. It's a case of the older bureaucrats imbedded in the system. One guy said, "I've been here through four mayors and I'll probably be here through two or three more, and if it doesn't get done today, it'll get done tomorrow."

JOHNSON: In one department I was told, "We're doing the job for you fellows, and I plan on being here for the duration of the project. Don't give me any flack or I'll retire." The younger guys are much more receptive. One guy said that they wouldn't be as far without project management. You have to depend on these guys because your job depends on their doing the work.

HAMILTON: I question the value of project management in relation to the cost of this office. There are a lot of high power people doing conceptually simple jobs. It doesn't take any real deep thought. But in the city projects are sometimes so fragmented, and the responsibilities so overlapping. . . . Because there is no guy that can look at the whole thing, it gets out of control. The technical part of the job is simple, but the total job you have to do through people—75 percent of this job is to motivate and get people responsive to the program.

HOMER: We can't measure the value in dollars and cents. We've helped the citizens with the things we've done. We may have been better off if we set better goals for this office. We are becoming a staff—absorbed in the line functions rather than project management.

HAMILTON: For what it is costing, we should not only do the job but also build an in-house capability to carry on. . . .

JOHNSON: Initially the people Carl works for couldn't tell him what they wanted. We tried to hit too much at once. . . . I disagree with Tom [Hamilton]. Although these are simple jobs, it is not an easy task; and it takes a lot of experience to be able to put it all on paper. It's a job to translate the plans and converse with the operating people.

Carl Allen commented on the past functioning of PMS and raised questions on the direction the group should take in the future:

We're a lot better at this now than we were a year ago. I learned a lot about the city and about project management. Under the project management umbrella, we can do a lot of things that aren't project management—and we have done them. For example, we ran the maintenance department of the parks department. We did it because it had to be done and there was no one else to do it. But it was a prop-up action. Many of our efforts are just good consulting jobs that we are doing—it makes me feel like a farmer going

around propping up his scarecrows. I want to initiate a management development program for each agency and design a management control system for
each agency so that there is a mechanism to run the city.

You asked me why we are effective. . . . We define the project and the expected end-results, and we're watchdogs to make sure things get done. We can
apply pressure in the agencies to alter their priorities. We're a communications link among agencies and between agencies and the bureau of the budget
—there we do a lot of coordinating. An agency that has principal responsibility for a program will get ignored by other agencies. The fact that a man is
a commissioner doesn't mean anything. The only way a guy can make any in-
roads is on a personal basis—and part of that is the perceived clout he has.
There is a lot of conflict between agencies and we spend a lot of time
mediating.

We also identify where additional resources are needed and where to go to
get them—often a commissioner doesn't know how to use consultants when
he gets them. We also provide technical skills and added manpower to fill in
the lack of talent in the agencies. We want to develop the talent in the
agencies rather than just solving problems and getting out. But how should we
do this? Do we hire guys to work on projects and then spin off into the
agencies? With the people in the agencies the question is how do you make
them results oriented. There is no profit objective. You have to define results
and measure people against them.

Texana Petroleum Corporation

DURING the summer of 1966, George Prentice, the newly designated executive vice president for domestic operations of the Texana Petroleum Corporation, was devoting much of his time to thinking about improving the combined performance of the five product divisions reporting to him (see Exhibit 1). His principal concern was that corporate profits were not reflecting the full potential contribution which could result from the close technological interdependence of the raw materials utilized and produced by these divisions. The principal difficulty, as Prentice saw it, was that the division general managers reporting to him were not working well together: "As far as I see it, the issue is where do we make the money for the corporation? Not how do we beat the other guy. Nobody is communicating with anybody else at the general manager level. In fact they are telling a bunch of secrets around here."

RECENT CORPORATE HISTORY

The Texana Petroleum Corporation was one of the early major producers and marketers of petroleum products in the southwest United States. Up until the early 1950s, Texana had been almost exclusively in the business of processing and refining crude oil and in selling petroleum products through a chain of company-operated service stations in the southwestern United States and in Central and South America. By 1950 company sales had risen to approximately $500 million with accompanying growth in profits. About 1950, however, Texana faced increasingly stiff competition at the retail service station level from several larger national petroleum companies. As a result sales volume declined sharply during the early 1950s, and by 1955 sales had fallen to only 300 million and the company was operating at just above the break-even point.

At this time, because of his age, Roger Holmes, who had been a dominant force in the company since its founding, retired as president and chief executive officer. He was replaced by Donald Irwin, 49, who had been a senior executive with a major chemical company. William Dutton,

EXHIBIT 1

Partial Organization Chart, 1966

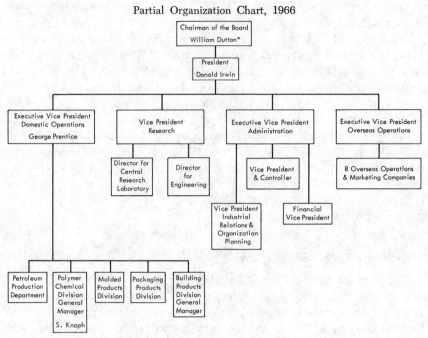

*Names included for persons mentioned in the case.

55, was appointed chairman of the board to replace the retiring board chairman. Dutton had spent his entire career with Texana. Prior to his appointment as chairman he had been senior vice president for Petroleum Products, reporting to Holmes.

Irwin and Dutton, along with other senior executives, moved quickly to solve the problems facing Texana. They gradually divested the company's retail outlets and abandoned the domestic consumer petroleum markets. Through both internal development and acquisition they expanded and rapidly increased the company's involvement in the business of processing petroleum for chemical and plastics products. In moving in this direction they were rapidly expanding on initial moves made by Texana in 1949, when the company built its first chemical processing plant and began marketing these products. To speed the company's growth in these areas, Irwin and Dutton selected aggressive general managers for each division and gave them a wide degree of freedom in decision making. Top management's major requirement was that each division general manager create a growing division with a satisfactory return on investment capital. By 1966 top management had reshaped the company so that in both the domestic and foreign market it was an integrated producer of chemicals and plastic materials. In foreign operations the company continued to operate service stations in Latin America and in Europe. This change in direction was successful; and by 1966 company sales had risen to $750 million, with a healthy rise in profit.

In spite of this success, management believed that there was a need for an increase in return on invested capital. The financial and trade press, which had been generous in its praise of the company's recovery, was still critical of the present return on investment; and top management shared this concern. Dutton, Irwin, and Prentice were in agreement that one important method of increasing profits was to take further advantage of the potential cost savings which could come from increased coordination between the domestic operating divisions, as they developed new products, processes, and markets.

DOMESTIC ORGANIZATION 1966

The product division's reports to Mr. Prentice represented a continuum of producing and marketing activities from production and refining of crude oil to the marketing of several types of plastics products to industrial consumers. Each division was headed by a general manager. While there was some variation in the internal organizational structure of the several divisions, they were generally set up along functional lines (manufacturing, sales, research and development). Each division also had its own controller and engineering activities, although these were supported and augmented by the corporate staff. While divisions had their own research effort, there was also a central research laboratory at the corporate level, which carried on a longer range research of a more fundamental nature, and outside the scope of the activities of any of the product divisions.

The *Petroleum Products Division* was the remaining nucleus of the company's original producing and refining activities. It supplied raw materials to the Polymer and Chemicals Division and also sold refining products under long-term contracts to other petroleum companies. In the early and mid 1950s this division's management had generated much of the company's revenue and profits through its skill of negotiating these agreements. In 1966, top corporate management felt that this division's management had accepted its role as a supplier to the rest of the corporation, and felt that there were harmonious relations between it and its sister divisions.

The *Polymer and Chemicals Division* was developed internally during the late 1940s and early 50s as management saw its share of the consumer petroleum market declining. Under the leadership of Seymour Knoph (who had been general manager for several years) and his predecessor (who was in 1966 executive vice president—administration), the division had rapidly developed a line of chemical and polymer compounds derived from petroleum raw materials. Most of the products of this division were manufactured under licensing agreement or were materials the formulation of which was well understood. Nevertheless, technical personnel in the division had developed an industrywide reputation for their ability to develop new and improved processes. Top management of the division took particular pride in this ability. From the beginning, the decisions of what products to manufacture was based to a large extent upon the requirements of the Molded Products Division and Packaging Products Division. However, Polymer and Chemicals Division executives had always attempted to market these same products to external customers, and had been highly successful. These external sales were extremely important to Texana since they assured a large enough volume of operation to process a broad product line of polymer chemicals profitably. As the other divisions had grown, they had required a larger proportion of the division's capacity, which meant that Polymer and Chemical Division managers had to reduce their commitment to external customers.

The *Molded Products Division* was also an internally developed division, which had been formed in 1951. Its products were a variety of molded plastic products ranging from toys and household items to automotive and electronic parts. This division's major strengths were its knowledge of molding technology and particularly its marketing ability. While it depended upon the Polymer and Chemicals Division for its raw materials, its operations were largely independent of those of the Packaging Products Division and Building Products Division.

The *Packaging Products Division* was acquired in 1952. Its products were plastic packaging materials, including films, cartons, bottles, etc. All of these products were marketed to industrial customers. Like the Molded Products Division, the Packaging Division depended on the Polymer and Chemical Division as a source of raw materials but was largely independent of other end-product divisions.

The *Building Products Division* was acquired in 1963 to give Texana a position in the construction materials market. The division produced and marketed a variety of insulation roofing materials and similar products to the building trade. It was a particularly attractive acquisition for Texana, because prior to the acquisition it had achieved some success with plastic products for insulation and roofing materials. Although the plastic products accounted for less than 20 percent of the total division sales in 1965, plans called for these products to account for over 50 percent of division sales in the next five years. Its affiliation with Texana gave this division a stronger position in plastic raw materials through the Polymer and Chemicals Division.

Selection and Recruitment of Management Personnel

The rapid expansion of the corporation into these new areas had created the need for much additional management talent; and top management had not hesitated to bring new men in from outside the corporation, as well as advancing promising younger men inside Texana. In both the internally developed and acquired divisions most managers had spent their career inside the division, although some top division managers were moved between divisions or into corporate positions.

In speaking about the type of men he had sought for management positions, Donald Irwin described his criterion in a financial publication: "We don't want people around who are afraid to move. The attraction of Texana is that it gives the individual responsibilities which aren't diluted. It attracts the fellow who wants a challenge."

Another corporate executive described Texana managers: "It's a group of very tough-minded but considerate gentlemen with an enormous drive to get things done."

Another manager, who had been with Texana for his entire career, and who considered himself to be different from most Texana managers, described the typical Texana manager as follows:

Texana attracts a particular type of person. Most of these characteristics are personal characteristics rather than professional ones. I would use terms such as cold, unfeeling, aggressive, and extremely competitive, but not particularly loyal to the organization. He is loyal to dollars, his own personal dollars. I think this is part of the communication problem. I think this is done on purpose. The selection procedures lead in this direction. I think this is so because of contrast with the way the company operated ten years ago. Of course I was at the plant level at that time. But today the attitude I have described is also in the plants. Ten years ago the organization was composed of people who worked together for the good of the organization, because they wanted to. I don't think this is so today.

Location of Division Facilities

The Petroleum Products Division, Chemical and Polymer Division, and the Packaging Products Division had their executive offices on separate floors of the Texana headquarters building in the Chicago "loop." The plants and research and development facilities of these divisions were spread out across Oklahoma, Texas, and Louisiana. The Molded Products Division had its headquarters, research and development facilities, and a major plant in an industrial suburb of Chicago. This division's other plants were at several locations in the Middle West and East Coast. The Building Products Division's headquarters and major production and technical facilities were located in Fort Worth, Texas. All four divisions shared sales offices in major cities from coast to coast.

Evaluation and Control of Division Performance

The principal method of controlling and evaluating the operations of these divisions was the semiannual review of division plans and the approval of major capital expenditures by the executive committee.[1] In reviewing performance against plans, members of the executive committee placed almost sole emphasis on the division's actual return on investment against budget. Corporate executives felt that this practice together with the technological interdependence of the divisions created many disputes about transfer pricing.

In addition to these regular reviews corporate executives had frequent discussions with division executives about their strategies, plans, and operations. It had been difficult for corporate management to strike the proper balance in guiding the operations for the divisions. This problem was particularly acute with regard to the Polymer and Chemicals Division, because of its central place in the corporation's product line. One corporate staff member explained his view of the problem:

This whole matter of communications between the corporate staff and the Polymer and Chemical Division has been a fairly difficult problem. Corporate management used to contribute immensely to this by trying to get into the nuts and bolts area within the Chemical and Polymer organization, and this created serious criticisms; however, I think they have backed off in this manner.

A second corporate executive in discussing this matter for a trade publication report put the problem this way: "We're trying to find the middle ground. We don't want to be a holding company, and with our diversity we can't be a highly centralized corporation."

Executive Vice President—Domestic Operations

In an effort to find this middle ground, the position of executive vice president, domestic operations, was created in early 1966; and George Prentice was its first occupant. Prior to this change, there had been two senior domestic vice presidents, one in charge of the Petroleum Products

---

[1]The executive committee consisted of Messrs. Dutton, Irwin, and Prentice, as well as the vice president of research; executive vice president, administration; and the executive vice president of foreign operations.

Division and Polymer and Chemicals Division and the other in charge of the end-use divisions. Mr. Prentice had been senior vice president in charge of the end-use divisions before the new position was created. He had held that position for only two years, having come to it from a highly successful marketing career with a competitor.

At the time of his appointment one press account described Mr. Prentice as "hard-driving, aggressive, and ambitious—an archetype of the self-actuated dynamo Irwin has sought out."

Shortly after taking his new position Prentice described the task before him:

I think the corporation wants to integrate its parts better and I am here because I reflect this feeling. We can't be a bunch of entrepreneurs around here. We have got to balance discipline with entrepreneurial motivation. This is what we were in the past, just a bunch of entrepreneurs, and if they came in with ideas we would get the money; but now our dollars are limited, and especially the Polymer and Chemical boys haven't been able to discipline themselves to select from within 10 good projects. They just don't seem to be able to do this, and so they come running in here with all 10 good projects which they say we have to buy, and they get upset when we can't buy them all.

This was the tone of my predecessors (senior vice presidents). All of them were very strong on being entrepreneurs. I am going to run it different. I am going to take a marketing and capital orientation. As far as I can see, there is a time to compete and a time to collaborate, and I think right now there has been a lack of recognition in the Polymer and Chemicals executive suite that this thing has changed.

Other Views of Domestic Interdivisional Relations

Executives within the Polymer and Chemicals Division in the end-use divisions, and at the corporate level, shared Prentice's view that the major breakdown in interdivisional relations was between the Polymer and Chemicals Division and the end-use divisions. Executives in the end-use divisions made these typical comments about the problem:

I think the thing we have got to realize is that we are wedded to the Polymer and Chemicals Division whether we like it or not. We are really tied up with them. And just as we would with any outside supplier or with any of our customers, we will do things to maintain their business. But because they feel they have our business wrapped up they do not reciprocate in turn. Now let me emphasize that they have not arbitrarily refused to do the things that we are requiring, but there is a pressure on them for investment projects and we are low man on the pole. And I think this could heavily jeopardize our chances for growth.

．　．　．　．　．

I would say our relationships are sticky, and I think this is primarily because we think our reason for being is to make money, so we try to keep Polymer and Chemicals as an arm's length supplier. For example, I cannot see, just because it is a Polymer and Chemicals product, accepting millions of pounds of very questionable material. It takes dollars out of our pocket, and we are very profit centered.

. . . . .

The big frustration, I guess, and one of our major problems, is that you can't get help from them [Polymer and Chemicals]. You feel they are not interested in what you are doing, particularly if it doesn't have a large return for them. But as far as I am concerned this has to become a joint venture relationship, and this is getting to be real sweat with us. We are the guys down below yelling for help. And they have got to give us some relief.

. . . . .

My experience with the Polymer and Chemicals Division is that you cannot trust what they say at all, and even when they put it in writing you can't be absolutely sure that they are going to live up to it.

Managers within the Polymer and Chemicals Division expressed similar sentiments:

Personally, right now I have the feeling that the divisions' interests are growing further apart. It seems that the divisions are going their own way. For example, we are a polymer producer but the molding division wants to be in a special area, so that means they are going to be less of a customer to us; and there is a whole family of plastics being left out that nobody's touching, and this is bearing on our program. . . . We don't mess with the Building Products Division at all, either. They deal in small volumes. Those that we are already making we sell to them, those that we don't make we can't justify making because of the kinds of things we are working with. What I am saying is that I don't think the corporation is integrating, but I think we ought to be, and this is one of the problems of delegated divisions. What happens is that an executive heads this up and goes for the place that makes the most money for the division, *but* this is not necessarily the best place from a corporate standpoint.

. . . . .

We don't have as much contact with sister divisions as I think we should. I have been trying to get a liaison with guys in my function, but it has been a complete flop. One of the problems is that I don't know who to call on in these other divisions. There is no table of organization, nor is there any encouragement to try and get anything going. My experience has been that all of these operating divisions are very closed organizations. I know guys up the line will say that I am nuts about this. They say to just call over and I will get an answer. But this always has to be a big deal, and it doesn't happen automatically, and hurts us.

The comments of corporate staff members describe these relationships and the factors they saw contributing to the problem:

Right now I would say there is an iron curtain between the Polymer and Chemicals Division and the rest of the corporation. You know, we tell our divisions they are responsible, autonomous groups, and the Polymer and Chemicals Division took it very seriously. However, when you are a three quarter billion dollar company, you've got to be coordinated, or the whole thing is going to fall apart—it can be no other way. The domestic executive vice president thing has been a big step forward to improve this, but I would say it hasn't worked out yet.

. . . . .

The big thing that is really bothering the Polymer and Chemicals Division is that they think they have to go develop all new markets on their own. They are going to do it alone independently, and this is the problem they are faced with. They have got this big thing, that they want to prove that they are a company all by themselves and not rely upon packaging or anybody else.

Polymer and Chemicals Division executives talked about the effect of this drive for independence of the divisional operating heads on their own planning efforts:

The Polymer and Chemicals Division doesn't like to communicate with the corporate staff. This seems hard for us, and I think their recent major proposal was a classic example of this. That plan, as it was whipped up by the Polymer and Chemicals Division, had massive implications for the corporation both in expertise and in capital. In fact, I think we did this to be a competitive one-up on the rest of our sister divisions. We wanted to be the best-looking division in the system, but we carried it to an extreme. In this effort, we wanted to show that we had developed this concept completely on our own. . . . Now I think a lot of our problems with it stemmed from this intense desire we have to be the best in this organization.

. . . . .

Boy, a big doldrum around here was shortly after Christmas (1965) when they dropped out a new plant, right out of our central plan, without any appreciation of the importance of this plant to the whole Polymer and Chemicals Division's growth. . . . Now we have a windfall and we are back in business on this new plant. But for a while things were very black and everything we had planned and everything we had built our patterns on were out. In fact, when we put this plan together, it never really occurred to us that we were going to get it turned down, and I'll bet we didn't even put the plans together in such a way as to really reflect the importance of this plant to the rest of the corporation.

A number of executives in the end-use divisions attributed the interdivisional problems to different management practices and assumptions within the Polymer and Chemicals Division. An executive in the packaging division made this point:

We make decisions quickly and at the lowest possible level, and this is tremendously different from the rest of Texana. I don't know another division like this in the rest of the corporation.

Look at what Sy Knoph has superfluous to his operation compared to ours. These are the reasons for our success. You've got to turn your guys loose and not breathe down their necks all the time. We don't slow our people down with staff. Sure, you may work with a staff, the wheels may grind, but they sure grind slow.

Also, we don't work on detail like the other divisions do. Our management doesn't feel they need the detail stuff. Therefore, they're [Polymer and Chemical] always asking us for detail which we can't supply, our process doesn't generate it and their process requires it, and this always creates problems with the Polymer and Chemicals Division. But I'll be damned if I am going to have a group of people running between me and the plant, and I'll be goddamned if I am going to clutter up my organization with all the people that Knoph has got working for him. I don't want this staff, but they are sure pushing it on me.

This comment from a molding division manager is typical of many about the technical concerns of the Polymer and Chemicals Division management:

Historically, even up to the not too distant past, the Polymer and Chemicals Division was considered a snake pit as far as the corporate people were concerned. This was because the corporate people were market oriented and Polymer and Chemicals Division was technically run and very much a manufacturing effort. These two factors created a communication barrier; and to really understand the Polymer and Chemicals Division problems, they felt that you have to have a basic appreciation of the technology and all the interrelationships.

Building on this strong belief, the Polymer and Chemicals Division executives in the past have tried to communicate in technical terms, and this just further hurt the relationship, and it just did not work. Now they are coming up with a little bit more business or commercial orientation, and they are beginning to appreciate that they have got to justify the things they want to do in a business or commercial orientation, and they are beginning to appreciate that they have got to justify the things they want to do in a business sense rather than just a technical sense. This also helps the problem of maintaining their relationships with the corporation as most of the staff is nontechnical; however, this has changed a little bit in that more and more technical people have been coming on and this has helped from the other side.

They work on the assumption in the Polymer and Chemicals Division that you have to know the territory before you can be an effective manager. You have got to be an operating guy to contribute meaningfully to their problems. However, their biggest problem is this concentration on technical solutions to their problems. This is a thing that has boxed them in the most trouble with corporation and the other sister divisions.

These and other executives also pointed to another source of conflict between the Polymer and Chemicals Division and other divisions. This was the question of whether the Polymer and Chemicals Division should develop into a more independent marketer, or whether it should rely more heavily on the end-use divisions to "push" its products to the market.

Typical views of this conflict are the following comments by end-use division executives:

The big question I have about Polymer and Chemicals is what is their strategy going to be? I can understand them completely from a technical standpoint, this is no problem. I wonder what is the role of this company? How is it going to fit into what we and others are doing? Right now, judging from the behavior I've seen, Polymer and Chemicals could care less about what we are doing in terms of integration of our markets or a joint approach to them.

. . . . .

I think it is debatable whether the Polymer and Chemicals Division should be a new product company or not. Right now we have an almost inexhaustible appetite for what they do and do well. As I see it, the present charter is fine. However, that group is very impatient, aggressive, and they want to grow, but you have got to grow within guidelines. Possibly the Polymer and Chemicals Division is just going to have to learn to hang on the coattails of the other divisions and do just what they are doing now, only better.

. . . . .

I think the future roles of the Polymer and Chemicals Division is going to be, at any one point in time for the corporation, that if it looks like a product is needed, they will make it. . . . They are going to be suppliers because I will guarantee you that if the moment comes and we can't buy it elsewhere, for example, then I darn well know they are going to make it for us regardless of what their other commitments are. They are just going to have to supply us. If you were to put the Polymer and Chemicals Division off from the corporation, I don't think they would last a year. Without their huge captive requirements, they would not be able to compete economically in the commercial areas they are in.

A number of other executives indicated that the primary emphasis within the corporation on return on investment by divisions tended to induce, among other things, a narrow, competitive concern on the part of the various divisional managements. The comment of this division executive was typical:

As far as I can see it, we [his division and Polymer and Chemicals] are 180 degrees off on our respective charters. Therefore, when Sy Knoph talks about this big project we listen nicely and then we say, "God bless you, lots of luck," but I am sure we are not going to get involved in it. I don't see any money in it for us. It may be a gold mine for Sy but it is not for our company; and as long as we are held to the high profit standards we are, we just cannot afford to get involved. I can certainly see it might make good corporate sense for us to get it, but it doesn't make any sense in terms of our particular company. We have got to be able to show the returns in order to get continuing capital and I just can't on that kind of project. I guess what I am saying is that under the right conditions we could certainly go in but not under the present framework; we would just be dead in terms of dealing with the corporate financial structure. We just cannot get the kinds of returns on our capital that the corporation has set to get new capital. In terms of the long run, I'd like very much to see what the corporation has envisioned in terms of a hookup between us, but right now I don't see any sense in going on. You know my career is at stake here too.

Another divisional executive made this point more succinctly:

Personally I think that a lot more could be done from a corporate point of view, and this is frustrating. Right now all these various divisions seem to be viewed strictly as an investment by the corporate people. They only look at us as a banker might look at us. This hurts us in terms of evolving some of these programs because we have relationships which are beyond financial relationships.

The remarks of a corporate executive seemed to support this concern:

One of the things I worry about is where is the end of the rope on this interdivisional thing. I'm wondering if action really has to come from just the division. You know in this organization when you decide to do something new it always has been a divisional proposal—they were coming to us for review and approval. The executive committee ends up a review board—not us, working downward. With this kind of pattern the talent of the corporate people is pretty well seduced into asking questions and determining whether a thing needs guidelines. But I think we ought to be the idea people as well, thinking about where we are going in the future; and if we think we ought to be getting into some new area, then we tell the divisions to do it. The stream has got to work both ways. Now it is not.

Printer, Inc.

In the summer of 1969, the management of Printer Incorporated were evaluating the recent change to "industry specialization" in the company's organization. The company's internal marketing and engineering departments, located at the Watertown, Wisconsin, headquarters, and several of its field sales regions had been reorganized by industry groupings of Printer's customers. Since the implementation of the organizational change, Printer's sales had increased substantially. One of Printer's executives commented:

As long ago as 1964 we had a fairly clear notion of the need for industry specialization. Now, five years later, we have gone a long way down that road. By and large, it has been a good thing, but we are not sure if we are all the way down the road or only part way. Is the implementation of the change finished? Should we push further in the manufacturing area? Did we push far enough or too far in our field sales organization?

The Company

Founded in 1926 and based in the countryside of Wisconsin, near Milwaukee, Printer produced and internationally marketed specialized production printing machinery and supplies. The "Basic Statement from Board of Directors" indicates:

. . . The company shall, for the present, concentrate its efforts in helping industry to effectively identify or decorate its products and packages. In general, this will require selling, manufacturing, installing, and servicing special printing machinery, coloring materials, design applying elements and associated supplies.

Printer's customers were in several diverse industries, each of which had its own unique problems in printing directly onto its products a company or other type of product identification. Traditionally, a customer with a special printing problem came to Printer, who met the customer's needs with a standard or specially designed machine and combination of printing supplies. Although in specific industries several companies competed with Printer, there were no other companies which sold printing products to customers in the wide range of industries that Printer served.

Several members of management explained to the case writer that the company's strategy was to meet a customer's specific needs with a combination of machines and supplies with the objective of selling highly profitable supplies over a long period of time. The company had established a reputation for its ability to supply the package of equipment and supplies that would solve the customer's special printing problems, and it continued to market its products under a high-quality, high-price image.

Printer's customers were in industries that presented different types of technical printing problems and which were characterized by different product life cycles. For example, the shoe industry, for which Printer held a substantial part of the market for printing requirements, had few basic product changes and a very stable production process technology. From one year to the next it had generally the same printing requirements. The production process utilized little sophisticated equipment; and the operation of printing the company name, shoe size, and identification numbers could be handled as an additional batch operation in the process of shoe manufacturing.

The electronics industry presented printing requirements at the other end of the spectrum. Rapid technological advances brought changing product sizes and characteristics, resulting in rapidly changing printing requirements. High-volume production utilizing sophisticated production equipment required high-speed printing equipment that could be integrated directly in the production process.

Thus, in serving the needs of these different types of customers, it was necessary not only to produce printing equipment and supplies that met the technical characteristics demanded by the customer's product characteristics but also to understand different customers' production process requirements and characteristics of his industry.

Meeting the technical requirements of a special printing problem required the selection and often design of a combination of machine, printing element, and ink or foil. Technical considerations in making this choice included such factors as the speed of operation, surface characteristics of the item to be printed, drying time requirements dictated by the production process, ability of the product to withstand heat of a drying oven or the necessity for air drying, and the unique characteristics of the combination of ink, printing element, and machine. Improper selection of printing supplies and equipment resulted in problems such as smearing of the impression, inconsistency in printing quality, or gumming of the printing elements. For some printing requirements, a foil printing machine best met the demands of the situation. In this case, foil passed under a printing head and the compound was thus pressed against the item being printed, eliminating the steps of feeding liquid ink from a reservoir onto the printing element and then transferring it onto the surface being printed.

Organization

As shown in Exhibit 1, the company was organized along the lines of marketing, engineering and research, and manufacturing. Of the 550 em-

EXHIBIT 1

Organization Chart

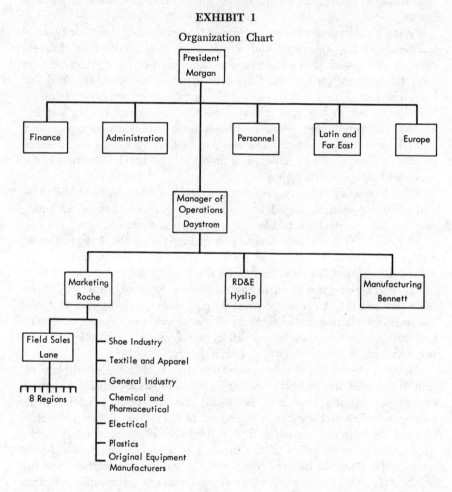

ployees in the company, 170 were in the marketing organization, and several of Printer's managers explained to the case writer that the company had a "marketing orientation." The Marketing Division was organized into a field sales organization of 85 people and an industry sales organization, as shown in Exhibit 2. The field sales organization, responsible for customer contacts for sales and service, was organized geographically into eight regions. Each region had a regional office with regional manager and a small office staff and several regional field salesmen.

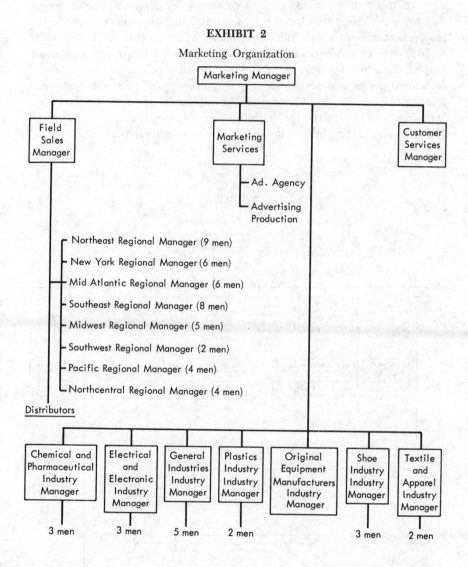

EXHIBIT 2

Marketing Organization

The industry sales organization, divided into seven industry groupings, provided inside support for field salesmen, the marketing manager explained. The internal sales organization handled order processing and other sales record keeping, and worked with engineering and manufacturing to meet the needs of the field salesmen's customers.

The Research, Development and Engineering Division was organized, as shown in Exhibit 3, into research, four technical groups, and some support groups. The research group concentrated on chemical research, and each of the four chemists worked primarily with one technical group. This research group was formerly a separate company, and except for the research manager, whose office was located next to that of the manager of R D & E, the chemists and research group were located in a separate part of the building from the other engineering personnel. Each of the technical groups was responsible for engineering products for customers in one or two industries. Comparison of Exhibits 2 and 3 shows the correspondence of industry specialization in engineering and marketing. Exhibit 4 shows the physical layout of the engineering department.

EXHIBIT 3

R D & E Organization

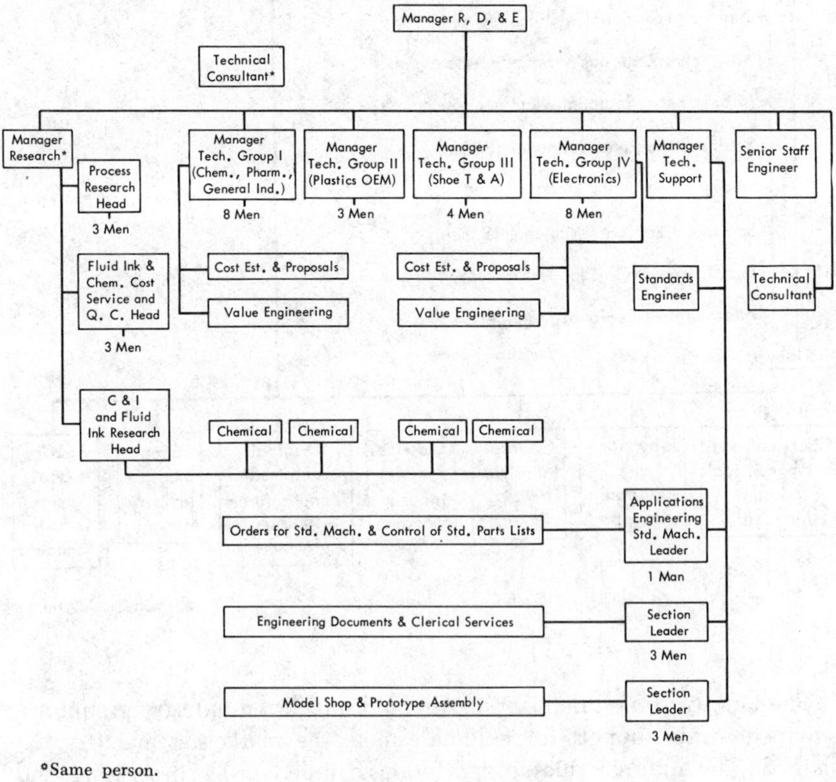

*Same person.

The Manufacturing Division was organized into machining centers (90 people), equipment assembly (28 people), printing elements manufacture (75 people), ink formulation (28 people), foil production (20 people), and miscellaneous support groups (total of 50 people). The ink formulation department prepared—often to customer order—over 10,000 different types of inks. The machining departments prepared from blueprints several different types of parts for stock, and the assembly department assembled these parts and those purchased from outside suppliers into equipment to fill customers' orders. The assembly area, which was 150' by 75' in area, contained several benches and few pieces of fixed equipment. Some assemblers worked on small batches of machines for stock, while others individually finished stock machines or specially assembled nonstock machines to customer order. They were familiar with a variety of different types of equipment and could switch from one assembly to another as orders and priorities shifted. The company followed the policy of not firing a man for lack of work, and the manufacturing manager indicated that this policy was the reason that they subcontracted 50 percent of their parts machining work.

Implementation of Industry Specialization

Prior to 1965 the Marketing Division was organized by region both internally and in the field, and the Engineering and Manufacturing divisions were organized along functional lines. In 1965 the internal marketing department was reorganized along industry lines, but it returned to a regional organization in 1966. In 1967 the Chemical Division, which was a separate company, was dissolved into the main company. The marketing manager commented, "You have to be secretive about chemical products. Until the reorganization I had never gone into the chemical plant, even though I had been marketing manager for four years." In 1967 the internal sales organization was once again reorganized along industry lines. Beginning in May 1968 the industry specialization concept was applied to the field sales organization, and shortly thereafter the technical division (R D & E) was reorganized. The "general industries" category applied to customers who were not in any of the other six industry groups. In the field sales organization salesmen in most regions, beginning with the north central region, were given responsibilities for specific industries rather than for specific geographical areas in their regions. In a few instances where there was a high concentration of one industry and a wide geographical diversion of the others, the field sales organization had much of a geographical breakdown of assignments. In those cases, the field salesman had to contact more than one internal marketing group to meet his customers' needs, whereas a purely industry specialized field salesman had one internal industry-specialized market-

EXHIBIT 4

Floor Layout of Engineering Department

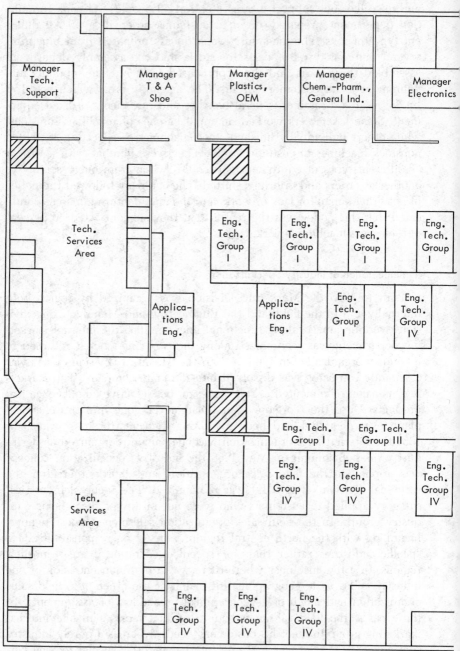

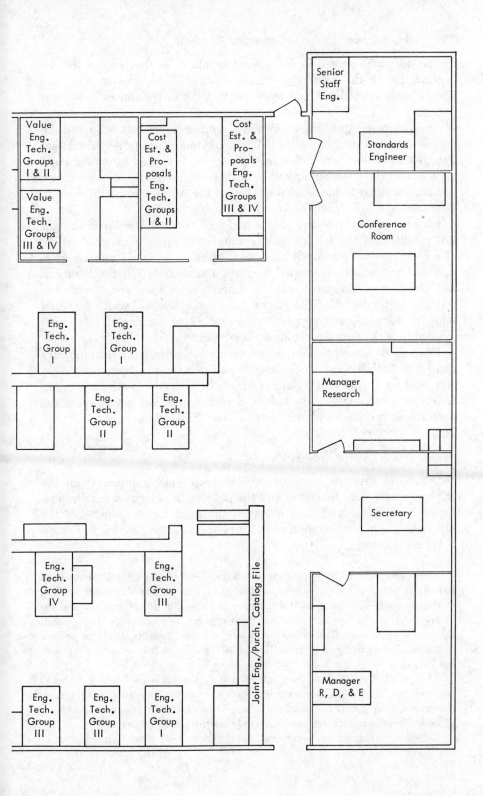

ing group which served as his internal contact. At the time of the reorganization of the field sales organization, the functions of sales and service were specialized and assigned to separate personnel in several regions.

The company also employed three product specialists who concentrated on the introduction of foil. The marketing manager explained that they felt foil sales were different because the field was extremely competitive and the large number of calls that were required to make a sale was discouraging to the salesmen. Most of the calls for foil sales were in industries in which Printer had not had active accounts.

Both the internal industry groups and field salesmen were paid straight salary, although the foil specialists were paid salary plus commission. The company had previously paid its field salesmen salary plus commission, but this was discontinued because management felt the additions and transfers of personnel and the differences in sales areas made the system inequitable. The company's information system, which reported sales of machines and supplies as compared to forecasted sales, was applied to both regions' and industries' performance.

Regional managers as a group were paid somewhat more than industry managers. Both the industry managers and regional managers were characterized by a wide range in age and length of service, with each group having at least one man who had been with Printer less than 4 years and several who had been with the company over 20 years.

Interviews with Printer Personnel

Several of Printer's management and employees commented on the implementation and functioning of the concept of industry specialization. James Roche, the marketing manager, prepared the description of the rationale and implementation of industry specialization shown in Exhibit 5. He commented:

1960 sales were 20 to 30 percent of today's. Most of this growth comes from growth in the industries Printer moved into. In 1911 it was shoes and textiles, in the 30s and 40s the electrical industry, in the 50s the pharmaceutical industry, and in the late 50s and 60s the explosion in electronics that pushed sales up. Top management is always looking for new markets. With 90 percent of the market in many industries, Printer is a leader as a broad-based marketing company.

The printing compounds—wet ink or dry carrier supported ink—are chemical, and machine design is mechanical with a small but increasing electrical requirement. The common denominator in all the technical groups is an appreciation of printing processes—you have to know the whole spectrum.

Different industries have different development lead times. The electronics

EXHIBIT 5

Rationale and Implementation of Industry Specialization

(July 1, 1969)

I. Recognition of a basic need to serve our customers with understanding of their needs and applications of our products.
    A. Field salesmen were having difficult time being experts in all fields. Growth meant less-experienced men in field compounding problem.
    B. Inside sales correspondents were jacks-of-all-trades—serving field and customers on purely geographical basis.
    C. No one was looking after or responsible for specific industry needs.
    D. New products were developed through instigation by top management or "market development groups," but no one was prepared to follow through. Market development people were "too" much of short-term experts.
II. First phase solution. Organize internal sales on major industry basis with industry sales managers. Advantages were:
    A. Developed expertise to benefit of field and customers.
    B. Made it easier to train new correspondents during growth situation.
    C. Made someone responsible for following industry trends, service, and worrying about new products to satisfy needs.
    D. Improved the transition from spec writing—development—and sales program stage of new product development. Smooth transition with continuity.
III. Second phase. Organize field force where market industry density warranted on an industry basis. Specialization with provision for general coverage and "new product" introduction on product lines crossing all industries.
    A. Benefits to customers since they were called upon by experts who talked to customers as if their industry was the only one we served.
    B. Easier for industry manager to serve men in field and receive input from specialists in field. Easier to develop specific industry sales programs.
IV. Third phase. Organize technical support groups on industry basis so the home office marketing–technical industry groups could operate as an industry-oriented team devoted to serving the customers of a particular industry.
    A. Many internal benefits. Marketing experts and technical experts talking the same language. Could make decisions and move faster.
    B. Better coordination in visiting field of marketing and technical teams to determine customer needs and find solutions.
    C. Could make impression on customers who could talk to marketing and technical teams at home office or field—answers to sales and technical problems.
V. Fifth phase. Include manufacturing personnel in the industry groups—particularly assembly groups working on specials or customs.

industry, for example, requires fast development and frequent calls on customers to keep up with their product developments. Customers in the electronics industry have a high technical ability themselves. At the other extreme the customer, say in the shoe industry, realizes post facto that he needs to mark his products. You have to tell him how to do it. He wants you to do the whole thing.

I had the industry concept fixed in my mind when I came with the company. From previous experience with another company I feel it is the way to organize. Sales this year are up 20 percent from last year and are 7 percent ahead of our goals, but we're having a hell of a time getting the products out. I would put a good measure of our success in 1969 due to our organizational change. The sales come from new products. We now have the technical people working and co-operating with marketing.

You can change things inside like a meat grinder and still survive, but you can't do it in the field. Many men in the field didn't want to change to industry specialization, but they agreed to do it on a timetable starting first in the north central region. Most of the negative aspects of industry specialization are in the field. For example, it results in higher travel expenses. The field sales force has men who have been with the company in their region for a long time. For them industry specialization means losing friends and contacts in those industries they would abandon in specializing. We took the stand of not specializing only where it is not practical—such as in the southeast region where the electronics industry is too scattered for specialization. We do have a good degree of specialization where it counts.

Donald Lane, the field sales manager, commented:

In addition to the southeast region, there is no industry specialization in the southwest region, where we only have two salesmen. In our other regions we are 95 percent specialized. Only two zones in the Northeast and two and half states in the Northwest are covered by men covering all industries. It's easier to train men only in one segment of the business [one industry], and training is more critical now with our growth speeding up.

William Hyslip, manager of R D & E commented:

This is a marketing-oriented company. In fact, it used to be that some of our engineers would take orders from nearly anyone in marketing without question. Industry specialization in both marketing and the technical group has created a more positive atmosphere. Now I think marketing feels they need the engineers. There are conflicts with field sales because they have a different orientation and they wonder what we are doing with our resources.

There are two types of work for engineering—customers' orders and new products. When the industry specialization came in, marketing was reorganized first, and they started dividing orders by industry. When engineering was reorganized, the industry technical groups got only orders for their industries, so they had to work with their corresponding industry group in marketing. Our best selling machines have developed from a machine designed for a specific application and then extended. Shot in the dark development hasn't been successful. We don't want to build first and then try to sell, but rather design what the customer wants. We're doing this better because engineering and the internal marketing men are getting more contact with the customer. The engineering requirements are getting highly specialized by industry, and the engineers must understand the customer's application. Almost 100 percent of our design work is initiated by marketing.

Problems do come up in allocating engineering responsibility for machine design on machines used in more than one industry. Generally, we assign responsibility to one industry technical group. The engineers know pretty much what's going on in other technical groups, but the responsibility for this falls back on me. Maybe we should hold regularly scheduled meetings for this, but now we have irregularly scheduled ones and I see all the men almost each day.

The R D & E Division has about 60 people of which one third are degreed, another third have taken a 2- to 3-year engineering course, and the remainder are "self-made." The industry specialization has allowed us to change the job content to give more of the men more of a "whole task." In contrast to a functional breakdown of work, we've tried at all levels to get development men to go with marketing men on customer visits.

With manufacturing, there is a need for coordination at the engineering stage and at the assembly stage. Manufacturing-engineering coordination is less than sales-engineering coordination. Plans are pretty well made by the time a product hits manufacturing. We sort our parts manufacturing problems at the value engineering stage—and get together with manufacturing to do this. What is left is problems that come up later—such as delivery or cost problems. I'd like to include [in industry specialization] assembly people who will learn to identify with an industry—at the assembly level there are people who generally work on the same type of equipment.

George Healy, manager of the electronics technical group, commented:

Salesmen sometimes get us into trouble because they are overzealous. Most of the salesmen are independent, whether they are technically competent or not. Engineering gets in after the fact. We should get into the field, but we don't do it enough. We should know where our machine fits into a customer's process, but often it is the salesman and customer that make this decision. So much depends on the salesman being knowledgeable, but some are practically illiterate. Yet some of these field salesmen even send us engineering drawings of how to make the machines. We have a tremendous problem with field sales. We don't have very much contact with them, and much of what we hear from them is negative.

Our problems are technical. After the salesman sells something we have to produce it. We are getting pushed all the time to advance the state of the art, but we get no support from the basic groups. I don't even know what projects they are doing. I have to coordinate the electromechanical machine design with the choice of ink. Sometimes this is done after the fact; but like other things with the research group, it is getting better.

About 75 percent of the engineering work in all industries uses some basic standard modules, but the applications are quite different and require different engineering skills. In organizing by industry, the men become stronger specialists through experience, but they also become less flexible. Another negative aspect about industry specialization is that when one group gets a surge in work it may not have the manpower to cover it. One of the advantages of it, though, is that now people know where to go in engineering to get some action when there is a problem. Problems used to get lost in the department. It was too hard for the marketing man to know what a technical man was doing, but now the marketing man gets more attention. We have a great relationship with our industry marketing group. Our priorities on work are based on Bill Williams' [industry marketing manager] knowledge of the industry and my estimates of how long it will take to do the work.

When asked how he allocated his time, George responded:

25 percent in the manufacturing area
25 percent on sales liaison
10 percent on service—fighting problems on customer-installed machines
40 percent on technical decisions and administration.

Manufacturing is a weak sister here—not that they aren't capable—but because they are loosely structured. It requires high personal attention on my part to get stuff out [of manufacturing]. When I came here, engineering was still going out on the manufacturing floor to get stuff working. Engineers even went out to try to track down parts. Some people confuse being a nice guy with doing other people's job.

One member of the electronics industry technical group commented:

There is quite a bit of contact with inside salespeople. 90 percent of the time I go to them to get more information about an order. The other 10 percent they come in with a question—usually on a machine they want to make a quote on. Only occasionally do we see field salespeople. A salesman will come in and say a customer wants to know why his machine is late and tries to get you to work it in sooner. I've never been in a customer's plant. Usually they send [degreed] engineers to impress the customer. Engineering handles order processing, and that is much of my work.

One disadvantage to the new organization is that we are divided into several small groups instead of one large group. If several orders come into one group, pressure is put on. Then we have to swap or borrow people among industry groups. Some guys come in nights at time and a half to help out others. I worked every night for two to three months when the new industry organization came in.

Tim James, manager of T & A and shoe technical group, commented:

Before industry specialization, our contact with sales depended on the project. There was one particular person in sales for each particular project. Now I get in right in the beginning on the specs. I'd write them if I could [marketing does]; as it is I bias them pretty heavily. Marketing lets me have my way until a machine is pretty much designed, then they come up with things we didn't put in—like a Monday morning quarterback. We are in an experimental stage now.

People in my group are out in the field only one or two times a year, but the work load is too high to go out more. With the new industry groupings there is narrowed communications. We can get around the technical shortcomings by trading people among groups.

Tim indicated that he spent 15 percent of his time with industry sales managers and 15 percent with manufacturing. He further commented:

With manufacturing I'd like to get more control. There are poor communications there. Manufacturing has problems with new equipment. They must go to engineering to get parts lists and to marketing to get sales forecasts. High-level people in manufacturing are not agreed on what they want and we're getting confusion coming back into engineering.

Tom Bennett, manager of manufacturing, commented:

This has been a very successful year for the company, so we are loaded with orders. We're also having a problem changing from a manual to computer system on scheduling and inventory control, so we have parts shortages and late deliveries. Both internal marketing and technical men from all seven industry groups come down to the assembly area and all seven marketing managers call me or see me pushing for their own product deliveries. If necessary, I can ask Jim Roche to set the priorities.

We are organized into two basic departments—machining and assembly. The machining department is organized into machine centers, each having a lead man. Jobs are allocated by machine center. The old-timers stay on one machine, and the apprentices spend time on all four. [Two thirds of the machinists are in the apprenticeship program.] We make three different types of parts: (1) batch stock order, (2) special one of a kind for a shipping order, and (3) special (custom) parts for customer's machine order. There is practically no contact between machinists and assemblers. Assembly has three sections: batch (6 people), where basic machines are put together in quantity; testers (12 people), who take the basic machines and add special features; and special assembly (5 people), where new designs and complex work is done. There's no gain in dividing batch assembly into industry groupings. To get economy, you need a large lot size. There is an informal grouping among the testers and special assembly men. Jobs for the electronics industry are tricky and take special assembly skills. One man does those orders and another handles all pharmaceutical work. If the guys on the floor have a better idea of what a machine is going to do, why they have to meet delivery, and what it means to Printer, they will do a better job. But I have a hard time seeing industry specialization, especially in machining. We don't have enough equipment to give to each industry.

On most applications there is no problem because we have done them before. If there are problems, a technical man comes over and helps. That happens mostly with new models. The engineering people are here for a total of six visits a day. Salespeople can be tied up and are not as quick to come—when they're worried, they come.

Others in the company say to me that I should bring my area in line with the others. Management would like to see industry specialization go as far as it can.

Ben Cabot, research manager, commented:

Having a chemically oriented man on the industry team facilitates its handling of specific problems and helping communications. They can solve problems earlier in the game. Sometimes you're unsure of whether a problem is with the ink or the machine. It requires a team effort attacking the problem from both ink and mechanical standpoints. The chemists have to work most closely with the industry technical groups, then with marketing, then manufacturing.

We need industry specialization. For example, in T & A one has to know dyes, dry-cleaning methods, history of the material, and technical terms of the industry. In electronics the terminology used to talk to the customer is quite different.

When a sticky problem is solved in one industry, it spills over into others. Bill Hyslip and I transfer information across industries. We sit in on technical marketing meetings and switch manpower around.

Bill Williams, electronics industry internal marketing manager, commented:

We had industry specialization a few years ago, but it was discontinued because someone favored geographical over industry. Field sales was still organized geographically, and they had to talk to several people inside to get answers to all their problems. There were complaints from the field salesmen calling in to Watertown.

The job of sales correspondent [internal sales] hasn't changed much through the reorganizations. He is a salesman and must sell as much as the guy outside. He takes care of the customer and field salespeople that are in his area. He has to write letters, give quotes on machines and parts, handle customer problems, and take care of field salesmen's problems, such as when they need a new price book.

Industry specialization has given 1,000 percent better communications between engineering, internal sales, and field sales. Giving the industry specialization to field sales makes it easier to communicate with the internal and field sales organizations. Marketing was specialized by industry first, and then engineering. When marketing was industry oriented way back, I loved it. I kept pounding the table to get engineering changed to it.

Now the engineers can better understand what the customer wants. The salesman's job is to make sure the customer gets a product that fills his needs, but sometimes engineering doesn't understand the application. A lot of times their design doesn't use common sense, generally when they haven't been in the customer's plant. There used to be no connection between the jobs the engineers would get. Two engineers could get the same job for different customers and come up with different solutions. Out in the field we see things others have done. We see what doesn't work well and feed that information back to engineering—sometimes too late. My 25 years' experience can save a young engineer from designing something I know won't work.

One of the problems we have here is where a machine design works OK here at Watertown but after two to three weeks in production it falls apart. Before we didn't know who to send. Now we take the man who engineered it. Generally a certain group in assembly does all the work for an industry, so we get together with them and engineering, and then we can send the man out with answer in hand.

It is engineering's job to coordinate with manufacturing in building a machine. On special orders the engineers sometimes spend up to a week on the assembly floor debugging a machine. I want engineering to take over our contact with manufacturing. Marketing people should be concerned only with selling—instead we find ourselves spending a lot of time with people in assembly—taking care of the customer. Assembly has the closest contact in manufacturing with us. INDUSTRY SPECIALIZATION SHOULD ALSO GO IN ASSEMBLY, and put that in capitals. The only reason not to do it is cost.

Ed Clark, internal marketing manager—general industries, commented:

Industry specialization makes it easier to have a man to contact for specific problems, but in general industries, we need a project orientation. We have to cover too much area, and it is hard to determine what to do daily. I don't feel responsible for daily sales, although officially I am responsible—it is projects [new product introductions] that I feel responsible for.

Field salesmen have much more prestige in this company than do inside salespeople, and the regional managers have more prestige than the industry managers. They have direct access to the president. According to field sales, inside sales doesn't know how the real world works. But our role in making the company go is significant. We are the guys that are going to come out with the new products and spot problems with the old. We have a larger field to cover than the other industry groups, which makes it the hardest to handle but also gives the most flexibility. The company's opportunities to broaden its scope of markets occur in general industries.

CASE WRITER: Do you have more trouble with field sales than engineering?

CLARK: Oh, hell yes. I can talk to engineering. Communications are very bad with field sales. We just keep them off our backs in servicing their requests. I can't win any battles I fight with them. We are all on the defensive with respect to field sales. We rarely go out and try to help them, although some of that is happening now. I don't work very much with manufacturing—mostly on sales forecasting, and when they screw up. When they are late, we holler to our boss and he gives it to them. We don't understand their problems, and usually I don't talk to them on anything except when I'm in trouble. Engineering often relays the information to us from manufacturing.

Frank Leonard, north central regional sales manager, who had joined the company in the 1940s, commented on the implementation of industry specialization:

Back in the 50s we had industry specialization inside and we abandoned it for geographical organization. The fellows in the field were not specialized, and they had trouble talking to many people in the plant. They weren't big enough to specialize in the field. In 1964–65 we went back to industry specialization inside. Many people in the field were getting older, and we questioned what we should do to give them incentives and opportunities—how could we exploit their strengths in certain areas? In the north central region we found that 80 percent of our sales came from 20 percent of our customers. We looked at the interests of the nine salesmen and tried to fit them with particular industries. Most salesmen know best the line that they sell most—a guy could be good in 5 of 90 basic types of equipment. Some guys are more well rounded, and we use them for general industries.

The most valuable manpower asset we have is in the field sales force. We knew that these men—as is always true—would have a natural resistance to a major change such as this, which would interrupt their established responsibilities and routines. We knew we had a selling job to do with these men, because if they were not enthusiastic the plan was sure to fail, as they were the doers. The most effective thing we developed was an outline of the advantages and disadvantages to them, the company, and our customers. [See Exhibit 6.] The reaction from the field salesmen varied from very negative to high enthusiasm, largely dependent upon the person's age, personal objectives, and capabilities. We lost no one. Only one man had to relocate, and he did.

Before the change, we were never able to get salesmen to schedule beyond one day. Because they had to do service, they couldn't plan. Now we have a separate service staff. The servicemen, who used to do less than one half of the service calls, now do about 88 percent of them. On a survey two months after specialization, sales calls were up 22 percent.

Field sales has little contact with other parts of the organization. The regional sales office should be able to handle all of the standard line requests. The farther out you get from Watertown, the more of the customers' needs are handled by the regional office. By habit some of the customers call Watertown. The primary contact for the field salesman is the internal industry man, who handles all the needed inside contacts. For the north central region only, the regional office is right here in the plant in Watertown. As a result, the salesmen often go directly to the internal marketing groups for things that in other regions would be handled by the regional office. I'd like to move the regional office out of the plant because of this.

It used to be that a field salesman would find a good application that needed a new machine and he would get little response internally. Now there is a more common interest between field salesmen and the internal people, and they get more interest and attention. I still get complaints from my salesmen that their requests are not done well enough—there seems to be a variance in the quality of service provided by the different industry groups.

Joe Benzing, New York regional sales manager who had been with the company for three years and had been regional sales manager for nearly two, commented:

When industry specialization was initially announced for field sales, the salesmen said that they were out of their minds to change. I had some questions and also saw some pluses—I knew many intelligent people had worked on it, and I gave the benefit of the doubt to the program. After the initial

EXHIBIT 6

Advantages to Customer

1. Served by an industry-oriented, more knowledgeable salesman.
2. Better recognition and response by Printer to customers' needs.
3. More attention from salesman on total requirements—including consumable supplies.

Disadvantages to Customer

1. Change of salesman—initially.
2. Possible slower response from salesman.
3. Small customer will receive fewer calls.

Advantages to Printer

1. Quicker market penetration for new products.
2. More efficient for new product introduction—fewer salesmen involved at first.
3. Deeper penetration of existing markets.
4. More flexibility in a company or market growth situation.
5. More effective sales calls.
6. Better communication between—
   a) Salesman and customer.
   b) Salesman and Watertown.
7. More field quoting.
8. Fewer field mistakes—credits.
9. Greater promotion of complete Printer package—more attention to consumable supplies.
10. Better administration and coordination of field activities by—
    a) Regional managers.
    b) Industry and product managers.
11. More alert to industry changes (market intelligence).
12. Easier and quicker to train salesmen.
13. Easier to assign men within capabilities.
14. Better selection and qualification of prospects.
15. Greater team effort among salesmen.

. . . . .

Doing a better job in fewer areas.

Disadvantages to Printer

1. Slower response to customer requests.
2. More sales travel time and cost—overlapping.
3. More difficult to adjust work load of salesmen.
4. Harder to deploy personnel geographically—where to locate?
5. Manpower planning more critical—replacement or transfer.
6. Possible higher turnover of sales personnel.

Advantages to Salesman

1. *Improved motivation*—greater proficiency and satisfaction by being more knowledgeable.
2. *Improved technical training*—easier to learn, and therefore become more effective, by concentrating on fewer products and industry areas.
3. *Improved job skills*—opportunities to work in areas of greatest interest and ability.

Disadvantages to Salesman

1. More travel and overnight.
2. Will lose customers of long standing—especially close to home.

reaction the men had very little reaction—they just started traveling different routes. I thought specialization would hinder me in doing my job because it would spread the men much thinner; they are hard to motivate to make calls, so why put roadblocks?

Specialization itself has made little impact on us. It raised travel costs from $35 to $40 per man per week. The number of calls settled to the same pattern as before. (It seems to be highly a function of the man.) There is no noticeable change in working with internal marketing and engineering, but what is noticeable is deteriorating communications with inside marketing people. I think that this is not because of specialization, but because the job of the internal marketing man is changing—they cannot go into the plant to expedite as much as before.

CASE WRITER: Do engineering personnel come out to visit customers?

JOE: Yes, but that's a result of specialization inside, not in the field. Relationships between our field men and engineering are still a function of the salesmen's work habits. Relationships haven't changed. Inside specialization has helped communications and I believe it will continue, but I haven't seen any bright flash of light.

Most of our sales are from replacements and expansion by our customers. I try to bring tremendous pressure to bear for new products because we're dying on the vine with no new markets. In this region the number of machines sold is actually on a slight decline because there are not enough new products. Sales dollars are relatively constant because of price increases. We see applications and send the information back, but the problem is the technical ability to do it. The technical people are not technical people at all; they are gadgeteers and good at it. But they don't understand the underlying process, so they can't give product training to the salesmen.

One reason I was so upset about industry specialization was they were completely switching things around based on reasons in conflict with the real selling situation. They said it would give (1) increased penetration in given industries (but how is that possible when we already have a substantial share of the market in many segments?); and (2) increased emphasis on consumable supply sales. But these don't take aggressive selling. With ink, customers try others, but Printer ink is so good that they come back. With rubber plate, price and delivery is what they want, and we cannot compete with competitors' overnight delivery. When you really analyze the selling situation and why they sell, you find that many reasons are outside the control of the salesman. If that is true, geography should be more important for organization than industry specialization; you can sell more economically.

One thing that is very much on my mind is the increased dependence of the field salesmen on the industry managers that weakens the role of the regional managers. I consciously do things for the fellows to head this off. There is a massive friction between the industry managers and the regional managers. I'm not convinced this is directly a result of industry specialization in the field, but I don't feel the boom in sales is from that either. I'd like to go back to the old geographical organization.

Index of Cases